October 25, 1962 at 5:00 p.m.

President John F. Kennedy issued **National Security Action Memorandum Number 199** to the Secretary of Defense Robert McNamara authorizing the loading of air launched ballistic missiles (ALBMs) onto strategic bombers ready to carry out the initial nuclear strikes to the Soviet Union.

"It shall be the policy of this nation to regard any nuclear missile launched from Cuba against any nation in the Western Hemisphere as an attack on the United States, requiring a full retaliatory response upon the Soviet Union."

John F. Kennedy [1917 – 1963] on October 22, 1962.

October 25, 1962; CIA reported that the Soviet missiles in Cuba were on the final preparation, instead of being dismantled. The Commander-in-Chief then **ordered US military to get ready to attack the Soviet Union, not just Cuba! It's real preparation for the nuclear war**!

The politics is a deception to counter another deception, the ultimate goal of politics is power, the ultimate goal of power is money; a politician is a businessman and the commodity is our weakness.

"When the government fears the people, there is liberty. When the people fear the government, there is tyranny."
Thomas Jefferson (1743-1826).

John F. Kennedy's Nuclear War

© 2013 by Abdul Rahman Bahry. All rights reserved.

No part or whole of this book may be reproduced, stored in retrieval system, or transmitted by any means, electronic, mechanical, photocopying, recording, or otherwise, without written permission from the author.

Copyright © of the photographs relating to atomic bomb victims, by Hiroshima Peace Memorial Museum, Japan

Copyright © of the photographs relating to Hiroshima before and after war, by the City of Hiroshima (Cultural Promotion Division, Culture and Sports Department, Citizens Affairs Bureau).

No part or whole of the photograph(s) may be reproduced, stored in retrieval system, or transmitted by any means, electronic, mechanical, photocopying, recording, or otherwise, without written permission from the Hiroshima Peace Memorial Museum, and the city of Hiroshima, Japan

Cover design and dollar bill illustration by the author

Warning!

This book contains the severe photograph(s) and illustration(s) which maybe not appropriate for the non-adult readers. Parental Guidance for up to 13 year-old youths (PG 13) is necessary. Any transcription in this book is not official one; the readers are suggested to check it in the original video media.

US Library of Congress Control Number: 2013902914

ISBN 978-0-9892988-0-3

Acknowledgment

This book is dedicated for those who love the peace and make every effort to maintain it for good.

Special acknowledgment attributed to Curatorial Division of Hiroshima Peace Memorial Museum and the staffs; Mayor of Hiroshima, the City of Hiroshima (Cultural Promotion Division, Culture and Sports Department, Citizens Affairs Bureau), and all parties who extended their hands helping the publication of this book.

A very special acknowledgment and appreciation attributed to createspace.com and amazon.com

受付 係 主任 副館長

8/22

※Please do not fill out the boxes above.

Atomic Bomb Material Publication Application Form

To: Hiroshima Peace Memorial Museum Curatorial Division	Date	08/17/2012

Applicant's address	6055 West 130th Street, Parma OH 44130 USA	
	Tel: Fax:1-216-362-0787 E-mail: abahry@hotmail.com	1-440-520-8142
Person in charge (name of organization)	Contact person	Abdul Rahman Bahry (author)

※Please fill in the blanks or tick the boxes as appropriate.

Purpose X publication ☐TV, movie, video etc. ☐exhibition ☐lecture/event ☐website X others Electronic Book Content	Title:	JFKennedy's Nuclear War
	Author/Editor/Producer:	Abdul Rahman Bahry
	Publisher/Broadcaster/ Sponsor:	Self published (if no sponsor available)
	Date of use:	From Now To print and reprint book
	Number of prints:	Unknown, min. 500, 100 free
	Retail Price:	Print $3.99 - 10.99 10

Description of the material(s) requested:	
Distinguishing code	Photographer's name/ Painter's name / Donator's name
HP135C	Gonichi KIMURA
SA017-2	Yotsugi KAWAHARA Courtesy of Association of the Photographs of the Atomic (Bomb) Destruction of Hiroshima
SA-001-2	Masami ONUKA Courtesy of Association of the Photographs of the Atomic (Bomb) Destruction of Hiroshima
SA-002-2	Masami ONUKA Courtesy of Association of the Photographs of the Atomic (Bomb) Destruction of Hiroshima

Offering means
☑Data ☐Print ☐Unnecessary ☐Others (   )

Special agreements:
1 The photo should not be used for any purposes not mentioned above. No alterations to the picture (color/composition) may be made.
2 In reproducing the photo,
☑Hiroshima Peace Memorial Museum (possess/offer) ☐Donator's name ☐Painter's name ☑Photographer's name must be expressed clearly.
3 One or more copies of the book including the photo you are applying for should be handed to the Hiroshima Peace Memorial Museum.
4 The applicant should apply again when reproducing the photo for any purpose not mentioned above.
5 The applicant is responsible for any problems that may arise from reproducing the photo.

Approval (Invalid without a seal)
許可 PERMISSION
2012. 8. 22
広島平和記念館
Hiroshima Peace ...

We grant permission to the applicant to reproduce the above-mentioned photos. Please abide by the agreements.
*When you use digital data, please be aware that some black-and-white photos were scanned in color.

For further information, please contact:
Hiroshima Peace Memorial Museum, Curatorial Division
1-2 Nakajima-cho, Naka-ku, Hiroshima 730-0811, Japan
Tel: 81-82-241-4004 Fax: 81-82-542-7941

Table of Contents

Preface x

Introduction xviii

Terms xxiv
    ALBM xxiv
    Bahia de Cochinos xxv
    "Bear", Soviet's Long Range Bomber xxv
    Boeing B-52 Stratofortress xxv
    BLA xxv
    Dictabelt xxvi
    ExComm xxvi
    ICBM xxviii
    IRBM xxviii
    MRBM xxix
    NATO xxix
    OLA xxix
    R-12 Dvina xxix
    SLBM xxix
    S-75 xxx
    San Cristobal xxxii
    Thirteen Days, Fifteen Days xxxii
    U-2 xxxiii
    UAV, Surveillance Plane xxxiii

Prologue 1

Part One: The Statesmen Doctrine 1
    1. Anaideia Doctrine 1
    2. Autonomism Doctrine 2
    3. Communism Doctrine 2
    4. Democracy Doctrine 3
    5. Dialectical Materialism Doctrine 3
    6. Hedonism Doctrine 4
    7. Ibn Khaldoun Doctrine 5
    8. Kennedy Doctrine 6
    9. Liberalism Doctrine 6
    10. Monroe Doctrine 7
        10.1. Argentina 9
        10.2. Bolivia 12

10.3. Brazil 12
10.4. Chile.. 13
10.5. Colombia... 14
10.6. Dominican Republic 15
10.7. Guatemala.. 15
10.8. Guyana... 16
10.9. Haiti 16
10.10. Honduras.. 17
10.11. Nicaragua... 17
10.12. Panama... 19
10.13. Peru.. 19
10.14. Venezuela 20
11. Neoliberalism Doctrine.. 21
12. Pre-emptive Doctrine... 22
13. Socialism Doctrine 22
14. Statism Doctrine 23

Part Two: The World around World War II 26

1. Freedom... 26
2. The Players on the World 30
   2.1. Eisenhower (1890-1969).. 31
   2.2. Lenin (1870-1924) 31
   2.3. JFK (1917-1963).. 32
   2.4. Nikita Khrushchev (1894 - 1971) 32
   2.5. Indonesian Communist Party.. 34
   2.6. Fidel Castro (1926-) 44
   2. 7. Oleg Penkovsky (1919-1963) 45
   2.8. Vasili A. Arkhipov (1926 – 1999) 46
   2.9. Robert Oppenheimer (1904 – 1967) 47
   2.10. Francis Gary Powers (1929 - 1977)..................................... 49
   2.11. Rudolf Anderson, Jr. (1927- 1962)...................................... 50
   2.12. Klaus Fuchs (1911-1988)... 53
   2.13 Julius and Ethel Rosenberg... 54
   2.14. Vilyam Genrikhovich Fisher (1903 –1971) 55
   2.15. Kitty Harris (1899-1966) 56
   2.16. Cambridge Five 57
      2.16.1. Kim Philby.. 57
      2.16.2. Donald Duart MacLean... 58
      2.16.3. Guy Burgess.. 58
      2.16.4. Anthony Blunt... 59
      2.16. 5. The Fifth Man 59
   2.17. Anatoly Mikhaylovich Golitsin 60
   2.18. Lev Vasilevsky 60
   2.19. Saville Sax (1924-1980) 61
   2.20. Morton Sobell.. 61
   2.21. George Abramovich Koval (1913 – 2006) 61
   2.22. Theodore Hall (1925 – 1999)... 63

Dialogue 65

Part Three: The Kennedys 65
1. Ireland 65
2. The Flaming Hearts 70
3. Hero of the Sea 73
4. A Futuristic Daddy 76
5. Pulitzer Prize 85
6. Superstition 89
7. Marilyn Monroe 99
8. Last Tango in The White House 104

Part Four: The Turmoil 110
1. Contradiction 110
2. The "Supreme Committee" 119
3. Dealing with the "Supreme Committee" 132
   3.1. Ronald Reagan (1911 – 2004) 132
   3.2. Colin Powell 133
   3.3. Condoleezza Rice 136
      3.3.1. nndb.com 137
      3.3.2. nymag.com 138
      3.3.3. huffingtonpost.com 139
      3.3.4. US Senate Hearing 140
   3.4. George W. Bush 140
4. Oswald the Radar Crew 143
5. Bahia de Cochinos 169
6. Cuban Missile Crisis 174
7. Crisis Time Table 192
8. Assassination of JFK 202
9. Warren Commission 227

Part Five: The Mystery Got Deeper 238
1. Zapruder Film 239
2. Dictabelt 246
3. Autopsy 258
4. Mysterious Bullet 265
5. The HSCA 272
6. The Possible Motives of Assassination 279
7. The Conspiracy Theory 287
   7.1. New Orleans Conspiracy 287
   7.2. CIA Conspiracy 287
   7.3. Shadow Government Conspiracy 288
   7.4. Military-industrial Complex 288
   7.5. Secret Agency Conspiracy 288
   7.6. Cuban Exiles Conspiracy 289

    7.7. Organized Crime Conspiracy 289
    7.8. Lyndon Baines Johnson Conspiracy 290
    7.9. Cuban Conspiracy 290
    7.10. Soviet Conspiracy 291
    7.11. Israeli Conspiracy 291
    7.12. Federal Reserve Conspiracy 291
    7.13. Decoy Casket 292
    7.14. Moon Flight 292
    7.15. Korean Air Lines Flight 007 293
  8. Perennial Cover up 295

Epilogue 302

Part Six: The Nuclear Jeopardy 302
  1. The Little Naughty Boy 304
  2. "Abel Archer" War Game 311
  3. Worst scenario: nuclear warfare 319
  4. Global Cooling 329
  5. Cyber War vs. Nuclear War 336

Closing Note 345

Bibliography 388

Index 394

Motoyasu River and the Dome before bombing. The Hiroshima landmark with the dome was severely damaged after atomic bombing in 1945. The dome was left "as is" and became the historic monument [Courtesy of the City of Hiroshima (Cultural Promotion Division, Culture and Sports Department, Citizens Affairs Bureau)]

Preface

Sometimes a pen is mightier than a sword, and a real story is more amazing than fiction. You may conceal your real intention but you can not conceal your glare of eyes; you can control your emotion but you can not control your glare of eyes since it is something beyond our ability to control; you can not hide your glare even by closing your eyes. If you own the ability to read the glare of someone eyes; you own a foolproof lie detector! Trust me. The ample stories relating to the publishing of this book are awful and in a same time are awesome.

One. Early 2002. When the war on terror was in the heyday, after publishing my book *"Jihad: Struggle or Terrorism"*, I started to collect the materials to write this book from the Public Library since it is a citizen university for free. Maybe it is a wrong time to start, but if I do not start an intention at any given time, I have never made. To read several books in a public library almost every single day for a long time and then to take a note in a composition book, of course, is to attract the attention of the library staffs. It is naturally; especially after the US government issued the warning about the possibility of the terrorists seeking from the public library the data about the vital installations for the bad purposes. So when almost every day I see the persons in uniform and in the plain cloths with the weird glare are walking and glancing to the tables where I am reading, I do understand. I do not blame on them; instead I go to the restroom just to give them the enough time to take a close observation over what is on the table, what am I reading and what am I writing on the composition book as well. As an author, I read a lot of books about the 35th US President John Fitzgerald Kennedy, a person I fully admire! Later, in December 2012 I have a rare chance to visit the crime scene where President Kennedy was assassinated; it was very sad moment. My previous book *"Jihad"* was published by the *AuthorHouse* of Bloomington, Indiana in 2002; now is self-published with new paragraphs, corrections, and ISBN 978-0-9892988-2-7. By publishing *"Jihad"* I have been trying hard to suppress the radicalism in order to fix the wrong understanding about jihad in the Muslim world and beyond. I believe I made it. They do not have to worry about what I do in the public library and elsewhere.

Two. May 4. You can not hide your glare of eyes. On a local newspaper advertisement, a 1999 European car was for sale for a couple of thousands. I called the number and asked "why did he want to sell it"; the answer was for preparing a newborn baby. The price was closed at far below the ad price –it turned to be necessary to spend a lot of money to fix– and we would meet at a parking lot of a local bank to pay. Whom do I meet first?

It's not the seller; instead a man, a Caucasian, below 55 years, about 5 feet 7 inches, 200 lbs, in American grey car staring at me, his glare of eyes was emanating a very deep curiosity. I do not blame on him, he's doing his job; I respect him. From this point I was convinced that my phone was monitored and he was watching who would come to see me "is he a car seller or a suspect"; since according to the human inter-relation theory "a person who meets a suspect, is likely a suspect, too". Never be in my life to think of harming my new country, America; ever. I already made a written statement to a US Government officer about this. Am I a religious activist in Cleveland? Yes. Do I pray at a public or open space like library, station, airport, etc.? Yes, it's obligation, whenever a time of prayer comes I have to pray. Do I have "the followers"? Yes, they are my inmate students, since I am the religious provider at 2 correctional centers. I always remind them that the US government is one among the good governments since it grants us the freedom to practice any religion while the Chinese government forbids the state employees to pray during business hours for 'counter productive reason; "The US government is still the best for hiring me to teach you and you spend nothing", I notify. As they reenter the community I urge them to avoid any violence even 'for a religious reason'; being an ex con does not necessarily mean that they are easy prey to recruit as an agent of violence; "Please report immediately to the authority as you find any religious leader preaching the violence". Am I a suspect because my first name is Abdul? Maybe, but Paula Abdul is not a suspect, for sure. "Bin Laden" is a big taboo; never mention these two words in any phone conversation. An innocent friend in Indonesia talked to me over the phone and he named "9/11" as "*peristiwa bin Laden*" in local language which means "bin Laden incident." The Americans name the attack on the WTC as "9/11" and they know how to pronounce it well. Since Indonesian people do not speak English they never said "*nine eleven*" nor "*sembilan sebelas*", but "*peristiwa bin Laden*" to refer the very same incident; does this (monitored) phone conversation make me a "suspect" because my friend mentioned a big taboo? May be, but one thing for sure; my friend and I are not terrorists!

Three. The Post Office, Hopkins International Airport, Cleveland Ohio; 2009.

The USPS is an important point in our life; we send and receive the mails through it. Never be in my mind to misuse USPS, ever; yet my visit to USPS could be considered something different from the other side by the other person. When I was sending the mail, a polite gentleman talked to me outside USPS about the climate and car, a common daily conversation everywhere. He was still outside when I came in to see the USPS clerk. As I came out I found him checking the USPS trash box in such a way so intensive to attract my attention on why a neat gentleman, not a homeless, was searching a dirty trash box with the risk of getting someone's vomit and spit? After praying a moment asking God's guidance, I was convinced that this gentleman was looking for a clue about me; he was looking for something inside the trash box to find out if I use it as a dead drop to blindly connect with a "suspect". As we know from the spy story, a *dead drop* is a point to leave and pick a message up to avoid the direct contact among the spies as Robert Hanssen a former Government agent used it to send the stolen US secret to Soviet spy (http://en.wikipedia.org/wiki/Robert_hanssen).

Alas, what are they thinking about me? I am not a spy, nor an agent for any government; instead a simple man to find a new life in America. What is the matter, is it phobia or hysteria?

Four. Trick is a dirty and abominable way to win a case if someone thinks that he would not prevail without cheating. When I was driving along Snow Road of Cleveland on a summer, two guys were smiling and waving at me as if they knew me for long time in their effort to be familiar and attracting my attention. When they were performing a sign to stop and talk, I made a right turn on Fry Avenue and stopped. Suddenly, one of two guys was approaching me and delivering a box of expensive sound system to give away; "It's free", he said and asked to open the trunk. He was a stranger I never knew before, so his action was seriously attracting my extra attention. After praying and asking a divine guidance I was convinced that it was a trick.

I believed whenever I accept his stuff then another group would report on me or even arrest me for receiving the stolen property; it is illegal to receive the stolen property for any reason. His action was too good to be true and honest; a stranger gives you something valuable? The sound system is expensive but the trick is cheap. Thanks God, You saved me.

Five. The most dangerous trick was in a worst Cleveland winter of this decade. After several attempts to trick me have failed; then someone invented a sophisticated way to entrap me. We are the workers, used to take a break in a small room where we read newspapers, magazines or just to socialize. It was almost the time to clock out when I saw a weird reading material on the table; it was the map with a title "Nuclear power plant", I do not care if it is real or fake, I have nothing to do with it. I asked one fellow worker to keep this paper for the office manager and not letting it on the table, and then I clocked out and went home. Alas, I was shivering to realize what if I take this map (but *for what?*), then someone would stop and search me and find the "strategic map" and detain me. Next morning, according to a scenario I believe were prepared for me, the local newspapers and local TV stations would display and broadcast the same headline "**A Nabbed Terrorist has map of nuclear power plant**", OMG. Frankly, I am still shivering anytime I remember this possible trick. I am not a terrorist; I do not need anything to destroy, I have nothing to do with any map and I do not even think about it; why does someone always set me up? Thanks God, You saved me.

Believe me, there are still some tricks to trap me during a 12-year span of time. The tricks were so intensive and for a very long time since "Toledo Incident" in 2001 where someone in an oncoming vehicle made abrupt U-turn to follow me during a trip to Michigan. This incident taught me that my vehicle was planted with an electronic device which compelled me to think on why someone has been focusing on me and singled me out for a very long time; is it because of my religion, race; discrimination or hatred, what else? I made some notes about the tricks I believe someone tried to get me; but I do not want to scare you now.

We are the common people; we have a question if someone has tried to block my comprehensive integration to the American society despite the fact that I did something beneficial for them. For ten years in row I teach so many inmates in preparing them to reenter the contemporary society they missed during incarceration; this is my dedication and loyalty to America, is it wrong? I was active in the interfaith group where the Moslem, Christian and Jewish join hands in hands to help the needy. Is this the reward I should get, do I deserved? Someday, maybe another book should have been written.

Seven years later after collecting the reading materials from the public library, the world is shocked by the malicious software (malware) ***Stuxnet*** and ***DuQu*** which infected the certain computers to stealing the data, taking the computer control over, recording the voice, reading the computer screen, monitoring the keystroke, and performing so many other complicated tasks. I believe I got a malware, not Stuxnet, but similar to this one. Here is the rationale:

(1) It is naïve to think that any computer is free from monitoring, so never make any bad intention and action, ever. Do not even think you are smart!

(2) A trustworthy friend sent email link, and without any suspicion I clicked it. It's totally wrong; it turns to be a confirmation for the malware to sneak.

(3) The malware is illegally attached to Microsoft Windows, but it does not work until you confirm it by clicking any link or program.

The good reason to click is when you received email from a very trustworthy name and you are tempted to click the available link. Once you click the link; that is the time the malware entering your computer. It happened to my computer.

(4) In August 2012 when the manuscript of this book is almost ready to print, I could not open my computer even with the correct password. There must be someone or something to change the password. Panic? Yes, it is naturally. After trying several times with so many possibility of "new password" I can open the computer; and soon I change the password.

(5) Any time I change the password; the malware knows and changes it again, and I beat on it again.

(6) I start thinking on how the malicious software knows my new passwords; it must be from the internet connection; and it's a clue that every single keystroke on my computer was monitored, otherwise how did they know the new password? Had he or she or they had the authority to do so, they should have come forward to present the warrant; and then I would voluntarily disclose the password and all contents of my computer, I guarantee one hundred percent there is nothing dangerous in my computer. So I disconnect the internet and change the password. Now, I challenge anybody to steal my password!

(7) After changing the password; it is naïve if to think that it's safe now. The infected computer is not good anymore to edit the manuscript ever since. Although we –you and I– never used computer to harm anybody else, ever; but to let a stranger to peep into whatever we are typing is not a good idea, either. With a complicated maneuver, I edit and keep the manuscript in a safe place, send it for publishing after obtaining ISBN; and now we may read it in a sense of freedom, American freedom. The question is "what is wrong with writing a book about US President?"

This book is a part of our past and the future history, and by reading this book you made the history already. This is life, and this is politics. The politics is a deception to counter another deception, the ultimate goal of politics is power, the ultimate goal of power is money; a politician is a businessman and the commodity is our weakness; if someone successfully scare you then you lost one half of your property and one half of your life; so what was left behind for you?

A.R. Bahry
Cleveland Ohio USA, April 2013

Introduction

"Kennedy" was an American mantra. Ted Kennedy passed away in August 2009; he was the last prince to bear the famous and success name of Kennedy. Even his natural death was a special "success" since he was not assassinated, unlike his two brothers Jack and Bob who were assassinated in 1963 and 1968 respectively. Ted Kennedy was not assassinated either from refraining himself from running for the presidency, or the would-be assassin decided to let him alive to prevent the Kennedy name from being more legendary. It is a matter of fact that John F. Kennedy and his brother Robert Kennedy were assassinated regardless of whether the assassination is a conspiracy or not. It is pretty challenging to write a short but "heavy duty" book about the late famous US President John Fitzgerald Kennedy. In this book his name was written as "US President John F. Kennedy" and sometimes as JFK his popular initial, both to refer to the famous and legitimate 35th President of the United States of America.

This book is an outcome of library research including the movies and websites; the analysis was made after comparing some sources thereof. It has been a long process from reading, resuming, comparing and analyzing of one source after another; and the most delicate process is to compile for the final manuscript. The first two chapters are prepared to be a comprehensive background for the next chapters to help us going back to the time when President Kennedy was assassinated.

About two thousand articles, books and movies had been released since a fateful day in Dallas Texas on Friday November 22, 1963. The JFK saga is a most narrated story in the modern history with the different depth and nuance. Most of the authors and analysts are leaning to blame on a certain government agency or officials within a reasonable doubt and without considering on why the assassination took place regardless of how wrong the assassination was.

Most of the authors, researcher and even New Orleans District Attorney Jim Garrison were so eager to find the villain -and failed-, while this book is seeking the answer on **why** the assassination happened without stressing who did; it's more analysis rather than merely synopsis. This book has a the different approach by considering that the triggermen never knew the motive of JFK's assassination, they just followed the instruction and got the payment for their work; and probably most of them had already gone; the time to prosecuting them is over.

Who did think that sixty to ninety million American people would have been vanished in a blink of eyes if the nuclear war between USA and Soviet breaks out? The world already had had 2 nuclear explosions which killed hundreds of thousand innocent people, plus 336 controlled nuclear explosions and a dozen of uncontrolled accidental nuclear explosions in the atmosphere. Both USA and Soviet Union have had more than 2,500 (two thousands five hundreds) operational nuclear missiles that more than enough to reduce this beautiful blue planet into irreversible rubble.

The so-called "civilized human being" had invented ICBM, ALBM, SLBM that are ready to destroy "the enemy" which in fact the extended family from the descendant of same father Adam and same mother Eve. In China only, there are 1,600 nuclear warheads and soon would be 2,000 according to the BBC report on July 2010.

This planet and the human being were in an impending danger to extinct; in 1960's the world was in political crisis, the most probable solution to the crisis is to prevent the nuclear war in order to save millions of people both in USA and Soviet Union. Whenever the nuclear war erupts, there will be absolutely no winner, both parties will be losing and suffering from the irreversible damages for decades long. The USA already used West Germany and Turkey to place nuclear missiles to strike the Soviet Union. The Soviet Union already used Cuba as a nuclear base to attack USA, the SS-3 medium range ballistic missiles (MRBMs) arrived on September 8-16, 1962.

The Soviet Union military technicians were building at least 9 out of 40 planned sites to launch the SS-4s and SS-5s with 2,500 mile-range capability. Had all available nuclear weapons simultaneously been launched from Cuba within 6 minutes or less, it is more than enough to inevitably reduce Washington, New York and other possible target cities into irreversible rubles.

Never be, the human being were so close to the global nuclear war as happened in 1962. It was the incident of September 27, 1962 when **Major Rudolf Anderson** on board of **U-2** spy plane was shot down over Cuba; the USA issued a final warning that the next shooting down of any US plane would be considered as the escalation of conflict.

It was a last warning before the real war. The Soviet Union then immediately ordered its Army Commander in Cuba to stop shooting the US planes. Another incident was on October 26, 1962 when **USS Beale** surrounded a Soviet submarine around Cuba with *the depth bomb* without realizing that the nuclear torpedo were on board of sneaking submarine, its captain **Valentin Savitsky** upon thinking that the real war already started then ordered his seamen to prepare the nuclear torpedo launching right away. He might be thinking that it would be "better off" to let nuclear torpedo go off on the American target(s) rather than to go off on board altogether with him and his seamen hit by American depth bomb. Fortunately, he was stopped by Commander **Vasily Arkhipov**; the world was already on the brink of nuclear war.

When Khrushchev "the communist" decided to send the nuclear missiles to Cuba, he did not just make a fun; it's deterrent and a real preparation to destroy America "the capitalist". His predecessor Iosif Stalin already killed five million fellow folks just to make sure the Soviet main land reform of *kholkoz* works, so why not taking seriously Khrushchev's plan to kill about millions of American on the initial nuclear strike launched from Cuba?

The estimation for the first nuclear blast on the American soil - maybe Washington DC- at least forty million people in DC and adjacent states would be killed; and the responding nuclear attack to the Soviet Union will take sixty million people. It should have been an absolute turmoil and the beginning of doomsday.

To avoid England and France from collaborating with the USA, the chairman of Soviet Communist Party might decide to act a "pre-emptive strike" against London and Paris. Another sixty million people should have been died. Because the Soviet Union has been thinking in such a way, then the USA should have prevented China from collaborating with the Soviet Union. The USA next action would have been launching a couple of nuclear weapons to China mainland as a part of "pre-emptive strike and preventive defense"; the result would be one hundred and twenty million Chinese people die. It's absolutely not a fantasy, it's a rational tally, it's a strategic calculation and it does make sense.

It takes hundred millions of dollar to prepare a US President, however a US President is not everything, there is still someone or something above the US President; the case of VENONA project was a perfect example. Two US Presidents Franklin D. Roosevelt and Harry S. Truman did not know anything about VENONA project, a secret method of encrypted communication. If the US President did not know a very important project, he might not know another secret project; and it does make sense if the secret group –such as what so-called "The Supreme Committee"– or below-the-line administration within the administration might be exist as an administration backup in case of the on-the-line administration fails.

Had you been on the compelling position at "The Supreme Committee" to keep millions of American people safe, do you think that sacrificing something or someone was not "justified" to protect sixty to ninety million American people from nuclear disaster?

John F. Kennedy might have been not the first nation leader to order the first nuclear strike against Soviet Union, but Nikita Khrushchev's daring action to place dozens of Soviet's nuclear weapons in Cuba was a terrorism; the real nuclear terrorism, he was the first terrorist to threaten America. Why does the terrorist want to harm America; because of hatred, envy, insanity, or something else?

It was provocative; it was an imminent danger since the nuclear missiles could be launched from Cuba to American soil as soon as necessary without enough time to warn the civilians and business centers to protect themselves. The USA never stepped back against any threat and enemy, but to let some million innocent people to die is another issue. The Khrushchev's action had been considered as the *passing action* over the USA at the time where the communism was blooming while the domino theory was looming (although this theory itself is now disputable as a tool of psywar).

John Fitzgerald Kennedy was too perfect to be the US President, and too many politicians to worry about their future political careers had Robert Kennedy assumed to succeed the Presidency, and afterward Ted Kennedy to succeed his brothers. Had they run for the presidency and prevailed, and each of them reigned for two terms then 3 Kennedys would have occupied the White House for 24 years in row, and the political career of other politicians would be closed for good.

In 1963 **President** Kennedy, **Attorney General** Robert Kennedy and **Senator** Ted Kennedy were photographed outside the Oval Room of White House as the US government officials and not just as the member of Kennedys; three Kennedys were in one time one place; one of them already occupied the White House and another two were ready to replace one after another. Never be in American history or any history of the world three brothers to hold the high position in the government after being elected democratically!

Joseph and Rose Kennedy must be very proud of their phenomenal sons, the Three Musketeers! Therefore from the cons side, the paradigm to terminate the reign of Kennedy's clan became a milestone of future America. However to avoid the nuclear war is far more important than the President election. This paradigm may explain on why Robert Kennedy was stopped! By understanding this rationale and paradigm, Ted Kennedy did a perfect choice, and he had a smart decision. He preferred to be alive as a common citizen rather than to be a US President but dies within days.

Was the assassination of US President John F. Kennedy a conspiracy? Either it was or it was not, the more important questions are **what, why, who** and **when. What's** the concealed motive behind the assassination of millennium? **Why** was US President John F. Kennedy assassinated? **Who** did successfully carry it on? **When** was the nuclear war overdue? **Was** JFK too dangerous to incite the Armageddon? **Was** he too young to understand the consequence of nuclear war? **Should** he be stopped before delivering order to launch a nuclear warhead?

Was his assassination justified? Find them out in this book, and also find out the result of "investigation" by the author on the crime scene at Dealey Plaza, Dallas Texas 50 years later that would definitely answer the long time question "Did Oswald killed JFK?"

The assassination had been an absolute solution when we have been unable to find the "win-win solution", it happened since very long time ago at the second generation of mankind when Qabel killed Abel –the sons of Adam and Eve– to solve their dispute rather than sharing the world dominion side by side peacefully; and ever since we used to resolve our inability and incapability with murder while thinking we shall not accountable on the judgment day. Why did we do that, because we are all the descendants of Qabel the assassin? A nice Abel had gone, long time ago without any single offspring. We came from belligerent Qabel, not peaceful Abel.

Terms

It is necessary to briefly explain the important terms and the influential persons in this book. It will also mention some sophisticated weapons which were ready in 1960's for the preparation of nuclear war then and now. The similar weapons, even more sophisticated, are ready today in global tension where the certain powerful nations are preparing to eliminate the rival just to proof to the world that they are legitimate to say "We are the most powerful nation in the world. Look, we eliminated our enemy already!" They were not preparing the defense as they claimed; they were ready to eliminate the rival by destroying its homeland and civilians with the nuclear weapon. They argued that ***the best defense is the pre-emptive attack***. This is the paradigm of so-called the civilized human being. "They" are actually "we", you and me. According to Stockholm International Peace Research Institute [SIPRI], since early 2012, 8 nuclear countries have reduced their arsenals from 4,400 nuclear warheads to 2,200. The 8 nuclear countries are China, France, India, Israel, Pakistan, Russia, United Kingdom and USA. Although they reduced the amount of their nuclear weapons; yet the alert is still high [1].

We are civilized people yet we have a built-in self destructive mechanism we always exercise it over the time, otherwise why did we make the nuclear weapons and deadly gadgets?

In the nuclear war -as our self destructive mechanism works- there is no winner whatsoever; it would be a mutual assured destruction [MAD] where all adversaries will be the losers; and the next generations would curse us because we put them on the ruble and genetically destroy them; is this the way we love our sons and daughters?

ALBM

Air-launched ballistic missile [ALBM] is a ballistic missile deployed from a special equipped aircraft, a B-52. This kind of missile was never be commissioned in the defense system due to high risk of its operation. One among the reason is the vulnerability of the aircraft that used to launch it. The use of ALBM is a double jeopardy for the user, if the aircraft is fail to airborne then the missile is fail too; and if the aircraft is successful to airborne then the aircraft itself is an object to intercept. With so many considerations and difficulties, then this missile was cancelled in 1962. The program is to be continued with SLBM.

Bahia de Cochinos

Bahia de Cochinos is a Spanish name for a small passage on the southern coast of Cuba, it was known as the Bay of Pigs. Bahia de Cochinos incident was an attempt by about 1,500 Cuban exiles under the command of US troops to topple communist Cuban leader Fidel Castro in April 1961.

"Bear", Soviet's Long Range Bomber

The Bear normally does not fly, but this "Bear" has four powerful turboprop engines capable to go to any place in the world. It is **Tupolev Tu-95**; it has capability to launch the deadly missile. It used to go back and forth from Eastern Russian military base to Tokyo; therefore it was nicknamed Tokyo Express.

Boeing B-52 Stratofortress

The long-range bomber operated by the USAF since 1955 with capability to carry nuclear weapons for Cold War Era. It is capable of carrying 70,000 pounds (32,000 kg) of weapons. The B-52 has been in active service with the USAF since 1955. It was operated for long time for its superior performance and low operating costs; it was the longest operated aircraft in service, and its debut reached 50 years in 2005.

BLA

Below-the-line administration is an intangible administration within the existing administration that might be serving as an administration backup in case of the over-the-line administration fails.

Dictabelt

Dictabelt is the old model of portable sound recorder as a part of police equipments in 1960's; it was used by the policeman in Dallas, Texas during the time of JFK escort. Dictabelt became important topic to discuss since one Dictabelt unexpectedly recorded the sound of gunshot during the fateful time when JFK was shot in Dealy Plaza, Dallas, Texas on Friday at 12:30 p.m. Central Standard Time on November 22, 1963.

From this dictabelt, the scientists are competing to unveil what direction the gunshot came from and what kind of weapon used by assassin to kill JFK. The dictabelt investigation became so important because there were some doubts that "the magic bullet" came from The Texas School Book Depository at the corner of Houston Street and Elm Street where the alleged assassin Lee Harvey Oswald worked.

ExComm

The Executive Committee of the National Security Council was a special committee of US government's top officials that helped and advised President JFK during 13 days of the October 1962 Cuban Missile Crisis. This committee was commonly referred to as the Executive Committee, or its short the ExComm. It was established on October 22, 1962 in rush due to the emergency situation of impending nuclear war between US and Soviet Union after US intelligence was convinced that Soviet Union had installed the medium range ballistic missile in Cuba. The ExComm meeting was intensified after USAF Major Rudolf Anderson's spy plane U-2 was shot down over Cuba on October 27, 1962.

The definitive information about the Soviet nuclear installation in Cuba came from Oleg Vladimirovich Penkovsky [1919 – 1963] a high rank Soviet military Colonel worked for Glavnoye Razedivatelnoye Upravlenniye [GRU, Military Intelligence Agency] [2]. This information was long time before the "official acknowledgement" by the US on October 14, 1962 that the Soviet nuclear weapons were installed in Cuba.

The October 14, 1962 revelation by a U-2 spy plane that the Soviet nuclear weapons were installed in Cuba was just a strategic cover-up to keep the role of Penkovsky in secret. U-2 Mission on October 14, 1962 was to take the aerial photographs of Soviet missile installation in Cuba, without U-2 the US knew the secret of Soviet missiles were already in Cuba. Most historians refer the Cuban Missile Crisis to as "Thirteen Days Crisis" that started from U-2 revelation on October 14 (not October 16, the first ExComm meeting) 1962 until ExComm meeting on October 27, 1962. Actually, it was "Fifteen Days Crisis" since ExComm held another important meeting on October 29, 1962 at the White House Cabinet Room during the Cuban Missile Crisis.

The ExComm had had 25 members of various high rank US officials including the members of the National Security Council (NSC) plus White House staffs, CIA, Department of Defence, Department of State, US Ambassador, US Special Envoy, and Information Agency (now similar to White House spokesman).

The 25 members of ExComm were [3]
John F. Kennedy, US President, NSC
Lyndon B. Johnson, Vice President, NSC
Dean Rusk, Secretary of State, NSC
Douglas Dillon, Secretary of Treasury, NSC
Robert McNamara, Secretary of Defense, NSC
Robert F. Kennedy, Attorney General, NSC
McGeorge Bundy, National Security Adviser, NSC
General Maxwell Taylor, Chairman of Joint Chiefs of Staff, NSC
John McCone, CIA Director, NSC
Ray S. Cline, CIA
Arthur Lundahl, CIA
George Ball, Undersecretary of State
Roswell Gilpatric, Deputy Secretary of Defense
Dean Acheson, Former US Secretary of State, US Special Envoy [4]
Paul Nitze, Department of Defense
Edward A. McDermott, Department of Defense
Alexis Johnson, Department of State
Edwin Martin, Assistant Secretary of State
Llewellyn Thomson, US Ambassador to Soviet Union
Adlai Stevenson, US Ambassador to the United Nation
Donald Wilson, Information Agency
Kenny O'Donnell, White House Staff
David Powers, White House Staff

Theodore Sorensen, White House Staff [5]
Bromley Smith, Secretary of the NSC

ICBM

Intercontinental ballistic missile is the 3,500 miles long-range weapon of mass destruction [WMD]; it's designed to kill the huge number of people abroad. The use of this weapon indicates that the war is entering the highest stage of destruction; it is an all-out war where each party knows for sure that using of this weapon will carry the ultimate irreversible destruction. Yet, we are the civilized nations produced total more than 10,000 ICBM. The Soviet's first ICBM was tested in August 1957; it has several advantages over the conventional bombers to deliver the nuclear warhead since it's much faster and more economic than a bomber, it travels the high altitude and high speed which would be difficult for the adversary to intercept. The variation of ICBM is MIRV [Multi Independently-Targetable Reentry Vehicle], a single missile with the capability to deploy several nuclear warheads to kill at least 10 million people; each warhead has 375 kiloton explosive more than 20 times stronger than atomic bomb detonated in Hiroshima, Japan on August 6, 1945. If an ICBM has 5 different warheads then it may kill 50 million people, meanwhile the amount of MIRV is more than enough to wipe the human being out from this beautiful planet. Who does have this WMD with capability to reduce this beautiful planet into junk? China, France, India, Israel, Iran, North Korea, Pakistan, Russia, United Kingdom, and USA do. North Korea is pursuing this kind of weapon.

IRBM

Intermediate-range ballistic missile has a range below 3,500 miles; it was designed to kill people of another country; its operator is intending to wipe a nation out easily from remote area. Who are the operators of this Weapon of Mass Destruction? They are China, France, India, Israel, Iran, North Korea, Pakistan, Russia, United Kingdom, and USA.

MRBM

Medium-range ballistic missile has a range below 1,900 miles yet still deadly; it was intended to "settle" the local, regional, and sub-continental conflicts like the Cuban Crisis in 1962. Who does have this WMD with capability to destroy the neighboring countries? China, India, Israel, Iran, North Korea, Pakistan, Russia, and USA do.

NATO

NATO (North Atlantic Treaty Organization) is the military alliance between some European governments and the USA for a collective defense against the Soviet Union and its ally.

NATO is the legacy of the Cold War Era; as the Soviet Union collapsed, NATO should have been dissolved or transferred into the economic alliance to face the China domination in the global spreading of cheap price products. NATO is also expected to be wary of the possibility of cyber war and computer hacking.

OLA

Over-the-line administration is an official regular administration.

R-12 Dvina

This Soviet's MRBM is designed to launch from an open mobile platform and from a silo; its nuclear warhead has 2 megaton of destroying capability about 10,000 times than "The Little Boy" a nuclear weapon that destroyed Hiroshima in 1945. North Atlantic Treaty Organization [NATO] code named R-12 Dvina as SS-4 which originally was designed to destroy the European countries; and its installation in Cuba incited the Cuban Missile Crisis in 1962.

SLBM

Submarine-launched ballistic missile, a missile launched from a submarine. The early program of this missile was Polaris missile, developed in 1962. China, England, India, Israel, France, Russia and the US are the owners of SLBM. The Germany does not have it, but has built the submarines with the capability to launch the SLBM and sold it to another country. SLBM is a very sophisticated WMD due to its capability to elude the conventional detection and its agility to move from one to another point of the sea. It has very long range between 4,000 to 5,000 miles. A SLBM may also be a MIRV with the capability to destroy multiple targets in the same time. This Satan may kill the huge amount of innocent people in a certain country without even being detected where its WMD was launched either from under the sea surface or from a submerged submarine. Some countries have this elusive WMD. Israel, Iran, North Korea, and Pakistan are either developing or operating this WMD; one of them is reported to have this capability after receiving the nuclear powered submarines from West Germany in early 2012. In general, The US outnumbered Russia in the intercontinental ballistic missile by tenfold or more, when US had had several hundreds, in fact, Soviet Union had only four [6].

S-75

The S-75 is a very sophisticated Russian surface-to-air missile. It was developed in 1953 by Pyotr Grushin's [7] team of military strategist. NATO code named it as SA-2 Guideline. It was commissioned in 1957 and became the most successful and widely used air defence missile in Soviet block history. It surprised the Western military analysts when it shot down a Taiwanese spy plane over China on October 1959; and ever since it became a focus of the Western military planner on how to tame it, even though the US still lost two very sophisticated spy planes over Sverdlovsk Russia in 1960, and Cuba in October 1962. The superiority of S-75 always becomes a serious threat to the strategic bombers such as B-47 and B-52. Since China shot a Taiwanese spy plane down to Gary Powell's fate in 1960 to 1962 during Cuban crisis until Vietnam War that ended in April 30, 1975; the superiority of S-75 never be defeated. It was later developed to be more sophisticated in 1993. The western strategists estimated that 4,600 S-75s were produced and deployed in 35 countries, and became the most deployed missile defense system in the military history.

Since S-75 is considered the most dangerous missile defense system, the US has developed three systems to conquer it:

(1) AGM-45 Shrike missile. It works based on S-75 system itself. S-75 consists of an integrated system including the missile, the launcher and the radar system to detect the target aircraft. When a hostile aircraft is approaching, the S-75 system knows it from the radar. From this point the US developed the Shrike missile to destroy the S-75 system by tracking the origin of S-75 radar.

(2) ECM [Electronic Counter Measure], including the powerful jamming device to blind the early warning radars of S-75; and the smaller device to impair S-75 radar from obtaining the range information. The ECM installed in the bomber and fighter jets.

(3) A Wild Weasel aircraft to find and destroy the S-75 installations. The main course of Wild Weasel is to use the sophisticated radar to seek missiles then destroy S-75 radar system.

Here the list of S-75 stunning victims:

(1) Taiwan's [Martin RB-57D] spy plane on October 7, 1959 over China mainland,

(2) Gary Power's U-2 on May 1, 1960 over Sverdlovsk Russia,

(3) Rudolf Anderson's U-2 on October 27, 1962 over Cuba,

(4) McDonnell Douglas F-4 Phantom II on July 24, 1965 over North Vietnam,

(5) Russian Sukhoi Su-27 jet fighter near Gudauta [Georgia, a part of ex-Soviet Union] on March 19, 1993. The latest incident is the first Soviet-made jet shot down by Soviet-made missile.

San Cristobal

San Cristobal was one of two nuclear launching sites in Cuba; the other was Sagua la Grande. On October 27, the CIA reported to the US President that three missile sites at San Cristobal and the two sites at Sagua la Grande were fully operational. This report seemed to be a relay from Colonel Rudolf Anderson who flew over Cuba in U-2 spy plane before being shot down.

Thirteen Days, Fifteen Days

Thirteen Days refers to the tumultuous days from October 14, 1962 to October 27, 1962 during the Cuban Missile Crisis which put the world on the brink of nuclear war between Soviet Union and United States of America. Actually, chronologically, and completely it was 15 days from October 14, 1962 to October 29, 1962 where the ExComm held the very important meeting in the White House discussing the Cuban Missile Crisis and the impact of last offer from Soviet Union Prime Minister Khrushchev in *quid pro quo* settlement.

October 14, 1962 was the day where a U-2 spy plane confirmed the secret previous information delivered by Soviet's KGB Colonel Penkovsky that Soviet Union had placed the MRBM in Cuba; and October 27, 1962 was the day Major Rudolf Anderson on the board of U-2 spy plane flew over Cuba to confirm that Soviet nuclear missile were fully ready to launch. It was the fateful day for Major Anderson since he was shot down to his death; it was also the day US President JFK issued the ultimatum to Cuba –and also Soviet– that any other U-2 were shot down then the US would invade Cuba in a full scale war. It was also a decisive day for the future fate of JFK since his ultimatum drew the huge question "would he bring the US to the direct confrontation with the Soviet Union in the nuclear war?" If so, why not to "stop" him before it's too late?

U-2

U-2 is the spy plane designed by Clarence Johnson [1910-1990], manufactured by Lockheed and made its first flight in August 1, 1955 [8]. It is a very important spy plane before the development of spy satellite in 1970's. This "Dragon Lady" has the ability to reach a very high altitude up to 70,000 feet beyond the average ability of anti-aircraft artillery. Even though, at least two U-2s were shot down i.e. Gary Power's U-2 on May 1, 1960 over Sverdlovsk Russia [9], and Rudolf Anderson's U-2 on 27 October, 1962 over Cuba. The death of USAF Major Anderson [10] in 1962 on the mission to detect the installation of Soviet Union nuclear weapon, had triggered President JFK to send ultimatum to Cuba that one more time an U-2 were shot down then the full scale war will start.

JFK considered the shooting down any U-2 over Cuba has only one meaning: to cover up the nuclear installation in Cuba; and the installation of nuclear weapon in Cuba has only one meaning: to launch a surprise nuclear war against the USA since Cuba has some strategic and geographic advantages. There was no doubt that JFK's threat to invade Cuba in a full scale war would have the direct impact on the nuclear installation in Cuba. The "full scale war" will drag Soviet Union into the Cuban war and in turn will force both SU and US to use the nuclear weapon. Therefore, JFK's threat on Cuba is still debatable until now on how it has a direct impact to his fate in Dallas, Texas on Friday, November 22, 1963.

UAV, Surveillance Plane

UAV is a surveillance aircraft has a special task to collect information either for military or civil purposes. Normally, it does not carry the weapon, but the later version does carry the deadly weapon as operated in Afghan-Pakistani borders. The latest development of surveillance plane is the use of drone or Aerial Unmanned Vehicle [UAV] to avoid the pilot as victim but it generates more civilian victims. UAV is a sophisticated satellite guided spy planes which remotely operated and armed with deadly weapons for multi military purposes; some countries are operating the UAVs.

[1] "Republika" online newspaper; Republika.com, June 06, 2012
[2] http://en.wikipedia.org/wiki/Penkovsky
[3] http://en.wikipedia.org/wiki/ExComm
[4] He had a special assignment to obtain the support from France President Charles de Gaulle during Cuban Missile Crisis.
[5] Later before his death in 2011, he wrote an important book about JFK. Some critics considered it was not necessary since it may undermine the legacy of JFK.
[6] Tim Weiner, "Legacy of Ashes, the History of CIA", Anchor Books, New York 2008, ISBN 978-0307-38900-8; p. 183
[7] http://en.wikipedia.org/wiki/S-75_Dvina
[8] http://en.wikipedia.org/wiki/U-2_Dragon_Lady
[9] http://en.wikipedia.org/wiki/Gary_Powers
[10] http://en.wikipedia.org/wiki/Rudolf_Anderson

Prologue
Part One: The Statesmen Doctrine

The statesman doctrine or political doctrine is a political guideline which influences the way a country works relating to its surroundings area. The political doctrines grew because the **followers** of mainstream religions [Christianity, Judaism and Islam] failed to accommodate the contemporary need to govern the society. These religions are not fail but rather their followers. The political doctrines have a wide and long term impact over the certain nation and its vicinity. The impact including but not limited to behavior, politics, and economics; it may also affect the peace or war. The political doctrine has its own rule, the politics is a deception to counter another deception, the ultimate goal of politics is power, the ultimate goal of power is money; a politician is a businessman and the commodity is our weakness. The power is another side of money; like a same coin with two different faces. Money may also be used to obtain the power; and power may also be used to obtain the money; money may not far away from politics and politics may not far away from money.

1. Anaideia Doctrine

Anaídeia derived from the Greek "a" or "an" (means "without") and *"aidos"* (means "shame") Anaideia does mean *"no shame"* or *"shameless"*. The world becomes the witness that lot of world leaders and businessmen practicing this doctrine (or suffering from it) since they assert that the strength is truth and weakness is fault; the lie is their daily menu. The real men who understand the meaning of shame are Japanese; if they made a grave mistake they would commit "hara kiri" and in some cases they commit "seppuku" the act of self inflicted wound to death sometimes with intentional suffering to reflect their remorse and sorry, and to guarantee that it would never happen again for good. In our modern era, a lot of war crimes happened.

When those who were responsible for war crime in the massacres of Balkan, Shabra-Chatila, Timor, Rwanda, Babri, Meikhtila Myanmar etc. would be brought to justice to stand trial? When would the defendants stand trial at International Criminal Court in The Hague?

2. Autonomism Doctrine

The Autonomism is a doctrine which adopts acquiring political autonomy of a certain region.

The democratic movement in Canada adopted this doctrine to acquire the title of autonomous State to the province of Quebec [11]. The Aceh [pronounced "Atjehh"] movement was also a democratic action to acquire the title of autonomous province in Indonesia, it's not separation; this movement successfully acquired the autonomy from the central government in Jakarta after struggling for a very long time. The East Timor province should have adopted this doctrine instead of separation from the Indonesian Unity, unfortunately during the tenure of President **Baharudin Habibie**, East Timor province lost from Indonesia in a frame of Australian oil interest in the Timor gap. **Habibie** is only a politician by a chance, not a statesman.

3. Communism Doctrine

Communism is an extreme version of socialism [12]. Its revolutionary movement was intended to establish a certain community with no class, no gap within community, no more poor or rich where everyone would be equal with the mutual ownership of the means of production, and no more exclusive capital ownership since all capitals are belong to the proletariat. This movement gained a significant influence a couple decades before and during almost entire 20th century, and became a root of deep rivalry between the socialist world lead by the Soviet Union and capitalist world lead by the US of America. If each party, socialist and capitalist, did not restrain themselves; the **World War III** should have went off in November 1963.

4. Democracy Doctrine

Democracy derived from Greek "demos" (people) and "kratia" (rule); it does mean the rule of the people. It has its root from $5^{th} - 4^{th}$ century BC [13]. Democracy is a form of government system in which all the citizens together in the same position to determine public policy and the law applied to every citizen. The core of democracy is a **consensus** among the people involved in any given case. It dated back to **Abraham** the Forefather of all believers when he asked his son **Ishmael** about his son's opinion when the God commanded him to sacrifice. It also dated back to **Queen Sheba** when she asked her board of experts what to do pertaining to a letter she just received from **Solomon**. It also dated back to **Jesus** when his disciples demanded him the food from heaven right away. Democracy became a mantra in the 21st century to overcome the various doctrines that have been proven unsuccessful. Sometimes democracy has also been misused. It was also democracy which some states legalized same-gender marriage without being prosecuted by federal government while the federal government did not recognize the same gender marriage due to Defense of Marriage Act of 1996. Obama Administration in 2011 determined that Section 3 is unconstitutional. Democracy is the foundation of the United States of America, not the religion. Under the democracy all religions enjoy the religious freedom in the USA which is not even found in the birth place of religion itself.

5. Dialectical Materialism Doctrine

Dialectical materialism is a branch of Marxism synthesizing Hegel's dialectics which suggests that every economic order grows to a state of maximum efficiency, while it simultaneously develops the internal contradictions that contribute to its systemic decay [14]. Dialectical materialism at the end tends to see everything from "material perspective", and therefore the Marxists do not belief in God since God is immaterial.

In its development, Marxism contradicts the capitalism since it asserts that capitalism is a kind of "sucking blood from the poor to feed the rich" while Marxism -and socialism- supports and defends the rights of working class. The dichotomy Marxism – Capitalism never be resolved, ever. From this perspective we may understand the background of Cold War between the Soviet Union Block and US Block for 44 years.

6. Hedonism Doctrine

Hedonism derived from the Greek "hedone" or pleasure and "ismos" or ism suffix [15], it does mean the attitude to be pleasure. It is a *mazhab* or school of thought that promotes the joy of worldly life which may be described in the phrase of "enjoy it now before it's gone since you do not know if you find it next time". The root of hedonism dated back to nation of **Aad** who lived after Noah's major flood when the dignitaries among them declared "This is our world, we live and we enjoy right here right now". During the Roman Empire, the last emperors preferred hedonism more than anybody else; and it brought them down.

Today's hedonism may be represented in the common attitude to enjoy the free sex that leads to the spread of STD (sex transmitted diseases), the kids who never knew their fathers, and blind incest where a couple get legally married but they are actually have the same father without their knowledge since their mothers are single parent; that's all the kind of parental neglect.

This kind of hedonism led to the California HIV horror in August 2011 which forced the creation of a new law passed in January 2012 mandating that Los Angeles porn companies ensure the porn actors to use condoms [16]. It is hedonism which brings California to syphilis outbreak in August 2012; while existing California workplace laws already mandated the use of condoms by porn performers [17]. In this case, more than 1,000 porn actors are tested.

The number of syphilis prevalence in California raised 18% from 2010 to 2011 and still counts. Syphilis, if left untreated, may cause the permanent damage to the heart, brain, and other body organs; [18] it is not free anymore since it costs the health of the performer. It's also hedonism that brings us to enjoy tobacco that leads to the emphysema and lung cancer on the government burden to cure; and to enjoy the alcohol that leads to DUI conviction, fatal accident and the cancer since alcohol is carcinogenic agent. It's also hedonism that brings us to drug abuse and smoke the pot that leads to the problem of nerve system. Hedonism is punishable only under the religious rules but free under the constitutions. Since we live in a free country, it's legitimate with hedonism unless someone breaks the law. It is still disputable if sport is a branch of hedonism.

7. Ibn Khaldoun Doctrine

Ibn Khaldoun [1332-1406], the father of socio-history, was a prominent scholar in 14th century; his popular book "Al-Muqaddimah" was translated into several languages.

He made a simple formula in socio-history "the history is always written by the winner; and the people tend to emulate the winner." Only the winner may write a new history, the people tend to believe the winner; no matter he is right or wrong, since nobody trusts the loser's story. From this point, the people prefer to be the winner in any subject including economics, science, politics, world hegemony, war etc.

Despite his success and popularity, it's irony for Ibn Khaldoun; first, the people built his statue without his authorization in Tunis defying the religious teaching he embraced; second, the world where he's still popular, do not read his book since most of them, even though were born and live in Arab countries, do not understand the standard Arabic used in his book.

8. Kennedy Doctrine

John Fitzgerald Kennedy was a second youngest US President. The critics undermined him as had no experience, but as a crisis mounted during the Bay of Pigs invasion he bravely forced Director of CIA Allen Dulles to resign. Never be in the CIA history a Director was fired no matter the reason. The dismissal of Allen Dulles indicated that Kennedy had his own doctrine, yet it does not mean that Dulles revenged by killing JFK, as the conspiracy theory suggests. JFK, the leader of the most powerful country in the world during the Cuban Missile Crisis issued the stiff warning against the Soviet Union.

His decision to impose the naval quarantine around Cuba, his ultimatum to invade Cuba with full scale war, and his no-retreat position when Khrushchev asked him to dismantle Jupiter missile system from Europe in lieu of Soviet nuclear withdrawal from Cuba; clearly indicated that JFK had his own doctrine "never stepped back from the enemy even it would cost his life".

This is Kennedy Doctrine that was proven to be sharp against the Soviet Union who already installed nuclear missile in Cuba. He's John F. Kennedy, whose ultimatum to Khrushchev tipped the balance in Cuban Missile Crisis and subsequently forced the Soviet Union to withdraw its missiles, fighter jets, and anti aircraft missiles from Cuba. The world owed him, which by his ultimatum; the nuclear war was averted in 1963.

9. Liberalism Doctrine

Liberalism is an ideological plague based on individual freedom and egalitarianism. **Liberals** espouse a wide array of views that generally support the ideas such as constitutionalism, liberal democracy, free and fair elections, human rights, and free exercise of religion [19]. They also agree on fornication, abortion, same gender marriage and contraception. Liberals do and do not honor any religious value but selective along with their preference. Liberalism became a prominent adversary for every major religions (Judaism, Christianity and Islam) since it systematically disobeys the basic teaching of religion. Liberalism makes any religious teaching upside down if it contradicts the individual freedom and egalitarianism. Pope Benedict (resigned in 2013) strongly opposed the same gender marriage [20], abortion [21], but proposed the contraception [22] which strongly proposed by the liberals, even by President Obama with his support on gay marriage. In this spirit, Mary Cheney a daughter of former US Vice President Dick Cheney got married her lesbian partner in June 2012 and she has two biological kids Samuel and Sarah. When her partner was publicly known, the biological father of her kids is unknown. The liberals may do or do not embrace any religion; but their first credo is liberty-equality. The world becomes the witness that liberalism crossed any political border, Obama and Cheney are on the different side of political affiliation yet they do agree in the same gender marriage.

Since US is a country separating religion from the state then liberalism is not a problem; the US Constitution grants freedom for the liberals to act as they wish.

10. Monroe Doctrine

The **Monroe Doctrine** is a basic policy of the USA against any potential adversary. It was proclaimed on December 2, 1823 and named after the fifth US President **James Monroe** (1758-1831) whose tenure was from 1817–1825. The doctrine stated that further efforts by European nations to colonize land or interfere with North or South America states would not tolerated and would be considered as aggression which lead to the US intervention [23]. It seems targeting the Spain Empire –and the Soviet Union later during the Cold War- who had some colonies in North and South America. To assess this doctrine would help us to understand the US policy especially the Cuban Missile Crisis and its political impact on the long run since this doctrine was applied to Latin America in the US foreign policy.

To understand this doctrine may also help us to explain on why the US involved in the *coup d'etat* of **Jacobo Arbenz**, **Salvador Allende**, the effort to topple **Fidel Castro**, and most recent involvement in the **Iran-Contra** scandal.

During the presidential campaign 2012, the Latin America became a hot topic between **President Obama** and **Mitt Romney** the Republican Presidential candidate. The issue is Iranian President Ahmadinejad visit to Venezuela, Cuba, Nicaragua and Ecuador in January 2012; should Ahmadinejad's visit be put on the frame of Monroe Doctrine?

On January 9, 2012 Iranian President Mahmoud Ahmadinejad and Venezuelan President Hugo Chavez (1954 - 2013) pledged a closer cooperation to fight poverty and imperialism together; Iran and Venezuela both are the oil-exporting countries while the oil still matters. The two leaders vowed to form a united front in their opposition to the United States. "It's clear they are afraid of our development. Our weapon is logic. Our weapon is culture. Our weapons are human values," Ahmadinejad said. Chavez said would join hand-in-hand with Iran to stop the "imperial insanity" of the United States, which he described as a "threat for the world". "We are not warmongers," Chavez said [24].

He also pledged to help Iran to connect with other members of the Bolivarian Alliance of the Americas, a block of eight Latin American nations sponsored by Chavez. A question sparks in this context "Is Iran as dangerous as Soviet Union during Cold War?"

President Obama on July 10, 2012 asserts that Ahmadinejad visit to Venezuela to meet President Hugo Chavez is NOT a serious threat to the US. While Mitt Romney claims on next day that Ahmadinejad's visit may be a starting point of Bolivarian movement against the US. The Obama spokesperson emphasizes how the Republican becomes worry about Chavez (1954-2013). Both parties missed the point. The point is **Monroe** doctrine.

Here the list of US alleged involvements in Latin America where the Monroe Doctrine was implemented:

10.1. Argentina

Argentina is another example of Latin American country which applied the military junta in 1970's since it was a simple way to control the left-wing movement. The military participation in the politics indicates the military jealousy and distrust against civilians who reached the high level governmental position without military experience. It also indicates the military assertion that the military is above everything and everybody. This phenomenon happens everywhere in the developing countries around the world, from Argentina to Panama to Mexico, and from Indonesia to Myanmar to Egypt and all Africa. Fortunately or unfortunately, this "military taste" becomes an open gate for the foreign power to plant the political influence. That's a simplest way to contain the Soviet influence over any given region.

In 1976, like the military in Indonesia, Myanmar and Egypt; the Argentinean military took control almost everything. Argentinean military suspended or semi-suspended the constitution, dissolved or dismantled Congress, imposed strict censorship especially the corruption news and banned all political parties or just squeezed several political parties into two official parties to make easy to control. Argentina; furthermore embarked on a campaign of terror against left-wing elements as Indonesia did over the so-called Islamic terror. In Indonesia, the Soeharto's New Order administration in order to silence the democratic movements invented the various term to put them in the corner. Soeharto labeled Muslim democratic movement as "Komando Jihad" and launched a massive manhunt to some Muslim leaders. A group of Lampung peasants who defended their lands soon got labeled "Terrorist" and were wiped out by Soeharto military forces within days and nobody asks. Another incident happened in Aceh. The Muslim boarding house with a small mosque lead by Teuku Bantaqiyah in Aceh was raided; and Bantaqiyah was shot to death along his all 40 more students. The charge? First, the government said Bantaqiyah and his students cultivated the marijuana; later was corrected that it was a grave mistake and a pure accident. The real story is; Bantaqiyah in his prayer invoked a divine punishment for Soeharto since he imposed the martial law of *Daerah Operasi Militer* (DOM, the Territory of Military Operation, a cover and euphemism for local war declaration) over Aceh province for years with so many innocent victims got raped, killed or just disappeared. Unfortunately, a spy overheard Bantaqiyah prayer and reported to the local authority. Another incident happened when a group of Indonesian students who supported democracy have been disappeared or shot to death, and nobody assumed responsibility. Like in Indonesia under Soeharto, so many Argentinean opposition supporters were persecuted, illegally imprisoned, tortured, disappeared and executed without trial. While Argentinean military dictatorship lasted until 1983, the Indonesian military power lasted until 1998 when the wider grass root movement, including the university students, publicly demanded the Soeharto resignation. Still like Indonesia, during the years of dictatorship, the main role of the Armed Forces in Argentina was condensed form defending the country against external infiltrator to just defending it from its internal democratic movements.

Argentina is romantic only when we watch it in the movie where Madonna sang "Don't Cry for Me Argentina".

"Don't Cry For Me Argentina"
From "Evita" movie, sung by Madonna
Music: Andrew Lloyd Webber
Lyrics: Tim Rice

It won't be easy, you'll think it strange
When I try to explain how I feel
That I still need your love after all that I've done
You won't believe me
All you will see is a girl you once knew
Although she's dressed up to the nines
At sixes and sevens with you

I had to let it happen, I had to change
Couldn't stay all my life down at heel
Looking out of the window, staying out of the sun
So I chose freedom
Running around, trying everything new
But nothing impressed me at all
I never expected it to

Don't cry for me Argentina
The truth is I never left you
All through my wild days
My mad existence
I kept my promise
Don't keep your distance

And as for fortune, and as for fame
I never invited them in
Though it seemed to the world they were all I desired
They are illusions
They are not the solutions they promised to be
The answer was here all the time
I love you and hope you love me

Don't cry for me Argentina
Have I said too much?
There's nothing more I can think of to say to you.
But all you have to do is look at me to know
That every word is true

As the democratic government assumed the power in Argentina, the members of the military Juntas were tried and convicted for the atrocities they committed during the years of dictatorship [25] [26]. Unlike Argentina, Indonesian military juntas never be tried and now even enjoy the political preference since the top Soeharto military aides are running for the top government jobs and enjoying the business boom with the money they "made" during Soeharto tenure.

10.2. Bolivia

In the spirit of Cold War, everything which has the ties with Soviet Union should be eliminated; and that what happened when Bolivian President **Paz Estenssoro** who was democratically elected then overthrown by General **Rene Barientos Ortuno** (1919-1969) and Army Commander **Alfredo Ovando** in a *coup d'etat* of 1964 [27]. It was only just three months earlier when Ortuno was sworn in as Vice President along with President **Paz Estenssoro**. Ortuno was later elected President in 1966 only to die in a helicopter accident during his tour to the remote area in 1969. Later on, after a long exile the former President Paz Estenssoro ran for the presidency again and won.

During his short tenure, Ortuno suppressed the opposition groups including an organized insurgency under the Marxist guerilla leader **Che Guevara** of Argentina which later was captured and executed in October 9, 1967 while he was 39, too young to die. The world remembers him as a international guerilla leader who together Fidel Castro to topple **Fulgencio Batista y Zaldívar** (1901-1973) a US-backed military leader who was elected the Cuban President from 1940 to 1944 and dictator from 1952 to 1959. **Guevara** death marked the end of Marxist insurgency in Bolivia and the success of US foreign policy.

10.3. Brazil

João Belchior Marques Goulart (1919 - 1976) was democratically elected 24th President of Brazil when he was deposed by military *coup d'etat* on April 1, 1964. The US President Lyndon B. Johnson ordered Goulart to have deposed in the context of the Monroe Doctrine. It was reported that President Johnson so eager to depose Goulart since he kept his independent foreign policy and opposed the US invasion to Cuba; Goulart also opposed the Cuban decision to allow Soviet missile installation [28]. The motive behind the coup became vague after the disclosure that an American phone company ITT operating in Brazil was worry from being nationalized by Goulart; the ITT CEO Harold Geneen was friend of John McCone the Director of Central Intelligence. McCone a few years later went to work for Geneen's ITT. That was Washington's concern. The true story of actual operation remains classified [29]; and there was only one thing to know, Goulart the "leftist leader" has gone. The coup put Marshall Humberto de Alencar Castelo **Branco** into power and the start of military dictatorship until March 1967. On July 18, 1967 Branco died when his aircraft was allegedly "shot down by accident" by another Brazilian Air Force six month after leaving his presidency [30].

10.4. Chile

Since the time of President James Madison, the United States has long history in Chilean politics. The US influence and involvement in Chile intensified in the beginning of the 20th century, and after World War I it replaced Britain role in controlling the Chile's resources especially copper. The copper is a strategic mine product, but at a same time is the source of conflict since the workers demanded the higher wage; at this point the socialist/leftist movement gained its base to influence the people of Chile.

Long before Salvadore Allende came to power, the US has designed programs and strategies to contain the rise of leftists in Chile. In 1958 and 1964 Allende was defeated only with heavy campaign funded by the US. According to the **US Select Committee to Study Governmental Operations with Respect to Intelligence Activities** of 1975 (which was known as Church Committee since it was chaired by **Senator Frank Church** in the wake of Watergate scandal), the US covert actions in Chile between 1963 and 1973 was extensive and continuous; $8 million has been spent between 1970 and 1973 prior to the military coup in September 1973 [³¹]. In 1970, Salvador Allende a leftist presidential candidate ran again for the third time since 1958 and won! President **Richard M. Nixon** was worry "Chile became another Cuba" since Allende openly criticized the US invasion to Cuba in 17–19 April 1961 which was known as the **Bay of Pigs** invasion. The Nixon administration was so eager to topple Allende; and in September 1970, President Nixon authorized $10 million fund to stop Allende from rising to power or depose him. On September 11 *), 1973 the world became the witness that the military *coup d'etat* put Augusto Pinochet into power in Chile for long time and long abuse. The Pinochet administration ever since implemented the strict and harsh treatments against the opponents; some 3,200 people were killed, 80,000 were detained and 30,000 were tortured by Pinochet regime [³²].

10.5. Colombia

The US Government at least has two legitimate reasons to get involved in Colombia. First, to prevent the US soil from being the big market for Colombian drugs; since Colombia has abundant source of drug with powerful drug cartel such as Medellin Cartel to smuggle drugs to the vicinity including the US. Second, Colombia has a leftist organization FARC (*Fuerzas Armadas Revolucionarias de Colombia,* Revolutionary Armed Forces of Colombia). The Los Angeles Times on March 25, 2007 and George Washington University's National Security Archives on July 1, 2007 reported that General **Mario Montoya Uribe** the head of Colombia army to cooperate with a right-wing militias *Autodefensas Unidas de Colombia (AUC,* the United Self-Defense Forces of Colombia) which the US government designated as a terrorist organization [³³] [³⁴]. The US State Department added AUC to the list of Foreign Terrorist Organizations as early in 2001, not before [³⁵]. On July 2, 2008 the Colombian commando freed 15 hostages including 3 US military contractors and **Ingrid Betancourt** [36] a Colombian politician and presidential contender kidnapped in 2002 by leftist guerrillas *Fuerzas Armadas Revolucionarias de Colombia* (**FARC,** the **Revolutionary Armed Forces of Colombia**).

In July 2012, a Colombian general Mauricio Santoyo Velasco was arraigned in Alexandra Virginia on the US Federal drug charge; he pleaded not guilty after surrendering himself to US DEA agents in Colombia and subsequently was flown to the US for September 2012 trial [37] [38]. The US effort to bring the Colombian officer to justice is a serious effort to fight the drug abuse.

10.6. Dominican Republic

The official name of Dominican Republic is Commonwealth of Dominica; it is a tiny island in the Caribbean, one half of this island is Dominican Republic and the other half is Haiti. In May 30, 1961 President Rafael Trujillo of the Dominican Republic was assassinated in a *coup d'etat* after 30 years in office. During his tenure, Trujillo was estimated to kill around 50,000 people to keep him in power. The involvement of the US under Monroe doctrine was not clear since there was a contradictory report [39] [40].

10.7. Guatemala

The records on US involvement in the 1954 *coup d'etat* that took the life of President **Jacobo Arbenz** of Guatemala were released on May 23, 1997. The Truman administration initially considered Arbenz was good since he took care of the poor people, but as he continued the policy of previous government which was not friendly to the US, and then an action should be taken especially in the Cold War era to contain the influence of Soviet Union. The U.S. State Department, warned:

"Guatemala has become an increasing threat to the stability of Honduras and El Salvador. Its agrarian reform is a powerful propaganda weapon; its broad social program of aiding the workers and peasants in a victorious struggle against the upper classes and large foreign enterprises has a strong appeal to the populations of Central American neighbors where similar conditions prevail [41]."

Ever since, between 1954-1990; the repressive military regimes murdered more than 200,000 civilians; while 100,000 "disappeared", the human rights groups estimated [41].

10.8. Guyana

Guyana was a former colony of the Dutch for 200 years from 1616 – 1814, and became British colony for over 130 years from 1831-1966 [42]. It is the one and only member of the Commonwealth Nations in South America where its 700,000 more citizens adopt the English for its long relation with British colonist while the adjacent countries speak Spanish. The US has the interest in Guyana after British left in 1966; the focus is to prevent **Cheddi Jagan** from being leader since he had declared himself a Marxist, he was Premier from 1961-1964 during British occupation [43]. However, he was elected as President of Guyana and served from 1992 to his death in 1997. During the first period of Guyana independence, the US supported Forbes Burnham from 1966 to his death in 1985. He was elected Premier from 1964 to 1966, Prime Minister from 1966 to 1980 and President from 1980 to 1985. Since the political activity in Guyana is not crucial as Nicaragua, then the US involvement is not intense unlike in Panama and Cuba.

10.9. Haiti

Since 1959 Soviet influence on the Caribbean nations was increasing, it started with Cuba, and might spread to other country. The US policy maker to decide that entry to Haiti should start with dollar aid; and 1963 was the turning point in relationship between Haiti and the US. The further action to "enter" Haiti is not declassified yet [44].

10.10. Honduras

In 1984, General Gustavo Alvarez Martinez, head of the Honduran military, according the declassified files, ordered the establishment of the Military Intelligence Battalion [MIB] which was later notoriously known as death squad. The death squad has a special job to deal with the leftist guerrillas and to kill them whenever necessary. It seems to be the remnant of Cold War. In June 1995 the Baltimore Sun newspaper published previously classified documents and interviewed former MIB members. However, after an investigation, Inspector General revealed that the CIA did not participate in the torturing or killing the leftist guerrilla by the MIB [45]. The case became more complicated since Father Carney, an American priest died under questionable circumstances in Honduras.

10.11. Nicaragua

Sandinista is socialist movement and socialist party in Nicaragua led by **Daniel Ortega**, now the democratically elected President of Nicaragua (1985-1990, 2007-2011, reelected November 2011). Its official name is *Frente Sandinista de Liberación Nacional*, or FSLN; it was communist in 1980. Therefore no wonder if the US wants to contain FSLN especially in relation with Monroe Doctrine. This party was named after **Augusto Cesar Sandino** who led the guerrilla to fight the US occupation in 1930. Sandinista considered the Somozas were dictators, it successfully overthrew Anastasio Somoza **Debayle** (ruled 1967–1972, 1974–1979) the third and the last of Somoza presidents in 1979. There were 2 other Somoza presidents: Anastasio Somoza **Garcia** (ruled 1937–

1947, 1950–1956) and Luis Somoza **Debayle** (ruled 1956–1963).

During Ronald Reagan tenure, the opposition group in Nicaragua was established in 1981; this group was internationally known as **Contra** and of course it received the support from the US as a continuation of Monroe Doctrine. In 1982, the US Congress prohibited the government from supporting Contra to overthrow Sandinista [46]; but as the world knew the show must go on, and the Monroe Doctrine never be stopped. The policy maker should invent the way to make money beyond Congress authorization; that was selling the weapon to Iran and the money goes to Contra. Iran was the adversary who held 52 American diplomats on November 4, 1979 for 444 days, yet the money still talks even when related to the adversary. The relationship between **Contra** and the US under Monroe doctrine is one of the most complicated issues in the US foreign policy because of its complex inter-relation with other Latin American countries. At least there are three countries Panama, Nicaragua and Costa Rica to have the inter-relation along with Contra – US issue. The issue of **Contra** was on the spotlight when in 1984 **Dr. Hugo Spadafora** a former Panamanian Health Minister who fought along with the Contra, charged that a very high level Panamanian officer was involved in drug trafficking. When Spadafora entered Panama from Costa Rica in September 1985 he was arrested by General **Manuel Noriega** forces. Spadafora was severely tortures and beheaded; and the official effort to investigate his tragic death only triggered Noriega to force Panamanian **President Nocholas Ardito Barletta** to resign. Noriega, a Military Governor from 1983 to 1989, has had the absolute power until US invasion to Panama to arrest him. In a subsequent move dubbed as "Spadafora curse" in 1989 Noriega was captured, detained as a prisoner of war and brought to US to stand trial on the charges of drug trafficking and money laundering. As his sentence ended in 2007 he was extradited to France over the charge of money laundering; and as his France sentence ended, on December 11, 2011 he was extradited back to his country Panama to serve 20 years for murder [of Spadafora] [47].

10.12. Panama

Panama is a strategic position either during peace or war. Panama is the point to separate Pacific and Atlantic Oceans. The first country to realize this strategic position is the United States of America; therefore it built the Panama Canal between 1904 and 1914. In 1977, Panamanian President General Torrijos and US President James Earl Carter reached an agreement to transfer the Canal from US to Panama by the end of the 20th century. As Torrijos died in a plane crash in 1981; General Manuel Noriega controls the military and the civilian government. After a 1987 civil disobedience which was repressed by the military; the Reagan administration imposed the economic sanction especially after an attack on the US Embassy.

President George HW Bush on December 19, 1989 decided to invade Panama for 4 reasons [48] [49]: (1) To safeguard 35,000 US citizens in Panama after Noriega declaration that Panama and US was in state of war. (2) To defend democracy and human rights in Panama. (3) To combat drug trafficking and money laundering (in 1988, Noriega was indicted in Florida for drug related charges). (4) To protect the integrity of the Carter-Torrijos Treaties concerning Panama Canal. In this invasion, General Manuel Noriega was arrested and flown to US to stand for trial.

10.13. Peru

Like most Latin American countries in 1960's, Peru was under a military dictatorship (junta) that seized power in July 1962. The reason to seize power from the civilians was classic: to prevent the left-wing movement from rising to power. "Left–wing" in the political terms does not necessarily mean communist. This time the reason was to prevent the *Alianza Popular Revolucionaria Americana* (APRA, the Alliance of Popular Revolutionary American) a radical leftist but **anti-Communist** party from winning the election in June 1963. The US Department of State starts to pay a serious attention when the report on human rights emerged in 1997. The human right abuse was allegedly committed by Peruvian *Servicio de Inteligencia Nacional* (SIN, the National Intelligence Service) under Vladimiro Montesinos. He fled to Panama on September 24, 2000 after a videotape discovery showing him to bribe an opposition legislator; he was also accused of selling the arms to FARC (*Fuerzas Armadas Revolucionarias de Colombia,* Revolutionary Armed Forces of Colombia) a Colombia leftist organization [50]. Panama denied his asylum request and he went back to Peru on October 23, 2000 to stand trial in 2004.

10.14. Venezuela

Venezuela, like most Latin American countries in 1960's received the US assistance to train its police and military personnel; one of them was **Luis Posada Carriles** who trained at Fort Benning military academy in Georgia [51]. The US never tolerated any Latin America to lean on the Soviet block; therefore as Hugo Chavez a socialist reformist was democratically elected as president of Venezuela in 1999, the intensive efforts have been implemented to remove him from power. He was internationally acknowledged as a prominent adversary to the US foreign policy [52]. On April 11, 2002 a *coup d'etat* has removed him from the presidency for 47 hours only being restored by a coalition of military force and mass demonstration [53], since he is a popular public figure in Venezuela. After being detained by the military, he was restored as President of Venezuela. Chávez re-installation as president ended a 47-hour **Pedro Carmona** presidency. Carmona, a businessman was a President with shortest tenure in the history. The coup was publicly condemned by Latin American countries, only two countries, the US and Spain acknowledged but ended up soon by condemning the coup after it had been defeated by the popular movement to restore Chávez. There is no perpetual friend or enemy; there is always a perpetual interest.

As the history goes on, there is no single doctrine satisfies all. Each doctrine has its own followers, every doctrine is partial, it never solved social problem as a whole. Later, the desperate people would come back to the religion since they learned from their mistakes for generations.

11. Neoliberalism Doctrine

Neo-liberalism or neo-lib is "an ideology based on the advocacy of economic liberalizations, free trade, and open market". It supports privatization of state-owned enterprises, deregulation of markets, and promotion of private sector's role in society. [54]" The idea of neo-liberalism is to speed up the slow productions and services; it takes a longer process if following the certain rule in a country. Unfortunately, in the developing countries such as Indonesia the neo-liberalism shifted into taking the state-owned enterprises over and owned by the private companies under the pretext of privatization. This is not privatization but embezzlement since taking state property over without compensation to the state is a crime. Privatization in the context of privatization is participation of the private company to do business in the area where it was exclusive for the state only, such as port management, railways, airports etc.

Whenever a state-owned enterprise is taken over by a private company with the help of a high level government officer that is collusion and corruption; not privatization.

12. Pre-emptive Doctrine

This doctrine says "before the adversary attacks, it is better to attack it first because it is adversary". If, later on a mistake is found, then the correction would be made, and the history would be fixed. The nuclear war *always* adopts pre-emptive strike to maximize the victim and reduce the counter attack.

The victim of atomic bomb in Hiroshima, August 6, 1945
Photo by Yotsugi Kawahara, courtesy of **Hiroshima Peace Memorial Museum**, Japan

13. Socialism Doctrine

The experts agreed there is no a single definition of **Socialism** [55]. In a common understanding it is defined as economic system with social (or mass) ownership and the control of production. In the socialist state, social ownership and control of production are owned and controlled by the state; no private ownership and no private control of production to ensure the public wealth would be evenly distributed to all citizens without any discrimination. On the other way, if the state needs a public good such as defensive tools to protect the state then the citizens should participate even without (proper) payment except for daily life such as state housing, food for the working family, public school and public transportation. The other consequence of socialism is the absence of religious freedom since to practicing any religion and belief would be considered counter-productive and anti-socialism and therefore the state officially bans any religion. This condition is a common practice in China mainland, a part Taiwan and Korea with an exception in China where a certain people were allowed to own the private company due to the world market demand for the cheap merchandise.

At this point China put the US on the **socialist trap** where the American hi-tech products are produced in China with the possibility of sacrificing the production secret. Let us be honest and ask where does China obtain the technology to build smart phones, computers, telemetry, gyroscope, assault satellite, space aircraft, stealth technology etc.? The US keeps bowing down to China, happily maintains the deficit trading and absorbs merchandise worth billions of dollars to fill up the "Dollar Stores" across America. Almost everything is imported from China. It seems that the US would only stop importing someday when another Cuban Missile Crisis happens; responding to China nuclear threat, the President of the United States of America orders to launch a ballistic missile to **Que Moy** island at 24.4400° N, 118.3300° E coordinates to warn Beijing that next time a second missile would be sent to **Tian An Men** square. A couple of seconds before the first missile launching, a General from Join Military Chief abruptly calls the President that it is impossible to launch a missile attack to China. The President scolds "Why?" The General answers "Because the missile electronic gyroscope is not yet shipped from China!" It's also imported. It's made in China like most of American flags today.

14. Statism Doctrine

Statism of Japan during Shōwa period was a political amalgamation of Japanese nationalism, Imperial militarism, and state capitalism [56]. It is still disputable on whether this statisme brought Japan to the World War II or there was an external factor to attract Japan to enter World War II. Japan might lose in the World War II, but it wins in the world business today. "**Sogo shosha**", a business philosophy, provides a strong bond within this political amalgamation since it refers to "Great Japan as a major capitalist" which bring a pride to Japanese nation.

[11] http://en.wikipedia.org/wiki/Autonomism_ (political_doctrine)
[12] http://en.wikipedia.org/wiki/Communism
[13] http://en.wikipedia.org/wiki/Democracy
[14] http://en.wikipedia.org/wiki/Dialectical_materialism
[15] http://en.wikipedia.org/wiki/Hedonism
[16] http://www.bbc.co.uk/newsbeat/19368744
[17] http://www.reuters.com/article/2012/08/22/entertainment-us-usa-porn-moratorium-idUSBRE87K12Q20120822
[18] http://articles.latimes.com/2012/aug/20/local/la-me-syphilis-20120821
[19] http://en.wikipedia.org/wiki/Liberalism
[20] http://www.huffingtonpost.com/2012/03/09/pope-denounces-gay-marriage_n_1334504.html
[21] http://www.lifenews.com/2011/02/28/pope-benedict-delivers-abortion-message-to-pro-life- leaders/
[22] http://www.bbc.co.uk/news/world-europe-11804398
[23] http://en.wikipedia.org/wiki/Monroe_doctrine
[24] http://www.cnn.com/2012/01/09/world/americas/venezuela-ahmadinejad/index.html
[25] http://en.wikipedia.org/wiki/History_of_Argentina
[26] http://en.wikipedia.org/wiki/CIA_activities_in_Argentina
[27] http://en.wikipedia.org/wiki/CIA_activities_in_Bolivia
[28] http://en.wikipedia.org/wiki/CIA_activities_in_Brazil
[29] http://en.wikipedia.org/wiki/1964_Brazilian_ coup_d%27%C3%A9tat
[30] http://en.wikipedia.org/wiki/Humberto_ de_Alencar_Castelo_Branco
[31] http://en.wikipedia.org/wiki/CIA_activities_in_Chile
*) Why does September 11 become significant moment for most violence?
[32] http://en.wikipedia.org/wiki/Pinochet
[33] http://en.wikipedia.org/wiki/CIA_activities_in_Colombia
[34] http://www.gwu.edu/~nsarchiv/NSAEBB/ NSAEBB223/index.htm
[35] http://www.state.gov/j/ct/rls/other/des/123085.htm

As of January 27, 2012 the **US Department of State** issued the list of FTOs (Foreign Terrorist Organization):
1. Abdallah Azzam Brigades (AAB)
2. Abu Nidal Organization (ANO)
3. Abu Sayyaf Group (ASG)
4. Al-Aqsa Martyrs Brigade (AAMS)
5. Al-Shabaab
6. Ansar al-Islam (AAI)
7. Asbat al-Ansar
8. Aum Shinrikyo (AUM)
9. Basque Fatherland and Liberty (ETA)
10. Communist Party of the Philippines/New People's Army (CPP/NPA)
11. Continuity Irish Republican Army (CIRA)
12. Gama'a al-Islamiyya (Islamic Group)
13. HAMAS (Islamic Resistance Movement)
14. Harakat ul-Jihad-i-Islami/Bangladesh (HUJI-B)
15. Harakat ul-Mujahidin (HUM)
16. Hizballah (Party of God)
17. Islamic Jihad Union (IJU)
18. Islamic Movement of Uzbekistan (IMU)
19. Jaish-e-Mohammed (JEM) (Army of Mohammed)
20. Jemaah Islamiya organization (JI)
21. Jemmah Anshorut Tauhid (JAT)

22. Kahane Chai (Kach)
23. Kata'ib Hizballah (KH)
24. Kongra-Gel (KGK, formerly Kurdistan Workers' Party, PKK, KADEK)
25. Lashkar-e Tayyiba (LT) (Army of the Righteous)
26. Lashkar i Jhangvi (LJ)
27. Liberation Tigers of Tamil Eelam (LTTE)
28. Libyan Islamic Fighting Group (LIFG)
29. Moroccan Islamic Combatant Group (GICM)
30. Mujahedin-e Khalq Organization (MEK)
31. National Liberation Army (ELN)
32. Palestine Liberation Front (PLF)
33. Palestinian Islamic Jihad (PIJ)
34. Popular Front for the Liberation of Palestine (PFLP)
35. PFLP-General Command (PFLP-GC)
36. al-Qaida in Iraq (AQI)
37. al-Qa'ida (AQ)
38. al-Qa'ida in the Arabian Peninsula (AQAP)
39. al-Qaida in the Islamic Maghreb (formerly GSPC)
40. Real IRA (RIRA)
41. Revolutionary Armed Forces of Colombia (FARC)
42. Revolutionary Organization 17 November (17N)
43. Revolutionary People's Liberation Party/Front (DHKP/C)
44. Revolutionary Struggle (RS)
45. Shining Path (Sendero Luminoso, SL)
46. United Self-Defense Forces of Colombia (AUC)
47. Harakat-ul Jihad Islami (HUJI)
48. Tehrik-e Taliban Pakistan (TTP)
49. Jundallah
50. Army of Islam (AOI)
51. Indian Mujahideen (IM)

[36] http://www.nytimes.com/2008/07/03/world/americas/03colombia.html?_r=1&hp
[37] http://latino.foxnews.com/latino/news/2012/07/06/colombian-genl-pleads-not-guilty-to-us-drug-charges/July 6, 2012
[38] http://abcnews.go.com/US/wireStory/colombia-general-pleads-guilty-drug-case-16725433, July 6, 2012
[39] http://en.wikipedia.org/wiki/CIA_activities_in_the_Dominican_Republic
[40] http://en.wikipedia.org/wiki/Rafael_Trujillo#The_Downfall_and_Assassination
[41] http://en.wikipedia.org/wiki/CIA_activities_in_Guatemala
[42] http://en.wikipedia.org/wiki/Guyana
[43] http://en.wikipedia.org/wiki/CIA_activities_in_Guyana
[44] http://en.wikipedia.org/wiki/CIA_activities_in_Haiti
[45] http://en.wikipedia.org/wiki/CIA_activities_in_Honduras
[46] http://en.wikipedia.org/wiki/CIA_activities_in_Nicaragua
[47] http://en.wikipedia.org/wiki/Manuel_Noriega
[48] http://en.wikipedia.org/wiki/Panama
[49] http://en.wikipedia.org/wiki/Panama_Invasion
[50] http://en.wikipedia.org/wiki/CIA_activities_in_Peru
[51] http://en.wikipedia.org/wiki/CIA_activities_in_Venezuela
[52] http://en.wikipedia.org/wiki/Hugo_Ch%C3%A1vez
[53] http://en.wikipedia.org/wiki/2002_Venezuelan_coup_d%27%C3%A9tat_attempt
[54] http://en.wikipedia.org/wiki/Neo_liberalism
[55] http://en.wikipedia.org/wiki/Socialism
[56] http://en.wikipedia.org/wiki/Statism_in_Sh%C5%8Dwa_Japan

Part Two: The World around World War II

We are not assuming that lynching, colonialism, racism and cold war have been totally over

1. Freedom

For those who were not born yet in the 1950's, it would be rather difficult to imagine what the world was, in 1950's we still inherited the remnant of the violence of the World War and even the Medieval Darkness. Today, in a modern age everything is available with a reasonable price; but when the world wars just ended in 1932 and 1945 the world was covered with the recession; everything was difficult; consumer products, public utility, highway, television, internet, global telecommunication were scarce or not found yet. Every country was introvert and considering themselves the best, the chauvinism was an absolute value, and the segregation was still considered as the heroism. The mindset of most people was still dual-colored and not yet open-minded as we see today. And as of today, we tend to willfully repeat the past catastrophe by doing the very same mistakes. World War II just ended, every head of state had a very tough job ever. It is hard to say were the Presidents in the post World War II "lucky" to get elected as the leaders of their nations. Or, were they unfortunate to inherit the trouble and big mess ever? Economics, education, transportation, communication, technology, engineering were not sophisticated as we find today. No television, no cell phone, no internet available.

After the World War II, many new countries in Asia and Africa emerged and freed themselves from the former colonialists. Given the fact that the Asian and African new countries acquired their independence after Japan and European colonialists lost their powers, we may consider that the World War II was a blessing for the then-occupied countries. Several new countries to gain their freedom from their former colonialists in Africa and Asia:

(1) China, Formosa, Indonesia, Korea, Manchuria, and Vietnam declared their independence from Japan.

(2) India and Pakistan declared their independence from Great Britain.

(3) The African nations: Algiers [Aljazair], Burundi, Congo, Egypt, Ivory Coast August, Madagascar, Morocco, Republic of Central Africa, South Africa, and Zambia liberated themselves from the various European colonialists.

(4) Latin American nations were struggling to manage themselves amid the political rivalries after Spain lost the control most of the Latin American territory. As for Cuba, the Soviet Union was supporting Fidel Castro to topple Batista and put Castro as the new leader; however there was a hidden agenda behind the Soviet Union support; to prepare a long range strategy for the USA.

Amid this world situation, the United States of America was still suffering from Pearl Harbor attack, the involvement in Europe and Pacific battle zones; even it had not been fully recovered yet from the 1936 great depression. The mindset of some Americans is changing from double color to colorful vision. They need time to change.

In 1955 Emmett Till (1941-1955) a 14 year old African-American boy from Chicago Illinois visiting his relative in Money Missouri had been a victim of lynching, an execution-style killing characterized with the severe torture like cutting the hand off or gouging the eyes out while the victim was still alive. His destroyed body was dumped at Tallahatchie River with his neck tied to the heavy object with the barbed wire. Emmett Till eye was mercilessly gouged out alive; he was brutally beaten and shot at his head. A total brutality committed by uncivilized creature named the human being. During the funeral service his lamenting mother insisted to keep the coffin of Emmett Till open to let the world know the severe injury her beloved son suffered from and how cruel the killers were.

Now, lynching is very rare to find inside the USA but rather exported abroad as happened to Abeer Qasim Aljanabi a 14 year old Iraqi girl who was gang raped, murdered and burned along her mother, father and sister (see the Box: al-Janabi). We are not assuming that lynching has been over; John F. Kennedy might have been a victim of lynching, too.

> **Rosa Louise Parks**
>
> **In 1955, Rosa Louise Parks (1913-2005) an African-American woman was arrested in Montgomery Alabama because he refused to offer her seat to a white passenger even after the bus driver ordered her. Because she was a member and secretary of Montgomery NAACP (The National Association for the Advancement of Colored People) --one of the most influential civil rights organizations in the USA-- her action sparked the bus boycott in Montgomery. After Rosa Parks incident and bus boycott, on May 4, 1961 two buses carrying both whites and African-American people left Washington, DC for New Orleans, Louisiana by May 17, 1961; they're named "Freedom Riders".**
>
> **Their main mission was to intentionally test the southern enforcement of the 1960 US Supreme Court ruling against segregation of bus terminals that were legally open to interstate travel. The mobs attacked the "Freedom Riders" in Birmingham and Montgomery, Alabama. In Anniston, Alabama the white people burned one bus and attacked the riders both white and black people. President John F. Kennedy ordered 600 Federal Marshalls to guard the bus riders. More than 50 years later, President Obama on February 28, 2013 unveils the statue of Rosa Parks at the Capitol.**

The story of possible hate crime and lynching are still going on. James Byrd, Jr. (1949-1998), a black man, was beaten and urinated. He was dragged alive around his ankle for 3 miles to his death by the white males in Jasper Texas in June 1998. The murderers are Shawn Allen Berry, Lawrence Russell Brewer, and John William King. They were tried and convicted. Brewer and King were sentenced to death, and Berry was sentenced to life [57]. There is still another dragging story in June 2010. USA Today newspaper reported that the authority is investigating the black man's death. The newspaper makes a sub-headline "Shooting, dragging in S.C. being assessed as possible hate crime". It's another tragedy when Anthony Hill, a 30 year old black man was allegedly shot to death by a white man Gregory Collins, 19 year old in Newberry, South Carolina. The Sheriff said that the races of both victim and defendant and the dragging of the corpse lead police into investigating the killing as a hate crime. Anthony Hill died from a gunshot to the head; his corpse was dragged behind a truck for about 10 miles and left on the highway [^{58}].

In 1961 America still segregated in the south although US Supreme Court in 1960 ruling against the segregated bus terminals, this turmoil was severely disturbing the African-American where so often they were beaten or kicked for a simple reason because they were considered as sub-human as depicted in "Mohammad Ali" DVD movie.

Dr. Martin Luther King Jr. (1929-1968) and Attorney General Robert Kennedy (1925-1968) were so eager to end the segregation but it was not easy, the public still in their undeveloped vision. The efforts of Dr. King and Robert Kennedy to abolish the inhumane segregation that still tightly hold by the majority of American, might have been leading to their tragic deaths.

In this kind of segregation era, John F. Kennedy was elected to be the 35th President of Unites States, an extra heavy job ever for the US President after the World War II. His heavy burden might be compared, although not exact the same, with President Obama who inherited $1.2 trillion deficit and another problem including Bernard Madoff 50 billion dollar Ponzi scheme [http://www.nytimes.com/2012/09/26/us/politics/obama-faces-test-as-deficit-stays-above-1-trillion.html?pagewanted=all].

However, on the other side; America flooded hundreds of billion of dollars to support the foreign policy rather than spending it inside the country.

President Obama inaugural speech on January 20, 2013 "A decade of war is now ending and economic recovery has begun" marks the end of unlimited spending outside the US for the war, and also marks the start of economic recovery and may be economic boom. This is the most inspiring speech a US President ever delivered to end the money-draining war.

2. The Players on the World

The world was still not fully recovered from the wound of World War I when some people invented more sophisticated methods and tools to kill each others. On the name of technology they invented fighter airplane, machine gun, cryptography, incendiary bomb, phosphor bomb, biological weapon, atomic bomb and so forth which their ultimate goals were to kill as much as they can. Every single new invention is used as the war machine to make more victims; the spirit to kill the adversary was still so high; every nation was trying any tactic to steal the adversary's invention and innovation in order to defeat each other.

The world was still in the continuation of their uncivilized mindset, maybe until today, to kill and to kill and to kill; if a government does not have the external enemy to kill, then it kills its own people on the name of stabilization since we have a built-in self destructive mechanism. It's a lot of question which no need for us to answer on why one third of Chinese population were killing each other during the last century, or why Hiroshima and Nagasaki were razed down, or why Hamburg was showered with so many bombs till a single inch of asphalt on the road was burnt out, and the dead bodies just stacked up like charcoal. Or why London received a set of V-1 rocket, or why seven Army Generals were killed in one night and two million people were slaughtered in Indonesia in 1965, or why the deadly poison was spread in Tokyo railway station, or why three million people were killed in Middle East since the World War II until now and still counts with no sign to recede.

Or why the foreign countries put their troops in Afghanistan one after another, or why Vietnamese killed each other for long time, or why the African nations always kill each other until now, or why the very civilized Europeans destroyed each other in two World Wars, or why an Austrian man lead Germany to mess Europe up. Or why three thousand five hundreds refugees most of them were women and children were slaughtered in one single night in Shabra and Chatila in 1982, or why two or three beautiful tall buildings have to be destroyed altogether with the people still inside. Or why do the Latin American leaders love so much to kill their own people, or why two lovers and two families were separated by the hopeless wall, or why if one wall was razed down then a new one should be built in another place and another time like Gaza wall after Berlin wall, and so forth and so on? Here, some famous and notorious people who were involved in the various trick around World War II and even though they passed away long time ago yet they left the trails and impacts behind which sometimes are still dangerous until today. Who is famous and who is notorious; depends upon whom, where and when a person to look at. They, directly or indirectly, contributed to the Cuban Missiles Crisis that almost incited another World War.

2.1. Eisenhower (1890-1969)

Dwight David "Ike" Eisenhower was a hero in World War II, the first supreme commander of North Atlantic Treaty Organization (NATO), a five-star general in the US Army who was elected as 34th President of the USA from 1953 until 1961.

2.2. Lenin (1870-1924)

Vladimir Ilyich Lenin was a leader of Russian Bolshevik Party during October 1917 Revolution. He was also a prominent Russian communist leader who served as the Premier of Soviet Union from 1922 to 1924. He had an important role to transform Russian Empire into the Soviet Union which later became a world superpower beside the USA.

2.3. JFK (1917-1963)

John Fitzgerald Kennedy was the 35th President of the United State of America, he was 43 when elected and became the second youngest US President ever. He prepared a special bunker in his home town for the nuclear radiation protection. It was a private bunker, funded by his family money, not from the US government; he really knew the risk of confrontation with the Soviet Union.

On the way to Vienna to meet Soviet Prime Minister Khrushchev during the Cold War, President John F. Kennedy stopped by in Paris to meet France President Charlie de Gaulle to discuss the nuclear disarmament. Before the France public, John F. Kennedy --who accompanied by his France-speaking wife Jacqueline Bouvier-- casually made a statement "I do not think it entirely appropriate for me to introduce myself. I am the man who accompanied Jacqueline Kennedy to Paris, and I enjoyed it". His popularity soaring as the Europeans understood how to respect the wife.

2.4. Nikita Khrushchev (1894 - 1971)

Nikita Sergeyevich Khrushchev was the Secretary General of Soviet Union Communist Party from 1953 to 1964. He was also the Soviet Union Prime Minister from 1958 to 1964 replacing previous Prime Minister Nikolai Bulganin his comrade in the ousting of Lavrentiy Beria. Khrushchev was the one and only political leader in the world to take his shoes off and knocked it to podium while addressing at the United Nation General Assembly. Khrushchev shoes on the UN assembly should have been better than Montadhar Al-Zaidi's. Al-Zaidi home town, Tikrit, just completed building the huge bronze statue of Al-Zaidi "shoes #10" in January 2009, a tribute to his "botoola" بطولة, a local language for the heroism for hurling his shoes to President George W. Bush who visiting Bagdad in November 2008 (see Box: Al-Zaidi).

Khrushchev met US President John F. Kennedy in Vienna, Austria on June 3-4, 1961 less than 2 months after the Bay of Pigs incident --an attempt by about 1,500 Cuban exiles under the command of US to topple communist Cuban leader Fidel Castro--. One among the important result of the summit was Khrushchev promise to stop nuclear testing unless the USA did first. However, on August 30, 1961 the Soviet Union announced to resume the nuclear test, soon after the USA did the same thing.

Meanwhile President John F. Kennedy realized that the nuclear threat was real, he called the Army reservists for duty and urged American to build nuclear shelter at home equipped with sufficient food and water supply for a certain period. This momentum became a selling point for businessmen to sell the "portable nuke shelter" and it was a good business taking an advantage from the murky situation. For today's young generation who were not living in the Cold War age, it will be hard to understand how the life during the nuclear hysteria was.

Khrushchev was the father rather the heir of the Cold War, after Iosif Stalin he was the most active Soviet leader to spread the communism on the piggy back of the poverty around the globe. It spread very fast and drew President **Dwight Eisenhower** to describe the situation like domino game, and therefore the spreading of communism was dubbed as "domino theory", a fear that one country will adopt communism after another. The launching of "domino theory" was a part of psychological war to win the public opinion during the Cold War. It was described that communist coming from Russia to China going south to North Korea, sneaking into North Vietnam, to Indonesia, leaping forward to Latin America before finding the best terminal in Cuba and Latin America; therefore –according to this theory- a big part of the world becomes communists.

2.5. Indonesian Communist Party

The Indonesian Communist Party, the focus of Khrushchev and Eisenhower, was the biggest communist organization in the world after Russia and China, and in the 1955 election it surprisingly won the fourth majority after Indonesian National Party (**PNI**), *Majelis Syura Muslimin Indonesia (**Masyumi**)* and *Nahdlatul Ulama* (**NU**) political parties.

It's more than enough to open the world eyes especially the US which was trying hardly to contain communism during the Cold War. In the election of 1955, the Indonesian Communist Party (**PKI**) won 39 out of 257 House of Representative (DPR) seats and 80 out of 514 Constituent Assembly seats.

The PKI surprise in leading achievement of 16% overall votes in a democratic election in the most populous Muslim country in the world was a red alert for the domino theorists. This condition leads to an attempt to topple Ahmed Soekarno in 1958 in the "Operation Stronghold" where Lee Harvey Oswald was allegedly involved. Luckily, the CIA found a young, energetic, smart and all-season politician **Adam Malik** to whom it funneled lot of money [59]. Later, Adam Malik became Secretary of State and the Indonesian Vice President under Soeharto presidency at the onset of New Order. Adam Malik (and if Soeharto included) became the highest ranking Indonesian national leader who also served as CIA operative.

When Tim Weiner's **Legacy of Ashes** first published in 2007 where Adam Malik was named CIA agent (p. 298-301), Adam Malik's family responded negatively stating that Weiner was wrong. The history sometime was late but is always truthful. The proponents of Adam Malik and Soeharto have a good question "What's wrong if they were CIA agents in the context of containing communism in the South East Asia?" They argued that the both were "wrong" only if their status became a way to kill around two million Indonesian peasants in 1965-1967.

During Soeharto tenure, the deadly rumors were not rare; two of them were about the mysterious deaths of high profile officers. *First* of two was Rear Admiral **Sukarton Marmosujono** the Indonesian Attorney General and a member of the Fifth Soeharto Cabinet who mysteriously died on June 29, 1990. He died in his office after pledging to investigate the alleged corruption in a company related to Soeharto family. The *second* was Lieutenant General **Ali Moertopo** the Secretary of Information who also found dead mysteriously in his office May 15, 1984. Here the story goes. When Soeharto was preparing the official trip abroad, he called his generals and asked a simple and routine question "What will you do if the chaos happens during my temporary absence?" Every general answered according his authority, and Ali Moertopo answered "*Sir, I'll mobilize my special force to restore the order and make sure you are safe whenever coming home*".

It seems a heroic and loyal answer from a close aide? No, his answer was blatant wrong! Yes, it **was** right Moertopo had the special force when he was a Director of Indonesian Intelligence [*Ba*dan *K*ordinasi *In*telejen, BAKIN], but it was a time when he was a Secretary of Information; to have a special force as a civilian incumbent could be suspected as the preparation for a *coup d'etat*; and Soeharto was very wary and worry about, since he had a special experience against previous President Ahmad Soekarno; and therefore Moertopo should have been stopped; as the inner circle source said.

The Indonesian people once upon a frightening situation endure the rumors such as about **Bagio** [3/3/1933 – 8/14/1993] a prolific Indonesian comedian who died after two weird incidents. Firstly, he was the host of a TV commercial for a furniture company saying "*[This chair is so good] when you sit down then you forget to stand up*". His TV commercial soon goes viral and quoted by many politicians to refer that Soeharto was too long as a sitting President and "…*forgot to stand up";* it's time to replace.

It was allegedly reported that Soeharto was so upset especially the next Election in 1996 would be very crucial since the economic and political problems were mounting; although he won the presidency at last he resigned in 1998. Secondly, Bagio just jokingly said that *Paguyuban Lawak Indonesia* (The Association of Indonesian Comedians) "was infiltrated by the CIA". It was one hundred percent joke, he did not mean; but it was allegedly reported that Soeharto felt he was fingered out; and that's a time when **Bagio** mysteriously died in 1993. The Indonesian new generation did not care if **Adam Malik** or **Soeharto** or both were the CIA agents; their concern is how to sustain minimum daily requirement plus the basic education for their future.

The strategy to replace Soekarno with Soeharto was a significant mistake since Soeharto is not better off than Soekarno. Later in 1996-1998 when Soeharto felt abandoned, to win the support of US Government he allegedly arranged the raid of the American citizens at mining site of Tembagapura West Papua killing a US citizen teacher. This move was intended to discredit **Kelly Kwalik** who wanted the autonomy in West Papua and distribution of mining proceed to this province. Later, Kwalik was killed by the Indonesian forces; the reason was "he resisted the arrest". However, according to the reliable source, an intensive investigation by the American government concluded that Kwalik had nothing to do with the raid and killing of a US citizen in Papua, instead the allegedly mercenary did. The US government did not buy Soeharto administration's story, and he's done.

Despite his nickname of "smiling general", Soeharto was allegedly known as a blood thirst soldier, when he initially joined the military he just wanted to get paid; whoever does pay does not matter; he was a member of KNIL Dutch occupation army. In 1942 he enlisted as a member of KNIL (*Koninklijk Nederlandsch Indische Lagere*, Legion for Dutch's East India Occupation) in Chimahi West Java.

It's absolutely not right that Soeharto was a hero for Indonesia during the revolution for independence; he was on the opposite side, he was a KNIL member (http://vithakom.wordpress.com/2011/09/20/mantan-presiden-indonesia-ternyata-bekas-tentara-belanda/; http://id.wikipedia.org/wiki/Soeharto). KNIL in Indonesian history was listed as a group of mercenary. Therefore, if he had something with the killing of a US citizen in West Papua, nobody wondered.

In 1994, Soeharto started to build his family museum emulating the US Presidents who built the libraries and tombs. He hired some experts to build "**Museum Purna Bakti Pertiwi**" in Kramat Jati, a small district of Jakarta East side. The museum visitors may use the computer at the entrance as interactive guide to explore the contents of museum and the biography of Soeharto family. The computer display was equipped with a touch screen technology the first kind applied publicly in Indonesia; it was a state-of-the-art technology in 1994. The expert who worked for this project should have been careful to avoid the previous unpleasant experience of a journalist who was sent to jail because his article about Soeharto "true family tree".

> Excerpt from
> http://www.tribunnews.com/2011/06/10/benarkah-ibu-tien-soeharto-meninggal-diterjang-peluru
>
> Mrs. Soeharto died from Gun Shot; Is it True?
>
> Jakarta, April 28, 1996 04:00 AM. Indonesian First Lady Mrs. Soeharto was suffering from heart attack at her residence Cendana Street. She was admitted to Military Hospital under the supervision of General Sutanto the special adjutant to President Soeharto and her two sons Bambang and Sigit. Unfortunately, the doctors were unable to save her life. 70 Minutes later, she passed away at 05:10 AM, she was 72. Soon after her burial in Solo Central Java, the rumour was spreading from one whisper to another that she died from gunshot during her intervention into a deadly gun duel between Bambang her second son and Tommy the third son over the project of national car. The rumour, of course, was denied but not before 16 years has elapsed. The denial is among the content of a newly published book to commemorate the 90th birthday of Soeharto.

> Excerpt from
> http://us.nasional.news.viva.co.id/news/read/225443-duar--ada-ledakan-saat-makam-soeharto-digali
>
> Thundering Sound Over the Burial of Soeharto
>
> Astana Giribangun Mausoleum; Solo Central Java, Sunday January 27, 2008 15:30 PM. A group of local workers under the supervision of Begug Purnomosidi the Mayor of Karanganyar district were digging the graveyard for Ex-President Soeharto. The first and second strokes were normal, but at the third a thundering sound was striking the mausoleum roof. The workers were rushed to find out, but nothing wrong, no damage and no sign of thunder strike. Every one was looking each other until Purnomosidi broke the tension "It's a sign that the earth is welcoming him". How does he know? This memoir is also a part of a newly published book to commemorate the 90th birthday of Soeharto.

Soeharto was married to Siti Hartinah on December 26, 1947. She was born on August 23, 1923 in Solo Central Java and passed away in Jakarta on April 28, 1996 from allegedly gun shot when she was trying to stop the fight between her two sons over "the national car project". This rumor had widely spread since the day one but never be denied until June 2011, fifteen years later. Soeharto passed away on January 27, 2008.

On the day of his burial, a terrifying loud sound went off over the roof of **Astana Giribangun** mausoleum in Solo Central Java where he supposed to be interned by the side his beloved wife. This mysterious sound obviously frightened the workers and local officials who were preparing the burial, yet after a thorough search no damage ever found.

There are too any witnesses to ignore and too hard to say it is superstition. The pros said that he was welcomed by the earth while the cons were convinced that it was the time when the divine decision was coming. This incident was tightly kept secret until June 8, 2011 when ***"Pak Harto The Untold Stories"*** was published to commemorate Soeharto's 90th birthday.

Soeharto's Last Supper

Every nation has the tradition of family gathering. The Westerns have Year End, and Soeharto family have Hari Raya. In this annual occasion, Soeharto used to ask his kids about their resolutions, and he usually made a surprise to make their dreams come true. In the family gathering of 1996, after supper, he asked his kids one after another about what their resolution. The first kid answered "*Sendika Rama* *), I want a telecommunication company". Soeharto reprimanded "I already provided you the *Palapa* telecommunication satellite, do you remember when *Palapa* was still good then I declared that it was out of service and due to replacement with *Palapa II* just to give you a chance to sell it to the Republic of Tonga for some million dollars since this good satellite also covers a part of Pacific. Do you share a couple dollars with the Secretary of Communication? By the way; you; do not even think to ask permit to go to Las Vegas again. Ask something else, good boy! Next". The second kid came, paid a deep traditional respect and asked "I dream of a national car project, *Rama*", Soeharto responded "Good, I have it and it's for you." The third kid came next and asked "I dream of another national car project", "Good, I have it and it's for you", Soeharto praised this cool kid. The fourth kid did not ask immediately, instead Soeharto got massaged first to show him how much this kid loves him. Soeharto understood, and then he said "I have the highway project, and it's for you." Next, the fifth kid politely stated that the health and longevity of Big Daddy are more important than any resolution. Soeharto was so happy and kissed this loyal kid on the forehead as a sign of greatest love ever; then Soeharto said "I have the mega mall project in *Senayan* the heart of Jakarta, it's for you".

For a moment all kids were surprising over the tip and trick of the fifth kid. At the same time Soeharto was surprised over the reluctance of his sixth kid to ask even a piece of cake. "*Tjah Ayu* **), why do you not ask me anything?" She replied politely "Thank you Daddy, you already provided me everything. It would be a shame for me to ask anymore!" Soeharto retorted "Shame? I do not have it. Dismiss!"

*) "*Sendika Rama*" is a high level Javanese language for "I obey you my respected Daddy".
**) Soeharto nicknamed her "*Tjah Ayu*" a local language for "the most beautiful daughter".

In October 1965, Soeharto successfully took the Soekarno administration over after the *coup d'etat* that never be publicly admitted. Four years before, in 1961, **Ethel** and **Robert Kennedy** with a special mission from President John Kennedy, visited Jakarta to negotiate Soekarno in order to avoid Indonesia from falling into the communism under the frame of "the domino theory". Robert Kennedy was welcomed with a big poster "KENNEDY GO HOME" and another unwelcome criticism against President John Kennedy; unbeknown by the Indonesian people that the Kennedy's main mission was to avoid the war between Indonesia and Dutch over West Papua which was still not integrated to Indonesia yet.

The spirit of anti-America was still high in 1962 when an American journalist in Jakarta asking President Soekarno "why were the Indonesian people not allowed to criticize their President (Soekarno) while American people are free to criticize their President (Kennedy)", Soekarno casually answered "*Right here, right now, the Indonesian people are free to criticize American President!*". Ahmad Soekarno the first President was a very popular and a good leader, he did not kill his folks nor oppressed them, every Indonesian citizen loved him. Soekarno along with Mohammad Hatta proclaimed the Indonesian independence from the Dutch after being colonized for 350 years.

The public animosity against Robert Kennedy -and America- in 1960s was generated by the Indonesia Communist Party (PKI) under the leadership of Dipa Nusantara Aidit who ever lived in Soviet Union for several years after the PKI incident in Madiun, East Main Java Island in 1948. Aidit, a secretary in the Soekarno administration, was considered as the KGB extended hand to infiltrate Soekarno administration. The infiltration even still persists during the Soeharto administration and might be until today. The KGB had been successfully infiltrating the Indonesian Army and planted Army **Colonel Soesdaryanto** as a KGB mole who successfully sent to Moscow the classified Indonesian naval information.

Upon receiving information from Embassy in Jakarta and the tip from Aidit about the mission of Robert Kennedy, the Soviet Union abruptly sent the Secretary of State Anastas Mikoyan to Jakarta to contain the American influence over Soekarno; Indonesia soon received a lot of Soviet weapons including AK-47 assault rifles, bazookas, T-30 tanks and MiG-17 fighter jets. The result was the (unnecessary) war between Indonesia and Dutch over West Papua in 1962, a kind of war which Robert Kennedy tried peacefully to avert. The Indonesian people should have been thankful to Robert Kennedy. The spirit of "killing the Dutch" was still high fueled by Soekarno's rhetoric, and Mikoyan just added a spark to incite the war between Indonesia and Dutch. Mikoyan's weapon diplomacy surpassed Robert Kennedy's peace diplomacy amid the continuance of Indonesian independence revolution over the Dutch occupation for more than 350 years.

Had Robert Kennedy provided the *assurance to Indonesian government that West Papua would be handed over from Dutch government*, his diplomacy would prevail and naturally **contain the communism** in Indonesia. The course of history might be different and it would not necessary to topple Ahmad Soekarno, killing seven Indonesian Army generals and killing two million peasants. The strategy to replace Soekarno with Soeharto was a grave historical mistake.

In such political situation in early 1960, John F. Kennedy won the presidency over Richard Nixon; later in 1968, Nixon ran for presidency and used the communism hysteria to win his presidency after President Lyndon B. Johnson term ended. However, Indonesia is still a point of interest for the US, and the tireless effort by American Embassy in Jakarta resulted in Soekarno's acceptance to the invitation by President John F. Kennedy, they met in a friendly reception in Washington, DC; and the press reported "Kennedy's smile had **tamed** Soekarno", but Indonesian press suspected that "Kennedy **bribed** Soekarno with a beautiful woman".

The accusation was not baseless, a declassified information 25 years later revealed that "a dirty brief amateur movie" had been made over "Soekarno" using a impersonator and a beautiful woman in action, this was the one then Indonesian journalists watched as "a leaking critical information"; in fact it's a perfect disinformation. However it's the other historical mistake for the planner, Soekarno did **not** fall because of such rumor and disinformation around the women because he officially already married **nine wives.** They are Dewi Oetari, Inggit Garnasih, Fatmawati, Hartini, Kartini Manoppo, Haryati, Yurike Sanger, Heldy Djafar, and Ratna Sari Dewi Soekarno aka Naoko Nemoto aka Madame Syuga a Japanese woman whose photograph with almost naked tattoo-covered body was banned in Indonesia in 1998 but has been circulating on the internet.

From these 9 wives Oetari, Garnasih, Manoppo, Sanger and Djafar did not have any child, while Hartini has had a son Taufan Soekarno, Haryati has a son Bayu Soekarno; Sari Dewi has a daughter Kartika Soekarno, and Fatmawati had had several children including Megawati Soekarno the fifth Indonesian President. When Soekarno was threatened with the publication of such fabricated movie, instead of being scary he was very happy and should have been given a copy to reproduce and distribute in Indonesia as a pride, because an Indonesian President with tan skin to have a white woman!

Soekarno's natural inclination as a woman lover was well exploited by Aidit to obtain a political gain; Aidit indirectly used to prepare the party where the attendants were arranged in a circular human fence so-called "*pagar ayu*" which literally means "the fence of beautiful women"; one night Soekarno personally provided a ride home to one among the "*pagar ayu*" members, **Yurike Sanger**. In such of situation, Aidit and Khrushchev were planting the influence inside Soekarno administration, a perfect infiltration.

Khrushchev did not obtain university education as John F. Kennedy did, but as a naturally talented leader he succeeded Iosif Stalin and even he corrected some Stalin's major errors. His address on February 25, 1956 at the 25th Congress of Communist Party shocked the communist party members by accusing Stalin of committing the crime during his tenure where he ordered to "purge" his opposing politicians and the peasants resisting their farms from being transformed into *kolkhoz*, the collective farm by abolishing the individual ownership. The critics said that during the major purge more than three million peasants and the political opponents had been killed. Khrushchev transformed the Soviet farming system to be a self-sustained country, and modernized the Soviet military power as well to emerge as a superpower with the bargaining power against the USA. Under his leadership Soviet Union launched **Sputnik** the first earth-orbiting satellite and launched Yuri Gagarin the first man into space in the spacecraft **Vostok** on April 11, 1961 (the USA launched Alan Sheppard to the space later on May 5, 1961).

Beside his tight schedule as Prime Minister, he still paid attention to the literature. The publication of Aleksandr Solzhenitsyn's "*One Day in the Life of Ivan Denisovich*" in 1961 was Khrushchev personal request; he was lauded by both friends and foes. Although he was born in Ukraine, he ordered the murder of the Ukrainian nationalist leaders Dr. Lev Rebet in Berlin 1957 and Stepan Andriyovych Bandera also in Berlin 1959 to prevent the separation of Ukraine from the Soviet Union; **the politics justify the tactics and the ends justify the means** (see the box: Stashinsky).

He has the gut when he bravely cancelled the Paris summit with US President Eisenhower in the wake of the shooting down of American U-2 spy plane over the airspace. His critics described him as stubborn, but he was a leader who knew what to do for his country; and he was not corrupt unlike some leaders of the developing countries.

He was the man behind the building of Berlin Wall to separate West Berlin and East Berlin in 1961; this infamous wall later was dismantled during the tenure of US President Ronald Reagan. Because of Khrushchev the world was in the highest alert of nuclear war when he shipped several nuclear missiles to Cuba in 1962, from which the missiles could be launched to reach American soil less than 1 hour, a point of no time to intercept. The nuclear placement in Cuba could have been just a watch dog to prevent John F. Kennedy from sending the troop (again) to Cuba retaliating the failed Bay of Pigs, but he set this world in the brink of the nuclear confrontation.

Khrushchev was removed from power among other thing because for the consideration of mishandling the 1962 Cuban Missile Crisis, his son is now living in America the country which his father so eager to destroy. It's the kind of Soviet leader to whom John F. Kennedy facing on the opposite side during his very short term. It's not easy for JFK to face Khrushchev, and it's the heavy burden John F. Kennedy had to endure prior to his assassination on Friday November 22, 1963 in Dallas, Texas.

2.6. Fidel Castro (1926-)

Fidel Alejandro Castro Ruz is a most popular leader in Latin America regardless of whether the people like or dislike him. He is the Cuban Communist leader who was the Prime Minister of Cuba during Cuban Missile Crisis of 1962. The world knows him more than Cuban President **Osvaldo Dorticós Torrado** (1919 –1983). Castro was Prime Minister of Cuba for 17 years from 1959 to 1976, and President of Cuba for 32 years from 1976 to 2008. In the international political movement, Castro served as the Secretary-General of the Non-Aligned Movement for 6 years in a separate tenure, from 1979 to 1983 and from 2006 to 2008. President Kennedy might dislike Castro and Cuba, but right away before the naval quarantine, he ordered to buy lot of Cuban cigar.

Castro is also the General Secretary of the Cuban Communist Party; no wonder if the US, the most anti-communist country in the world, never ever had intention to normalize the bilateral relationship for five decades under ten US Presidents!

> **Bogdan Stashinsky**
>
> Nobody knew for sure what happen to Dr. Lev Rebet the leader of Ukrainian nationalist leader in Berlin 1957, but one thing everybody knew is he's dead. Stepan Andriyovych Bandera was also Ukrainian nationalist leader lived in Berlin when found dead in 1959. The investigation revealed that he was died from poisoning; but it never revealed who did until a KGB agent Bogdan Stashinsky defected to the West and confessed that he did the murder of both Dr. Rebet and Bandera to prevent the independence of Ukraine from the Soviet Union. Stashinsky, as he confessed, used the cylindrical metal canister to deploy the arsenic poison gas to kill both victims (source: Intisari Indonesian magazine)

2. 7. Oleg Penkovsky (1919-1963)

Sometime, the humanity prevails over the belligerence even during the war. **Oleg Vladimirovich Penkovsky** [1919-1963] knew from his job that the Soviet Union was placing the medium range missile in Cuba of 1962, and therefore he contacted the British intelligence in his attempt to avoid the direct war between the Soviet Union and the US that might lead to World War III. It is hard to say who the hero is. Is he a person who betrays his own country and discloses a secret to the enemy of his country on the name of humanity? If the answer is "Yes", then Oleg Vladimirovich Penkovsky was the real hero for the humanity. He prevented the possibility of the nuclear war between his country Soviet Union and the USA in 1962. He was a colonel in *Glavnoye Razvedyvatelnoye Upravlenniye* (*GRU*, Soviet Military Intelligence) when provided USA the ultra secret information about the placement of Soviet nuclear missiles on Cuba [60]. His information led the global missile crisis, not just Cuban missile crisis. In 1962, the Soviet Union was convinced that the "the capitalist" USA should be destroyed, and therefore the Soviet leader shipped the medium-range nuclear missiles to Cuba in preparation to destroy the USA in a surprise attack with the minimum possibility of defence. Penkovsky provided the USA information of this shipment to prevent the global nuclear war. In order to prevent the covert source and to obtain the first hand evidence, the USA sent U-2 spy plane over Cuba to identify the missile sites. The possibility of nuclear war was so close; Penkovsky's early and accurate information led the USA to realize the proximity of nuclear danger (see Cuban Crisis). He also provided the other important information about the Soviet nuclear arsenal which convinced the US that the Soviet tactical weapons were smaller than the US previously expected. Penkovsky was arrested, tried and sentenced to death; yet the free world lauded him as the hero without country border. Penkovsky heroic action to help preventing the nuclear war was only betrayed by George Blake the British spy who sold the information to Soviet Union for money. Penkovsky was arrested on October 22, 1962 and executed on May 16, 1963. It was not clear on how he was executed; some sources said he was shot on the back of his neck, and some said he was bound to the board and burnt alive. Even, during the Cold War era; not every Soviet Union citizen is bad; the world still has the good heroes like Penkovsky and Vasily Arkhipov who were so eager to prevent the world from nuclear war. Penkovsky never defected to the West, and unfortunately his heroic action to stay in the Soviet Union to face the high risk, became a base of accusation that he was a double agent.

2.8. Vasili A. Arkhipov (1926 – 1999)

Vasili Alexandrovich Arkhipov was a high rank Soviet Naval Officer aboard a B-59 Soviet submarine off Florida coast during the Cuban Missile Crisis of 1962 [61]. On October 27, 1962 he bravely prevented the submarine commander Savitsky from launching the nuclear weapon to the US soil.

During the most apprehensive Cuban Missile Crisis, on October 20, 1962 the US imposed the naval defensive quarantine over Cuba to prevent Soviet ships from delivering the more supplies to Cuba; albeit a Soviet B-59 submarine armed with the nuclear torpedo successfully sneaked to Cuba as a backup whenever the nuclear strike from Cuba failed. In this submarine Arkhipov was with the submarine commander Valentin Savitsky and the high rank political officer Ivan Semonovich Maslennikov representing the government of Soviet Union. These three officers were disputing the launch of nuclear weapon over the depth bomb attack by the US destroyer imposing the naval quarantine. Subsequently, this B-59 submarine went to surface and cancelled the launching of nuclear torpedo. When **Penkovsky** prevented the nuclear war by issuing the early warning about the Soviet nuclear installation in Cuba, then **Arkhipov** stopped **Savitsky**'s hand from pulling the nuclear trigger.

They were the heroes deserved the Nobel Prize. It's only by God's blessing the world was safe from the nuclear war in 1962.

2.9. Robert Oppenheimer (1904 – 1967)

J. Robert Oppenheimer was the scientific director of the Manhattan Project, an ultra secret Laboratory at Los Alamos, New Mexico to develop the nuclear bomb during the World War II. He was a professor of physics at University of California, Berkeley. For his role to develop the first nuclear bomb, he was known as the father of Weapon of Mass Destruction. His team work at Los Alamos at last tested the first nuclear bomb on July 16, 1945. Oppenheimer, after his success in developing the A-bomb, then opposed the development of the H-bomb. He estimated about two hundred million people would be killed if the nuclear war erupted.

The combination of A-bombs dropped in Nagasaki and Hiroshima were like a fire cracker when compared with today's sophisticated H-bomb.

The very first H-bomb was tested in 1952 to have the destruction power of 10.4 megatons, more than 650 times the strength of the A-bomb developed by Oppenheimer in his Manhattan Project [62]. On January 26, 2009 PBS TV aired the documentary of Robert Oppenheimer being interviewed by the government agent. He was suspected in passing the secret information about the A-bomb to the foreign country.

He was a victim of suspicion and misinformation; the US counter-intelligence might find a clue after intercepting the high traffic of encrypted communication from Colonel **Rudolf Abel** in New York to Soviet's **NKVD** [Narodnyy Komissariat Vnutrennikh Del, People's Board for Internal Affairs] a precursor of **KGB**. It must be the atomic secret either leaked by **Theo Hall** or **George Koval** that worked at Los Alamos Laboratory.

Hall or Koval or both provided the secret of US atomic bomb to Abel spy ring; Oppenheimer did not. For some reasons he was suspected as a "communist", he was placed under tight scrutiny and his security clearance was revoked in 1954. The suspicion that he was a communist might be resulting from a fact that in November 1940 he married Katherine "Kitty" Harrison a former Communist Party member. Moreover, his former girl friend Jean Tatlock was active in the Communist Party in the '30s or '40s [63].

> "The FBI recorded that J. Robert Oppenheimer attended a meeting in the home of self-proclaimed Communist Haakon Chevalier, that Communist Party's California state chairman William Schneiderman, and Isaac Folkoff, West Coast liaison between the Communist Party and the Intelligence, attended in the Fall 1940, during the Hitler-Stalin pact. Shortly thereafter, the FBI added Oppenheimer to its Custodial Detention Index, for arrest in case of national emergency, and listed him as "Nationalistic Tendency: Communist." [64]

Long after he was "interviewed" by the government agents on the suspicion of passing nuclear secret to the other government, he was awarded the Enrico Fermi Prize by President Lyndon B. Johnson as a sign of his rehabilitation.

> "In a seminar at the Woodrow Wilson Institute on May 20, 2009, and based on an extensive analysis of the Vassiliev notebooks taken from the KGB archives, John Earl Haynes, Harvey Klehr and Alexander Vassiliev confirmed that Oppenheimer never was involved in espionage for the Soviet Union. The KGB tried repeatedly to recruit him, but never was successful. Oppenheimer did not betray the United States. In addition, he had several persons removed from the Manhattan project who had sympathies to the Soviet Union. [65]"

He never be tried; and the proof of his treason, if any, never be found; he was one of McCarthyism victims, a wave of communism phobia. Such of phobia always repeats itself over the times; it was Christianity phobia that led to inquisition, then Jewish/Judaism phobia that led to Hitler's death camps; and now Islam phobia; the next will be Maya phobia.

The first Soviet's nuclear weapon was tested on 29 August 1949 in Kazakhstan. One month later, the US President Harry Truman on September 23, 1949 notified the world of the first Soviet nuclear test: "We have evidence that within recent weeks an atomic explosion occurred in the U.S.S.R." [66]

This is the end result of the spy team who stole the nuclear secret from the US and later would be used against it. The US was like a young beautiful girl in the summer which the bad boys are on lane to harass because nobody seriously protects her.

2.10. Francis Gary Powers (1929 - 1977)

Francis Gary Powers was on a secret mission to photograph the Soviet military installation including the site of 1957 nuclear disaster at Kyshtym when his U-2 spy plane was shot down by S-75 missile over Sverdlovsk. He was captured and sentenced to three years in imprisonment plus seven years of hard labor [67].

Powers was supposed to activate the U-2's self-destruct mechanism prior to parachuting to the ground and he was supposed to take cyanide pill before being captured, but he "forgot". He was sentenced to hard labor but later released from the prison and sent home in "the spy exchange" with Soviet Colonel Vilyam Fisher alias Rudolf Abel who was in US custody after being caught by Federal Bureau of Investigation [FBI] for espionage. The swap place was Berlin, Germany on February 10, 1962. The U-2 incident set back talks between Soviet Prime Minister Khrushchev and US President Eisenhower. Both parties were upset; Khrushchev was so upset over why US sent a spy plane while a summit meeting is on the way; while Eisenhower was so upset over why did spy agency sent U-2 after being told not to do so prior to the summit meeting.

The U-2 incident might be a determinant factor for Khrushchev to send the medium range nuclear weapon to Cuba 2 years later "to teach USA" just in case another U-2 "strayed off course" over Soviet air space. Khrushchev might be thinking that the summit meeting was just a cover to shift the focus while the US was preparing a real war; otherwise why did US send U-2 deep into SU airspace? From this point we may understand the motive of nuclear deployment to Cuba, and also from this point we may understand on why JFK threatened to invade Cuba without considering first "Why did Soviet Union send the nuclear weapon to Cuba." This point may bring us to understand on why JFK "should be stopped" to prevent the Cold War from being the Open War.

2.11. Rudolf Anderson, Jr. (1927- 1962)

Major Rudolf Anderson, Jr. was a 35-year old pilot in USAF and became the only American casualty during Cuban Missile Crisis when his U-2 spy plane was shot down over Cuba on 27 October, 1962. His wrecked plane was displayed at Museum of Revolution in Havana, Cuba; and his remain was sent back to US on November 6, 1962 [68]. Based on Gary Powers' experience, Major Anderson might be still alive upon landing on Cuban soil, but he soon took a cyanide pill to protect him from being forced to confess or from being tried like Gary Powers, or based on the SOP (Standard Operating Procedure) he had to take his own life. After this incident, JFK threatened to invade Cuba if another U-2 were shot down. This was quite different with Gary Powers' incident where the US President did not threat to invade the Soviet if another U-2 were shot down.

Here's the **vicious cycle**: Khrushchev sent medium range nuclear weapon to Cuba in August 1962 because he was convinced that US would start the open war first, his consideration was based at least on four crucial incidents:

(1) In 1959, the US installed Thor IRBM in England and in 1961 installed Jupiter IRBM in Italy [69]. The deployment of nuclear missiles in England and Italy that had the capability to destroy Moscow within **18 minutes** [70] had made Soviet worried most. Therefore, the Soviet Union demanded first to uninstall the Jupiter missile in lieu of uninstalling the nuclear weapon from Cuba. This was the essence of ***quid pro quo*** in October 1962.

(2) US sent Gary Powers on U-2 spy plane to penetrate deeply into Soviet airspace; it was shot down on May 1, 1960;

(3) US invaded Cuba on April 17-19, 1961; Cuba was a Soviet ally.

(4) On July 9, 1962 the US tested the nuclear weapon in the outer space over Johnston Atoll, in the Pacific Ocean [71]. *This test was monitored unexpectedly by 2 Soviet "expedition boats" at the nearby island.* This test more convinced the Soviet Union that US was preparing the open war using the nuclear weapon. The flash created by the outer space nuclear test reached Honolulu 1,500 kilometers away although it went through the dark cloud. The US was still doing some tests in 1962 as the response to the

announcement of Soviet government on August 30, 1961 that they would resume the nuclear test after a three-year self moratorium.

On the other hand, on 14 October 1962 a U-2 spy plane found that the medium range nuclear weapon was installed in Cuba, and on 27 October, 1962 the US sent another U-2 to check the last development of the Soviet nuclear installation in Cuba, this spy plane was shot down. JFK considered this incident as a proof that Soviet leaders would deliberately launch the nuclear weapon first to US soil and therefore they kept the nuclear installation in secret. **Had the Soviet Union let the US to monitor the nuclear installation in Cuba, JFK would have been considering Cuba as a "regular" nuclear station** for Soviet like Germany as a "regular" nuclear station for the US where the both stations would be just the "watchdog" because both parties knew each other. But when Soviet kept the nuclear weapon in Cuba in secret, JFK considered it as a real preparation to launch to US; and therefore he issued ultimatum to invade Cuba in a full scale war anytime another U-2 were shot down. That's the vicious cycle which put our planet on the brink of the nuclear war in 1962.

The Vicious Cycle of SU and US that culminated in the Cuban Missile Crisis

Post World War II, 1945: The suspicion and distrust each other between the Soviet Union (SU) and the United States (US). The root of distrust is different system of administration (communist vs. capitalist) and competition over world hegemony

Initial Cause/New Cause
▼

Adverse Action

1942 – 1949: Klaus Fuchs and Julius Rosenberg stole the US nuclear secrets which enabled the Soviet Union to produce its first nuclear bomb and tested on 29 August 1949.

1953 – 1957: The Soviet spy ring led by Colonel Vilyam Fisher alias Rudolf Abel operating in US to steal the US military secrets.

> ***Adverse Reaction***
> 1958- April 1962: In the wake of Soviet capability of building the nuclear weapons, the
> US started to deploy the missile system in Europe (England, Germany, Turkey, and Italy)
> April 17, 1961: Under Monroe doctrine, US invaded Cuba to topple Fidel Castro a Cuban communist leader in order to eliminate the Soviet Union hegemony over Latin America
> ▼
> ***Adverse Action***
> May 1962: Soviet Prime Minister to order the deployment of nuclear weapon to Cuba
> ▼
> ***Adverse Reaction***
> October 14, 1962: US spy plane to take the pictures of SU missile in Cuba
> October 27, 1962: US spy plane was shot down over Cuba. The US threatened to
> Invade Cuba (again) in the full scale war
> ▼
> Distrust increased---- back to *Initial Cause/New Cause* ----- ▲ ▲

2.12. Klaus Fuchs (1911-1988)

Klaus Emil Julius Fuchs was German and British national, he was born in Germany and worked United Kingdom and USA in nuclear research facility at Los Alamos. In 1950 he was convicted of spying and providing the secret atomic weapon to former **Soviet Union of Socialist Republics (USSR)**. The significance of his treason is the capability of the Soviet Union to develop its first atomic bomb; he was held responsible for proliferation of the weapon of mass destruction. This success was credited to then-leader Lavrentiy Beria. Fuchs was sentenced for 14 years, but to serve only for 9 years; and after his imprisonment he moved to East Germany where he taught the Chinese scientist to make a more sophisticated atomic bomb. He did not stop proliferating the WMD until he died, for which he received the Karl Marx medal [72].

2.13 Julius and Ethel Rosenberg

Julius Rosenberg (1918 – 1953) and **Ethel Greenglass Rosenberg** (1915 – 1953) were also atomic spies; they were executed in 1953 after being convicted of providing the atomic bomb secret to the Soviet Union. As the result of their treason altogether with Fuchs', the USSR was able to make the atomic bomb in 1949 despite the (unsuccessful) effort of the USA to protect its nuclear secret.

The Rosenbergs were honored and recognized in the memoir of former leader Nikita Khrushchev (1990). The interesting part of their case is the legal consideration of **Judge Irving Kaufman** that the Rosenbergs made the Korean War possible with 50,000 casualties because the Communist now has the atomic bomb, and they changed the course of history to make millions of Americans in the tension under the threat of nuclear attack. The political impact of their trial was the rise of a young **Senator Joseph McCarthy**; he was inspired by the trial and launched a campaign of anti-communism.

Had he survived, he could be preparing a long run for the presidency, but he died from an acute disease; and later, Richard Nixon used the tip and trick of McCarthy and won the presidency in 1969. Although the Rosenbergs were dubbed as "American Communist", in fact they came from the Jewish family; and therefore their lawyer filed a complaint prior their execution that the execution on Sabbath would be offending their Jewish heritage [73].

It is still disputable about Fuchs and Rosenberg's action. Some critics considered them as worst traitor; and some considered them as balancers since without them the nuclear hegemony would be in the US hand only.

2.14. Vilyam Genrikhovich Fisher (1903 –1971)

Vilyam Genrikhovich Fisher was a leader of Soviet spy ring operated in New York [74]. His main mission was to steal the US atomic secret and smuggle them to the Soviet Union. Born in England to Russian immigrant parents, his birth place provided him a benefit of perfect English ability as "natural American" in New York. He moved to Russia and served in the Soviet military in 1921 to 1927; his fluency in English, Russian, German and Polish brought him to be translator for GRU. He was the most important person to collect the US atomic secrets from various sources and to smuggle them out of the US. He successfully coordinated the spy ring in the US and never be caught until he was betrayed by **Häyhänen** one of his ring member. His qualification as a master spy was so high and his success team consists of the high quality spies, couriers, and scientists such as:

(1) Special courier Kitty Harris

(2) Courier Lona Cohen, the courier for Julius and Ethel Rosenberg

(3) Maurice Cohen the courier for Julius and Ethel Rosenberg

(4) Ethel Rosenberg's brother **David Greenglass** who worked for US atomic laboratory at Los Alamos

(5) Harry Gold courier for **Greenglass** and the German scientist, **Klaus Fuchs**

(6) Scientist **Morton Sobell** (1917-) an American engineer worked for General Electric

(7) Manhattan scientist **Theodore Hall** who used **Saville Sax** and **Lona Cohen** as couriers

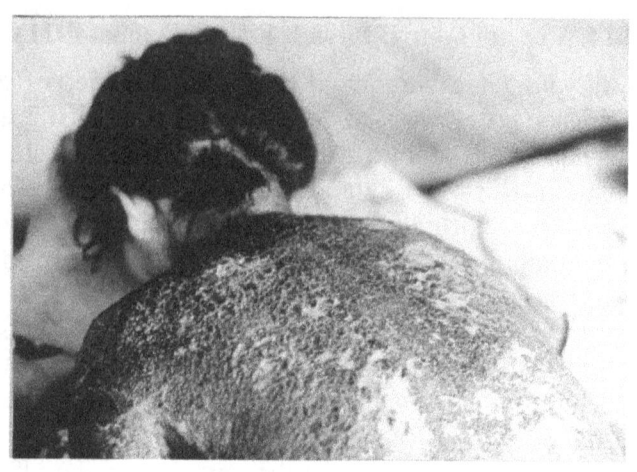

The victim of Atomic bomb in Hiroshima; August 6, 1945
Photo by Masami Onuka, courtesy of **Hiroshima Peace Memorial Museum**, Japan

His success may be described in one phrase "Soviet knew how to produce the atomic bomb from the work of Vilyam Fisher". When he was arrested on charges of conspiracy he used his real name Colonel **Rudolf Ivanovich Abel** to convey the signal that he did not betray the Soviet. He was arrested on June 21, 1957 and tried; the jury found him guilty on October 25, 1957 and the Federal judge on November 15, 1957 sentenced this master spy to thirty years for first count, ten years for second count and five years for third count a total of 45 years, and $3,000.00 fine. After four years, on February 10, 1962 he was exchanged with Gary Powers a USAF pilot shot down over Soviet airspace in 1961.

2.15. Kitty Harris (1899-1966)

Kitty Harris was a Soviet spy who was involved in the Colonel Rudolf Abel spy ring as a dependable courier. She was born in London to a poor Russian Jewish family, moved to Canada and later moved to China in 1928 [75]. To track her movement and activity, we have no doubt that she was long prepared to be a very high quality spy. She was very active in the "socialism" activity and later was sent to

Germany, England and eventually to USA 1941 after some years of experience. When she was in England, she became a very important courier to **Donald Duart McLean** one of five England spy ring. In 1943 she was sent to Mexico to contact Lev Vasilevsky a KGB agent in Mexico City. The various activities she was involved with might explain how important she was. Her code name was "Aida", even though her code was found in 1956 and made public in 1986; her real identity was only discovered in 2001 long time after she passed. She never be captured, never be tried, never betrayed and never be betrayed; a perfect Soviet spy who successfully helped the Soviet Union to produce the atomic weapon.

2.16. Cambridge Five

The Soviet Union reached a big success in the spying activity during and after the World War II by infiltrating the Britain Secret Service. This success was credited to master spy **Arnold Deutsch** who extraordinarily recruited five top spies in the United Kingdom dubbed as the Cambridge Five. They were Kim Philby, Donald Duart MacLean, Guy Burgess, Anthony Blunt [76] and the fifth spy which his or her identity is still disputable until today. They passed the secret information on for the benefit of the Soviet Union after being recruited in 1930's during their education at Cambridge University.

2.16.1. Kim Philby

Harold Adrian Russell "Kim" Philby (1912-1988) was a high level intelligent British officer MI6 who betrayed his country to be a top spy for the Soviet Union, he was the most smart and elusive spy among five spies. He was forced to resign from MI6 based on suspicion from being a spy with crypto name "Stanley" [76]. After leaving MI6 he worked as a journalist a perfect job as a cover to his covert action, and fortunately for him but unfortunately for British intelligence. MI6 called him back into service despite the fact that the British counter-intelligence has suspected him for a long time as a spy for Soviet Union. It's s second success for the Soviet Union to re-implant its top spy inside the heart of British intelligence. In 1955 on a press conference he even publicly denied allegation that he was a spy for the Soviet Union. For his courage to call a press conference, British Foreign Secretary Harold McMillan cleared Philby from the suspicion, a grave mistake nobody realized until Philby defected to Soviet Union in 1963 without ever being caught.

2.16.2. Donald Duart MacLean

Donald Duart MacLean [London 1913 - Moscow 1983] was an important member of Cambridge Five which first sought by the British intelligence since the revelation of Venona secret code [76]. When Philby was posted in the British embassy in Washington DC after the World War II; he learned from his position that the US and the British counter-intelligence were looking for a Soviet spy working inside the British intelligence with a code name "Homer". He knew that he had to warn Donald Duart MacLean and Guy Burgess about the impending danger if they were unveiled by the British counter-intelligence. Soon afterward, in summer 1951 Burgess and MacLean shocked the international intelligence community by disappearing. Nobody knew where they were until five years later when in 1956 they attended a press conference in Moscow. They never be compromised or caught for creating a big mess they left behind in the British intelligence. **Katty Harris** was his handler and lover during his long time spying period.

2.16.3. Guy Burgess

Guy Francis de Moncy Burgess (1911-1963) was another important member of Cambridge Five which first sought by the British intelligence since the revelation of Venona secret code [76]. His British birth place enabled him to be British intelligent officer and provided him a perfect cover of his spying activity for the Soviet Union. From this point we know how important he was, and he made a big hole in the NATO strategy since he disclosed it to Soviet Union.

2.16.4. Anthony Blunt

Anthony Blunt was another important member of Cambridge Five altogether with Kim Philby, Donald Duart MacLean and Guy Burgess. He worked for the British intelligence in 1940 and later became a historian. The British counter-intelligence unveils his role as a Soviet Union spy in 1964 only after being tipped off by his friend for 30 years [76]. During interrogation he confessed as a Soviet spy, eventually he was not prosecuted in exchange of his confession and cooperation while at the same time was kept as a staff of British intelligent without access to the classified materials. The mystery of his freedom from prosecution might be explained only if the British counter-intelligence wants to use him as disinformation agent against the Soviet Union. Or, another Soviet spy in a high level British government defended him.

From this point we might understand Peter Wright's "*Spy Catcher*" published in 1987 where the former MI5 Director Roger Hollis and former British Prime Minister Harold McMillan were accused of being KGB agents. Blunt's identity as a Soviet spy was made public in 1979 by an investigative journalist.

2.16. 5. The Fifth Man

In 1961, Anatoly Golitsyn a high level KGB officer defected; he provided the important information about the fifth man among the Cambridge Five including MacLean and Burgess [76]. The fifth man is still a mystery until today while Golitsyn accused that the former British Prime Minister **Harold Wilson** (1916-1995, in office from 4 March 1974 – 5 April 1976) was a KGB agent. If he was, the British government never publicly disclosed it out of embarrassment. The legendary British super spy James Bond is only a fiction written by a former British Naval Officer and novelist Ian Fleming (1908–1964). Fleming died almost 50 years ago, yet his Bond character is still alive and written by the ghost writer to create the good image to the British intelligence agency. Had James Bond ever lived then the Cambridge Five had been caught long time ago. The classified document sold on an auction revealed that Cambridge Five actually were recognized since very long time ago, but the spy catcher intentionally let them escape to make a perennial periodical British humour alive.

2.17. Anatoly Mikhaylovich Golitsin

Golitsyn (1926-) is a high level KGB officer assigned as a diplomat at Soviet embassy in Helsinki, Finland. He defected to the CIA in 1961 and disclosed a lot of KGB strategies [76] [77]. He was awarded the British knighthood CBE (Commander of the Order of the British Empire and granted American citizen in 1984. The information about his residence, his life or death, if any, is kept in secret since the Soviet death squad is pursuing him. He provided super important information about many notorious Soviet agents including Kim Philby, Donald Duart MacLean, Guy Burgess, John Vassal and Alekandr Kopatzky. Golitsyn is to confirm that Philby was a Soviet super spy who worked for a long time inside the British intelligence, but before Philby was being arrested he defected to Russia in 1963.

2.18. Lev Vasilevsky

Lev Vasilevsky, alias **Leonid A. Tarasov**, was an important KGB agent in Mexico City who handled the flowing information about secret nuclear program from some sources at Los Alamos Laboratory in 1943. In 1950 after **Klaus Fuchs** arrest, Vasilevsky set the escape route from the US to Soviet Union for **Bruno Pontecorvo** who collected the atomic secrets from **Enrico Fermi** a senior researcher at Los Alamos Nuclear Laboratory. **Kitty Harris** was Vasilevsky's important courier in Mexico City in early 1943 [78].

2.19. Saville Sax (1924-1980)

Saville Sax was Theodore Hall's roommate and Hall's recruiter to be a Soviet spy in order to steal the nuclear secret from Manhattan Project where Hall worked. Sax was also a Hall's handler to transfer the nuclear secret to Soviet Union [79]. His parents were born in the Soviet Union, and most probably were prepared to have a US citizen son to become a Soviet spy. In his last years of his life he was addicted to drug and became hippie; he died in poverty.

2.20. Morton Sobell

Morton Sobell (1917-) was born into a Jewish family in New York City who worked for General Electric Company. He was a spy for the Soviet Union and found guilty of spying against the US along with Julius Rosenberg at 1951 espionage trial and sentenced to 30 years in prison. After spending 17 years in Alcatraz prison at San Francisco Bay he was released in 1969. He keeps his innocence for a long time and only admits as a Soviets spy after half a century when he is 91 and interviewed by the *New York Times,* published on September 11, 2008 [80].

2.21. George Abramovich Koval (1913 – 2006)

George Abramovich Koval was an American who secretly worked as Glavnoye Razvedyvatelnoye Upravlenniye [GRU] agent while served as engineer for the Manhattan Project a USA rush project to produce atomic bomb during 1940's [81]. Koval was born in Iowa, USA to the Jewish immigrant, and as the young American with the Soviet root he visited the Soviet Union with his parent where he was recruited and trained as a GRU spy upon his return to the USA. Koval was the most important Soviet spy to steal the nuclear secret from the US. His infiltration into Manhattan Project was to speed up the Soviet ability to copy what the US was doing to produce the first atomic bomb. It was Koval –not **Klaus Fuchs**, not **Julius Rosenberg** and not **Ethel Rosenberg**- the real teacher who taught the Soviet on how to produce the atomic bomb from scratch, from producing plutonium and uranium to designing and detonating the atomic bomb since he was a US-born intern worked unsuspected in the Manhattan Project and then transfer his whole knowledge to produce the Soviet first atomic bomb. At the time the US realized what happened, it was too late, even too late to catch him.

His extraordinary infiltration to the ultra secret US program enabled the Soviet Union to produce plutonium and uranium for deadly weapon almost the same time the US was producing. His role was so important that the Soviet called him back right away after the World War II in October 1948 under the disguise "to travel to Poland and Israel" to prevent from being caught by the US counter-intelligence.

To analyze his tracks since his parent immigrated to US, born in US, traveled to Soviet as a young adult, came back to US in 1940, drafted into the US Army until he worked at atomic research laboratories showed us a very meticulous plan of GRU to preparing Koval to infiltrate to the heart of the US ultra secret program. It was almost impossible to consider that Koval parent immigrated to US just for the reason of seeking a new life; it must be a precise plan to send Koval parents to US, to have a US-born son to eliminate the suspicion of being a foreign spy because he was born and raised in the US soil. It must be a long and meticulous plan designed accordingly by GRU. Later on, this method was copied by another intelligence agency in the case of **Jonathan Pollard** to steal the US secret communication system since the GRU method was proven effective and nobody suspected. The Russian Federation as the continuation of the Soviet Union awarded Koval the highest recognition as Russian Hero; he deserved it as he deserved the US death penalty. The free world split decision over his action. Some critics considered him as the worst traitor; and some considered him as the balancer, as Theo Hall did, since without them the nuclear hegemony would be in the US hand only.

2.22. Theodore Hall (1925 – 1999)

Theodore Alvin Hall also known as **Theodore Alvin Holtzberg** was an American atomic scientist worked for Manhattan Project and became the voluntary spy for the Soviet Union. He provided the Soviet the detail information about the first plutonium bomb and the process to produce plutonium. His father changed the family name to avoid anti-Semitic sentiment and make easy finding a job during the Great Depression.

At the same time, another physicist of Manhattan Project, **Klaus Fuchs**, also provided the atomic secret from Las Alamos laboratory. Unbeknown, their information and activities were handled by the same master spy Colonel Rudolf Abel from an art studio in New York who never be caught for year if his ring member **Reino Häyhänen** did not betray him. Theodore Alvin Hall did not betray the US for money, not for an ideology; he sent the Los Alamos secret to the Soviet handler for free just for a simple reason: "American monopoly on nuclear weapons was dangerous and should be avoided" [82]. He was so anxious if the US falls into abusing the atomic weapon and "turn it loose on the world as Nazi Germany developed".

[57] http://en.wikipedia.org/wiki/James_Byrd,_Jr.
[58] *USA Today* newspaper, Friday June 4, 2010 page 3A
[59] Tim Weiner, *"Legacy of Ashes, the History of CIA"*, Anchor Books, New York 2008, pp. 298 – 301
[60] http://en.wikipedia.org/wiki/Oleg_Penkovsky
[61] http://en.wikipedia.org/wiki/Vasily_Arkhipov
[62] http://en.wikipedia.org/wiki/J._Robert_Oppenheimer
[63] *ibid.*
[64] *ibid.*
[65] *ibid.*
[66] http://en.wikipedia.org/wiki/Joe_1
[67] http://en.wikipedia.org/wiki/Gary_Powers
[68] http://en.wikipedia.org/wiki/Rudolf_Anderson
[69] http://en.wikipedia.org/wiki/Cuban_Missile_Crisis
[70] http://en.wikipedia.org/wiki/Thor_IRBM
[71] http://en.wikipedia.org/wiki/Starfish_Prime

[72] http://en.wikipedia.org/wiki/Klaus_Fuchs
[73] http://en.wikipedia.org/wiki/Ethel_Rosenberg
[74] http://en.wikipedia.org/wiki/Rudolf_Abel
[75] http://en.wikipedia.org/wiki/Kitty_Harris
[76] http://en.wikipedia.org/wiki/Cambridge_Five
[77] http://en.wikipedia.org/wiki/Anatoliy_Golitsyn
[78] http://en.wikipedia.org/wiki/Lev_Vasilevsky
[79] http://en.wikipedia.org/wiki/Saville_Sax
[80] http://en.wikipedia.org/wiki/Morton_Sobell
[81] http://en.wikipedia.org/wiki/George_Koval
[82] http://en.wikipedia.org/wiki/Theodore_Hall

Dialogue
Part Three: The Kennedys

"Ask not what your country can do for you; ask what you can do for your country", JFK on the inauguration day January 20, 1961 *)

1. Ireland

Ireland is the land of Kennedy forefathers; an overview on Ireland will add our understanding to the Kennedys. In the mid-sixteenth century, the spirit of adversary between Catholic and Protestant was still dominating a part of Europe. The England, Scotland and Ireland were ruled by King Charles I (1600 - 1649) who considered himself as absolute and divine king, and nobody would remove him. The dispute about the taxes had caused the friction between him and the Parliament and subsequently led to his abdication and execution on January 30, 1649. The man behind this action was Oliver Cromwell (1599 - 1658), he was also known as the man behind the massacre of 2,800 Irish Army in 1652, and the seller of thousands of Irishmen as the slaves to West Indie (the predecessor of Indonesia); he seized almost of Ireland farms and redistributed to the Protestant soldiers.

The animosity between Catholic and Protestant lasts for centuries even until the era of Prime Minister Margaret Thatcher when she labeled Bobby Sands "criminal" and "terrorist" on a very day he died in North Ireland prison. Sands was a working class Catholic and member of Irish Republican Army (IRA) who struggled against the violence and repression, a political reason.

Sands died from hunger strike for 66 days on May 5, 1981. More than 100,000 people attended his funeral in Belfast since he was lauded a hero for the Irish people. The people remember two things from him; his starving to death and his quote "…. *beidh bua againn eigin lá eigin*" (we would win someday).

Around one-third of Ireland population had died in a various wars, famine, and plague; the living peasants had to pay the rent for their own redistributed land to the foreign owners. The poor tenant farmers and their families used to live in the worst huts we never imagined. The Irish language was forbidden, the catholic practices had been banished, no school and no teacher available. To keep Irish docile, the British enforced "illiteracy" [83]; this condition might have increased their ability of speech tradition.

The deteriorating condition forced them to immigrate to America, under this situation Thomas Fitzgerald and his wife Rose Mary Murray in 1840 emigrated from Ireland to Boston, Massachusetts. They had had eleven children, their third kid was John which was popular with his nickname "Honey Fitz" because his good social life. He was a future-envisioned person, an excellent organizer to build the future career, and ever aware of his environment.

In 1892 he was elected City Council, 1893 was State Senator, from 1895 to 1901 was US Congressman from Boston, and at last in 1905 was elected Mayor of Boston and was re-elected in 1910. From his marriage to Mary Josephine Hannon in 1889 he had had six children; Rose Fitzgerald was the oldest, she got a good education and graduated from High School in 1906.

On another side, Patrick Kennedy on 1848 decided to immigrate to Boston; he married Bridget Murphy and had had the son Patrick Joseph Kennedy who later in 1887 married Mary Augusta Hickey from a well-known family. Patrick Joseph was a nice person who used to offer a loan for the needy, in 1886 was elected Massachusetts House of Representative, and 6 years later was elected State Senator. In 1888 his wife delivered the first child Joseph, and later Loretta and Margaret; Joseph graduated from Harvard in 1912. Joseph Kennedy and Rose Fitzgerald met first time when they were children, while in the High School they secretly met each other, and they engaged in 1914; four months later they got married.

From this family root, it was obvious that both Joseph Sr. and Rose came from the political family of Boston. In 1915 Rose gave birth to the first child Joseph Patrick Kennedy Jr., at his birth his grandfather Honey Fitz announced that the baby was decided by his parent to be the "next President of United States", and in 1917 John "Jack" Fitzgerald Kennedy was born who later to carry the family mission on to be the US President.

Joseph Kennedy Sr. was talented and fortunate person, he bought 15,000 shares of Hayden, Stone and Co of Boston at $16 each and sold the 9 months later for $42 each and netted $675,000 when he was under 40. He knew how to maintain a good relation with everybody especially with Franklin D. Roosevelt who knew him during the war era. Roosevelt appointed Joe Kennedy Sr. as a chairman of SEC in 1932 and he resigned in 1935 to campaign for Roosevelt. To quit a good job for campaigning someone else is a bet, but Joe Kennedy Sr. knew what to do; in 1937 he was appointed for a higher position, the US Maritime Secretary, and later in 1938, the Ambassador to Great Britain where his wife Rose remembered as a best part of her life.

Joe Kennedy Sr. was an attentive father and thought nothing more important than the future of his children, he paid attention to each of his children to understand their potential and weakness and encourage them how to utilize their talents. He hired Alice Cahill "Keela" Bastian to supervise his children. He provided her a job description in the sentence of "Miss Cahill, do not hesitate to interrupt me, whether I am at a meeting, in conference, or visiting with friends, if you wish to consult me about my children" [84]. Some years later in 1938 when Joe Jr. and Jack were involved in a bout with the other boys and police incarcerated both, their father Joe Kennedy Sr. refused to bail them out, "Stay where you are", he said [85]. However, Joe Kennedy Sr. at any chance prepared his children future, when a German U-2 boat sank SS Athenia in September 3, 1939 he sent Jack Kennedy to Glasgow to comfort the victim relatives; this action soon praised by the British newspapers.

No doubt it was one among the popularity for the future of the Kennedys. Another chance came in 1940, Jack Kennedy raised the fund of $1,700 sent to the Red Cross to help Europe; this money was $500 over the designated amount. Jack Kennedy graduated *cum laude* from Harvard University with the thesis "Appeasement in Munich" in June 1940 while his father was still the Ambassador in London and was not able to attend the graduation ceremony. He sent a telegram congratulating his son. The thesis was published under the title of "Why England Slept" a deliberate paraphrased of Winston Churchill's "While England Slept", it was sold almost 100,000 copies and became a pride for the Kennedys; the US Ambassador happily sent the copy to the Queen of England and British Prime Minister Churchill. However, behind this popularity and success of "Why England Slept", there was a slanting story; Harvey Klemmer the Ambassador's speech writer and Arthur Krock a family friend were allegedly helping Jack Kennedy to write the thesis, and later in 2008 Theodore Sorensen admitted that he helped to write Jack Kennedy's "Profile in Courage".

In 1940 Roosevelt was reelected in a hard time when the world was preparing the World War II. The United States of America was still neutral in the European conflict. However in March 1941 the US Congress passed the **Lend-Lease Act** to help the Great Britain, Soviet Union, France and China in the World War II with war supplies worth of $50.1 billion equivalent to about $700 billion at 2007 prices [86] [87]. The war supplies were everything necessary to win the war including trucks, locomotives, landing craft, airplanes, etc. The Lend-Lease Act was a tricky maneuver by the Republicans. Everett Dirksen a Republican US Representative to secure the passage of the bill by introducing it while 65 of the House's Democrats were at a luncheon [88]. The Land-Lease Act was a respond to the outbreak of European war in September 1939.

Under the Lend-Lease Act, the United States of America supplied the Allied nations with big amount of war supplies between 1941 and 1945 to help them in the war against Germany under Hitler leadership. After **Lend-Lease Act** the Great Britain allowed the USA to build the military bases in Newfoundland, Bermuda, and the British West Indies in return for the war supplies it received. When Hitler learned this situation he ordered to attack SS Robin Moor the US civilian merchant steamship on 21 May, 1941 outside of the war zone. Hitler specifically mentioned the Lend-Lease Act when he declared war on the US on 11 December 1941 [89]. The Lend Lease Act which had been passed by the Congress and was signed by President Roosevelt in March 1941; was a **determinant factor** to bring the USA into the World War II *far before* the Pearl harbor attack by the Japanese troops on December 7, 1941.

The history should have been rewritten *on why* the Japan attacked the headquarters of US Pacific Fleet at Pearl Harbor on Oahu island, Hawaii regardless of whether how wrong this attack was.

*)   This quotation is originating from Lebanese poet Kahlil Gibran (1883-1931)
[83] O'Brien, Michael, "*John F. Kennedy*", Thomas Dunne Books, St. Martin's Press, NY 2005; pp. 1 - 2
[84] *ibid*. pp. 36 - 45
[85] *ibid*., pp. 82 – 83
[86] *ibid*. pp. 109 – 110
[87] http://en.wikipedia.org/wiki/Lend-Lease_Act
[88] O'Brien, *loc.cit.*
[89] *ibid.*

2. The Flaming Hearts

> "I am not going to try and make you change; it would be without result anyway..." Inga Arvad Fejos's love letter to JF Kennedy

Jack Kennedy had an extraordinary attractive performance and personality, during his time as a student at Harvard University, he maintained his relationship with his High School sweetheart **Olive Cowley**, and during 1938-1939 he had a relationship with **Frances Ann Cannon** who in 1939 introduced him to a popular writer **John Hersey** and is also her future husband; in 1944 Hersey won a Nobel prize for his novel "A Bell for Adano".

Every father always wants his children to be success in the life, so did Joe Kennedy Sr., he helped Jack Kennedy to have his first job at the US Government's Office for Naval Intelligence (ONI) in Washington October 1941 before being trained and assigned as a commander of PT-109 boat to the Pacific War in 1943. He was a young and handsome Navy officer when he met 28 year-old **Inga Arvad Fejos** a columnist at Washington Times-Herald where Jack's sister Kathleen worked as a reporter. His relationship with Inga became the important news when a reporter found her photograph with **Adolf Hitler**; it's a questionable relationship in regard what if Inga were a suspect of Nazi spy who tried to build a functional relationship with a US Naval officer.

Inga was young and beautiful while Jack was young and handsome, however after their relationship was revealed on January 12, 1942 by yellow columnist **Walter Winchell** on **New York Mirror** [90], his father Joe Kennedy Sr. reminded Jack that Inga has already married. Joe Kennedy Sr. must be arranging his spy ring to investigate who is Inga; and it was found that she separated with her husband but has not yet divorced at that time of relationship.

Jack Kennedy was removed from Washington to Charleston afterward with the "help" of his invincible father power; Inga seemed to understand the situation and wrote a letter on January 27, 1942 "*I am not going to try and make you change, it would be without result anyway because Joe has a stronger hand than I*" [91].

Did their relationship ended after Jack's transfer to Charleston? On February 1942 a Charleston hotel room assigned to be the *rendezvous* for two lovers was bugged with a hearing device to make sure Inga and Jack did not talking about the government secret; instead the device disclosed a lot of premarital relationships, a lot of sighs and groans. Michael O'Brien the author of "John F. Kennedy" (2005) wrote in a poetic passage:

> ".... a kind of love Jack had never known before. Inga tormented Jack with a depth of maternal, womanly affection he would never experience again in his starlet -studded life- an appreciative, forgiving, understanding, tantalizing, humorous, intuitive, feminine love that made every other relationship seems small and artificial..." [92].

Inga is an unforgettable woman, when Jack Kennedy went home from the war he visited her a couple times before she married actor Tim McCloy who was 30 years elder. Six months later she delivered a baby **Ronald**; however 20 years later she complained herself "I do not know who your father for sure, I really do not know if it was Jack or Tim" [93]. It is not a bad idea to have the DNA test for the paternity to determine who Ronald is, as it is necessary for **Lisa Lanett**, a 87 year-old Texas woman who claims in 2009 that she had a baby boy from her relationship with then-26 year old John F. Kennedy after returning from Pacific war. She claims she was pregnant in early 1945, and Jack wanted to marry her, however she turned him down [94].

This is life; every hero has his own relationship with some women as a part of his flaming life; from Emperor Shih Huang Ti, Mussolini, Soekarno to Kennedy, we might not blame on them for having some relationships with several beautiful women; the only question is "were their relationships legitimate?"

[90] O'Brien, *ibid.* p. 121
[91] *ibid.*
[92] *ibid.*, p. 122
[93] *ibid.*, p. 125
[94] Jim Nelson, "*Globe*" Magazine, April 13, 2009 edition, p. 44

3. Hero of the Sea

> Unmindful of personal danger, Lieutenant Kennedy unhesitatingly braved the difficulties and hazards of darkness to direct rescue operations... (US Navy)

John F. Kennedy in 1940 completed his thesis at Harvard University "Appeasement in Munich" discussing the British participation in the Munich Agreement, he graduated *cum laude* in the international affairs. As a futuristic father, Joseph Kennedy Sr. encouraged John F. Kennedy to publish his thesis as a book; in July 1940 it was published with the title "Why England Slept", this book amazingly became a bestseller.

The Munich Agreement was an accord regarding the Czechoslovakia's Sudetenland which mainly inhabited by "Czech Germans", the Agreement was signed on September 29, 1938 by Germany, France, Britain, and Italy allowing Germany to annex the strategic Sudetenland without Czechoslovakia's consent; it was the cutting of a cake without its owner's permit. Therefore, some analysts said it was a cowardice action against Czechoslovakia, but then-British Prime Minister Neville Chamberlain called it "appeasement" the euphemism for "cowardice" or "to avoid the war"; the agreement is good until now. "Appeasement" is the domain of political science; sometimes the international politics allows the injustice action shrouded with a good word like "genocide" for "mass killing", "pre-emptive strike" for "bloody occupation", etc.

John F. Kennedy's thesis was published in clearer message without using the euphemism; "Why England Slept" is to questioning the England "permit" for Adolf Hitler to annex a part of Czechoslovakia territory.

John F. Kennedy joined the US Navy in July 1942; he enrolled midshipmen's school at Northwestern University before assigned as a lieutenant to command a PT-109 boat a Patrol Torpedo with twelve crew members. His education at the Naval Reserve Officers Training School and Motor Torpedo Boat Squadron Training Center lead him to his position as a commandant of Patrol Boat at Pacific war. During World War II; Japan had stationed the troops and supplies on a base named Vila close to Kolombangara Island in the Pacific. On August 1, 1943 Lieutenant John F. Kennedy on PT-109 as a part of the fleet of fourteen PT boats were ordered to patrol nearby Kolombangara Island to search the Japanese destroyer.

A couple hours after midnight on early August 2, 1943 2:30 AM a crewman on PT-109 spotted a huge dark shape about 200 yards away. It was a Japanese destroyer Amagiri under the command of Let. Com. Kohei Hanami, it was too short to avoid the crash, Amagiri crushed Lieutenant John F. Kennedy's PT-109 boat and left two crewmen died instantly. Lt. John F. Kennedy ordered his crewmen to swim to a nearby island about 3 miles away for five hour in the dark and cold night.

Crewman Patrick McMahon was injured and could not help himself, Lt. John F. Kennedy with his teeth had to clench McMahon's strap of life jacket to tow him to Plum Pudding Island. No water or food available; and fortunately there were coconut trees; and they found some Japanese food hidden on the island. Lt. John F. Kennedy had no communication tools, everything sunk along with his PT-109, but he had to send message to his superior. He found a coconut shell and scratched the message on it using his knife and asked two Solomon Islanders to convey his message to Lt. Arthur Evans the Australian naval officer, he then radioed the Allied Forces about the Japanese boat as well informing US PT-boats base for victim rescue mission [95][96]. For this heroic action Lt. Kennedy received the US Navy and Marine Corps Medal with praise:

"For extremely heroic conduct as Commanding Officer of Motor Torpedo Boat 109 following the collision and sinking of that vessel in the Pacific War Theater on August 1–2, 1943. Unmindful of personal danger, Lieutenant (then Lieutenant, Junior Grade) Kennedy unhesitatingly braved the difficulties and hazards of darkness to direct rescue operations, swimming many hours to secure aid and food after he had succeeded in getting his crew ashore. His outstanding courage, endurance and leadership contributed to the saving of several lives and were in keeping with the highest traditions of the United States Naval Service [97]".

Under the effort of Joe Kennedy Sr., John Hersey a Nobel laureate was asked to write the heroic story of Jack Kennedy during the Pacific war; the story of PT-109 commanded by Jack Kennedy which was crushed by the Japanese destroyer Amagiri, however, was declined by the popular *Life* magazine; fortunately The New Yorker accepted it instead. After Joe Kennedy Jr. died in the World War II, Joe Kennedy Sr. never gave up propelling the popularity of Jack Kennedy in the effort to place Jack as the future President of USA. Joe Kennedy Sr. lobbied the ***Reader's Digest*** to reprint the story of Jack Kennedy and his PT-109 ordeal in Pacific; it was successful and after the reprint on the Reader's Digest August 1944 edition, Jack Kennedy became a national hero [98]. A straight path to the presidency had been paved on him. He received some Awards including the Purple Heart that made him the most decorated US President in the history. He was honorably discharged in 1945 a couple of months before the Pacific war ended and Japan surrendered to the Allied Forces. His coconut shell which was used to deliver a message to Lt. Arthur Evans the Australian naval officer was kept on the presidential desk during his tenure, and now is displayed at the John F. Kennedy Library.

[95] Karen Bornemann Spies, "*John F. Kennedy*", Enslow Publishing Inc., Berkeley Height, NJ, 1999, p. 35
[96] O'Brien, *ibid.*, pp. 130 - 143
[97] http://en.wikipedia.org/wiki/John_F._Kennedy
[98] O'Brien, *ibid.* p. 171

4. A Futuristic Daddy

> (John F. Kennedy) had a tremendous and well-deserved popularity and he was an extraordinary likable man (Henry Cabot Lodge, a rival)

Back from the sea, a big job was awaiting John F. Kennedy. His lovely daddy Joe Kennedy, a man with the futuristic view, was preparing a very nice future; either for Mayor, Governor, Congressman, Senator, or President. Joe Kennedy was so eager to make his children's future prosperous and success; he meticulously prepared and supported his three sons Jack, Bob and Ted to be US Senators; never be in the history a father had three sons and they were all the US Senators. They dedicated their lives to the people without expecting the rewards. When a young John F. Kennedy was sick and still using the walkers, he campaigning while his lovely mother Rose Kennedy watched; later the photograph of his campaign with Rose Kennedy on the background became the historic photograph the Kennedy clan kept with pride. However, a rumor spread about this campaign to win a representative seat, that Joe Kennedy lobbied the sitting US Representative James Michael Curley to resign in lieu with Kennedy clan's effort to place John F. Kennedy as a new US Representative. It was not true, but even if this rumor turned to be true, then Joe Kennedy was a real ideal father everybody wants to be his son. The real story was a US Representative seat was vacant; and it's a time for the Kennedy clan to place John F. Kennedy as US Representative.

In 1946 U.S. Representative James Michael Curley resigned to run for mayor of Boston, this was a golden opportunity for John F. Kennedy as a Democrat to run for the vacated US House of Representative seat; he easily beat the Republican opponent to represent Massachusetts's 11th congressional district from 1947 to 1953. He was a congressman for six years; and in 1952 he defeated incumbent Republican Henry Cabot Lodge Jr. for the U.S. Senate from 1953 until 1960.

From this point, the father's mission almost be accomplished as John F. Kennedy became the US Senator; next step would be running for the Presidency. John F. Kennedy was only 35 years old when he beat Henry Cabot Lodge [99] and won 51.5 % votes to be sworn into Senate office on January 3, 1953. Later, in 1978 Henry C. Lodge a former rival in the Senate race, praised John F. Kennedy as someone who "had a tremendous and well-deserved popularity and he was an extraordinary likable man. In fact, I liked him. So often in a campaign you look for a man's faults and then campaign on them. Well, in this case you did not do that" [100].

The future was already open for him; and on January 2, 1960 he announced his candidacy for the President of USA. His presidential debate with Richard M. Nixon was the first debate aired on the television ever. Thank to Theodore C. Sorensen for his futuristic strategy. John F. Kennedy's strategy to attract the votes was to make American aware about some key issues facing the nation like ending arm and nuclear race with Soviet Union, improving the science and education for every citizen, and increasing the nation's economic growth.

John F. Kennedy's campaign theme was "Responsibility and Action". Later, the theme of every presidential campaign will be a key factor to win the votes and in turn the presidency. The Barrack Obama presidential campaign theme in 2008 "Yes, we can" has became a mantra and in turn helped him to win the presidency, while John McCain was busy to place negative campaign on the televisions and radios; he should have learned from Henry Cabot Lodge – John F. Kennedy in 1953. The sympathy always comes from the warm heart and not from sowing the hatred to the public. Mr. Obama theme of campaign has been tested when he met Mitt Romney in the 2012 Presidential Race. For this election, it looks too much negative campaign commercial on the media from every side.

The American public still remembers how Richard M. Nixon used the hysteria of Soviet spy in his campaign as George W. Bush used the hysteria of terrorist in his campaign, the both strategies worked but with a certain price. For the future presidential campaign, it would be beneficial if a candidate could find Theodore C. Sorensen's style and tactic ever applied to prepare JFK for the presidency in 1960.

Kennedy clan hired Theodore C. Sorensen a 24-year old gifted and talented writer who prepared so many steps for John F. Kennedy on his way to Senate and later to the White House. When JFK moved to Washington, Sorensen was appointed the White House Counsel a special advisor to the President, and became a credible source of history about what happened around the Bay of Pigs incident.

Six years after being diagnosed at London Clinic with Addison's disease, John F. Kennedy married Jacqueline Lee Bouvier on September 12, 1953. They met at a dinner party and were introduced by a friend. A couple years after their marriage, John F. Kennedy underwent spinal surgeries and received Roman Catholic Church's last rites when he was nearly dying; his health was kept in secret during his lifetime. During his recovery in 1956, he published "Profiles in Courage" for which book he was awarded the Pulitzer Prize for Biography in 1957. When the rumors were spreading that John F. Kennedy did not write this book by himself but coauthored by Ted Sorensen, the futuristic father Joseph Kennedy Sr. hired the lawyer to deny the allegation (Part Three: Chapter 5. Pulitzer Prize).

In 1956 John F. Kennedy failed to get nominated as Vice Presidential candidate, he lost to Senator Estes Kefauver of Tennessee, but the Big Daddy Joseph Kennedy Sr. was happy because it was very hard to defeat Dwight D. Eisenhower. The failure of John F. Kennedy to be running mate of popular Adlai Stevenson brought a specific bliss to John F. Kennedy to run for the presidency on the next season.

In 1960 the real battle began for John F. Kennedy, he officially announced his candidacy on January 20, 1960; in the primary he defeated Senator Hubert Humphrey of Minnesota and Senator Wayne Morse of Oregon. As Humphrey and Morse were out, the main rival was only Senator Lyndon Baines Johnson of Texas for the nomination at Democratic Party convention in Los Angeles.

He knew the religion was something to consider in the nomination, and therefore he addressed "I am not the Catholic candidate for President. I am the Democratic Party's candidate for President who also happens to be a Catholic. I do not speak for my Church on public matters — and the Church does not speak for me. [101]" The party convention is always a display of the candidate bright idea, and he launched "New Frontier" idea in his speech which described how the America and the world would be changing. The Democratic Party convention of 1960 nominated John F. Kennedy as the Presidential Candidate with Lyndon B. Johnson as the running mate.

In September and October 1960, John F. Kennedy met his main opponent Richard M. Nixon the Republican candidate and the incumbent US Vice President in the very first televised US presidential debates in US history. John F. Kennedy was well prepared while Nixon on the television looked tired and unprepared, this condition brought the big influence to the audience and they easily decided that John F. Kennedy would be a winner. On the Big Tuesday November 8, 1960 John F. Kennedy defeated Richard Nixon in a very tight presidential election by a thin margin; for the national popular vote Kennedy won only 0.2 percent over Nixon (49.7% to 49.5%), and for the Electoral College Kennedy won 303 votes (34 votes more than minimum 269 to win) over Nixon who got 219 votes. Until now, JFK was the only Roman Catholic ever elected as US President; he was the second-youngest President after Theodore Roosevelt, who was elected to be US President at 43.

Among all forty four US Presidents there was only JFK ever won the prestigious Pulitzer Prize in 1957 for his book "Profile in Courage". Some important international events happened during his tenure including the Bay of Pigs Invasion, the Cuban Missile Crisis, the Berlin Wall, the Space Race, the African-American Civil Rights Movement, and early stage of the Vietnam War with the casualties of more than 50,000 US servicemen. His first 100 days in the White House was a record never be surpassed by any President before or after him in sending 277 requests to Congress. Along with John F. Kennedy the White House became the glamour, a combination of Hollywood and Harvard. He invited World Class celebrities like painter George Catlin, composer Leonard Bernstein, Igor Stravinsky, Aaron Copland, violinist Isaac Stern, cellist Pablo Casals, novelist Pearl S. Buck, poet Robert Frost and 49 Nobel laureate winners in the different occasions.

John F. Kennedy came from a very rich family, his father Joe Kennedy was a smart and fortunate businessman, and his grand father was sweet and generous Mayor of Boston which nicknamed "Honey Fritz". With this background, we can understand when John F. Kennedy signed an executive order to double the food program up; it's the food assistance to four million needy Americans. The first year in the office President John F. Kennedy created the Food for Peace Program for India, Algeria and Egypt. He signed an executive order to establish the Peace Corps for the overseas mission to help the developing countries.

He also created the President's Commission on Equal Employment Opportunity (EEO), and as it went into effect, it's illegal for the employer to differentiate the employees based on race and gender. This is his extraordinary legacy along with the Medicare. American people got sick and had no enough money for medication? President John F. Kennedy introduced the *Medicare* to help million Americans in need of medication and hospitalization; it's a futuristic thought for the sake of Americans.

Unfortunately, just for the politics; his opponents knocked this medical aid proposal down. Later on as he deceased, his successor Lyndon B. Johnson signed the Medicare bill into law.

After Cuban Missile Crisis ended, the popularity of President John F. Kennedy was "sky-rocketing high"; the school teachers around the globe narrated the famous story of Kennedy to their school children, they knew Kennedy and America are inseparable name; it's a time when America was lauded as a hero. Even the Soviet Union's school children and common citizens knew him since it was the very first time a US President's radio address was broadcasted from *Radio Moskwa*. It was June 10, 1963. Never be in the international relationship before and after Kennedy, the United States President's address was broadcasted live from *Radio Moskwa* and never ever the Soviet Union leader address was broadcasted live to American public.

America owed JFK, he brought lot of developments for the US; and here the excerpts of his address at American University in Washington, DC:

> "I speak of peace because of the new face of war. Total war makes no sense in an age where great powers can maintain large and relatively invulnerable nuclear forces and refuse to surrender without resort to those forces. It makes no sense in an age where a single nuclear weapon contains almost ten times the explosive force delivered by all the allied air forces in the Second World War. It makes no sense in an age when the deadly poisons produced by a nuclear exchange would be carried by wind and water and soil and seed to the far corners of the globe and to generations yet unborn". "....Some say that it is useless to speak of peace or world law or world disarmament, and that it will be useless until the leaders of the Soviet Union adopt a more enlightened attitude. I hope they do."

"I believe we can help them do it. But I also believe that we must reexamine our own attitudes, as individuals and as a Nation, for our attitude is as essential as theirs. And every graduate of this school, every thoughtful citizen who despairs of war and wishes to bring peace, should begin by looking inward, by examining his own attitude towards the possibilities of peace, towards the Soviet Union, towards the course of the cold war and towards freedom and peace here at home" [102].

On the very next day June 11, 1963 there was another incident that accumulated to JFK popularity. The segregation spirit still covering the south when two African-American **Vivian Juanita Malone** (1942-2005) and **James Hood** were enrolling to the University of Alabama but blocked by then-segregationist Governor of Alabama **George Wallace**. Later, Vivian Malone's brother-in-law **Eric Holder** was the Deputy US Attorney General under President **William Clinton** and is US Attorney General under President **Barrack H. Obama**. Had George Wallace still alive today hopefully he should not be incinerating.

George Wallace in a futile June 11, 1963 ceremonial demonstration; stood still in front of the university auditorium and addressing the campus to support "the sovereignty of state". Vivian Malone an instant celebrity arrived at the all-white university to pay the tuition fee altogether with James Hood accompanied by US Deputy Attorney General **Nicholas Katzenbach** while Governor Wallace accompanied and backed by the State Troopers. It was so dramatic; Wallace refused them to entry. **Henry Graham** a National Guard General was sent by President Kennedy to escort the African-American student enrolling to Alabama University, Graham with four sergeants confronted Governor Wallace and said "*It is my sad duty to ask you to step aside under the orders of the President of the United States.*"

On the same day President Kennedy took the command over and put the Alabama National Guard under Federal Government, stripping the governor authority over the Alabama National Guard; Kennedy also appointed himself University of Alabama Temporary **Registrar** overruling the existing university administration. The Guards then escorted Vivian Malone and James Hood back to the auditorium while Wallace had to set aside rather than defying the orders of the President of the United States. The dramatic incident was later reenacted in the **"Forrest Gump"** movie with Tom Hank as the leading actor. Two years later Vivian Malone achieved her BA in business management and joined the U.S. Department of Justice until her transfer and retirement in 1996 as a director at US Environmental Protection Agency [103][104][105].

Eight days after June 11 incident, on June 19, 1963 President John F. Kennedy addressing the civil rights before the US Congress, and three days later on June 22, **1963** visiting Europe to meet **Giovanni Battista Enrico Antonio Maria Montini** who just one day earlier elected as a new Pope, Paul VI. Three days later on June 26, 1963 President Kennedy visited Berlin where he addressed a popular quote *Ich bin ein Berliner*, "I am a Berliner".

On July 15, 1963 he secured his position as a top leader among the world leaders by visiting Moscow and discussing the nuclear testing ban either in the atmosphere, ocean or outer space; meanwhile the underground nuclear testing was let open [106]. The popularity of President Kennedy was so high both in USA and in the world.

Everybody loves John F. Kennedy; he was handsome, young, popular, smart, and rich, Pulitzer Prize winner, Harvard educated, and taking care of the needy. No one single previous US President has had this quality ever; and no one single political analyst has any doubt that JFK would have won the second term. But, God the Almighty has another will.

[99] Henry Cabot Lodge was appointed by President John F. Kennedy as the US Ambassador to South Vietnam; Lodge was in Vietnam when President Ngo Dinh Diem and his brother Ngo Dinh Nhu were assassinated in a *coup d'etat* by General Duong Van Minh in 1963

[100] Karen Bornemann Spies, "***John F. Kennedy***", Enslow Publishing Inc., Berkeley Height, NJ, 1999, pp. 55-75

[101] http://en.wikipedia.org/wiki/JFK

[102] http://americanrhetoric.com/ jfkamericanuniversityaddress.html

[103] http://en.wikipedia.org/wiki/Vivian_Malone

[104] Spies, ***ibid***. p. 116-117

[105] In 1996 she retired from the U.S. Environmental Protection Agency as Director of Civil Rights and Urban Affairs. In October 1996 the George Wallace Family Foundation named her as the first recipient of Lurleen B. Wallace Award of Courage. It might be an apology or might be sincerity, but Wallace said at the ceremony "Vivian Malone Jones was at the center of the fight over states' rights and conducted herself with grace, strength and, above all, courage."

If it's an apology, it's long overdue for 33 years, and if it's sincerity the award should have been sustaining.

[106] According to wikipedia.org, on May 1, 1962 French underground nuclear test under mount Taourirt, Algerian Sahara was leaking and spreading the radioactive dusts to the Algerian Sahara atmosphere. If so, the government of Algeria should have demanded the compensation from French government.

Between 1963 and 2007, there are some additional facts that about 30 more nuclear explosions tested by China, India, Pakistan, and North Korea. The other countries with the capability of producing nuclear weapon like Iran, Israel, Japan, South Africa, South Korea and Taiwan are not tallied yet; while Iraq and Libya have been ruled out.

5. Pulitzer Prize

> "The author of *Profile in Courage* is Senator (JF) Kennedy..... To assert that one of us who supplied such materials "wrote the book" for Senator Kennedy is clearly unwarranted and in error" (Ted Sorensen)

Pulitzer Prize was awarded to those who had the extraordinary talent in writing; and one of it was awarded to John F. Kennedy in 1957 for his book *Profile in Courage*. There was always a story behind any prestigious award. May 7, 1957 was a decisive day for the Pulitzer Prize Advisory Committee (PPAC) to discuss who would be the winner. Two members of jury were the professors at leading universities; Prof. Julian Boyd the Editor of Thomas Jefferson Paper at Princeton, and Prof. Bernard Mayo of the University of Virginia. They were checking the list; and on the top list was **Harlan Fiske Stones: Pillar of the Laws** by Alpheus T. Mason, the second was James M. Burns' ***The Lion and the Fox***, and John F. Kennedy's ***Profile in Courage*** was the third. So why did it come first and win the prize?

The PPAC was supposed to decide Mason's book as the winner when a member **Donald Ferguson** the Editor of *Milwaukee Journal* came forward with an influential voice: "Gentlemen, I read Kennedy's ***Profile in Courage*** aloud to my grandson and he was absolutely fascinated. I think; we should give the prize to Kennedy". The critics said that John F. Kennedy inner circle with the power of money lobbied for this award, one of them was Arthur Krock, he boasted that he lobbied [107] the PPAC for this purpose.

A Smoking gun? Gilbert Seldes claimed in ***Village Voice*** on May 15, 1957 that Kennedy's ***Profile in Courage*** was written with "collaborator", unfortunately this hot claim got a little publicity even after The Mike Wallace Interview was aired on ABC TV station on December 7, 1957 [108].

The beloved father Joe Kennedy a couple days later called attorney Clark Clifford to prepare a lawsuit against ABC TV station for $ 50 M; even though John F. Kennedy remained cool unlike his father. It's not really clear why columnist **Drew Pearson** picked the name of Theodore C. Sorensen, but John F. Kennedy acknowledged later that Sorensen had been paid for $6,000.00; the dispute suddenly became a huge fire. How much this money did worth? Meanwhile the annual salary of President Dwight D. Eisenhower was only $ 100,000.00. This payment did **not** necessarily mean that Sorensen wrote *Profile in Courage* for John F. Kennedy. What did Sorensen say about this? He signed an affidavit:

> "The author of *Profile in Courage* is Senator (JF) Kennedy, who originally conceived its theme, selected its character, determined its contents, and wrote and rewrote each of its chapters. The research, suggestions and other materials received by him in the course of writing the book from me and the others listed in the Preface were all considered by the Senator along with his own material, and in part rejected by him and in part drawn upon by him in his work. To assert that one of us who supplied such materials 'wrote the book' for Senator Kennedy is clearly unwarranted and in error [109]."

John F. Kennedy himself appreciated those who aided him including two secretaries, Editor Evan Thomas, Jules Davids, and James F. Landis for assisting him in preparation of his book. The criticism by two Harvard scholars Arthur Holcombe and Arthur M. Schleisinger, and Walter Johnson of University of Chicago has substantially improved and enriched Kennedy's book, still; he acknowledged that "the greatest debt is owed to my research associate Theodore C. Sorensen for his invaluable assistance in the assembly and preparation of the material upon which this book is based" [110].

Now, the question is, "Did John F. Kennedy write the book or edit it, was he an author or editor?" Attorney Clifford is smart and well prepared, he refers to Preface in ***Profile in Courage*** that John F. Kennedy acknowledged his "greatest debt" and research associate Theodore C. Sorensen. Furthermore, Clifford told ABC that he was preparing a legal action; ABC did not want any trouble nor to fight in long legal battle in the court because it will take a lot of time and money; and opted to retract the story. On Saturday evening December 14, 1957 at the very beginning of Mike Wallace program, Oliver Treyz the ABC Vice President read a well prepared statement:

> "The company has inquired into the charge made by Mr. Pearson and has satisfied itself that such charge is unfounded and the book in question was written by Senator Kennedy. We deeply regret this error and feel it does a grave injustice to a distinguished public servant and author and so the excellent book he wrote, and to the worthy prize that he was awarded. We extended our sincere apology to Senator Kennedy, his publishers, and the Pulitzer Prize Committee. [111]"

According to Michael O'Brien the author of "***John F. Kennedy***" wrote that this statement was prepared by Kennedy's attorney Clark Clifford. It's a wise decision, the case closed; and the show must go on. Later on, one year after swearing in, John F. Kennedy invited Nobel laureates to the White House for dinner. A night in April 1962 became an unforgettable night for all Americans and the guests when 49 Nobel Prize winners packed the White House. It was an indirect publicity that an American citizen at the same time was a President, a Pulitzer-winning author and an intellectual.

John F. Kennedy always knew how to lift his popularity up. However, in May 2008, Sorensen confirmed the rumor in his autobiography that he co-authored "*Profile in Courage*" long time after JFK deceased; an unnecessary confirmation after he was involved in the covering up and signing an affidavit 52 years ago. Based on the affidavit, we know who did lie and to whom we can trust in; should Sorensen be prosecuted for signing an untrue -if not fraudulent- affidavit 52 years ago; and when did the statute of limitation end? Ted Sorensen died on October 31, 2010.

[107] O'Brien, Michael, "*John F. Kennedy*", Thomas Dunne Books, St. Martin's Press, NY 2005; p. 332
[108] *ibid.*, p. 333
[109] *ibid.*
[110] *ibid.*, p. 336
[111] *ibid.*, p. 334

6. Superstition

> Even, after the liquor ban had been cleared, the consequence of liquor drinking still brings the tragedy

It is not good enough to discuss the misfortune or misery of a person unless to complete the biography with due respect to another side of someone's life. Honey Fitz the Mayor of Boston and the grand father of John F. Kennedy already announced that a new baby born, Joe Kennedy Jr., was decided by his parents to run for President of the United States of America. Everybody has his own plan and the God has his own; on August 12, 1944 Joe Kennedy Jr. was aboard a bomber stuffed with almost 10 tons explosive when it went off, and he vanished. The original mission of Joe Kennedy's team was to destroy the German V-3 weapon system which was placed in Northern France to destroy England. The Allied successfully dropped bombs to the V-3 site and German abandoned the system before Joe Kennedy's mission. Had the Allies known that the German abandoned the weapon system in Northern France, the unnecessary Joe Kennedy's mission were cancelled.

The people named a lot of tragic moments that happened to some members of the Kennedy family "The Kennedy Curse"; some people did not believe in the "curse", they said it just a bad luck or a misfortune, while a cleric said it was a consequence of the liquor business the Kennedy Family did for years.

The US government in 1930's in the "Capone Era" banned the liquor beverage with regard that liquor might cause some crimes. Even, after the liquor ban had been cleared, the consequence of liquor drinking still brings the tragedy e.g. the motorist entered the wrong direction of highway killed another motorist and himself, a popular sport star after a party hit and killed the pedestrian, a husband abused his wife, and so forth we never imagined.

Some bad things might happen after consuming the alcoholic beverage; and every religion banned the liquor drinking. Since the USA is a free country and not a state of religious administration, the alcoholic beverage eventually was allowed to sell with some restrictions. However, some people did believe that the liquor business has nothing to do with the Kennedy Family; it was just a destiny, a predefined life line that already assigned even before someone's birth.

The well-knows tragedy was the assassination of John F. Kennedy in 1963, Robert Kennedy in 1968, and the tragic death of John Kennedy Jr. along with his wife and his sister-in-law in 1999. Here the Kennedy saga was compiled from some sources such as Edward Klein's "The Kennedy Curse", O'Brien's "John F. Kennedy", and wikipedia.org [112].

1858: November 22; around 10 years after immigrating to Boston in 1848, Patrick Kennedy died; this date was significant, it was exactly 105 years before his great-grandson assassination in Dallas, Texas. Is it a superstition or coincidence?

1873: Jossie Hannon the mother of Rose F. Kennedy was involved in an accidental drowning of her sister Elizabeth and her friend.

1881: Michael Hannon, the uncle of Rose Fitzgerald died of alcoholism when he was 21.

1885: Thomas Fitzgerald, 62, died and left Honey Fitz behind to take care of all his eight brothers. Honey Fitz, the father of Rose Fitzgerald, was a true patriarch of his future clan, the Kennedys, through his popular daughter, Rose.

1888: Jimmy Hannon, 25, the uncle of Rose Fitzgerald died of alcoholism.

1890: John Edmond Hannon, 13, the uncle of Rose Fitzgerald, had his leg amputated after a train accident; the medical procedure was without anesthesia.

1936: Mary Agnes Fitzgerald Gargan, 43, the sister of Rose Fitzgerald died when her oldest child Joseph Gargan was 6; her three children were raised by Rose and Joseph Kennedy Sr. Thirty three years later when the Chappaquiddick incident occurred, Senator Edward Kennedy asked Joe Gargan to take the blame of the accident.

1941: Rosemary Kennedy was considered to have a problem with her mental health, her father Joseph Kennedy Sr. decided to get her underwent a special procedure "lobotomy" a procedure to slice or remove a part of the lobe of brain.
The Family sent her to psychiatrist Dr. Egas Muniz for a medical procedure [113]; the surgery had impaired Rosemary's cognitive abilities and she remained at her family hospice until her death in 2005. Dr. Muniz had performed a first lobotomy at the University of Lisbon, Portuguese in 1935 to relief of severe mental disorder; and later he won a Nobel Prize. After the invention of the antipsychotic drugs, the lobotomy was considered "as one of the most barbaric mistakes ever perpetrated by mainstream medicine" [114]. The lobotomy; even was kept secret for twenty years from Rose Kennedy, her own mother [115] [116].

1944: August 12, Joseph Patrick Kennedy Jr. the eldest son of Joe Kennedy Sr. and Rose F. Kennedy was aboard a bomber stuffed with almost 10 tons explosive when it went off and he vanished during the World War II. It was decided that he should have been a US President when he was born in 1915.

1948: May 13, 1948; Kathleen Kennedy-Cavendish, 28, and his boy friend Peter Wentworth-Fitzwilliam, 37, died in a plane crash in France on their way to ask the permit from Joseph Kennedy Sr. for the marriage.

In May 1944 Kathleen, a Roman Catholic, married William John Robert Cavendish the Marquis of Hartington without the blessing of Kennedy Family because Cavendish was a Anglican; and therefore none of her relatives but Joseph Kennedy Sr. her eldest brother to attend the marriage ceremony. Four months later, William Cavendish the Marquis of Hartington was killed in the World War II. Joseph P. Kennedy Jr., the only family member of the Kennedys who attended the marriage ceremony of Cavendish and Kathleen, was also killed during the World War II. Was everybody who close to Kathleen killed: Cavendish, Fitzwilliam, and Joe Kennedy Jr.?

1954: Jacqueline Kennedy suffers from a miscarriage, it was supposed to be a baby boy who would have carried on the family name and political career along with his brother John Kennedy Jr.; in 1956 Jacqueline gave birth to a stillbirth daughter.

1955: Ethel Kennedy parents were killed in a plane crash in Oklahoma. Were Ethel, her parents and her children -Joseph P. Kennedy II and David Kennedy- got cursed after her marriage to Robert Kennedy, or Robert Kennedy got killed after married Ethel?

1961: In the first year of John F. Kennedy tenure as the US President, his father Joseph P. Kennedy Sr. suffered from a stroke that made him unable to move and communicate well.

After years of planning for his son's presidency and was successful he was unable to enjoy the result, instead he had to accept the reality that his beloved son, the 35th US President, was killed. He died in 1969, six years after his son John F. Kennedy's death.

1962: Marilyn Monroe, a blond beautiful movie star who was linked to Robert and John Kennedy, was found died from "overdose". Was she got cursed from her close relationship with the Kennedy brothers, who the both later were killed in 1963 and 1968 respectively?

1963: August 9; Jacqueline Kennedy gave birth to Patrick B. Kennedy, a premature boy and died within two days.

1963: November 22; President John F. Kennedy, 46, was assassinated in Dallas, Texas on the 105th anniversary of his great-grandfather's death of 1858.

1964: June 19; Senator Edward "Ted" Kennedy (Democrat - Massachusetts) to have a plane accident that killed the pilot. He was "lucky" to be alive but had to spend some weeks in the hospital. It was believed that he gave up the family mission to be the next US President to keep himself alive. To be alive as a citizen is better off than to be a US President but dies within days.

1964: Mary Pinchot Meyer, one of John F. Kennedy's lovers was found mysteriously murdered near the Potomac River in Washington, DC. Was she got cursed from her close relationship with John F. Kennedy? What's in her diary, and why it's so important to find?

1967: George Skakel, Ethel Kennedy's brother was killed in a plane crash. Was he got cursed from his kinship with the Kennedy?

1968: June 5; omitting the advice of his close friends that to be alive as a citizen is much better than to be a US President but dies within days, Robert F. Kennedy, 43, run for the presidency. After his victory in the California Democratic presidential primary, he was shot to death in a Los Angeles hotel kitchen on his shortcut way to his room from a meeting room.

He was warned by his guards and the FBI not to take the kitchen shortcut. The public believed that the assassin Sirhan Bishara Sirhan did not know what he did because he was "drugged and made a robot" like "Manchurian Candidate" movie. Sirhan's handgun had only *eight* bullets, but there were *thirteen* bullets altogether on Robert Kennedy body, head and doorframe of the hotel kitchen.

The coroner Dr. Thomas Noguchi ruled that the deadly shot "was caused by .22 bullet that went into the back of Robert Kennedy's head".

"The gun powder burn indicated that the gun was fired from a distance of no more than three inches; the bullet came from a couple of feet behind Senator Kennedy" [117]. Sirhan was *in front* of Senator Robert Kennedy but the fatal shot came from *behind* Robert Kennedy's head. Dr. Noguchi wrote "The existence of a second gunman remains a possibility. Thus, I have never said that Sirhan killed Robert Kennedy" [118].

The American public demanded a formal investigation, but the result never answered on why there were *thirteen* bullets altogether on Robert Kennedy body, head and doorframe of the hotel kitchen while Sirhan's handgun had only *eight* bullets. Do we need another investigation? It would not bring Robert Kennedy alive.

1969: July 18; the Chappaquiddick Island car incident killed Mary Jo Kopechne a secretary of Senator Ted Kennedy on their way to Martha Vineyard, Massachusetts. Some people suspected Ted Kennedy was intoxicated, but some people suspected it was a ploy to stop Ted Kennedy from running for the presidency.

1973: November 17; Edward Kennedy Jr. son of Senator Edward Kennedy, loses his right leg to the bone cancer when he was 12 year-old.

1973: Joseph P. Kennedy II; the son of late Robert Kennedy and Ethel had an accident that leaves the passenger Pamela Kelley paralyzed for life. Was Miss Kelley got cursed from her close relationship with Joseph P. Kennedy II?

1975: Martha Elizabeth Moxley, 15, was murdered in Greenwiich, Connecticut; the suspects were Thomas and Michael Skakel, the nephews of Ethel Kennedy. Thomas was cleared from the murder case, however 27 years later in June 7, 2002; Michael Skakel was convicted.
Was Miss Moxley got cursed from her close relationship with Kennedy extended family, or was Michael Skakel got cursed from his kinship to Ethel Kennedy?

1982: Senator Edward Kennedy was divorced by his first wife Joan Bennett Kennedy; she was later admitted to the alcohol rehabilitation center; was she got cursed from her kinship to Edward Kennedy?

1984: April 25; David Kennedy another son of late Robert Kennedy and Ethel, dies from drugs overdose in a Florida hotel.

1997: December 31; Michael Kennedy another son of late Robert Kennedy dies from ski sport accident in Aspen, Colorado.

1999: July 16; John "John" Kennedy Jr., his wife Carolyn, and her sister Lauren Bessette died in private plane accident piloted by John Kennedy on the Atlantic near Martha Vineyard, Massachusetts.
Were Carolyn and Lauren got cursed from their kinship to Kennedy Jr.?

1983: September 11, Robert F. Kennedy Jr. was arrested for allegedly drugs possession.

1986: Patrick J. Kennedy; the son of Senator Ted Kennedy was treated for drugs addiction.

1988: Christina Onassis, 38, died of "pulmonary disorder", too young to die for a young rich lady. She lost all her immediate relatives within only 24 months.

Her brother Aleksadros Onassis was killed in a plane crash in 1973, her mother committed suicide for a desperate grief of losing his only son; and her father Aristotle Onassis was ailing after losing his only son, and later Aristotle Onassis died in 1975. Aristotle Onassis suffered from a rare eye disorder; one of his eyes could not be opened and kept closed. Were the Onassis' got cursed after his marriage to Jackie who got married before to one of the Kennedys?

1994: Jacqueline Kennedy Onassis, 64, died of cancer.

1999: August 12; Anthony Radziwill, nephew of John F. Kennedy and Jackie Kennedy, dies of cancer.

2001: September 11; Robert Speisman the son-in-law of Maurice Templesman, the companion of Jacqueline Kennedy was one among the victims aboard American Airlines Flight 77 on 9/11 tragedy.

Was Speisman got cursed from his father-in-law companionship with Jacqueline who ever got married to one of the Kennedys?

2002: June 7; Michael Skakel a nephew of Ethel Skakel Kennedy is convicted in the 1975 murder of Martha Moxley when he was a teenager.

2003: Kara Kennedy, a daughter of Edward and Joan Kennedy was admitted to the hospital for the lung cancer.

2006: May 4; Patrick J. Kennedy underwent the treatment for drug addiction.

2006: Senator Ted Kennedy plane was struck by lightning and survived although the plane had to be diverted.

2008: May 20; Senator Ted Kennedy was diagnosed with a brain tumor after a seizure in Massachusetts.

2009: January 20; Senator Ted Kennedy suffers from another seizure during the luncheon at President Barack Obama inauguration.

2009: Caroline Kennedy declined the Family request to run for a US Senator replacing Senator Hillary R. Clinton who was appointed the Secretary of State by President Obama.

The people made up the amazing "13 coincidences" between President Kennedy and President Lincoln; this coincidence is not for those have *triskaidekaphobia*:

1. Kennedy was riding *Lincoln* limousine on the fateful day in Dallas.
2. Kennedy and Lincoln had had the deep concern about the civil rights, Lincoln emancipated the Afro-American in the South; and Kennedy sent the National Guard to Montgomery Alabama to defend the Afro-American civil rights (Part Four Chapter 7).
3. The last two digits of the years where they were elected are the same 60, Lincoln in 1860 and Kennedy in 1960
4. The last two digits of the birthday years of Lincoln and Kennedy successors are the same 08 with different order, Lincoln successor in 1808 and Kennedy successor in 1980.
5. The last two digits of the years where the suspect were born are the same 39. John Wilkes Booth was born in 1839 and Lee Harvey Oswald's in 1939.
6. Both suspects were killed before stand for trial.
7. "Lincoln" and "Kennedy" are 7-letter name.
8. The successors of Lincoln and Kennedy had 13-letter name; Andrew Johnson and Lyndon Johnson.
9. Both suspects had 15 letter-full name; John Wilkes Booth and Lee Harvey Oswald.
10. They got fatal shot in the head, Lincoln from the back and Kennedy from the front.
11. The last names of Lincoln and Kennedy successors were Johnson.
12. Both Lincoln and Kennedy lost the child while in the White House.
13. Both Lincoln and Kennedy were Democrats.

Despite any superstition and coincidence which some people believe in, John F. Kennedy accepted the presidential job to serve his beloved country, even without expecting any single penny of salary. He was the first and the last President in this planet –maybe in this whole universe- who did not receive the salary. A most wanted top job in this planet without salary; unbelievable! Consider someone who wants a presidential job to get served and benefited; or to acquire the government contracts or even intentionally incited a war to generate a new government contract for his crony. This is the point we missed to teach our children. The US became a famous and popular country because of John F. Kennedy. God Bless America.

[112] http://en.wikipedia.org/wiki/Lobotomy, http://en.wikipedia.org/wiki/Kennedy_Curse
[113] O'Brien, *ibid*. pp. 172 - 173
[114] http://en.wikipedia.org/wiki/Lobotomy
[115] Edward Klein, "*The Kennedy Curse*", Thorndike Press, Waterville Maine, 2003, p. 53
[116] http://en.wikipedia.org/wiki/Kennedy_Curse
[117] James McConnachie and Robin Tudge, "*The Rough Guide to Conspiracy Theory*", Rough Guided Ltd., London, 2005, p. 39
[118] McConnachie, *ibid.*

7. Marilyn Monroe

> ... Was killed by administering chloral hydrate by enema; this theory may explain on the lack of tablet residue in her stomach...

When we watch the ***Seven Year Itch*** movie, no doubt that Marilyn Monroe role was very attractive and sensual, her pose in front of a theater when the gusty wind blew her blouse up was legendary; although the real wind never existed but a powerful blower instead to make such effect. Steward Johnson created her statue and posted it in Chicago July 2011 only to be dismantled on May 5, 2012. She was unknown actress; she gained the significant role in the movie with the help of the Chicago Outfit boss Tony Accardo who asked the Outfit member Johnny Roselli to lobby Harry Cohn the president of **Columbia Pictures** to give her a contract. Cohn was unable to decline the request because he obtained his position in Columbia Pictures with the support of the Outfit Family.

Roselli, who had had a special relation with the organization, later was summoned to testify on the murder investigation of John F. Kennedy. On June 24, 1975 and September 22, 1975 he testified before the United States Senate Select Committee on Intelligence (SSCIA) -which was known as Church Committee because it was led by Idaho Senator Frank Church- about the plan to kill Fidel Castro. He testified for the third time before a government committee on April 23, 1976 about the conspiracy to kill President John F. Kennedy, and then afterward he had been missing.

On August 9, 1976 Roselli's body was found in a steel fuel drum floating on the sea near Miami, Florida; he had been strangled and shot, and his legs were cut off. It was said he broke ***omerta*** the silence pledge by testifying before the government committee [119]; the cutting of his legs off was a sign that he was not supposed to go.

Marilyn Monroe was born **Norma Jean**, she was glamorous, successful, had enough money, easygoing, and looked happy; however Los Angeles County coroner declared she committed suicide. On the day she died, August 4, 1962; Joe Jr. her stepson, a son of her second husband Joe DiMaggio, called her and she was fine. She was happy and was getting back to DiMaggio, and at the same time was obtaining a new contract with 20th Century Fox film studio for her role in *Something's Got To Give*. It is hard to understand that a popular lady, happy, had enough money, was getting back together with her husband then committed suicide.

There were some strange facts around her death:

(1) Police was just called around 4:30 AM on early August 5, 1962 six hours after her manager came to Monroe apartment; the Police Station was only 3 miles away.
(2) The incident scene was so well organized; the bed cover had been laundered.
(3) The empty pill bottles were arranged by her side; however the autopsy revealed that no such residue of drug in her stomach. So where did the deadly dose of sodium barbiturate on her blood come from?
(4) Her diary and notes were missing.
(5) No medical explanation about the bruise at her body.
(6) The body tissue taken from her for laboratory analysis mysteriously disappeared.

James McConnachie and Robin Tudge in their popular book "The Rough Guide to Conspiracy Theory" (2005) citing the conspiracy theory that Monroe was the danger to the Kennedy Brothers John and Robert because they had had a special relationship with her:

> "The Kennedy therefore unceremoniously set about ditching Monroe before the affairs could be revealed. For her part, Monroe felt shabbily treated, and was reportedly about to "blow the lid off of Washington" before she died."

" .... The first ambulance driver to arrive at Monroe's house, James Hall, subsequently wrote 'Peter Lawford: The Man Who Kept Secrets'. He contended that Robert Kennedy persuaded Monroe's psychiatrist Dr. Ralph Greenson -who arrived with the ambulance- to inject her with a lethal dose of Nembutal. 'Just as Marilyn started coming around, the doctor arrived .... I believe it was Dr. Greenson. He pushed her breast to one side and gave her an injection'. That would account for the lack of tablet residue [120]."

The sudden death of a high profile person always followed by the conspiracy theory which is not always true; it was said that Monroe's death has been arranged by Robert Kennedy "on the grounds that information she had picked up from the Kennedy as pillow talk made her a threat to national security." [121] If so, who was a threat to national security; Monroe or someone who did reveal the government secret, if any?

The other theory said that when the public knew that the Kennedys had had a special relationship with Monroe, then her "necessary" killing will subsequently disgrace them and put them out of Washington power. The another said that she had to be stopped to protect the secret of the plot against Fidel Castro, if it is true there was a question how did she knew the classified information about Castro?

Several books have been written concerning Monroe's death, her unnatural death when she was young, beautiful and popular has generated various conspiracy theories:

(1) She was killed because she had picked the classified information up from the Kennedys, and her possibility to reveal such information would be a threat to national security, i.e. the plot to overthrow Fidel Castro from the power over Cuba.
(2) DiMaggio, her husband, believed that she was killed because she had had a detailed conversation with Robert Kennedy about the plot of poisoning Castro. She talked over the phone with DiMaggio's son that she was about to reveal everything on the day when she died.

(3) She was killed in order to put the Kennedy Brothers out of Washington power as a retaliation against their effort to prosecute the mob Family; by killing Monroe it was supposed Robert Kennedy would by implicated, or at least their affair would be publicly revealed to make the Kennedys resign in disgrace. It was said that Joseph Kennedy Sr. the Kennedy patriarch had asked the mob Family to help his son John F. Kennedy to win the Illinois primary during the presidential election; but as he won the presidency then Robert Kennedy and John F. Kennedy prosecuted the mob Family and deported the mob figure Carlos Marcello to Guatemala. Marcello was actually born in Tunisia, he falsified his birth certificate as to be born in Guatemala, then-the Attorney General Robert Kennedy deported him to Guatemala. He eventually came back to USA and died naturally in 1993.

(4) Monroe was killed by administering chloral hydrate by enema (through the anus); this theory may explain on the lack of tablet residue in her stomach and the bruise on her body due to the deadly struggle before her death.

The conspiracy theory is going on and on, and this is a weird one; Robert was trying to persuade Marilyn to severe her relationship with John, instead of being successful Robert fell on her lap. Upon knowing his two sons to share a same woman, then what if Joe Sr. hired a team to stop her?

Although every theory is still theory and could not be verified, yet Marilyn Monroe had had the unique position in the American history, she was a popular and beautiful movie star with the endorsement of the Chicago Outfit. As the wife of a baseball star Joe DiMaggio, she had had a close relationship with Robert Kennedy and John F. Kennedy; she attended John F. Kennedy's birthday party at Public Square wearing a very tight gown. She was declared died with "pills" while not such pill residue in her stomach.

Despite her well-known relationship with the Kennedys, there was no official government reinvestigation such as Warren Commission, HSCA, or AARB; the American public had accepted the "verdict" that Monroe committed suicide; period.

After the assassination of John and Robert Kennedy, the weird question spreads "Who got cursed, Monroe for her relation with Kennedy, or Kennedy for the relation with her?"

However, another startling question rises "What if you have had two handsome sons, both were the public figures and popular, they have had the very good chances to be the next US Presidents. Unfortunately, they stumbled and fell down on the lap of a very same beautiful woman; do you think that to stopping her was not an option to prevent them from falling down with disgrace?"

[119] http://en.wikipedia.org/wiki/John_Roselli
[120] James McConnachie and Robin Tudge, *ibid.* p. 18
[121] *ibid.*

8. Last Tango in The White House

A latest surprise about John F. Kennedy came in February 8, 2012 when Mimi Alford, 68, released her book *"Once Upon a Secret: My Affair with President John F. Kennedy and Its Aftermath."* Alford, a former White House intern detailed in her book about 18-month "imbalanced relationship" with then 45-year old President Kennedy when she was 19-year old working for the White House press office. The initial story dated back to 2003 when historian Robert Dallek disclosed in *"An Unfinished Life"* about a mysterious yet slender and beautiful intern who allegedly had a special relationship with the late President Kennedy. After publication of this book, she just simply disappeared. Fortunately, or unfortunately, the investigative reporter of The NEW YORK DAILY NEWS was able to identify her as Alford who subsequently confirmed the relationship. After an interview with NBC's Meredith Viera then the story goes viral. The Americans so wondered on how come she ended up at JFK bedroom? She was a newspaper editor of Miss Porter's School in Connecticut who are interested to interview the First Lady who graduated from this school some years before. In 1961, instead of interviewing the First Lady, she interviewed the White House social secretary who eventually offered her an internship one year later when she studied at Wheaton College in Massachusetts. After a pool party, JFK provided her a special tour to the White House including the First Lady' bedroom where Mimi lost her most valuable crown as an innocent 19-year old girl.

For the next 18 moths she enjoyed being included in JFK inner circle. It could be imbalance in age, but she really enjoyed. She confessed later that the Secret Service knew what happened between her and the President but she felt that the relationship was "natural" [122] [123] [124]; no one single woman in the world declined to be close to the President. Never. Is the internship an artificial cover for young girl(s) to privately serve the President as Mimi Alford and Monica Lewinsky did? Who's the next? Who did confess and who did not?

The Congress should have passed the special permit for the US President to have more than one woman legally if the USA is a real democratic state and not a religious state or theocracy. He deserved; it would be better off. The American Mormon has a tradition of polygamy, Presidential candidate Mitt Romney's grandfather had had three wives and 35 children yet they were happy and nobody prosecuted him.

Only modern Christianity forbids the polygamy while other most religions allow it, however the polygamy could be traced back to **Abraham**, David, Solomon and Moses the forefathers of main stream religion of Judaism, Christianity and Islam. The ban of polygamy is a manifestation of syncretism, a blend of Christianity and democracy, it is not a true Christianity and not a true democracy either; while the USA adopts the separation between church, synagogue, mosque and state, the best interest for a US President --to live peacefully-- is to allow him to have more than one lady legally. He deserves.

Whenever the US Congress to issue special permit for the sitting US President to legally marry more than one woman, it would avert the "official embarrassment" such as an incident of unmarried Secretary of State who named a US President as "my husband", or a US President official statement "I did not have the relations with that woman", or a US President who allegedly had had six children with Sally Hemings out of wedlock. The latest case of General Petraeus resignation in 2012 due to his relationship with Paula Broadwell, a 40-year old married woman, has added the list of high profile regrettable tragedy. The lost of General Petraeus from the CIA is too costly for the USA, everyone regrets to lose a decorated General, it's **not** his absolute fault, it's ours; had he had another woman legally which accompanies him during his non-stop 5-year hard time of war then the history will be different, very different. Let the high level officers to have more than one woman legally; as for President Obama himself, what if his father did not have more than one woman, did the USA ever have the first African-American president in 2008 and 2012?

Both presidential candidates of 2012, Mr. Obama and Mr. Romney are the brilliant descendants of the gentleman with multiple ladies, do we forget this fact?

James Strom Thurmond (1902 – 2003) a US Senator for 48 years; was a best example of segregationist who hated the color, not the taste. At 22 he fathered Essie Mae Washington-Williams (1925– 2013) with then a 15-year old black girl, Carrie Butler. It's questionable on why he was not prosecuted. We are the civilized nation, we respect the women, we do not abuse them; let them have their status and dignity as the wives rather than just "the biological mother". We do not treat a woman like a **napkin**, to use once and then dispose. Do we?

The Americans do not need to be shy and hide behind the stiff formality; they should have admitted that the relation between the man and woman is natural and should have been conducted in a natural manner under the legal and legitimate boundary for the sake of woman dignity. The history recorded that the leaders at any century always had had more than one lady since they were the special persons with the special talent and ability; therefore they deserved to do it openly and legally. The US President should have been entitled to some privileges such as living in the White House for free, using Air Force One for the official visits, to live with more one lady, etc. This is not discrimination but a privilege, it is just in the context of maintaining the dignity of a sitting US President and to prevent from the embarrassing incident such as happened in the past which is not necessary to elaborate. We knew already. The polygamy option is not necessary anymore if there is a guarantee or pledge that such an embarrassing incident would not happen again. The sitting US President may file a lawsuit, if he wants, that marrying only one woman and holding a Scripture instead of the Constitution during a swearing in ceremony are against the US Constitution since they originated from a certain religion while the US government does not formally embrace any religion.

America separated religion from the state, and then using a Scripture during a swearing in ceremony? The USA is not a religious state; it is a democratic state where everything is based on **consensus**, not religion. The Americans should have come forward instead of concealing the stink scandal that the people would recognize sooner or later. If the union between two men, the union between two women, and the union between a man and a woman with or without marriage are legal; so why the union between one man and two women, or the union between one woman and two men are not legalized? Is it because of moral hazard, moral issue or political issue?

The democracy never dealt with the moral issue, democracy always deals with the consensus. Even if an issue is contrary to a religious moral teaching like gambling but the majority do agree then it is democracy. This is the base for nine states Connecticut, Iowa, Maine, Maryland, Massachusetts, New Hampshire, New York, Vermont and Washington to legalize the same gender marriage.

Now, where is the Defense of Marriage Act of 1996 known as DOMA; is it really unconstitutional? If two different laws (DOMA and 9-state laws) are opposing each other, which one is constitutional under the Constitution? If the same genders can be married, if a man and a man can be married, if a woman and a woman can be married and legalized by the court, so why not the polygamy?

The Americans respect the women. The true Americans are not abusing the women and not using them as napkins; the US President should have been granted the special right to marry more than one woman. This special circumstance does not apply either to Obama's SS detail escorting him in Cartagena Colombia April 2012 who turned awry with beach girls, and does not also apply to Prince Charles of England and the other British Royal family since Queen Elizabeth II is the leader of Anglican Church.

The Britain is not a full democratic state, it is a theocracy. According to the political science, we do not know the difference between Britain and Iran.

Democracy is a consensus; and marriage is a religious practice. Regardless of the sexual orientations, if the marriage is democracy, then the marriage of a Governor to his recent wife might be annulled whenever the US citizens in the aforementioned nine sates preferred a gay or a popular actress as Governor's spouse or partner of life. If the majority of US citizen casting ballots to decide that a Governor has to marry someone then he has to do, this is democracy as the US citizens decided him to be the Governor. From this viewpoint we exactly knew the difference between **democracy** and **religious practice**.

The USA officially regulates the marriage and divorce in the court while the both are the religious teachings and not the democratic domain; the democracy includes the rights to live together either for the same or different sexes with or without marriage based on consensus. This is the essence of the Constitution.

Within the democratic boundaries, the mutual living without marriage and the gay marriage are legal, and now several states have legalized it. A true democratic American —not the religious one— will never oppose the living together, gay marriage and even prostitution since they are religious domain while democracy is a consensus. Within democracy, if the majority did agree over something then the minority should follow, while the religion does not consider the majority-minority dichotomy; a ban in religion is still not permissible even the majority considered it as permissible.

Under the Obama administration, a federal mandate is requiring the employers to provide their employees with insurance coverage. The employers under the term of "religious-affiliated organizations" opposing contraception may decline the insurance coverage for birth control since birth control is forbidden in the Christianity.

The obligation of the religious institutions to provide their employees with insurance coverage for birth control is unconstitutional, since the state does not interfere the religious rules, therefore the birth control should have been excluded from the insurance coverage. The religious institutions which are forced to provide their employees with the insurance coverage for the birth control should have filed the lawsuit to challenge the insurance rule. This is true democracy, and this is true America we proud of.

[122] http://today.msnbc.msn.com/id/46325984/ns/today-today_news/t/former-intern-jfk-affair-was-imbalanced-not-abusive/
[123] TODAY.com, 2/9/2012
[124] http://www.huffingtonpost.com/2012/02/06/mimi-alford-jfk-affair_n_1257759.html

Part Four: The Turmoil

Conspiracy is an act by two or more people to do any inconvenience thing against someone else from his back because they can not afford to do face to face

1. Contradiction

The history of conspiracy started as early as ancient Egypt kingdom when the historians discovered the trace of conspiracy to assassinate King Tutankhamen. Most people do not like the terminology of "conspiracy theory", they prefer to believe the "magic bullet theory" instead. The sudden shock arose from the stunning death of a young, flamboyant, smart and lovely President in turn to resemble that of *tsunami* propelling the devastating wave around the globe and at certain point generating the promulgated conspiracy theory until today, five decades later. Before and after his death, John F. Kennedy became a world symbol of equality, sacrifice and popularity for fellow Americans and aspiring youths around the globe. The world never accepted why the popular President was assassinated in such a way, even his enemies in the Soviet block countries never understood, ever. Most people did not remember where they were when a member of their close relative passed away, but most of us remember exactly where we were when firstly learning that John F. Kennedy was shot to death. It's hard to imagine how the American people lost a beloved John F. Kennedy.

Some people opposed the conspiracy theory, but accepted another, the single bullet theory. The segregation that JFK strongly opposed especially in the case of black student at Alabama University had been wiped out, but John F. Kennedy himself was segregated; his files were kept in a most tight segregation ever. To keep the file on John F. Kennedy in tight secrecy would only support the conspiracy theory, while some people claimed they were involved in the assassination.

Chauncey Marvin Holt (1921–1997) became an important name along with **James E. Files** since Holt was the only one among "three tramps" who confessed to have the relationship with the assassination. Holt was one of "three tramps" photographed in Dealey Plaza after JFK assassination; [125] their photograph became mystery for decades since it may implicate the certain person(s) to the assassination of JFK.

He testified that he went to Dallas, Texas from Peter Licavoli's *Grace Ranch* in Arizona with Charles Nicoletti and Leo Moceri. In Dallas, according to his confession, Holt (1) delivered the forged Secret Service badge to Homer Echevarria an anti-Castro exile, (2) handgun and ID to Charles Harrellson on the Dealey Plaza's parking lot behind the grassy knoll.

After the tragedy; Chauncey Marvin Holt, Charles Harrelson and Charles Rogers were nabbed from a boxcar in the railroad yard next to the Dealey Plaza where they were hiding and detained by the Dallas Police; they were released on that day.

No any information available on why they were easily released while the investigation on the assassination of President John F. Kennedy was underway. Some years later, their picture became best-known as "the three tramps" and they were positively recognized by the forensic sketch artist Lois Gibson who worked for the Houston Police Department. The story of "the three tramps" --which Holt considered as "three derelicts", the poor homeless-- did not end with Lois Gibson's recognition that they were Chauncey Marvin Holt, Charles Harrelson and Charles Rogers. The story of mysterious "three tramps" was revived by *Newsweek* Magazine in December 23, 1991 issue after Chauncey Holt's interview with researchers John Craig, Phillip Rogers and Gary Shawon October 19, 1991. Soon after this publication, it got the hot respond in 1992 from the Dallas Police Department which revealed that real "three tramps" actually were Gus Abrams, John F. Gedney and Harold Doyle.

It is not clear why the undermining revelation on Holt's story came only after his interview for *Newsweek* Magazine while the Dallas Police Department kept silent for almost 30 years and such fingerprints and/or mug shots of the three tramps are **not** available. Is it another perennial cover up, one after another?

The three-hour Holt's interview was later published by Wim Dankbaar the author of "*Files on JFK*" on his website *jfkmurdersolved.com* after obtaining the copyright on transcript of interview. The hot controversy arouse in 1993 after the publication of Gerald Posner's "*Case Closed*" about who they really were. Posner an investigative journalist mentioned in his book that they were Gus Abrams, John F. Gedney and Harold Doyle. Holt was still alive and responding to *San Diego Union Tribune* review on Posner's "*Case Closed*". His very long letter to *San Diego Union Tribune* is a proof that he knew what really happened more that Posner did. Here the excerpt of his letter:

> "On page 273 Posner made the following statement regarding me in regard to the "tramps", which he claimed were arrested on 22 November 1963: Some self proclaimed adventurers, like Chauncey Holt, have confessed to being one of the tramps and spun long tales about their purported roles in the assassination. But in February 1992, researchers discovered that the Dallas police files released in 1989 showed that three tramps had indeed been booked on November 22, 1963. The records identified the suspects as Harold Doyle, Gus Abrams and John Gedney. Two of the men, Gedney and Doyle, were still alive, and it turned out they were real tramps that had been to the local rescue mission the night before the assassination and were sleeping in the railroad car when the police arrested them. The men had no connection to the events at Dealey, and the conspiracy press suddenly and quietly abandoned the issue."

"Mr. Posner's allegations, couched in the same demeaning, sarcastic language he resorted to throughout the book, is replete with misstatements of fact. Mr. Posner alludes to me as a "self proclaimed adventurer". To proclaim is to announce officially and publicly. I have no need to do this. I have knife and bullet wound scars and broken bones to establish my bona fides. As far as I know I am the only person who has come forward and admitted to being one of the tramps or "spun a long tale" about his role in this matter. The "police records" were not released in 1989, but only after Newsweek printed a lengthy story about me in the December 1991 issue. There were also articles appearing in other newspapers, and my account of that fateful Friday was aired on television in Houston, Dallas, and San Diego. It is interesting to note that the Dallas television reporters asked me if I would be willing to confront Marvin Wise, one of the police officers in the now famous photograph of the "tramps". I readily agreed to this confrontation, but Marvin Wise, who is now a rent-a-cop, refused to appear with me. I provided numerous photos of myself, taken in the sixties, which Lois Gibson, a nationally recognized forensic artist with the Houston Police Department, used to compare with photographs taken in Dealey Plaza on Friday, 22 November 1963. To the best of my knowledge, no photographs of Abrams, Gedney, or Doyle, taken in the sixties, have been furnished to researchers or the police.

Furthermore, the statements of Gedney (Florida Today, 7 March 1992) and Doyle (A Current Affair, 25 February 1992) differ from those of Posner in his book, demonstrating again that Posner is very reckless in his claims as to what he was told by various witnesses. Doyle and Gedney told essentially the same story."

"This is what Gedney said: He and two drifters had gotten cleaned up at a homeless shelter in Houston. The train stopped in Dallas on November 22, 1963. They were returning to the railroad yards from another soup kitchen near Dealey Plaza when the sirens began howling. Somebody said the president had been shot. Suddenly a police dragnet was sweeping the streets for suspicious characters. Gedney says more than 100 people were hauled in for interrogation, but only he, Harold Doyle and Gus Abrams got caught by a photographer. We were taken away, put in jail for three or four days and found not guilty of anything but vagrancy. Does this sound like three tramps sleeping in a boxcar? The records released by the Dallas Police Department after almost thirty years indicated that Abrams, Doyle, and Gedney were charged with burglary and remained in jail for four days, but, incredibly, have provided no fingerprints or mug shots of these three derelicts. I realize that the Dallas Police Department in 1963 was appallingly inept, but does this really make sense?" [126].

Holt's letter to **San Diego Union Tribune** unfortunately, without any explanation, never be published while Holt reserved his rights to publicly answer over the **San Diego Union Tribune** review, and fortunately **James Fetzer** a Professor at Minnesota University and the assassination researcher made it available on his website [127]. The question is whether **San Diego Union Tribune** accidentally neglected Holt's letter as an indirect outcome of the pressure from the Supreme Committee or it's just an editorial issue. Who's right? Holt was, Posner is, and Dallas Police Department is. The explanation is Holt, Harrelson, and Rogers were detained by the Dallas Police Department on Friday afternoon November 22, 1963 and were released on the very same day; while Gus Abrams, John F. Gedney and Harold Doyle were detained for 4 days and NOT released on November 22, 1963.

It is a matter of fact that the Dallas Police Department apprehended more that 50 suspicious people from the railroad yard near the Dealey Plaza for interrogation. Most of them have been caught from an "*open flatbed railroad car*" but Holt, Harrelson, and Rogers were caught from the hideout a "*boxcar*". A boxcar is a railroad car with the closed roof, while open flatbed railway car is a railroad car without roof which used to transport coal or bulk product.

The arrest of Holt, Harrelson, and Rogers was made possible by a Lee Bowers a Union Pacific Railroad dispatcher who spotted them and called Dallas Police station which sent Sergeant DV Harkness and several officers to railroad yard just behind Texas School Book Depository. Soon they were in Dallas Police custody, they were missing mysteriously as the missing of their record from Dallas Police in 1975 [128].

Holt's partial respond could be found at http://en.wikipedia.org/wiki/_Chauncey_Marvin_Holt_ while the full and very long text could be found at http://assassinationresearch.com/v3n2/v3n2holt.pdf copyrighted by Karyn Holt Halcourt.

Another researchers, Ray and Mary LaFontaine conducted their own research and claimed that the three tramps were Gus Abrams, John F. Gedney and Harold Doyle; they successfully traced Doyle and Gedney who confirmed they were two of the tramps; while Gus Abrams was dead; her sister was available to identify the third person in the photograph as her late brother Gus Abraham. John McAdams a researcher on John F. Kennedy assassination reported the findings of this research on his website [129].

The other credible researchers James Fetzer and Wim Dankbaar [130] point out to the inconsistencies in this research and suggest it was an intentional attempt to discredit the story of Holt moreover after Lois Gibson confirmed that the three tramps were Holt, Harrellson and Rogers. In a hard tone Wim Dankbaar stated [131]:

"Chauncey's revelations were largely ignored by the mainstream media. The few media that did report on it, left it with a conclusion that cast doubt on his story. I could believe that Doyle, Gedney and Abrams were picked up from a train and taken into custody."

"So in that regard they may well have been telling the truth. I just don't believe they are the men in the tramp photographs. As Chauncey said, several individuals were picked up that day from the railroad yard. The shadows in the photographs indicate a time around 2:30 PM or later. The shadows have moved two hours compared with the time of the shooting. This is consistent with Holt, who said they were hiding in the boxcar for 2 hours before they were found. It is not consistent with what Doyle and Gedney were telling. In the photographs you can also see that the crowds of people are gone, which is also indicating a time well after the assassination. All the documents and statements (also from the arresting officers) say that the arrests occurred very shortly after the assassination, within an hour, well before 1:30 PM. Read the interviews with the arresting officers. The sun and shadows don't lie. It's just the law of the earth's rotation. Also, Doyle and the others said that they were picked up from an open flatbed coal car, known as a gondola, not a boxcar.

This is in their FBI statements. The man that is supposedly Harold Doyle looks to be much older than 32. This is also more consistent with what Holt is telling. Charles Rogers, aka Richard Montoya was 43 at the time."

> "Two good acquaintances of Rogers identified him immediately from those photographs. One was an ex girlfriend that he dated, the other was Charles Rolland, manager of the Houston ice-skating rink where Rogers frequently used the pay-phone."

Wim Dankbaar -beside James Fetzer- is a most credible researcher among all researchers of John F. Kennedy assassination, he also made Holt's video documentary ***Spooks, Hoods and The Hidden Elite*** available on his website http://jfkmurdersolved.com. His comment on this documentary is short but meaningful "*... This is not another conspiracy theory; it's just the confession of a man who claims involvement and knowledge about the JFK assassination...*"

Here the synopsis of the documentary reads:

> "**Spooks, Hoods and the Hidden Elite** is the video memoir of ..... Chauncey Marvin Holt as he operated in the twilight world of bootlegging, bookmaking, gun running, money laundering, espionage and assassinations, using secret identities, serving many masters. Holt's amazing story chronicles his participation in Top Secret "black operations" conducted during the Cold War, and reveals his clandestine role in the events surrounding the assassination of President John F. Kennedy."

> "....... Early in his criminal career, Holt connected with Meyer Lansky, chairman of the board of organized crime, and Peter Licavoli, a ruling "Don" of Detroit's Mafia family. His versatility earned him Lansky's praise as a renaissance man of crime. As a money manager and fine art connoisseur, Holt was affiliated with some of the most influential members of the "hidden elite."

"In *Spooks, Hoods and the Hidden Elite*, he unmasks their identities - including a senior counsel to the Warren Commission - and exposes the long-standing incestuous relationship between Intelligence, Organized Crime and a shadowy group of elites. In this video interview - made one week before his death - Holt provides a chilling account of ...... team ...... were in Dealey Plaza, and the truth behind the mysterious "three tramps" picked up behind the Grassy Knoll after the assassination. ...... **Spooks, Hoods and the Hidden Elite** presents persuasive evidence of the existence of a powerful, interlocked cabal that orchestrated the removal of a president with frightening resolve. Most importantly, this video reveals the footprints of a renegade covert network, a Secret Government; that has exerted untold influence over U.S. policy from World War II until today... [131]"

The real agent never told his past job as a covert agent, most -if not every- covert agent was sworn in secrecy for the entire life, if he/she got killed the government would never acknowledge anything. Based on this premise we should have been cautious to accept any confession from anyone who claimed as a former government agent especially if we know there is any monetary gain behind the confession. Holt was loyal to Licavoli and Lanski and declined to testify against them for a "payoff" and "witness protection program", so why did he came forward to confess that he had a relationship with the government agency? Holt was convicted of mail fraud, 20 years after his conviction he died at 75, just eight days after completing the film narrating his life story.

[125] http://en.wikipedia.org/wiki/Chauncey_Marvin_Holt
[126] http://assassinationresearch.com/v3n2/v3n2holt.pdf
[127] http://en.wikipedia.org/wiki/James_Fetzer
[128] Fetzer, James H. (ed.), "*Murder In Dealy Plaza*", Catfeet Press, Chicago, 2000, pp. 64-68
[129] http://mcadams.posc.mu.edu
[130] http://jfkmurder.com
[131] http://jflmurdersolved.com

2. The "Supreme Committee"

Its special mission in 1960's was to protect US from nuclear disaster during the Cold War

The method of JFK assassination, covering it up for a very long time, the influence over the Warren Commission, the crazy single bullet theory that does not make any sense; and the influence over the Senate and Congress in a certain time has inevitably suggested us that there's a huge, invisible and invincible power behind the JFK assassination. We simply name it the "Supreme Committee".

In the management science we know the "discretional right" similar to veto right in the UN; it exists but it is not daily used. What is in a name, the name may vary but the goal should be achieved without sacrificing the safety of people. It could be so-called Super Agency, Supreme Agency, Emergency Committee, Umbrella Board, or Executive Board. It was not the **ExComm** which was established in October 1962 in the wake of Cuban Missile Crisis; but its main function is to protect America from any harm, its special mission in 1960's was to protect US from nuclear disaster during the Cold War. The main mission may change in any different time and situation. In the politics there is no perpetual friend or perpetual enemy; there is only one that never changes: the change itself.

The CIA, FBI, Mafia and Warren Commission are **not** the subject to blame in the assassination of President John F. Kennedy. "The Supreme Committee" as an invisible administration could do everything necessary for the sake of US people, and it **did** as we knew according to available indications.

It is a common knowledge that the House Select Committee on Assassinations [HSCA] in 1979 officially issued a final report concluding that President John F. Kennedy was assassinated probably as a result of an [unidentified] conspiracy.

The HSCA believed that the conspiracy *did not include* the governments of the Soviet or Cuba, anti-Castro group, organized crime, *nor* the government agencies (the FBI, the CIA, the SS, the US Departments); but the HSCA "could not rule out individual members of either of *those groups acting together*" [132]. "***Those groups acting together***" refers to an invisible and invincible "Supreme Committee" that exists some time some place, but its existence never be confirmed nor to be denied any time any place, ever. It is safe to us to assume that "Supreme Committee" still exists hitherto with different personnel and program but with the very same mission, to make America safe. In JFK assassination, the issue is not about right or wrong, but how to protect innocent Americans from being victims of nuclear weapon.

The Supreme Committee is **shadow government** alike; it is not secret government which the conspiracy theory suggests or **Peter Dale Scott** indicates. This Committee is unofficial or semi official group which has the concern about the safety of all Americans and the dignity of US government as well.

The USA never stepped back against any threat and enemy, ever; but to sacrifice forty to ninety millions innocent citizens is another issue. To describe more clearly on how this unofficial group has tried hard to make America safe, let us listen to Robert McNamara's narration in a documentary film "***The Fog of War, eleven lessons from the life of Robert S. McNamara***". He was a former Secretary of Defense serving under President Kennedy during the Cuban Missile Crisis and under President Johnson during Vietnam War. In this movie of "Lesson #1 Empathize your enemy", he said:

> "Any military commander who honest with himself over those he will speaks to admit that he made mistake on application of unauthorized power. He has killed people unnecessarily, he sends his troops and other troops through error judgment, killed hundreds, one thousand, 10 thousands maybe 100,000; but he has not destroyed the nation."

"And the conventional wisdom is "don't make same mistake twice, learn from your mistakes", we all do, we make the same mistake three times, four, five; but will be no learning period with nuclear weapon; **you make one mistake you destroy the nation**... Soviet Union introduced the nuclear missiles into Cuba targeting 90 million Americans."

"The report said the warhead not deployed yet... We mobilized 180,000 troops. The first day of air attack was planned, ten hundred ninety sorties, a huge air attack... General LeMay whom I served as sergeant during the World War II was saying 'Let us go on, let us totally destroy Cuba'."

As tension between the US and Soviet mounting and Khrushchev offering two different messages; the soft one was demanding a guarantee that the US would not invade Cuba in lieu of dismantling nuclear weapon from Cuba; and the hard one was "if you attack we prepare to confront you".

It was known from Khrushchev's letter to Kennedy declaring that the US naval quarantine as "reckless" and Khrushchev instructed the Soviet Naval to ignore it; thus keep shipping another weapons to Cuba. The hard message i.e. "combat ready" was demanding US to dismantle the US-made Jupiter missiles from Europe in lieu of dismantling Soviet missiles from Cuba. On this option, McNamara explained what happened:

"On a critical Saturday October 27 (1962), we have two crucial messages in front of us: one was coming Friday night, it was dictated by a man either drunken or under the tremendous stress. Basically, it said 'if you guarantee won't invade Cuba then we take missiles out'. Then before we can respond, we have second message dictated by the hardliner and it said 'if you attack we prepared to confront you in a military power'."

> "So what to do ….. the soft message and hard message?" "At the elbow of President Kennedy was [Llewellyn "Tommy"] Thompson a former US Ambassador to Moscow….. Tommy Thompson said "Mr. President, I urged you to respond to soft message", the President said to Tommy "We can not do that…." Thomson said "Mr. President you are wrong…."

On the black and white screen of McNamara documentary movie, it was displayed an official transcript of Kennedy-Thompson dialogue:

> October 27, 1962:
> President Kennedy: "We're not going to get these weapons out of Cuba, probably anyway with negotiation."
> Thompson: "I don't agree Mr. President. I think there's still a chance."
> President Kennedy: "He (Khrushchev) will back down?"
> Thompson: "The important thing for Khrushchev it seems to me is to be able to say 'I have saved Cuba, I stopped invasion'."

McNamara went on his narration explaining his Lesson #2 "Rationality will not save us":

> "In Thompson's mind was this thought: Khrushchev got himself in how to fix (the situation and saying) 'If I can get out this with a deal that I can say to Russian people "Kennedy was going to destroy Castro and I prevented it"….' Khrushchev would accept that (solution). Thompson was right; that's what I call (the) empathy. We must try to put ourselves inside their skin and look at us through their eyes just to understand the thought behind action and interaction….I participated in two wars and I know what the war is….sowing death and destruction, such illogical war."

"If people do not display wisdom they would clash like blind mules and then the mutual annihilation will commence. I want to say and it's very important; at the end we're locked out, **it was locked** [McNamara said in exclamation!] to prepare nuclear war, we came to that close to the war game [his thumb and point finger made a sign of very narrow gap]. [There're] rational individuals, Kennedy's rational, Khrushchev's rational, Castro's rational, [why] rational individuals came to that close to total destruction......and that danger exists [until] today. Major lesson is.......nuclear weapon will destroy nation. It's right and proper that today there are 7,500 offensive nuclear warheads on alert....**to be launched by the decision of one human being.**"

Now, we get the points from McNamara legacy "... will be no learning period with nuclear weapon; **you make one mistake you destroy the nation** (America)" and "... *7,500 offensive nuclear warheads on alert to be launched by the decision of one human being*". This is a clue on why President Kennedy was "unofficially" assassinated, or at least he was assassinated under the agreement of silent majority of individuals within the Supreme Committee. McNamara was **not** a part of the decision makers, most probably he was an inspiration for them to stop JFK --who had the authority over "*7,500 offensive nuclear warheads*"-- since in the time of crisis McNamara was the one of only two members of "the war committee" inside the ExComm known by the public as the cool statesman beside Llewellyn "Tommy" Thompson a former US Ambassador to Moscow. It absolutely does **not** mean that McNamara got involved with the assassination. The majority members of ExComm, as McNamara acknowledged, were calling for Cuba invasion especially General Curtis LeMay to whom McNamara yelled "We lost and we're wiped out today!"

> **Tommy Thompson**
>
> **Llewellyn E. "Tommy" Thompson Jr.** (1904-1972), was a US diplomat served a long time [1957-1962, and 1967-1969] in Moscow during the Cold War. He was a member of the "war committee" during the Cuban Missile Crisis who knew Khrushchev more than anybody else; he had more information and was able to provide his cool consideration to President Kennedy. When the US received two messages from Soviet leader Khrushchev during the Cuban Missiles Crisis; first was soft and conciliatory and the second was hard and threatening, Thompson urged Kennedy to accept the first one. Since he knew Khrushchev, he believed that Khrushchev had intention to withdraw the Soviet missiles from Cuba in lieu of the assurance that the US would not invade Cuba; and he was right. He was also present at a very important Glassboro summit between US and Soviet Union. He was a dependable advisor to President Johnson pertaining to Non-Proliferation Treaty on the nuclear weapon; he also testified before the Warren Commission during the investigation of the assassination of President Kennedy. He was an actor and witness of the US modern history.

McNamara surprisingly just knew lately about the number of nuclear weapons in Cuba and their impending danger, he just aware 30 years later in 1992 that the Soviet nuclear weapons in Cuba were **not** only 9 [nine] as previous reports suggested or as observed by the U-2 spy planes, but far more than this number:

> "It was not until January 1992 in a meeting chaired by Castro in Havana Cuba that I learned 162 nuclear warheads including 90 tactical warheads were on the island at the time of critical moment of crisis. Uh.. u.."

At this point, McNamara paused, his words are stopped and he was choking upon realizing that the number of Soviet nuclear warhead in Cuba was far more than the US knew at the time of crisis.

Had the US knew for sure how much nuclear did Castro have, the history might be different. With a hard effort McNamara continued his narration as a witness of history:

> "I could not believe what I was hearing; and Castro got very angry with me because I said 'Mr. President, let us stop this meeting I am not sure I got a right translation [from Spanish into English about number of nuclear warheads, 162]. Mr. President, I have three questions to you:
>
> (1) Do you know that nuclear warheads out there?
>
> (2) If you did, what do you have recommended to Khrushchev in the face of US attack?
>
> (3) If you have to use them [nuclear warheads], what would happen to Cuba?
>
> He [Castro] said '#1 I knew they were there, #2 I have not recommended [to Khrushchev, and it does mean that Castro let Khrushchev to launch nuclear warheads to US] and #3 we are totally destroyed" [Castro used 'We' and not 'I'].

McNamara paused again after commenting "**That's so close to war**." His face was so sad and he looked so guilty; it was not a face of [former] Secretary of Defense a powerful man, the first civilian to lead the US military, and second man in White House after Kennedy; it was a face a statesman who sensed so guilty over what happened had the nuclear war erupted when he was an incumbent to defense the US. So, when in an ExComm meeting a member said "Gentlemen, we know we will win", McNamara snapped right away "Won *hell*, we lost; we're wiped out today!" He was contemplating:

> "It's almost impossible for our people today to put themselves back to that period. In my seven years as Secretary of Defense we came close to war with the Soviet Union in *three* different occasions; 24 hours a day 365 days a year as Secretary of Defense. I lived the Cold War."

"During the Kennedy administration, they designed a 100 megaton bomb and it was tested in the atmosphere, I remember this. Cold War? It was a Hot War! I think the human race needs to think more about killing, about conflict; is that we want in the 21st century? [133]"

The "Supreme Committee" was a special group which has a deep vision about the future of America. Although they know that America never retreats when any adversary is coming, yet the safety of hundred million innocent Americans is their priority. They are committed to win or to avert the nuclear war at any cost, even if they have to stop a US President who was inciting a nuclear war. That's what happened; no matter it was admitted or declined.

Shadow Government

"One conspiracy theory suggests that a secret or shadow government including wealthy industrialists and right-wing politicians ordered the assassination of Kennedy. Peter Dale Scott has indicated that Kennedy's death allowed for policy reversals desired by the secret government to escalate the United States' military involvement in Vietnam. [134]" **Peter Dale Scott** (1929-) is a former English professor at the University of California, Berkeley, a former diplomat and a poet. As a poet he wrote *"Coming to Jakarta"*. He spent four years (1957–1961) with the Canadian diplomatic service, and retired from the University of California Berkeley in 1994 [135].

In the practical politics -not always according to the political science- it is a common practice that there is an invisible power within administration, (almost like) an administration within administration. The popular examples are the Khrushchev inner circle within Lavrentiy Beria administration, the Brezhnev clique within Khrushchev administration, Lin Biao group within Mao Zedong administration, and Aidit's "kabinet bayangan" (shadow cabinet) within Soekarno administration.

In the first two examples the invisible administrations prevailed, while in the third and fourth examples they failed. The administration is a matter of power, whosoever to have the power will prevail either democratically or not; the power is the ability to obtain or retain control while the presidency is a matter of democratic election and popularity.

A President is not always on the top; in Malaysia, India and Israel the role of the Prime Minister is more comprehensive both in the domestic and foreign policy. In some points the power overrules the democracy and popularity; there are some examples around the globe where a powerful person was elected as a president although he was unpopular like Soeharto in Indonesia, or even after a political party was officially declared as the winner in the election then was defeated by the power in a *coup d'etat* like in Algeria (Al-Jazair) in 1992 and Pakistan during Pervez Musharaf in 1999. The only common thing between the power and democracy in the ultra modern government is money, the time where a poor man but honest to be elected as a president like **Omar bin Abdul-Aziz** is over.

Omar bin Abdul-Aziz [682-720]

He was one of famous caliph of the Umayyad dynasty; still poor during his tenure beside the fact that he was abundantly paid for. When his children asked him the money he distributed only $70 for 11 children, that's all what he had; the rest of his salary goes to the needy; his 11 children were born from just one wife, they were properly educated and were successful and prosperous in their lives. Unfortunately, the corrupt and bad people in his time did not love him, and get him poisoned to death after three years only in power. No wonder if the God did not create the wise and just ruler like him anymore. God knows better. Who is the wise and just ruler ever since until today?

The fact that Soviet had placed the nuclear weapon "inside our backyard" which just needs some minutes to reach American soil was a horrible threat. Nuclear weapon is "normally" for deterrent and defensive purpose only, its practical deployment in any war after **Hiroshima** and **Nagasaki** needs a comprehensive strategic calculation where any given available time will be insufficient to decide unless for responding over the real initial attack. This is one among **two paradigms** of nuclear war; the other is MAD [mutual assured destruction].

The nuclear-owning states knew the long decade of devastating impact of it, and therefore they had a reciprocal ethic code and asserting language communicated over the hot line red telephone whenever a crisis happens. How devastating the nuclear weapon is, we may learn from the former US Secretary of State Dr. Henry Kissinger "*Our Nuclear Nightmare*" on **Newsweek** "*Any use of nuclear weapon is certain to involve a level of casualties and devastation* **out of proportion** *to foreseeable foreign-policy objectives*" [136].

The combination of atomic bomb dropped in Nagasaki and Hiroshima was like a fire cracker when compared with today's sophisticated hydrogen bomb. Robert Oppenheimer, the father of H-bomb estimated about **two hundred million** people would be killed if the nuclear war erupted, and therefore he opposed the use of H-bomb [137]. The combination of all nuclear weapons available today owned by the nuclear-operating countries is more than enough to completely destroy this beautiful tiny planet.

Want to live in another planet to be safe from nuclear war? It's empty dream, wasting money and time for nothing; it's good only to shift the public focus from critical issues such as teen pregnancy, drugs, violence, environment, unemployment etc. To be active in the international relationship is good, but it is not good to get distracted and dragged too far in the overseas cases and forgetting the war on enemy which is chiseling the economy slowly but surely.

Billons of dollars were spent overseas only to get stolen by "friendly regime" while the US Attorney General has not jurisdiction to prosecute.

The Americans are surprised when some financial institutions crumbling, they are stunning when the Wall Street --the kingdom of global financial institutions which most makes us proud of-- was slanting, and they are confusing when the auto makers as the lighthouse to indicate that America is ahead from other nations suddenly turned to be the needy where its CEO lamenting before the law makers in Washington asking for help with the tax payer money, our money, yours and mine. The law makers were so furious upon learning that the auto maker CEOs came to Washington asking for help flying the luxurious corporate jets. They are the most luxury beggars ever.

Aldrich Hazen Ames

Do you want to operate and own the superstore in the major cities in America with multi billion dollar asset as you retired from your government job? The KGB can arrange it for you, it is easy as ABC, sell your country's top secret. That's KGB offer to Aldrich Hazen Ames, a then-top US spy. The damage and loss of the US government resulted from his treason will never be compared to anything else in the history. The one and only comparison to the US loss maybe is the loss of nuclear secret stolen by the Rosenbergs in 1940's. If the loss of nuclear secret is only one entity, the loss of US secret sold by Ames was so many that the US government never could explain, ever. The secrets Ames traded in with money in a very long period were so complicated that they were almost at a point where the US **wins or loses** the Cold War to the Soviet Blocks. Ames was convicted in 1994; the secrets he sold were too many and too valuable; so the price is enough to build the superstores across the North America, if he wants. There was one "Ames" superstore in Cleveland in 2005, now defunct, but it's not clear if it has a connection with Aldrich H. Ames. The US and British government suspected that Ames also disclosed the treason of KGB agent Oleg Gordievsky who later defected to Britain; too many to record all Ames treasons.

> **Robert Hanssen**
>
> If you built a good home, you might stay in it or to rent it or at least to utilize it; but the Russian government never intended to use, lease or utilize its newly built embassy in Washington, DC. Why? Because it knew that under its construction there is a secret space where the US spy installed the sophisticated electronic device to overhear everything inside the Soviet Embassy. How does it know? Robert Hanssen told the KGB. Who is Robert Hanssen? He was a top US spy arrested in 2001. Hanssen's treason brings a huge loss to the US. Was Hanssen put in the death row? No, he was enjoying life in a federal prison; and some day he maybe released to enjoy his saving account of payoff from *Komitet gosudarstvennoy bezopasnosti* (*KGB*, Committee for the Security of State) as a direct result of his treason to his country, the United States of America.

The Cold War ended, and the USA come out from the arena as a big winner with the prize of world hegemony while the looser is breaking apart as its satellite countries cut the chains off from their necks. It could be good for them, but the worst thing is the Cold War ended with the **global irony**, the capitalist became socialist where the car industries, contrary to the business dogma, to ask for the government help because they lost the business war against Japan and German automakers. On the other side, the socialist became capitalist where the natural gas customers have to pay the bills right away or the gas pipe for former socialist comrades should be tightly closed as happened in 2005-2008 dispute between Ukrainian oil and gas company **Naftogaz Ukrainy** and Russian gas supplier **Gazprom**. The socialism and capitalism which five decades ago divided our pristine world into two parts and created the prolonged Cold War with the cost of trillions of dollars for both adversaries to produce the defense system and sophisticated offensive weapons, now suddenly became obsolete and lost their significance as the USA and Soviet Union joined hand in hand in the space laboratory and "war on terror".

The socialism is not bad, and the capitalism is not bad either; the bad is **Ponzi** scheme which was proven to be capable to rake $50 billions; and it is even worst when we were unable to catch **Bernie Madoff** for years; had the economics were good, he would never be caught.

The socialism-capitalism dichotomy is over; Francis Gary Powers one among thousands of participants in the Cold War must be rolling his grave; in 1960 his airplane was shot down over the Soviet Union airspace. However, now the American military airplanes such as jet fighter, military transport, spy plane, any kind are welcomed to use Kirgizstan's Soviet Union-built airbase. The US lost the Scorpion submarine in 1968 with the entire seamen on board either from accident or from the adversary action and nobody helped, now when Russian Navy is in trouble in the Arctic Sea, then the "capitalist" is extending the hand to help and to lend the sophisticated barge to salvage the sinking "communist" submarine without thinking of possibility that the Russia should have intentionally made two submarines sink to lure the Western top secret barge to come out to help. Did anybody ever think why two military submarines consecutively sank in a couple of months? During the Cold War this barge must be kept in secrecy to prevent the spy from taking photograph, but now with an allegedly made up accident, the Russian Navy could take the photographs of barge for free. Seaman brotherhood? Forget it. Under no any circumstances does a classified towing barge with the capability to pull submarine out from the seabed to come out helping the (former) enemy the "socialist" or "communist"; let them die as they let us die.

[132] http://en.wikipedia.org/HSCA
[133] Errol Morris Film, "*The Fog of War, eleven lessons from the life of Robert S. McNamara*", documentary 2003
[134] http://en.wikipedia.org/wiki/JFK_conspiracy
[135] http://en.wikipedia.org/wiki/Peter_Dale_Scott
[136] *Newsweek* Magazine, February 16, 2009
[137] PBS TV documentary, aired on January 26, 2009

3. Dealing with the "Supreme Committee"

It is hard to find the existence of the "Supreme Committee", although it is detectable but it is intangible; it is powerful, the perennial cover-up over the files related to the JFK unsolved mystery is among its amazing power. How come the files were sealed for 75 years? To trace its existence, we would start from the power of a US President. Contrary to the public opinion, the US President is not the single man to decide the foreign policy. If his policy is about to jeopardize the safety of American people, the "Supreme Committee" should have directed him. Ronald Reagan was a best example for a President who worked with the "Supreme Committee" in a harmony especially to save 52 American diplomats kept against their wills inside the American Embassy in Teheran for 444 days by Iranian Revolutionary Guard from November 4, 1979 to January 19, 1981. Although the diplomats were declared as "the guests of Ayatollah Khomeini", but the fact they were hold hostage with demand to send former Iranian ruler Reza Pahlavi back to Teheran to stand trial, and to release the frozen Iranian assets in USA. As for the foreign policy, it is still questionable if (a) Ronald Reagan's **SDI** [Strategic Defense Initiative] a new method of nuclear defense, (b) Collin Powel's **vial show off** in the UN, (c) Condoleezza Rice's **statement** "Let the smoking gun does not become the mushroom cloud", and (d) George W. Bush **war on Iraq** --where it turns to be no WMD found whatsoever-- were among substantiations of the Supreme Committee existence **if** we assume that it still exists. However, they did the designated jobs as mandated.

3.1. Ronald Reagan (1911 – 2004)

Ronald Wilson Reagan () was the 40th President of the United States of America; he was considered the best US President ever in accordance to his cooperation with "the Supreme Committee", if it still existed at that time. He was not a bellicose, after a briefing with Pentagon he wrote "We had many contingency plans for responding to a nuclear attack. But everything would happen so fast that I wondered how much planning or reason could be applied in such a crisis... Six minutes to decide how to respond to a blip on radar scope and decide whether to unleash Armageddon! How could anyone apply reason at a time like that? [138]"

He was handsome, smart, flamboyant, former Governor and former movie star; a combination to be a perfect public figure. Beyond the public knowledge, he suffered from Alzheimer disease; it was made public only after he openly wrote a farewell letter to the fellow Americans. Alzheimer is not an instant disease; if someone suffered from it; he must be suffering for a long time before the signs of Alzheimer becomes obvious to the public such as tremor, memory lost, etc. Once upon the weekend after leaving office he was walking on the park with his family member; he was so surprised when the people keep waving and greeting on him; he asked to his daughter "How come so many people know me?" He forgot that he was one among the popular US Presidents, and he forgot that his name was mentioned almost every day in the news for 8 years during his tenure as the US President. Most probably that during his "incapacitated" final years of his tenure due to the Alzheimer, the administration steering wheel was on the hand(s) of the Supreme Committee, and the US government was put on the auto pilot mode; yet it's successful. Everybody was happy.

3.2. Colin Powell

General Colin Powell (Retired) is a son of Jamaican immigrant who urged his children to pursue the higher education for their own future. Colin Powel went to Military Academy and has had war experience before his assignment as the Secretary of State in the Bush Administration first term (2000 - 2004). He is smart and diligent, when he reaches the top career in US military and became the general, his brother is still a bus driver.

Colin Powel is a true military cadre, he used to obey the command; he has a high discipline and has an advanced knowledge to know what to do even before his superior asks. Unfortunately, his advanced action sometimes brings an uncomfortable situation which the analysts say led to his decline as a political incumbent. Colin Powell is an example for those who do not understand what "The Supreme Committee" wants, assuming that it still exists at his time.

The power elsewhere always consists of two elements, tangible and intangible; Powell does not read the "road map". Only those who had a sharp analysis or those who ever studied the political science like Condi Rice knows how to cope with the agile maneuver in the politics. Fred Kaplan wrote about Colin Powel in *Slate* Magazine "The Tragedy of Colin Powell. How the Bush presidency destroyed him":

> "One of Powell's first acts as secretary of state was to tell a reporter that the Bush administration would pick up where Bill Clinton left off in negotiations with North Korea—only to be told by Vice President Cheney that it would do no such thing. He had to retract his statement. For the next nine months, he disappeared so definitively that *Time* magazine asked, on its cover of Sept. 10, 2001, "Where Is Colin Powell?" As George Bush's first term nears its end, Powell's tenure as top diplomat is approaching its nadir. On the high-profile issues of the day, he seems to have almost no influence within the administration. And his fateful briefing one year ago before the U.N. Security Council—where he attached his personal credibility to claims of Iraqi WMD—has destroyed his once-considerable standing with the Democrats, not to mention our European allies, most of the United Nations, and the media."

"The decline of Powell's fortunes is a tragic tale of politics: so much ambition derailed, so much accomplishment nullified. He seems to have launched a rehabilitation campaign, to escape this dreaded state. Last month, after David Kay resigned as the CIA's chief weapons inspector and proclaimed that Iraq probably didn't have weapons of mass destruction after all, Powell told a reporter that he might not have favored going to war if he'd known there were no WMD a year ago. He almost instantly retracted his words, as all internal critics of Bush policies seem to do." [139]

The critics said the vial that Colin Powell showed at the UN Assembly on February 5, 2003 was not the real anthrax spores found at Sadam Husein arsenal but an alleged sample of DNA discovered in Australia. America always has the unique anecdote like England does; as the world knew, the glowing object caught by astronaut Edwin Aldrin [1930-2012] camera was not an UFO but his urine packed in a small transparent plastic bag thrown out to the outer space!

As of Powel vial, fortunately, the audience at the UN Assembly kept quiet; nobody asked Powel what's he was showing to, it's a real anthrax powder or something else. As Powell realized that "Iraqi weapon of mass destruction" was a lie; he was very upset and regret.

If the vial he showed at the UN Assembly were true anthrax spore, it was questionable did he violate the law of transportation of the hazardous materials. His "vial show off" at UN Assembly is worst than Bernard Madoff $50 Billion scandal because it created more loss than Madoff did, it worst than the Cuban Crisis that claimed only one US service member, because his "vial show off" lead to the death of 24,219 US soldiers, supporters and contractors plus 117,961 total wounded and the death of hundred thousands of Iraqi civilians.

Colin Powell seems to get splashed Saddam Hussein's curse. Powell never shown any remorse and inclination to point out who allegedly directed him to the fatal mistake before the UN Council; when interviewed by ABC's Barbara Walters about whom should have been responsible for the "official" mistakes in his overall ("anthrax") presentation, he simply answered "I don't have the names." "….There's no question that Powell WAS consciously lying: he fabricated 'evidence' and ignored repeated warnings that what he was saying was false", Journalist Schwarz wrote for huffingtonpost.com (http://www.huffingtonpost.com/jonathan-schwarz/colin-powell-wmd-iraq-war_b_2624620.html).

Although he endorsed Obama for President during 2008 campaign heyday, the critics suggest that what Powell did was something else, still President Obama did not pick Powell as a member of the Cabinet. President Obama as a Democrat has nominated Judd Gregg a Republican Senator as Commerce Secretary. Had he would not withdraw himself [140], Gregg becomes the third Republican to join in President Obama's Cabinet along with Robert Gates (Defense Secretary) and Ray LaHood (Transportation Secretary); still Powell was not included.

3.3. Condoleezza Rice

Condoleezza Rice is a perfect example for those who do understand what The Supreme Committee wants, assuming that it still exists at her time. As a professor in the political science at Stanford University she knows that the power elsewhere always consists of two elements tangible and intangible; she has a sharp analysis and has been successful to adapt with the agile maneuver in the politics. Condi does understand not just the "road map"; she makes a part of it.

Condi Rice is a colorful Secretary of State that brighter than her predecessor Madeline Albright who was born in Europe and raised in the USA; Condi was born and raised in the USA.

She made a surprise on January 10, 2003 when she said about Saddam Hussein "Let the smoking gun does not become the mushroom cloud". "Mushroom cloud" refers to the nuclear explosion, and this is her mastery in expressing the political maneuver on the international stage.

The analysts know that her tone was soft when said about "mushroom cloud" but, the meaning was very sharp, very. That is Condi; let's see what the critics said about her:

3.3.1. nndb.com

"Her parents were both college professors. Her unusual first name is derived from the Italian for an opera stage instruction, *con dolcezza*, meaning "with sweetness". Rice was raised in segregated Birmingham during the civil rights movement. A childhood friend, 11-year-old Denise McNair, was one of the four young girls killed in the bombing of Birmingham's 16th Street Baptist Church in 1963. Rice never became involved in the civil rights movement, but she says, "My parents had me absolutely convinced that, well, you may not be able to have a hamburger at Woolworth's but you can be President of the United States. She mastered the piano at three, and was told that she could have had a career as a concert pianist. She skipped first and seventh grades, entered college at 15, holds three degrees including a doctorate in political science, and earned her Master's in just one year's study. She was a professor of Political Science at Stanford from 1981-93, and from 1993-99 she was also Stanford's provost, responsible for overseeing the school's budget and academic programs."

"She served as a mid-to upper-level member of the National Security staff during the first Bush presidency, and as National Security Advisor during the second Bush presidency, before succeeding Colin Powell as Secretary of State in 2005".

"Little is known of Rice's personal life, except that she has never been married. .... At a dinner party while Rice was National Security Advisor, she referred to President George W. Bush as 'my husband' before abruptly correcting herself [141]."

3.3.2. The Observer

"On another occasion, when Rice was an academic at Stanford, she was shopping for expensive jewelry with a friend when a white clerk made some hostile comments. 'Let's get one thing straight,' Rice reportedly told him. 'You're behind the counter because you have to work for six dollars an hour. I'm on this side asking to see the good jewelry because I make considerably more. [142]' "

3.3.3. nymag.com

Political Conversation: Condi's Slip

"A pressing issue of dinner-party etiquette is vexing Washington, according to a story now making the D.C. rounds: How should you react when your guest, in this case national-security adviser **Condoleezza Rice**, makes a poignant *faux pas*? At a recent dinner party hosted by New York *Times* D.C. bureau chief **Philip Taubman** and his wife, *Times* reporter **Felicity Barringer**, and attended by **Arthur Sulzberger Jr., Maureen Dowd, Steven Weisman**, and **Elisabeth Bumiller**, Rice was reportedly overheard saying, 'As I was telling my husb—' and then stopping herself abruptly, before saying, 'As I was telling President Bush.' "Jaws dropped, but a guest says the slip by the unmarried politician, who spends weekends with the president and his wife, seemed more psychologically telling than incriminating. Nobody thinks Bush and Rice are actually an item. A National Security Council spokesman laughed and said, 'No comment. [143]'"

3.3.4. huffingtonpost.com

Mike Schneider on August 28, 2012 wrote for huffingtonpost.com: "Police in Tampa stopped a dozen anti-war protesters from entering an event attended by former Secretary of State Condoleezza Rice after the group said it intended to arrest her for war crimes. The protesters from "Code Pink" carried handcuff Tuesday and tried to enter a performing arts center. Rice was attending an event in conjunction with the Republican National Convention. They said they wanted to make a citizen's arrest of Rice. She was George W. Bush's National Security Adviser when the Iraq War started in 2003. Officers told protesters to leave because they were on private property. "They went back to the sidewalk and some of them lay down on the ground to display their "blood-splattered" clothes. The group says it will try to arrest other members of the George W. Bush administration. [144]"

The incident of the attempt to arrest Condi was posted on http://www.youtube.com/watch?v=rmi7crM4LuI and soon becomes viral. Condi's mastery in the political science, however, is not a guarantee that she is not going to get splashed with Saddam Hussein curse. George Bush got one: Muntazar Al-Zaidi shoes #10.

Montazar Al-Zaidi

The Arabs are famous with their hospitality to host the guests, and Montazar Al-Zaidi an Iraqi journalist has had his own hospitality; he hurled his shoes one after another consecutively to President George W. Bush during a press conference with Iraqi Prime Minister Nur Al-Maliki on December 14, 2008. George W. Bush ducked to avoid the leather missile and jokingly said "It's number 10". When Al-Zaidi was standing for trial in February 2009 he argued that Bush was not a guest, a guest is not sneaking into Iraq without permission and announcement. March 12, 2009 the Iraqi court sentenced him for 3 years, a verdict that spurs a tumult across Bagdad. On his action, Al-Zaidi was considered by fellow Arabs as a brave hero. Do you think so? (from many sources)

3.3.5. US Senate Hearing

During Iraq invasion, as we know, the US lost lot of soldiers. When the number exceeds 4,500; the Americans start asking the government to bring the troops home. On January 11, 2007 during the US Senate hearing, Senator Barbara Boxer [Dem-California] was questioning Secretary Condoleezza Rice. A portion of it was posted on http://www.youtube.com/watch?v=3FdFf7_yUVc&NR=1&feature=endscreen here Senator Boxer grilling Secretary Rice especially with a startling question "who does pay the price [of Iraq invasion]?, I do not, because my son is too old and my grand son is too young. You do not."

3.4. George W. Bush

George W. Bush sometimes was nicknamed Dubya a simple pronunciation of his middle name "Double U". He was a president of the most powerful nation in the world with extraordinary military capability including the nuclear deterrent, and special force deployment to any point in the globe within some hours; yet he has to negotiate against a voodoo threat and pay some thousand dollars to be safe when he visited Indonesia in November 20, 2006; next time US President should have sent Navy Seals to solve this problem. Here the allegedly story goes:

Gendeng and George W. Bush

Ihsan Marsadi aka Issanmarsadi alias Ki Gendeng Pamungkas was born in Surabaya East Java on October 14, 1947; he learned the bad magic, African and Haitian voodoo for commercial purposes.

One of his rituals during learning the voodoo is to submerge his body up to the neck in the pool of cow dung and does not eat anything for a certain period unless he finds something from the cow dung. After a week or more he feels hungry and thirsty while nothing to eat but worms popping up from the pool, so he eats them up. After his success to learn voodoo, he reportedly charges up to $20,000 to kill someone with the voodoo and bad magic he learned in Africa and Haiti; he confessed to practice the voodoo to kill up to 800 persons in Indonesia. He makes a lot of money. He was a Muslim and knew the divine risk of practicing voodoo yet he did it anyway, later in 2002 he converted into Catholic. Prior to President Bush visit to Bogor on November 20, 2006; Marsadi publicly performed a voodoo ritual at *Kujang* Square, Bogor West Java, with intention to harm the US President George W. Bush who was expected to visit the Bogor Presidential Palace. The voodoo is intangible and complicated which gives hard time to the Secret Service yet the problem should have been resolved.

The Secret Service with some voodoo experts —which a Jakarta TV station reported up to "6 voodoo team members"—reportedly went to meet Marsadi in his Bogor residence to compromise with his voodoo plan to harm the visiting US President. After a friendly negotiation, the Secret Service team agreed to pay Marsadi a sum of $10,000 or equal to Rp 90 million a sweet deal for a couple days of work, plus bonus from the local Indonesian government leader in a compensation of Marsadi's voodoo cancellation. Unfortunately, Marsadi informed the voodoo team members and Secret Service that he already completed the voodoo ritual on November 16, 2006 and he was unable to retract the "ongoing curse" and he was not sure if President Bush would not be harmed. However, Marsadi said there was another ritual to evade his ongoing voodoo, President Bush had to jump with his 2 feet altogether from the limousine as he stepped out; he was not supposed to step either with his right or left foot first, but both of them.

On November 20, 2006 the world became the witness as TV cameras catch the image of President Bush to jump out from limousine on his two feet as he arrived at Bogor Presidential Palace. He had to be alive and not harmed, since he was negotiating the oil exploration of Natuna oil block, one among the biggest oil wells in the Southeast Asia.

The critics say that everything is negotiable in Indonesia including to twist the Constitution which is "Undang-Undang Dasar" [UUD] in local language; they stated UUD contemporarily stands for *Ujung-Ujungnya Dollar*, Under Unlimited Dollar." On May 11, 2012 an ad hoc tribunal in Malaysia has found former President Bush plus six administration members guilty of war crimes (http://www.youtube.com/watch?v=_KODyCouerE). Is this voodoo? *)

Reagan, Bush, Powel, and Rice etc. are the public officials who tried hard to have their jobs done, they are the dedicated government officers; yet the politics sometimes, in a certain time and a certain place to fracture the good people reputation as the bad railway crossing destroyed the good drivers.

[138] http://en.wikipedia.org/wiki/Able_Archer_83
[139] Fred Kaplan, "*The Tragedy of Colin Powell. How the Bush presidency destroyed him*", Slate Magazine website, Thursday, Feb. 19, 2004
[140] On February 12, 2009 Gregg withdrew his nomination for a specific reason other than tax problem unlike other did.
[141] nndb.com
[142] Paul Harris, "*How Condoleezza Rice became the most powerful woman in the world*", The Observer, Sunday January 16, 2005
[143] nymag.com
[144] http://www.huffingtonpost.com/2012/08/28/condoleezza-rice-protest_n_1837053.html?utm_hp_ref=elections-2012
*) http://www.youtube.com/watch?NR=1&v=OAQ6niJpk-c&feature=endscreen,
http://www.foreignpolicyjournal.com/2012/05/12/bush-convicted-of-war-crimes-in-absentia/

4. Oswald the Radar Crew

His Russian language course at the DLI was one of secrets hidden from public

TU-95 "Bear" is the Soviet Union's turboprop surveillance airplane stationed in Vladivostok the most eastern part of the Soviet Union. The "Bear" flew regularly back and forth from Vladivostok Soviet Union to Okinawa Japan, and therefore it was dubbed "Tokyo Express". The routine flight of TU-95 "Bear" for a long distance in the cold war era must be for reason. Okinawa, Japan meanwhile was an important US airbase in the Pacific. The most possible mission of TU-95 "Bear" was to detect if U-2 spy plane(s) still in its place at Atsugi airbase, Okinawa Japan and not roaming somewhere or breaching the Soviet air space. Even if Tu-95 "Bear" still finds "U-2" or mock U-2 sticks around at Atsugi it does not mean that it's accurate, because the another U-2 was already secretly deployed from Peshawar, Pakistan. If the long range Tu-95 "Bear" did not find any U-2, it still yields other information, its strategic mission was:

(a) to find out the U-2s whereabouts

(b) the training for the new pilots to be familiar with the Pacific region,

(c) to convey a political message to Japan that helping the USA posing a risk,

(d) to test if its 24,000 lb. payload is safely delivered over the target with/without refueling for 4,900 miles,

(e) to check the engine if it's ready anytime especially when a modification was made.

It's amazing, during its long time mission no one single Tu-95 "Bear" is involved in accident; it brings the sense of confidence to the Soviet Union that Tu-95 and its variant are ready to carry on the strategic mission such as delivering Air Launched Ballistic Missiles (ALBM), long range mission or aerial surveillance.

Both the Soviets and the USA meanwhile were in the early stages of developing the remote surveillance from satellite in the deep space; they still needed the "traditional surveillance" from the airplanes either TU-95 "Bear" or U-2. Meanwhile in September 1957 Lee Harvey Oswald (1939 - 1963) worked at Atsugi, he and his team worked at an ultra secret and very sophisticated radar station. He was one among handful staffs at Atsugi airbase, Okinawa Japan -and at Cubi Point airbase, Philippines- who had the "crypto clearance", a higher level than "confidential" clearance. Two times he stood for the trial in the martial court, once for inflicting "self wound"; and second from fighting; but this fact was suppressed from being included in the Warren Commission report [145]; nobody was able to explain why. Oswald was a self declared Marxist, he should have not been assigned to this sensitive position, radar station is a war control room and no one single communist should had been allowed to enter. The question became so deep over who Lee Harvey Oswald was. Was he a pawn of **Komitet Gosudarstvennoy Bezopasnosti** (KGB, The Committee for Homeland Security)?

Did he disclose the radar secret when he defected to Soviet Union with the direct impact for Francis Gary Powers' U-2 spy plane which was shot down over Soviet air space on May 1960 *less than one year* after Oswald defection? This incident had an unprecedented impact on the bilateral relationship between United States of America and Soviet Union; it was so tragic and made the summit meeting between President Eisenhower and President Josef Stalin was cancelled; it was an embarrassing incident. In May 1958 Lee Harvey Oswald radar crew was involved in another important role in the covert action to topple Indonesian President Ahmad Soekarno. It was a failed attempt to topple leftward-leaning Indonesian government under Soekarno. US President Dwight David Eisenhower (1890 - 1969) and Allen Welsh Dulles (1893 - 1969) the Director of CIA considered Soekarno (1901- 1969) as a dangerous leader because under his administration the Indonesian Communist Party (***Partai Komunis Indonesia, PKI***) in the 1955 elections reached the fourth majority after ***PNI, Masyumi*** and ***NU*** political parties.

PKI with around 1.5 million members obtained 16% votes to win 39 out of 257 seats in the *Dewan Perwakilan Rakyat* (the Congress) and to win 80 out of 514 seats in the *Konstituante* (Constituent Assembly, a predecessor of *Majelis Permusyawaratan Rakyat*, the Senate). The operation where Oswald was involved was code-named "Operation Strongback" [146] a kind of operation which was forbidden by the US Congress later in 1975.

The role of Oswald and his radar crew was not elaborated in McKnight's *"Breach of Trust"*, but most probably was to control and manage 15 B-26 bombers supporting the *PRRI/Permesta* separatist rebel. These USA-made bombers had formed AUREV (*Angkatan Udara Revolusioner*, The Revolutionary Air Force) based on Manado airfield in northern part of Sulawesi (Celebes) island; they bombed city of Makassar in the most southern part of Sulawesi island, city of Ambon in Ambon Island south eastern of Sulawesi, and city of Balikpapan in Borneo island 840 miles south western of Manado, Sulawesi island. On May 15, 1958 the AUREV rebel planes bombed the city of Ambon indiscriminately killing civilians attending church service on Sunday; the pilot who bombed them might be thinking it's romantic for Ambon people to die on a beautiful sunny tropical Sunday.

PRRI

PRRI stands for *Pemerintah Revolusioner Republik Indonesia*, Revolutionary Government of the Republic of Indonesia, it was a rebellion, a separatist movement (1956-1958) and treason led by Indonesian army officers in Sumatra main island against the central government in Jakarta during the administration of Indonesian first president, Ahmad Soekarno. At the same time on March 2, 1957, in the eastern part of Indonesian archipelago, there was another rebel movement; it was **Permesta** stands for *Piagam Perjuangan Semesta* (the Charter for Universal Struggle) which was declared by civil and military leaders in Manado a city in Sulawesi (Celebes) island. The Permesta was led by Colonel Ventje Sumual. Soekarno was a soft-hearted president, the rebels were given the amnesty after the re-education at Banyubiru, Central Java.

> Had the rebel occurred during Soeharto era, it is for sure they were shot to death or "eliminated" without any explanation where their graveyard are, as happened to some students and democracy activists who vanished since 1980's until now. Even, the person who advocated the missing activists was murdered by poison like Munir; and the court never revealed who was behind the serial murder over decades during the Soeharto administration. **Wikipedia.com** asserts that *"The most significant progenitor of the rebellion was the opportunism by local military leaders who during the Liberal Democracy Era in Indonesia (1950-1957), had developed a system of warlordism due to weakness and instability of central government in Jakarta. When the central military command under Armed Forces Chief General Abdul Haris Nasution tried to re-impose central military control and rein in the regional army chiefs' massive copra smuggling operations, the opportunistic regional military leaders in West Sumatera formed the PRRI movement and those in North Sulawesi formed the Permesta movement to counter the central government. To worsen the situation, the American CIA interfered in the affair by giving support to the rebellious movements. The reason was because US President Dwight David Eisenhower and CIA chief Allen Dulles was concerned that the success of Indonesian Communist Party (PKI) in winning fourth-place in the 1955 elections (most of these votes came from Java) might be precursor of Indonesia becoming a communist state".* This Wikipedia passage is NOT true since there was no warlordism, nor it was a factor in the rebel; however, from the very beginning there were the efforts to topple the Soekarno administration in the context of "domino theory", Eisenhower was anxious to see Soekarno was leaning into the left. For more explanation please read **Oswald the Radar Crew** Chapter.

Who did fly B-26 bombers when AUREV did not have any pilot? One of the pilots to fly B-26 bombers was **Allen Lawrence Pope** a CIA pilot whose plane on May 18, 1958 was shot down by Indonesian Air Force pilot **Ignatius Dewanto** over Ambon Island in the eastern part of Indonesia while supporting the PRRI/Permesta separatist rebel.

The other pilots were mercenaries from Philippines, Taiwan and Poland. When Allen L. Pope was in the Indonesian military custody, his belongings were confiscated including his special wrist watch. He insisted to take it back; one decade later when James Bond movie demonstrated the use of a watch for the communication it was too late for the interrogator to realize that Pope's watch concealing a special communication device to report his whereabouts to the nearest base, might be the Philippines where **Oswald** was on the assignment. However, after the Permesta rebellion; Soekarno, with a strong lobby from US Embassy in Jakarta did agree to meet President John F. Kennedy in Washington and release Allen Lawrence Pope [147] (see Box: **PRRI** for more story). It's a matter of fact that JFK was a President, statesman and diplomat at the same time.

Where Oswald's station during this rebellion was not clear, but most probably at US Naval Air Station Cubi Point, Subic Bay the Philippines, to operate the radar station controlling mercenary pilots aboard the rebel airplanes bombarding the Indonesian field targets in Ambon, Ujung Pandang and Balikpapan including the mass killing of Christians at Ambon market on their way from the Ascension service on Sunday. The mass killing of Christians at Ambon traditional market was most probably chosen to impress the world that "the Christians were not welcomed in the Muslim country" and to discredit the Soekarno administration.

The city of Ambon, Ujung Pandang and Balikpapan were chosen as the target most probably because they were on the reach of Oswald's radar coverage; and not Bali or Jakarta.

Meanwhile, at the western part of Indonesia, a synchronized Army rebel was on the way, starting from December 1956. They were led by **Lieutenant Colonel Ahmad Hussein**, **Colonel Mauluddin Simbolon** the commanders of Territorial Army in Sumatra, and **Lieutenant Colonel Barlian** the commander of Territorial Army in South Sumatra.

Three months prior to the Ambon bombing by Manado-based Permesta rebel, in February 15, 1958 Ahmad Hussein declared the establishment of PRRI (*Pemerintah Revolusioner Republik Indonesia*, The Revolutionary Government of the Republic of Indonesia). The commanders of Indonesian Territorial Army in Sumatra intentionally took the local government of Sumatra over in a rebellion against the central government in Jakarta NOT because "the political rivalry" inside the Indonesian Army as asserted in http://en.wikipedia.org/wiki/PRRI. They did because they were influenced and infiltrated by a foreign power, supported by foreign troops and foreign weapons. Wikipedia in another paragraph wrote "The US government, which supported the rebels, started to withdraw their forces immediately after one of their fighter planes was shot down and its pilot Allen Pope was shot over Ambon" [148].

The Indonesian troops who were assigned to regain control over Manado had captured the weapons from the rebel, however they were not able to use it because it was very sophisticated, it's made in USA. Both **PRRI** and **Permesta** willfully planned the rebellion against the legitimate Indonesian government; those who were involved, under the Constitution, should have been put on the death row; however Soekarno under the lobbying of "the beautiful women club" gave the amnesty to the rebels after reeducating them in the Army detention center in Banyubiru 25 miles south of Semarang the capital of Central Java.

After this successful assignment as radar operator in **Operation Strongback** of 1958, the other assignment was awaiting Oswald. On February 25, 1959 the US Navy tested Oswald ability in the Russian language skill, this is a fact that invited more question rather than an explanation. This testing happened just 8 months prior to his defection to Soviet Union. His Russian language course at the Defense Language Institute (DLI) was one of some secrets hidden from the public, therefore the request of Gerald D. McKnight the author of "*Breach of Trust*" to access Oswald file was declined by a staff at DLI at Monterey, California [149].

As Oswald discharged from US Marine, he "immigrated" to the Soviet Union on October 1959 when he was 19. He left New Orleans port on September 20, 1959 for Le Havre, France and at the same day on October 9, 1959 he left for England; and he flew to Helsinki, Finland and next trip was to Moscow by train, he arrived on October 16, 1959 and soon to seek the Soviet citizenship. On October 21, 1959 when his request was declined he "committed suicide" with a sharp object to scratch his arm to make a very superficial wound without cutting the main blood vessel on his wrist; a perfect drama.

He worked at an electronics company in Minsk; it was not clear why he settled in this city; is it possible that he thought the components of Soviet Union's nuclear weapon were made here? In 1962 he came back to USA with a Russian wife Marina Prusakova and a daughter. The more we learn about Oswald the more suspicion arouse. He was totally a mysterious person, his trail was zigzag, and his fate was tragic. His actions were contradictory, and from his conflicting actions he might provided a very different perception to the public:

(1) He was assigned to handle the top secret facility by US government in Subic Bay, the Philippines and Atsugi, Japan.

(2) He took a course of Russian language at an "official" school, Defense Language Institute (DLI) in California, prior his defection to Soviet Union.

(3) He was discharged from US Navy with "honorable" only later to be reversed into "undesirable" after immigrating to Soviet Union.

(4) In 1959, a high level KGB official Pavel T. Voloshin to lead the Russian Dancers to Los Angeles [150]. Voloshin's position as the leader of cultural performers has provided him a perfect cover to deflecting any suspicion that he was a KGB high officer sneaking into the US for reason. At the very same time Oswald was in Los Angeles to get

his US passport. Voloshin might have been in Los Angeles with a very special assignment to recruit Oswald and/or to prepare his defection upon KGB recognition that Oswald was a radar operator at Atsugi, Japan the base of U-2 superspy plane. Oswald was also a radar operator in the Philippines at the time of Alan Pope bombing Indonesia in support of separatist rebel in 1957-1958. Voloshin and Oswald were at the very same city at the very same time, it could be just a coincidence or meticulous *rendezvouz*.

(5) When Richard Helms was a Deputy, before appointed as Director of CIA, between 1958 and 1959 he had had a top secret report leaked by Pyotr Semyonovich Popov a KGB Colonel that the presence of American U-2 super spy plane had been recognized by KGB [151]. Everything about U-2 in 1958-1962 or beyond until its decommission is a top secret; so how did the Soviet know the exact altitude of this superspy plane and its schedule? In 1960 a U-2 was shot down over Soviet airspace, did Oswald inform the KGB so his defection was warmly welcomed?

(6) He was warmly welcomed in the Soviet Union and was showered with 5,000 rubles plus luxury apartment, as a defector he easily found a job with good salary of 700 rubles a month while another defector was treated poorly [152].

(7) After coming back to US, Oswald visited Carlos Bringuier a Cuban exile on August 5, 1963 and declared himself as anti-Castro only to get caught a couple days later that he distributed the pro-Castro leaflets. When a brawl between Oswald and anti-Castro Cuban exiles was about to erupt, and the Police was questioning Oswald, then suddenly a mysterious government agent John L. Quigley came to intervene.

"Do not dispose your used car to junk yard, you may sell it for price"; this proverb applies when we look at the shooting down of U-2. Did Oswald unintentionally disclose the secret of U-2 spy plane, or did he ***intentionally*** disclosed it to win the confidence of KGB while the U-2 technology itself was obsolete and will be soon replaced with SR-71 Blackbird or surveillance satellite? Was Gary Power's U-2 mission sacrificed? It's so many questions never could be answered until now because on November 24, 1963 he was murdered in Dallas while being accused of murdering police officer JD Tippit and President John F. Kennedy.

It was a perfect murder happened before many witnesses in the police station when he was being transferred to jail, Jack Ruby the murderer never escaped but never admitted who asked him to kill Oswald in Murder of The Millennium. Ruby died in jail in 1964, the rumor said he was poisoned with the carcinogenic substance by someone visiting him in jail.

Whosoever Oswald was, he was an important person who was confided by the government in a task force to handle some important missions like radar stations in the Philippines and Japan, and an attempt to topple Indonesian President Ahmad Soekarno [153].

In 1962 Soekarno met John F. Kennedy in Washington after the failure of PRRI/Permesta separatist movement; the circulating report in Indonesian newspapers said that Kennedy's smile had teamed Soekarno even after Allen Lawrence Pope a CIA pilot was shot down in Ambon supporting PRRI/Permesta.

Oswald still had another covert activity with David Ferrie, Judyth Vary Baker and others on a covert project to produce the carcinogenic substance that should had been used to stop Fidel Castro [154]. During this time Oswald had had an alleged affair with Judyth Vary Baker, a medical researcher, as she confessed later.

The official version put Oswald on the accusation that he fired his rifle to kill President Kennedy; did he fire his Carcano rifle from sixth floor of Texas Depository Building on Friday November 22, 1963? This is natural question; yet the answer is "No, for sure". This answer came from a self-declared assassin, **James E. Files**. He declared himself as the assassin who fired a fatal shot to John F. Kennedy with a powerful Remington Fireball gun caliber .222 from the grassy knoll. Did he felt sorry? His answer is "No" again. The only "regret" was, he missed one inch from main focus the right eye of John F. Kennedy and hit his front-right temple [155]. The witness is not available to confirm what **James E. Files** said, even if what he declared was true, he never knew the motive behind the assassination of John F. Kennedy, because a triggerman only "fires and forgets", he does not have to know for what he was ordered to. On the other hand, the confession without evidence would create more problem rather than solution.

We should be wary about the motive of any confession; it is possible that someone declared to be a killer of a famous figure for popularity or monetary gain or another unknown reason. Sometimes a certain person declared himself to be responsible for a high profile case such as in the case of JonBenet Ramsey murder that turned to be untrue and without DNA evidence. **James E. Files** a former hitman has said that he, Roselli and Charles Nicoletti were at Dealey Plaza, Dallas Texas on November 22, 1963 and fired the fatal shots killing John F. Kennedy. This claim, however, is without proof and witness; and could not be confirmed [156].

Another claim was made by Bill Bonnano a New York mob boss in his autobiography that he spoke to Roselli about the assassination of John F. Kennedy while they were in prison. According to Bonnano account, Roselli confessed about shooting John F. Kennedy from a storm drain on Elm Street in Dallas, Texas.

This claim was doubtful, among other things the Bonnano Family were forbidden from revealing the "family secret" or facing a death under *omerta* secret code. Roselli had allegedly been flown from Tampa, Florida to Dallas, Texas on November 22, 1963 morning by then-CIA pilot Tosh Plumlee; but on the different mission i.e. aborting the assassination of President John F. Kennedy.

The confession of **James E. Files** a former hitman could not be independently verified; it more arouse the question rather than the answer because amid the *death storm* sweeping over the persons who allegedly knew about the assassination of John F. Kennedy, James E. Files popped up voluntarily to be a target of bullet. Nobody could verify if Sam Giancana, Johnny Roselli, Charles Nicoletti were murdered in 1975, 1976, 1977 respectively because they were feared to testify before the House Select Committee on Assassinations; however one thing is sure they died unnaturally. Within such scary condition for years including the mysterious death of Rose Cherami, then James Files instead of hiding, he voluntarily confessed that he, Roselli and Nicoletti were at Dealey Plaza, Dallas Texas on November 22, 1963 and fired the fatal shot(s) killing John F. Kennedy. Everybody has the freedom of speech, but the risk is waiting either being summoned to testify before the grand jury or being prosecuted for perjury. It seems that some people were suffering from pop-up-popularity syndrome (PUPS) by confessing something that they never did just to gain an instant popularity.

James Earl Files

James Earl Files (1942-), alias **James Sutton**, is an American inmate at SCC Prison, Crest Hill, Illinois. During a recorded interview in 1994 he confessed that he was the shooter on the grassy knoll at Dealy Plaza in the assassination of President Kennedy. Ever since, he was interviewed by some researches and became topic in various books discussing the conspiracy theory of JFK assassination.

> However, in 1994, the FBI investigated James Files assertion and found it "not to be credible". In 2010, Hillel Levin wrote in ***Playboy*** magazine about James Files who implicated Nicoletti and Roselli in JFK assassination.
>
> Sources: http://en.wikipedia.org/wiki/James_Files; Dankbaar, "***Files of JFK***", 2008

The presence of three mysterious persons who caught by the Dallas Police from the railroad yard next to the Texas Book Depository Building around the same time John F. Kennedy was murdered was very suspicious. On their way to the Dallas Police Station the photographers took the images from them. They were initially known as "the three tramps", and after their mysterious disappearance from the police station, the investigative journalists found them as Chauncey Marvin Holt, Charles Harrelson, and Charles Roger [157] although another narration told different three names.

Oswald was a very important link in the investigation of JFK assassination. To assume that Oswald was a lone assassin, we need to ask "what's his motive?" He never threatened to kill John F. Kennedy, he never hated JFK, and even he was happy when JFK being elected as the President of United States as his wife Marina Prusakova testified before the Warren Commission.

Marina also testified that Oswald might have been shooting John Connally as the retaliation over Connally rejection to Oswald request to upgrade his Navy discharge from "undesirable" to "desirable". Connally was the (former) Navy Secretary from January 1961 to December 1961 under President John F. Kennedy.

Oswald was honorably discharged from US Navy, and when immigrated to Soviet Union he went to the US Embassy in Moscow on October 31, 1959 to renounce his US citizenship. He also explained that he ever informed the Soviet officials - most probably KGB officers- that he was a radar operator when he served in the Marine Corps.

US Navy, upon learning his actions -most probably US Embassy in Moscow informed Washington- then changed Oswald's Marine Corps discharge from "honorable" to "undesirable" [158] [159].

As for the discharge itself, it should be "undesirable", since if it is "honorable" then the Soviet government would be suspicious that the defector was listed as "honorable" which implies that Oswald defection is sponsored by the US government.

There're at least 2 additional benefits of Oswald's "undesirable" discharge:

(1) To provide undisputable proof that Oswald defection was strongly condemned by the US government, therefore his discharge was changed to "undesirable".

(2) To implant the hatred toward US government officer inside Oswald soul. These psycho game and disgusting situation someday might be used for strategic purpose. Oswald shot General Walker on April 10, 1963 out of his hatred to Walker a segregationist and outspoken anti-communist. Marina Prusakova testified before the Warren Commission that Oswald might have been shooting Connally as the retaliation over Connally rejection to Oswald request to upgrade his Navy discharge from "undesirable" to "desirable". Connally was the (former) Navy Secretary from January 1961 to December 1961 under President John F. Kennedy. The announcement of presidential motorcade route on the local newspaper and the possibility of Governor Connally presence, either on the same car with President Kennedy or separated, might trigger Oswald to take a chance to retaliate to Connally, not Kennedy. The worst possibility is: Oswald was lured to retaliate against Connally, and then the real assassin would piggyback to shoot JFK! The strategic purpose has been successful.

Since the information and or evidence about Oswald motive to kill JFK was NOT available, then any plausible version should have not been ruled out.

Oswald might have been ordered to shoot at a given time and place although he did not have to kill the target; therefore at the time of arrest in the theater he yelled "It's all over" indicating that he intended to disclose everything he knew. He also snapped back at the journalist who asked him about JFK assassination "I do not even know the charges until you ask me!" His word was quite different with his message to his wife Marina when he tried to kill General Walker "If I don't go home, please check the county jail". Had Oswald shot at JFK motorcade either targeting JFK or Connally or both, then the fatal gunshot on JFK should be from behind where Oswald was; but the fatal JFK gunshot was from the front. The powerful gunshot to blow JFK head came from the **front** as recorded in Zapruder film while Oswald was **behind** JFK.

It's hard to say that Oswald was the shooter of JFK from behind since based on Altgens' photograph a big tree with thick leaves was standing between Oswald and JFK motorcade. That is the fact. A tree is still standing over there in 2012; it could be the same or different tree, but this tree was blocking the accuracy of shooting.

To convince that Oswald was the assassin or not, in December 2012 I went to sixth floor of Texas School Book Depository, now the museum, to assure that the angle of shooting did or did not conform to the fact of the first crime scene. The first crime scene is the spot on Dealy Plaza in front of Texas School Book Depository at Elm Street where JFK was shot at the first time and he held his neck with his hand as photographed by Altgens. This spot is now marked with white "X" on the street a couple yards from Elm street intersection at the Dealey Plaza. The display on the sixth floor museum depicts that Oswald nest was next to the windows where the boxes were stacked and facing the small lot. The Texas School Book Depository is located on the west corner of Houston Street and Elm Street facing south; the building's left side wall is facing Houston Street just across Dal-Tex building.

If Oswald was next to the window on the right hand side of the building *facing parking lot* and not facing Elm Street when firing on JFK motorcade –and the effect as recorded in Altgen's photograph--, then it is absolutely impossible for Oswald to fire his rifle to JFK, because there are *the building corner and the tree* blocking him from JFK motorcade. Even if Oswald was facing Elm Street, it's still impossible to fire JFK's neck from behind, it should have been from the right side of JFK; the ballistic evidence never matched the available theory.

This condition may also be found at http://www.jfk.org/go/about where the tree was blocking Oswald nest and JFK motorcade. On the Exhibit No. 900 of The Warren Report, this tree is even very clear to be present at the right hand side of JFK motorcade [160]. If Oswald did, then his bullets would hit the building corner first and definitely have to penetrate the brick wall and/or glass window, going through the tree branches and/or tree leaves before hit JFK at a distance of 218 feet. Oswald nest on the sixth floor was conforming only to the second crime scene which was marked with the other "X" next to the grassy knoll before Stemmons Freeway, but it's too far for his Carcano rifle bullets to reach motorcade. Oswald's Carcano rifle only effective toward any target up to 200 feet while the distance between Oswald's nest and the motorcade next to the grassy knoll right before Stemmons Freeway is almost 307 feet which is beyond the range of Carcano rifle. He ever used it to shoot General Walker without lethal effect because the target was too far and behind the glass window.

On this second crime scene, *JFK head was moving backward and a portion of his head was scattered behind him on the limousine trunk* as the proof that the shot was coming from his front while Oswald was behind JFK. Even, if Oswald fired the shots from Texas School Book Depository *behind* JFK targeting the *second* crime scene and **his bullets made the amazing sharp U-turn to hit JFK from the *front***; then who did fire the shots targeting the *first* crime scene?

It should have been someone at **Dal-Tex** Building (now is the gift shop selling JFK memorabilia), from this position the sniper was **not blocked** by any tree since the tree was a couple feet on the right hand side of JFK motorcade. If Oswald was next to the window on the FRONT left side of the building *facing Elm Street* when firing on JFK motorcade –JFK held his neck as recorded in Altgen's photograph--, then it is absolutely impossible for Oswald to fire his rifle to JFK, because there are **the trees** blocking him from JFK motorcade.

Either Oswald's position inside Texas School Book Depository sixth floor was next to the window on the right hand side of the building *facing parking lot,* or next to the window on the FRONT left side of the building *facing Elm Street,* the Carcano bullets could not penetrate JFK's neck from the front or behind since Oswald was on the right hand side of JFK. If Oswald did, the bullets should have penetrated JFK's neck and groin (not back) from his right hand side to his left hand side not from behind to front. If Oswald shot JFK's head, then the bullet(s) should have penetrated his right temple to his left temple; not from right temple to the rear head (Part Five: Chapter 3. Autopsy).

Had Oswald fired his rifle from FRONT right side of the Texas School Book Depository sixth floor *facing Elm Street,* then the museum makes a confusing display of Oswald nest. To decide that Oswald was involved in JFK assassination is "That's a lot to think about!" *)

The ballistic **trajectory**

Exhibit 1   Exhibit 2

On Exhibit 1, the fact is JFK neck's wound from bullet entered his neck and penetrated his tie knot, indicating that the bullet either entered from his front or back side; while Oswald was on the right side of JFK. If Oswald fired on JFK then the neck wound must be from right to left side as displayed on Exhibit 2.

The other fact surrounding JFK assassination is the existence of a woman named Rose Cherami who told police that JFK would be killed, she worked for Jack Ruby night club and knew both Ruby and Oswald [161] [162] [163] [164] [165] [166]. She might overhear the plot and told police but no further follow-up.

The following paragraphs are the excerpts from Gary Richard Schoener's "A Legacy of Fear":

"Rose Cherami: On November 20, 1963 Rose Cherami (born Melba Christine Marcades) was thrown from a vehicle on highway 190 near Eunice, Louisiana. She was taken to the local hospital and then to jail, but moved to the East Louisiana State Hospital in Jackson when it appeared that she was having narcotic withdrawal. She told Dr. Victor J. Weiss Jr., a psychiatrist, that the President and other public officials were going to be killed on their visit to Dallas. After the President and Texas Governor John Connally were shot in Dallas on November 22, Dr. Weiss told at least one friend, Mr. A H. Magruder about the incident. Rose Cherami, who had a long-criminal record and 19 known aliases, told Lt. Francis Fruge of the Louisiana State Police that she had been part of a narcotics ring working between Louisiana and Houston. On November 26, four days after the assassination, she was released from the hospital in the custody of Lt. Fruge and Capt. Ben Morgan of the Louisiana State Police plus Anne Diechler of the Revenue Division."

"They flew to Houston to investigate the narcotics ring and on the flight Rose allegedly picked up a newspaper which had a story about Jack Ruby's murder of Lee Harvey Oswald in which Ruby was quoted as denying he had ever known Oswald. According to Lt. Fruge Rose laughed and stated that Ruby and Oswald were very good friends, had been in Ruby's club together, and were even "bed partners."

"Upon arrival in Houston she repeated this claim to Capt. Morgan but refused to talk to federal authorities saying she didn't want to get involved in this mess. According to Lt. Fruge, the information Rose Cherami supplied about the narcotics ring was "true and good information." "When an investigator working for New Orleans District Attorney Jim Garrison attempted to locate Rose Cherami in early 1967, he learned that she had been killed on September 4, 1965, when a car ran over part of her head near Big Sandy, Texas."

"The driver of the car, who reported the accident to the Texas Highway Patrol after taking Rose to the hospital, claimed that the accident had been unavoidable because the victim had been lying on the roadway with her head and the upper part of her body resting on the traffic lane. Due to the unusual circumstances and the lack of prominent physical evidence, Officer J. A. Andrews attempted to determine whether the driver and Rose had any relationship. He found no evidence of such and although he was allegedly not completely satisfied that he had all the facts, he closed the case since the victim's relatives did not pursue the matter.

Left unanswered was how Rose Cherami ended up lying on the highway, especially Texas highway 155, a "farm to market road." Had she been hitchhiking at 2 AM when the accident occurred, one would have expected her to have been on either of the two larger U. S. highways, 80 and 271, which parallel Texas highway 155. And, last but not least, was Rose Cherami's alleged prediction a lucky guess and were her statements about the Ruby-Oswald connection fabrications, or did she really know something of importance?" [167]

Let us transfer the long word describing this very important link in the investigation of Oswald into a computer algorithm and Boolean algebra, while the practical computer programming may utilize **dBase** or artificial intelligence **LISP**:

Line #01 *JFK was assassinated*
Line #02   *Do think while .True.*
Line #03
Line #04   *Facts*

Line #05	*Oswald was a suspect*
Line #06	*Rose Cherami told Police 2 days before*
Line #07	*FK would be murdered*
Line #08	*JFK FatalWound from Bullet entering TempleToBackhead*
Line #09	*Rose worked for JackRuby she knew Oswald*
Line #10	*Rose was killed by car*
Line #11	*EndFactsAvailable*
Line #12	
Line #13	*If he had a motive to do*
Line #14	*He left a message to Marina*
Line #15	*Find the motive*
Line #16	*Endif*
Line #17	
Line #18	*If he had no motive*
Line #19	*Someone had it*
Line #20	*He said "I'm a patsy"*
Line #21	*He denied killing TippitAndOrJFK*
Line #22	*If he was ordered a part*
Line #23	*Someone will complete job*
Line #24	*Endif*
Line #25	*Endif*
Line #26	
Line #27	*If he was targeting Connally for declining*
Line #28	*to change Oswald undesirable Navy discharge*
Line #29	*.And. telling someone*
Line #30	*Someone will complete job*
Line #31	*Endif*
Line #32	*EndDo*

Lee Harvey Oswald died and left behind some unanswered questions for us, his bizarre life story and death started **from** his discharge from the service to his unusual immigration and his come back to USA with a Russian wife and a daughter, **to** the day he was accused of shooting the President until his tragic death on November 24, 1963. Here some unanswered questions and mysteries shrouding his short but wavy life [168]:

(1) He was early discharged on September 11, 1959 "to take care of his mother"; but rather than taking care of his mother, he went to Cuba and Soviet before enrolling at Albert Schweitzer College and University of Turku in Finland instead. If he petitioned for "hardship discharge", then **from where** the money to enroll the college and moved to Russia?

(2) What did happen to Oswald's friend Pvt. Martin D. Schrand a 18-year old classmate at the electronic school and a fellow Marine team who died from gunshot when guarding a super secret vehicle at Cubi Point, the Philippines on January 1958?

(3) The Defense Language Institute (DLI) has a special Russian language class for Oswald. Why did he learn the Russian language at DLI? Was he prepared to "defect"?

(4) With a support of US Marine Corps, he applied for US passport a week before discharge, and was granted on September 10, 1959 just a day prior to his discharge on September 11, 1959. Who did really need the passport?

(5) Did he go to Russia on his own intention or on a duty?

(6) When he was in Minsk, he wrote "a scientific report" about his environment including radio and television plants, demography, regular resident meeting, *production schedule*, workers profile, population figures, the city layout, etc. This is not a simple report, it is a strategic one; it indicated his comprehensive skill and sharp observation which could not be performed by the common people. If he went to Russia on his own intention, why did he have to make a special report about Minsk? To whom this report should be submitted?

(7) Because Minsk is one among the centers of Russian electronic industry including the semi conductors, it does make sense if a strategic planner thinks that Minsk has a secret factory to produce the nuclear missiles.

Did Oswald intentionally compromise the information of **obsolete** U-2 spy plane to win the KGB confidence in order to eventually obtain the information of nuclear production later?

(8) If Oswald did not disclose the secret of U-2 spy plane, why was Francis Gary Powers' U-2 shot down over Sverdlovsk just a couple months *after* Oswald immigration to Russia? Was it a coincidence or correlation?

(9) Francis Gary Powers the U-2 pilot was sure that there was the treason behind his fate to get shot down over Russian airspace in May 1960. Who did inform Russia about the exact **altitude** of U-2?

(10) US U-2 super spy planes have three different airbases, Atsugi Japan, Adana Turkey and Peshawar Pakistan to make them easy to sneak into Soviet airspace. Did Oswald compromise the presence of these different U-2 bases to KGB?

(11) Oswald was devoted to Marxism since he was 15 [169]. Was he recruited by Soviet intelligence agency in early 1954? A Western citizen who declared himself Marxist would be recruited by KGB as happened to **Donald Duart MacLean** a high level officer of British Foreign service. McLean was recruited by Soviet intelligence agency when he was only 18 in 1931; he had a very good career and very long role as KGB mole inside British intelligence.

(12) Was Francis Powers sacrificed to prove that Oswald was truthful (and) to obtain the bigger secret, like a bait to catch a big tuna?

(13) Was Oswald a double agent and then "double-crossed"?

(14) On August 5, 1963 Oswald visited a Cuban exile Carlos Bringuier at his business store, Oswald said he was anti-Castro and offered the help. A couple days later Oswald distributed the pro-Castro leaflets, Bringuier confronted Oswald when learned that it was the same Oswald who offered help for anti-Castro group. When the Police was questioning Oswald, why did John L. Quigley a government agent intervene?

(15) Who did go to Mexico, Oswald or his impersonator?

(16) Henry Wade, the Dallas District Attorney heard from a reliable source that Oswald's official ID number was 110669 and his number on "a sanitized file" was 289248. Who did pay for him $200.00 per month?

(17) Why did Oswald leave the Texas Book Depository Building and go home after the Kennedy's assassination?

(18) Why did two persons driving a car tap the horn twice in front of Oswald home as he went home after leaving Texas Book Depository Building? Who are they?

(19) At the time of Officer Tippit was shot to death at 1:10 PM, Oswald was already inside the Texas Theatre building since 1:00 PM as the theatre manager Warren Burroughs witnessed; and he was still there until apprehended by the Dallas Police officer. Oswald went downstairs to buy popcorn [170] from Burroughs at 1:15 PM. Burroughs is a reliable witness. Who's the person resembled Oswald entering the Texas Theatre at 1:35 PM as John Brewer witnessed? It's absolutely impossible that Oswald were at two places at the very same time.

(20) Why did he work for William B. Reily company which very close to the government agency garage?

(21) Why Oswald name was not included in the security index prior to Kennedy's visit to Dallas, Texas?

(22) Why did he leave behind no message for his wife Marina just in case he did not come home, unlike he did before when he shot General Walker?

(23) Did Oswald and Jack Ruby know each other? If yes, in what occasion? Why the witness who knew their relationship mysteriously died e.g. Rose Cherami, Dorothy Kilgallen and Jack Ruby himself?

(24) Oswald did not shot officer JD. Tippit, instead someone else did. Warren Reynolds was the witness and he chased the killer of Tippit, two months after Reynolds failed to identify Oswald as Tippit's killer, Reynolds was shot to death on his head allegedly by Darrell W. Garner, later Garner died from "overdose". Why was Reynolds murdered while he intended to help the police to nab the shooter of officer Tippit? And why Garner the allegedly killer of Reynolds was also found dead mysteriously?

(25) George de Mohrenschildt was a Russian-born geologist and lived at Forth Worth, Texas; he was introduced to Oswald and his Russian-born wife Marina Prusakova in the summer of 1962.

Mohrenschildt had heard of the Oswald from the Russian-speaking immigrants in the Dallas area. After Kennedy was assassinated, de Mohrenschildt testified before the Warren Commission in 1964 about his relationship with Oswald. In 1977, prior to his due to testify before the HSCA, he committed suicide; shortly before his tragic death, he was interviewed by author Edward Jay Epstein who wrote in his diary dated March 29, 1977 that David Bludworth, the State's Attorney asked whether Epstein had de Mohrenschildt's black address book.

When he said "No", Bludworth politely asked the same question over and over a half-dozen times about de Mohrenschildt's black book. This black address book must be very important, what is in the book? Does it contain the plot to kill Kennedy?

(26) Sam Giancana (1908 – 1975) the underworld boss of Chicago in his biography stated that he knew Lyndon Johnson, Richard Nixon, and de Mohrenschildt. Was Giancana assassinated because he knew about the plot to kill Kennedy?

(27) Trenton Parker, a former government agent said he had the secret tapes recording the plot to kill Kennedy. Parker handled the tapes over to Congressman **Lawrence McDonald** shortly before he boarded on Korean Airline flight (KAL-007). This flight departed from Anchorage, Alaska on August 31, 1983 and its experienced pilot -with thousands of hours on Boeing 737- took the very unusual route over the Russian restricted airspace where the secret military training was going on. The aftermath dispute contending the KAL-007 was on international airspace, and another account accusing the pilot took a shortcut on his way from Anchorage to Seoul to save the fuel, while another account accusing this commercial plane was on a spy mission and loaded with the military gears to record the Russian military training; and therefore the Russian did not take any risk to let any party to peep into.

The Soviet government claimed that the KAL-007 real purpose of breaching the Soviet airspace was to peep into the air defenses of ultra sensitive Soviet military zone in the Kamchatka and Sakhalin. The Russian military training is always a secret mission, and only a handful people knew.

Whenever someone **knew** that Congressman Larry McDonald was about to board on KAL-007 flight while he had had on hand the secret tapes containing the plot to kill Kennedy –which in turn would have been exonerating Oswald- and then either these tapes should have been destroyed or McDonald should have been stopped from using the tapes for any purpose.

From this point, is it possible to assume that the KAL-007 **was intentionally** *misguided* to the Russian airspace with a certain consequence to get shot down? Why was the pilot so sure until the end that he never breached the Soviet airspace? Why the Anchorage Voice Operated Recording (VOR) beacon was "not operational" for any reason at that time although the KAL-007 got the Notice to Airmen (NOTAM)? To avoid another accident after the KAL-007 incident, President Ronald Reagan authorized to make GPS free for everyone, it was a secret project.

We are sure nobody could answer these questions. Lee Harvey Oswald never been tried in the court, he died from handgun shot by Jack Ruby just on his way to be transferred into county jail in front of journalists and police officers at Dallas Police Headquarter. Some people believed that Oswald killed police officer Tippit and US President John F. Kennedy while no single reliable proof and no single credible witness ever testified in the court. We may have a simple question: Is someone considered guilty until proven innocent, or considered innocent until proven guilty?

---

[145] McKnight, Gerald D., "*Breach of Trust*", University Press of Kansas, 2005, p. 299.
[146] McKnight, *ibid*.
[147] Bahry, Abdul R., "*Jihad: Struggle or Terrorism*" 1stBook Library, Bloomington IN, 2002, p. 40
[148] http://en.wikipedia.org/wiki/PRRI
[149] McKnight, *ibid.* p. 300
[150] Epstein, Edward Jay, "*Legend: The Secret World of Lee Harvey Oswald*" McGraw-Hill, 1978, p. 111

[151] *ibid.*, p. 107
[152] *ibid.*, p. 117
[153] Bahry, *ibid.*
[154] hubpages.com
[155] jfkmurdersolved.com
[156] http://en.wikipedia.org/wiki/John_Roselli
[157] Fetzer, James H. (ed.), "*Murder In Dealy Plaza*", Catfeet Press, Chicago, 2000, pp. 298-311
[158] http://en.wikipedia.org/wiki/Lee_Harvey_Oswald
[159] Fetzer, *ibid.*
*) This is Ike Altgens quotation as an actor on *Beyond the Time Barrier* movie
[160] The Warren Report, pp. 306-307
[161] http://en.wikipedia.org/wiki/Lee_Harvey_Oswald
[162] http://sport.acorn.net/JFKplace/09/Kelin34/fear.html
[163] mayferrell.org
[164] jfkonline.com
[160] spartacus.schoolnet.co.uk
[165] sport.acorn.net
[166] http://sport.acorn.net/JFKplace/09/Kelin34/fear.html
[167] The questions were summarized and inspired from many sources especially Smith's "*Conspiracy*", McKnight's "*Breach of Trust*", Dankbaar's "Files of Kennedy", Fuhrman's, "*A Simple Act of Murder*", and various sources including newspapers, magazines, radio/TV and movie.
[169] Posner, Gerald "*Case Closed*", Random House, New York 1993, p. 320
[170] Groden, Robert J. "*The Search for Lee Harvey Oswald*", Penguin Studio Books, New York 1995, p. 148

5. Bahia de Cochinos

The political magnitude of this invasion would be a subject to perennial discussion in the political science beyond the small area of Bahia de Coshinos

Bahía de Cochinos is a Spanish name for a small passage on the southern coast of Cuba, it was known as the Bay of Pigs. The name, the meaning and the geography of the Bay of Pigs sometimes is nothing compared to the political magnitude of the military-style invasion in 1961. In May 1959, the USA still did not know who is Castro, a senior US officer described Castro as "a new spiritual leader of Latin American democratic and anti-dictator forces" [171]. As the US realized that Castro was leaning to the Soviet Union during the Cold War, then the effort to topple him was well prepared. The Bay of Pigs or Bahia de Cochinos incident was an attempt by about 1,500 Cuban exiles in Miami under the command of US in an effort to topple Cuban communist leader Fidel Castro who just took Cuba over from Fulgencio Batista in 1959.

The common question relating to Bay of Pigs invasion is about "who led whom, and who invaded whom"; the most acceptable explanation is a CIA-sponsored attempt to overthrow the government of Cuban Prime Minister Fidel Castro in April 1961 using the Cuban exiles in Miami who did not like the socialist government that already made them the exiles in USA. The group of Cuban exiles did not have the weapon to invade their own country, and the CIA did not have the enough manpower to invade Cuba; the invasion looked bizarre in today's criteria, but in 1961 under the shadow of Cold War and within the socialism-capitalism dichotomy, a such invasion or "similar effort" to topple the "leftist" government was justifiable. The political magnitude of this invasion would be a subject to perennial discussion in the political science beyond the small area of *Bahia de Cochinos*. Some analyst concluded that the failure of *Bahia de Cochinos* invasion had led to the assassination of President John F. Kennedy in 1963 as retaliation against his unwillingness to fully support the invasion.

Although *Bahia de Cochinos* invasion was not Kennedy's idea, but he fully supported it; the problem is the coordinated communication which was not properly conducted in the "comprehensive" headquarters unlike today's ultra modern communication system.

The Cuban crisis was the legacy of John F. Kennedy's predecessor Dwight D. Eisenhower during the Cold War Era. In 1960 Eisenhower approved the covert action to invade Cuba in order to influence the dissatisfying Cubans to rebel against Castro. On March 1960, President Eisenhower on the recommendation of the Central Intelligence Agency to prepare the invasion of Cuba; for this effort a special forces originated from the Cuban exiles were established, the plan was code-named **Operation Pluto**. The plan was organized by Richard M. Bissell, Jr., CIA Deputy Director for Plans, under CIA Director Allen Dulles. John F. Kennedy never intended to invade Cuba even though he knew communist Castro took Cuba over from Fulgencio Batista is 1959. JFK approved this operation; however another report asserts that President John F. Kennedy disapproved the plan [172].

At the onset of his presidency, as a new President, within first 100 days in the office, in March 13, 1961 JFK hosted a warm reception for the Latin American Diplomats and announced the establishment of the Alliance for Progress to improve the quality of education and to promote the economic development for all Latin American countries, minus Cuba. This was a remarkable diplomatic approach from the USA toward the Latin American (poor) countries to win the warm hearts and to prevent them from being marauded by the communist. In the diplomacy language, the food and education should have come first before the weapon to deal with the designated poor countries.

Castro was initially considered a weak leader and easy to topple like those of Jocobo Arbenz Guzmán of Guatemala in 1954, however not less than **nine** US Presidents were unable to topple Castro until he tired and resigned from the power and replaced by his brother Raul Castro in 2008.

The assumption that assassination of John F. Kennedy as a result of retaliatory conspiracy over failure of the **Bahia de Cochinos** was questionable, President Kennedy already approved the invasion and he never declined sending the supporting troops, but due to the miscommunication between the top staffs, and then **George McBundy** *aborted* the invasion, President Kennedy *did not*. JFK never cancelled the Bay of Pigs invasion, George Bundy did. Some discrepancies happened in the crisis situation such as the confusing time zone since the atomic clock was not invented yet, situation room, central command, and communication system which are fixed later after the crisis.

Even though the origin of **Bahia de Cochinos** invasion was from Eisenhower administration; yet President Kennedy approved it. When a commander of beleaguered ship convoy sent a radio message to Washington asking for the Naval help, neither the CIA nor the Navy was aware of the latest development of invasion and nobody ever approached the President for this special message, the convoy was aborted instead. Theodore C. Sorensen a close aid to the White House declared that it was the ONLY request for help made by the ship convoy at the Bay of Pigs and it NEVER reached President. According to another account, the CIA requested President the Air Force cover for the convoy withdrawal but was refused [173], abandoning the Cuban exiles invading Cuba to their own fate where more that 1,000 men captured and around one hundred killed [174]. The invaders were left behind on their fate and later were released for 35 million dollars. The fiasco of Bay of Pigs invasion was a result of **miscommunication**, neither the ExComm members nor the invasion planners were at the **situation room** monitoring every single minute of the war development; this strategic mistake might have been fixed now. If there was any disapproval over the invasion outcome, then the Kennedy's decision to openly confront Cuba and Soviet Union altogether by preparing the combat ready troops on October 8 - 28, 1962 should have been a relief and a proof that JFK supported the mission to Cuba (please read Cuban Missile Crisis Chapter).

During two-week mounting tension, John F. Kennedy sent 11 destroyers, addressed the nation on October 22, 1962, cooperated with the Organization of America States (OAS) foreign ministers, directed the United States Armed Forces to prepare for any possibility, called the army reservists, warned Cuba and Soviet Union "technicians" about the hazards, called for emergency meeting of the OAS and UN Security Council, intensively discussed the crisis with the ExComm, and negotiated with UN Secretary General U Thant as well. These actions were more than enough to fulfill American need to respond the crisis; and there is no retaliatory conspiracy necessary over the invasion failure.

The latest analysis of *Bahia de Cochinos* Invasion reveals the possibility of "Cuban Chess Game" a deliberate intention of the Soviet Union to let USA invaded Cuba although the Soviet Union had had the available information prior to the invasion. The purpose of this action was to make Cuba more dependent to the Soviet Union so it could use Cuba as a jumping pad to strike USA; it's a tip of balance against the USA which used West Berlin and Turkey to place the nuclear missiles ready to strike the Soviet Union.

In the middle of April 1961 the invasion on the Bay of Pigs takes place anyway. The Bay of Pigs is a point of no return, it's to win or to die, no escape option available. The Bay of Pigs is southern Cuban shore with marshland. If something goes wrong nobody can escape to the nearby highland. Unfortunately, this crucial information **was withheld from President John F. Kennedy**. His last minute "approval with a note" was on 1:45 PM April 15, 1961 just **three** months after his inauguration. Soon, the US airplanes attacked Cuban airfield, but because there's the lack of accuracy then was only 5 out 50 Cuban planes destroyed.

On April 17, 1961 1,500 Cuban exiles under the supervision of US commando invaded the Bay of Pigs. More than 1,000 men captured and the others were killed, a total fiasco because the backup troops were unavailable and the Plan B was never made.

The invading troops asked the US President to send the additional troops, but *the request never reached him*; however he was still considered to decline the request; a mounting uproar and upset just awaiting to go off. It's not fair. Are we surprised when every investigation on his assassination always facing the dead end, even since the day one on the ground zero until now, 16,000 days later?

The decision to stop FJK may be understandable whenever we trace back to the comprehensive background during the Cold War under the threat of devastating nuclear war, but nobody ever explained this motive. The plan to stop JFK might be spreading among the certain people such as overheard by Rose Cherami; anyway the plan should have been executed on time. This thesis may explain J. Rosselli's mysterious death prior to his testimony before the HSCA; and also may shed the light on why Robert Kennedy was murdered just one step before winning the US Presidency. To let Rosselli to testify will disclose the secret job Rosselli knew; and to let Robert Kennedy to be a US President will imply to allow him to comb the clue of his brother's assassination. Also, this thesis may explain why Jimmy Hofa vanished until now after brokering a secret job for Rosselli's friends. The silence is golden, and let the history becomes the wise judge.

[171] Weiner, *ibid.*, p. 180
[172] Karen Bornemann Spies, "*John F. Kennedy*", Enslow Publishing Inc., Berkeley Height, NJ, 1999, p. 9
[173] Smith, *ibid.* p. 11
[174] *ibid.*, p. 11-12

6. Cuban Missile Crisis

> The USA is always ready to launch the nuclear
> weapons, but it never be ready to get launched on
> even a single nuclear weapon

The Cuban crisis was the legacy of John F. Kennedy's predecessor Dwight D. Eisenhower, not Kennedy's himself. John F. Kennedy never initiated to invade Cuba even though he knew communist Castro took Cuba over from Fulgencio Batista in 1959; and therefore this young and elegant 35th US President was considered by his opponents as too soft to the communism, the number one American enemy. The placement of Soviet nuclear missiles in Cuba in 1962 might have been changing John F. Kennedy, he never be same thereafter. He had a concern about nuclear missiles which were placed in the US "back yard", as a Supreme Commander of the US Army he had the rights to deploy the nuclear weapon as necessary. He was reported as having the deep concern about the safety of Americans especially the children and the future of America.

Prior to the Cuban Missile Crisis, when the tension between Soviet and America during Cold War was mounting, the world was surprised by the shooting down of U-2 a super spy airplane on May 1, 1960 over Sverdlovsk deep inside the Soviet Union soil. This shocking incident had destroyed the peace talk which was supposed to be held in Paris between Soviet Prime Minister Nikita Sergeyevich Khrushchev and President Dwight David Eisenhower on May 16, 1960.

In fact, President Eisenhower ordered the Defense Secretary to abstain from sending any U-2 flight over Soviet Union *after* April 1960 until further notice because he did not want to jeopardize the summit meeting, but nobody listened; it's a proof that a US President is **not always** an absolute Commander in Chief. When the world almost went off after U-2 incident, another shocking incident happened on April 15, 1961; the American bomber dropped the bombs on the Cuban airfield and destroyed Cuban airplanes.

The willful breaching of any country airspace with the military aircraft is a war, no matter what the reason is; as Japan did on the Pearl Harbor 16 years earlier. A couple days later on April 17, 1961 America **invaded** Cuba on the Bay of Pigs; no doubt that the war had really begun.

Nonetheless, beside some provocative incidents; President John F. Kennedy had successfully persuaded Nikita Khrushchev to meet in Vienna June 3-4, 1961 five weeks after April 17, 1961 unsuccessful invasion of the Bay of Pigs. Their meeting was extraordinary since the arm race between two superpowers the USA and the Soviet Union was soaring especially in the open air nuclear testing. The topics of Vienna meeting were:

(1) mutual involvement in Laos and to make it remain neutral,

(2) the nuclear disarmament, the reciprocal inspection was not necessary,

(3) Khrushchev to promise that would be no more nuclear test unless the USA did first,

(4) to agree in disagreement about the Berlin wall; it had been subject to the escape of 2.7 million people since 1949-1961.

The receding tension between the US and the SU after Vienna summit did not last longer when on August 30, 1961 Khrushchev announced to resume the nuclear test only three months after the summit; and the USA did the same; soon the world once more time was on the brink of the nuclear disaster. When President John F. Kennedy went home from the summit and realized how serious the world situation was, he ordered to call 200,000 army reservists and urged the American to build the portable nuclear shelter at home with sufficient food and water supply.

Two months after Kennedy-Khrushchev summit in Vienna, East Germany troops under the command of East Germany President Walter Ulbricht on August 13, 1961 set the roadblocks and barbed wires around East Berlin.

Willy Brandt the Mayor of West Berlin asked the immediate help, and President John F. Kennedy sent 1,500 more US soldiers to the West Germany. Around this critical moment, a group of US soldiers under the leadership of Sergeant Johnson who were assigned to guard the US missile command in West Germany were invited by a close friend for a party at a local night club. As soon they left, the Soviet's KGB plumbers entering the US super secret missile command to steal the military secrets. KGB, with a low cost bribery has successfully breached the security of US compound while the US never successfully stole the Soviet military secret with the low cost.

When the US under President Eisenhower decided to install the Thor and Jupiter missiles in Europe in 1959; the Soviet Union might perceive the US action as offensive since the missiles may reach Moscow within 30 minutes or less while no one single Soviet missiles may reach Washington DC within same minutes. Therefore, the Soviet Union decided to install the nuclear weapons in Cuba, a Soviet ally, under the disguise of "farming cooperation". According to surveillance plane, there were 9 missiles only to install, 6 R-12 MRBMs with 1,200 miles (2,000 kilometers) range, and 3 R-14 IRBMs with 2,800 miles (4,500 kilometers) range enough to reach Washington DC within 29 minutes which is 1,131 miles away from San Cristobal missile site. These US major cities might be other targets within minutes if the Soviet missiles have the speed of Mach 3:

Missile	Possible Target	Mile Distance	Minutes
R-14	Atlanta, GA	742	12
R-14	Raleigh, NC	900	23
R-14	Houston TX	924	24
R-14	Nashville, TN	935	24
R-14	Saint Louis, MO	1,166	30
R-16	New York, NY	1,307	34
R-16	Los Angeles, CA	2,292	60
R-16	Seattle, WA	2,770	72

This number turned to be wrong when Castro disclosed 30 years later to former US Secretary of State McNamara. It was not 9 [nine] only, the U-2 spy planes were not able to observe all Soviet nuclear weapons either due to rush to avoid the sophisticated **Dvina** anti aircraft or due to technology limitations at that time. In 1992, in an international meeting in Havana Cuba about Cuban Missile Crisis, former US Secretary of Defense Robert S. McNamara who attended the meeting was briefed by Fidel Castro that the number of Soviet warheads on Cuba Island was 162 [one hundred sixty two]! This number is more than enough to raze down all the US major cities. The Soviet Union decided to install the nuclear missiles in Cuba in August 1962 after considering these facts:

(1) April 15, 1961; the US dropped the bombs on Cuba airfield.

(2) April 17, 1961; the US invaded Cuba to topple Fidel Castro a Soviet ally.

(3) 1959-1961, the US installed Thor and Jupiter missiles in the UK, Turkey and Italy.

The first missile arrived on September 8, 1962 and soon on September 11 *) the Soviet Union publicly issued a warning that any attack against Cuba or Soviet ships delivering supplies to Cuba would be seriously considered the war. The Soviets initially stated that they were assisting Cuba in the irrigation and agricultural cooperation; they confidently denied any offensive weapon shipping to Cuba.

The Soviet's official sources such as Ambassador Anatoly Dobrynin and TASS news agency always declined that Soviet Union had had intention to install the offensive nuclear missiles in Cuba. Even a Soviet Embassy staff conveyed a personal message to President Kennedy from Soviet Prime Minister Khrushchev that no any missile would be sent to Cuba [175]. Therefore, when the US found the evidence that some Soviet missiles had been installed in Cuba, JFK had no plan on hand since he had been convinced that the Soviets would never install nuclear missiles in Cuba.

He called the EXCOMM to discuss several options including naval quarantine.

The world tension seemed never stopped, the incident came and went one after another; on October 16, 1962 U-2 spy plane revealed the presence of Soviet missiles placed in Cuba. The discovery of Soviet missiles in Cuba had drawn the hard reaction from the US; on October 20, 1962 US imposed the naval defensive quarantine over Cuba to prevent Soviet ships from delivering the supplies to Cuba. Quarantine is a blockade, a blockade is a war. A vast amount of B-52 bombers -some of them might be carrying the nuclear bombs- had been sent encircling near Cuban airspace; and 180 naval ships had been sent to Florida along with some hundreds of thousands of troops. It's a war! The world situation was frightening. For those who were not born yet in that year, it would rather delicate to understand the daily tension under the threat of the nuclear war and the possibility of World War III.

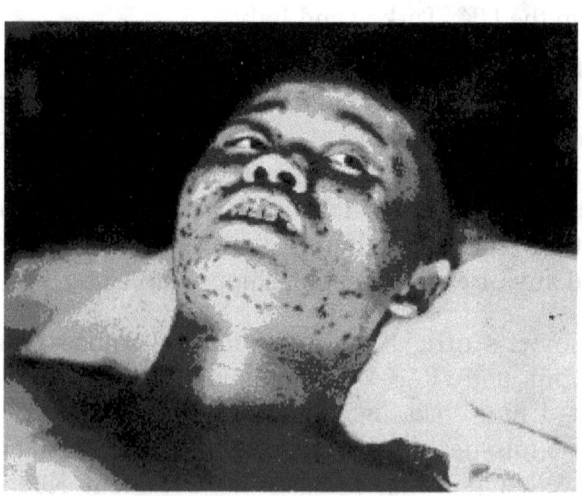

The victim of Atomic bomb in Hiroshima, August 6, 1945.
Photo by Gonichi Kimura, courtesy of **Hiroshima Peace Memorial Museum**, Japan. It seems that victim's face was severely dotted by the radiation.

Meanwhile in August 1962 the US intelligence obtained the information that the Soviet jet fighters and bombers were in Cuba already; it's a confirmation over the previous secret information obtained from Colonel Penkovsky a KGB officer that the Soviet Union had had a plan to install the nuclear missiles in Cuba. This was the time for the US to send U-2 spy planes over Cuba for a field confirmation and to photograph the missile sites. The US publicly acknowledged that it obtained the information pertaining to the Soviet missile installation from U-2 spy plane on September 14, 1962 and ever since sent another spy planes over and over to monitor the latest development of missile installation until October 27, 1962 when a U-2 was shot down and its pilot was killed during this mission.

Cuba is only 90 miles away from US soil; it takes only a couple minutes for a MRBM to destroy the main US cities whenever the nuclear war starts; if it happens then the Americans would be suffering from the nuclear explosion as the Japanese did. The consideration of using Cuba as a Soviet nuclear station is to tip the balance of US nuclear installation in Germany, Turkey and Italy. The Soviet Union decision to secretly install the nuclear weapon in Cuba was intended to surprise the USA; but Colonel Penkovsky a KGB officer provided this ultra secret information to the USA in advance to prevent the nuclear confrontation. By this action, Penkovsky put his life at risk and he knew this risk. In order to protect Penkovsky as a secret source, the USA publicly acknowledged that the information pertaining to the Soviet missile installation in Cuba was obtained by the U-2 surveillance plane over Cuba. It was unusual where the secret information about U-2 was publicly disclosed just to protect the higher secret, Penkovsky, only to be compromised by Jack Dunlap later on. **Dunlap** (1927-1963) was a US Army sergeant worked for National Security Agency and became a spy for the Soviet Union for money; when his role as an informant for KGB was revealed he "committed suicide". The other information asserts that he was assassinated by the carbon monoxide poisoning to make his death looks natural.

KGB soon arrested Penkovsky on 22 October 1962 just before President Kennedy's historic address to the nation informing the discovery of Soviet missiles in Cuba after sending U-2 spy plane to photograph the missile site [176]. The development of world tension was so fast and frightening; just about two years from **May 1, 1960 to October 26, 1962** several high profile incidents which might have led to the war had occurred. From a couple months before John F. Kennedy inauguration until his short tenure, the frightening incidents happened, one after another:

(1) May 1, 1960; the US spy plane U-2 was shot down over Sverdlovsk Russia, the impact was the cancellation of the summit meeting between Khrushchev and Eisenhower (just a few months before JFK inauguration).

(2) April 15, 1961; the US bombers bombed Cuban airfield.

(3) April 17, 1961; unsuccessful invasion of the Bay of Pigs.

(4) October 20, 1962; the US imposed the naval defensive quarantine over Cuba after the Soviet missiles in Cuba came into light.

(5) October 26, 1962; the confrontation between **USS Beale** a US warship and the **B-59** a Soviet submarine under the command of Savitsky which was loaded with the nuclear torpedo at the sea south of Florida.

These dangerous incidents all just took place within **2 years 4 months and 26 days**, based on these facts, it's most likely that the nuclear war will erupt soon within one year ahead. Therefore John F. Kennedy should have been **stopped** at any risk to save tens of millions of the American lives. The war is a harvest time for the arm producers and arm dealers, a satisfaction for the planners, and atrocity for the common people, women and children.

Four days after John F. Kennedy's quarantine announcement, on October 26, 1962 the Soviet Union Prime Minister NS. Khrushchev sent a very important letter stating that it would be no more weapons shipping to Cuba, and Soviet would voluntarily withdrew or destroyed them.

The tone of Khrushchev's letter seemed bowing down and the world might take a breath but, it was one day only. The very next day on October 27, 1962 under the pressure of members of Soviet Union politburo he sent another letter that was very different from the first. In this second letter, he demanded USA to remove the NATO's Jupiter nuclear missiles from Turkey under assumption that they could reach the Soviet Union much faster than from American soil. Under the military strategy, this demand was a real preparation for the Soviet Union to enter the nuclear war against the USA and NATO.

It was a very threatening situation; the world was expecting that the nuclear war between the Soviet Union and the USA would be erupting either today or tomorrow. The tension was still high when on the same day October 27, 1962 a U-2 US spy plane was shot down over Cuba and the pilot, Major Rudolf Anderson, was killed either during incident or killed as he was captured or to kill himself as instructed. As the world knew later, every U-2 pilot was instructed to kill himself rather than disclose the secret, Gary Powers another U-2 pilot who was shot down over Sverdlovsk Russia was instructed to kill himself, but he "forgot"; his suicide kit was displayed by the Soviet authority along with his gadgets.

Do we think that this tension was over? President John F. Kennedy asked the US Attorney General Robert Kennedy to call the Soviet Ambassador Anatoly Dobrynin to let him know that the USA declined the Soviet Union's request to remove the Jupiter nuclear missiles from Europe! The demand to remove the Jupiter nuclear missiles from Turkey as the NATO defense system was turned down; it does mean a step ahead to the nuclear war!

Amid the mounting tension, there was another tension. On November 2, 1963 Vietnamese President Ngo Din Diem was toppled in a *coup d'etat* by General Duong Van Minh, and the USA acknowledged the new Vietnamese military government under General Duong.

The Soviet Union consider the *coup d'etat* in Asia as an American strategy *to be closer to Laos* and at the same time to divide the Soviet concentration over its focus on American and European continents; now at a very same time the Soviet Union has three war fronts. President John F. Kennedy increased the number of U.S. military in South Vietnam from 800 to 16,300 although he might have considered of pulling out from Vietnam on his second term.

The speculation based on Secretary of Defense Robert McNamara's assertion about the seriousness of President Kennedy to pull the US troops out of Vietnam after the 1964 election. The Vietnam War seemed to be the urgent agenda of the Supreme Committee to contain Soviet in the Southeast Asia especially Laos where *a proxy war* was going on, if President Kennedy would stop it then it was an additional reason to stop him. The tremendous tensions came and went one after another during the very short tenure of John F. Kennedy! Under these so many decisive circumstances, do we still think that John F. Kennedy should have not been stopped?

In the US main doctrine as a derivative from Monroe doctrine, Fidel Castro should have been toppled, whether President John F. Kennedy did agree or not. The reason? It's safety of US people since Cuba is considered as a frog leap base for Soviet domination to the Latin America and at some points to touch the North America. Therefore, at least nine US Presidents John F. Kennedy, Lyndon B. Johnson, Richard M. Nixon, Gerald R. Ford, James E. Cater, Ronald W. Reagan, George H.W. Bush, William J. Clinton, George W. Bush, and Barack H. Obama never normalized the bilateral relationship with Cuba even after Fidel Castro resignation and succeeded by his brother Raul Castro in 2008.

Between September 5 to October 14, 1962 despite the increasing evidence of Soviet weapon delivery to Cuba, the US made no U-2 flights over Cuba to avoid another crisis yet on August 30, 1962 another U-2 flew over Soviet's Sakhalin Island "by mistake".

Luckily, the Soviets did not shot it down as it did on Gary Power's U-2 in May 1960; the US abruptly apologized but had to be worry if another U-2 flying over Cuba would be shot down; and that's what really happened on October 27, 1962.

Cuban President Osvaldo Dorticos on October 7, 1962 addressed the United Nation General Assembly:

> "If ... we are attacked, we will defend ourselves. I repeat, we have sufficient means with which to defend ourselves; we have indeed our inevitable weapons, the weapons, which we would have preferred not to acquire, and which we do ***not*** wish to employ. [177]"

On October 14, 1962 the American U-2 surveillance airplane took the photographs over Cuba and found that the Soviet medium range missile sites were under construction; when President John F. Kennedy saw the photographs on October 16, 1962 he was sure that Nikita S. Khrushchev was not playing around.

On October 18, 1962, President Kennedy discussed the important matter pertaining to the Soviet's Cuban missiles with Soviet Foreign Minister Andrei Gromyko in the Oval Office. In this meeting Gromyko stated that the missiles were for the *defensive* purpose only, not offensive.

Meanwhile, President JFK already knew from his previous briefing with his National Adviser Bundy that Soviet already built the missile sites in Cuba yet he did not disclose what he knew in this meeting to Gromyko or the public.

By next day, October 19, 1962 U-2 spy flights photographed 4 operational missile sites at San Cristobal, Cuba. Soon, the high alert to enforce the naval quarantine and to invade Cuba was imposed. The US military Armored Division and Strategic Air Command were well prepared for a real war. B-47 medium bombers and B-52 heavy bombers were on high alert to deploy; the war was expected today or tomorrow.

Once the war starts, it will not just the conventional war only, it would eventually become the nuclear war.

On October 22, 1962 President John F. Kennedy was addressing the nation about how serious the military danger coming from Cuba:

> It shall be the policy of this nation to regard any nuclear missile launched from Cuba against any nation in the Western Hemisphere as an attack on the United States, requiring a full retaliatory response upon the Soviet Union [178].

JFK appealed Khrushchev to stop his "reckless and provocative threat to world peace and to stable relations between our two nations.... The greater danger of all would be to do nothing ... Our goal is not the victory of might, but the vindication of right; not peace at the expense of freedom, but both peace and freedom... [179]". After his address to the nation, his popularity was soaring; Gallup poll showed that 84% Americans behind JFK action [180]. As the Soviet missile installation became obvious, the US considered attacking Cuba by air and sea, and in the ExComm meeting it was decided a military blockade should be imposed instead. Meanwhile, the Joint Chiefs of Staffs **unanimously** considered to launching a full-scale attack on Cuba; they were convinced that the [second] invasion to Cuba was the only solution; yet President Kennedy was skeptical since another invasion to Cuba after a 1961 failure would trigger the Soviet to *do the same over Berlin*. It was announced that the US would not permit any weapons delivery to Cuba; it was also demanded that the missile bases already under construction in Cuba have to be removed.

The Cuban Missile Crisis in fact was the confrontation between the US on one side and the Soviet Union plus Cuba on the other, but by the Rio Treaty, the Latin American countries might get involved as well. The Rio Treaty is the defense pact between the Latin American countries signed in Rio de Janeiro Brazil in 1947.

The core of this treaty is an attack against one among the members of Rio Treaty would be considered an attack against them all. This Latin hemispheric defense doctrine is actually an extension of Monroe Doctrine of 1823. The members of Rio Treaty are Argentina, Bahamas, Brazil, Chile, Colombia, Costa Rica, Cuba, Dominican Republic, El Salvador, Guatemala, Haiti, Honduras, Panama, Paraguay, Peru, Trinidad and Tobago, United States and Uruguay. Latin American "participation" in the US naval quarantine then involved two Argentine destroyers, one submarine and a Marine battalion; two Venezuelan destroyers and one submarine. Trinidad and Tobago offered its Naval Base for fellow Treaty Members imposing the naval quarantine against Cuba. Their involvement in this quarantine only to make the crisis more complicated rather than solving it.

At 7:00 pm, October 22, 1962, President Kennedy on the television addressed the nation publicly announcing the discovery of the missiles in Cuba. Now, the US is one hundred percent ready to war; the JFK address was a ***command sign*** for all US forces worldwide to be ready for the worst. On October 23, 1962, President Kennedy signed the Proclamation for Interdiction of the Delivery of Offensive Weapons to Cuba at the White House Oval Office. The real preparation for a nuclear confrontation with the Soviet Union has begun.

The Quarantine would be into effect on Wednesday morning 10:00AM October 24, 1962; and during the quarantine period 6 Soviet Union ships were stopped and turned back. According to the military doctrine, the quarantine is a first step prior to the military action. The successful outcome of naval quarantine had make John F. Kennedy cheering, he jokingly stated "I guess this is week I earn my first salary"; as the public knew that during his tenure John F. Kennedy never accepted any salary, his presidential salary was donated to the needy. A non-paid US President really deterred his political rivals since the Americans loved him dearly; he would surely win for second term. It's very sad; this generous President was assassinated.

The main purpose of his announcement was clear that quarantine was only a first military step before a real military invasion; it was a real challenge that the USA was ready to go to war with the Soviet Union at any cost, even if the nuclear missiles should have to be launched. This was a real danger to the world peace itself; from this point it is reasonable to assume that the Supreme Committee decided to "stop John F. Kennedy at any risk"; and that's what the world witnessed on Friday November 22, 1963 in Dallas, Texas.

On October 24, 1962 Khrushchev sent a letter to JFK arguing that the blockade is an act of aggression. On October 24, 1962 at evening; the Soviet TASS news agency broadcasted a telegram from Khrushchev to President Kennedy warning that the US "pirate action" would lead to war. This broadcast was followed by Khrushchev telegram to Kennedy at 10:52 pm EDT stating that the US blockade as an act of aggression and the Soviet ships were instructed **to ignore it**. It's an answer that the Soviet was also ready for the war.

Now, everybody preparing the food and water bottles ready to go the nearest government shelters like public library and city hall for protection from the nuclear fallout.

On October 26, 1962 the real result of quarantine was arising. Khrushchev sent the first letter to John F. Kennedy stating that **no more weapon** for Cuba, the Soviet Union would withdraw and destroy the missiles already sent to Cuba and "please do not invade Cuba", he added. But on the very next day the situation dramatically changed, **two** threatening incidents happened. The first incident was the very urgent letter from Khrushchev to John F. Kennedy demanding USA to remove the NATO's Jupiter missiles from Turkey in lieu of the missiles withdrawal from Cuba. The difference between Khrushchev's first letter and the second might be a result from the pressure of Politburo members. The second incident was the death of Major Anderson; he was the one and only casualty during Cuban Missile Crisis.

In the morning of October 27, 1962 Major Rudolf Anderson aboard U-2 spy plane was in special assignment to fly over Cuba. Around 12:00 pm EST the spy plane was shot down by S-75 Dvina Surface to Air Missile (SAM), this incident was increasing the tension that already mounted between the Soviet Union and the USA.

The shooting down of an U-2 should have been considered as the escalation of conflict into real war, the Soviet Union argued that it was an "accident", an order by local commander *without* authorization from Moscow, and therefore Nikita S. Khrushchev ordered General Pliyev the higher commander in Cuba *not* to shoot down the U-2 spy plane, but Major Anderson was already died; this incident made USAF General Curtis LeMay very upset, he was a member of "war committee" ExComm; he wanted USA to invade Cuba right away. Meanwhile the negotiation between two adversaries was tightly proceeding through the Secretary General of United Nation Organization, U Thant.

Upon receiving Khrushchev's letter John F. Kennedy was so eager to answer right away, he called Attorney General Robert Kennedy to meet the Soviet Ambassador Anatoly Dobrynin. The very emergency meeting was commenced on Saturday October 27, 1962 at the Attorney General Office. The answer from US President to the Government of USSR was NO nuclear removal from Turkey without European allies' approval while the USA accepted the Soviet offer to remove nuclear weapon from Cuba.

That's the message conveyed by Attorney General Robert Kennedy to the Soviet Union Ambassador to the USA Anatoly Dobrynin. At this point, Kennedy's answer was *a first step toward nuclear war* between the Soviet Union and USA; to decline the removal of Jupiter nuclear from Europe during Cuban missile crisis has only one meaning, conflict escalation.

President John F. Kennedy also demanded the Soviet Union to respond **within 24 hours** or would face a "further action"; this demand was the *second step toward a real war*, it does mean that the nuclear war should have been erupting on **Monday October 29, 1962**: Cuba and its whole contents including the un-launched nuclear missiles should have been eliminated. The World War III, nuclear war, was due on Monday October 29, 1962 00:01 AM.

Meanwhile if the war scenario goes on, the Cuban missile that already launched had reached Washington DC, and before Soviet Union having enough time, the Jupiter missiles were launched from Europe to the Soviet Union; a couple minutes later the Soviet Union Intercontinental Ballistic Missiles (ICBM) might have been deployed to Alaska and another targets. The nuclear warfare is a matter of *who does launch first will be credited with one-half win*, this is a paradigm in the nuclear war. It should be absolute apocalyptic catastrophe, and an irreversible detriment.

Therefore, before this disaster happens John F. Kennedy should have been stopped first. Less than 12 hours before the World War was supposed to erupt, III *Radio Moskwa* on **October 28, 1962** broadcasted that the Soviet Union had accepted the Kennedy proposal. The Soviet Union acceptance of President John F. Kennedy's ultimatum was publicly broadcasted because the Soviet Union had no time to send the official letter and they knew that *Radio Moskwa* was well monitored by the USA.

The placement of Soviet nuclear missiles in Cuba was intentionally and strategically calculated "to buy the time" just in case the nuclear war erupts; however the nuclear missile launched from Cuba would have reached American soil faster than from Vladivostok since Miami is only 228 miles away from Cuba. The Kennedy ultimatum "to respond within 24 hours or would face a *further action*" was *a very clear declaration to prepare either the war* or **nuclear war**, nothing else.

It was absolutely **not a bluff** against Soviet Union the country with the capability of using the weapon of mass destruction. Had a nuclear war erupted and the USA was hit first by the Soviet Union with weapon already installed in Cuba, who's the subject to blame?

It must be the person who opposed the effort to nip Castro in the bud! Although it might have been a misunderstanding, however the Supreme Committee and the decision maker thought that Kennedy "declined to eliminate Castro by declining to send the additional troop" during invasion on Cuba. From this point, **why not eliminating** this person first before the real disaster comes to take the life of sixty million Americans in a blink of eye? On Friday November 22, 1963 12:30 PM in Dallas Texas the mission accomplished, no one single American life lost due to the Soviet Union nuclear attack. The assassination of John F. Kennedy was an ultra **emergency salvage mission** by the Supreme Committee.

No doubt, the escalation of Bay of Pigs incident and Cuban missile crisis could have dragged the nations into the World War III; the Supreme Committee has successfully prevented it while the majority of ExComm members supported the invasion. It's still disputable until now should the Americans and the world have to be thankful to Supreme Committee for its critical role to avert the nuclear war.

On the other hand, JFK and his small group should have announced their decision to accept *quid pro quo* deal [181] they made at the Cabinet Room to McCone and his group. It's questionable on why this announcement was only for the limited very important persons –McCone was not included-- and they should have been sworn in secrecy. The official notice to the Director of CIA and the high Ranking Officials should have been conveyed by the White House Press Secretary to avoid any misunderstanding. The acceptance of quid pro quo is very important since it a beginning of war cancellation.

The Cuban crisis tension, communication chaos and deadlock might lead the plot to kill JFK, because everybody was guessing –or *suspecting*- what did Kennedy decide in the closed meeting at 7:30 PM with Attorney General Robert F. Kennedy and his close aides minus McCone the Director of CIA.

The decision to assassinate JFK was a very difficult and complicated choice ever, it's a better-off choice and not the best one; it's a **thorny choice** between eliminating one person or forty million US citizens as the ultimate risk if the Soviet Union to launch nuclear weapons from Cuba to American soil. If there was the ballot vote or referendum over what have to do, no doubt every US citizen decided unanimously what to do. "Is the assassination of JFK justified or not" is still disputable until now. If the answer is "yes" then it's no wonder if nobody would disclose the secret behind it because it was "an (un)official plan" to prevent JFK from authorizing nuclear war during his tenure, otherwise the US history should have been rewritten.

McCone (1902-1991), the CIA Director, and another ExComm members could have been presuming that JFK and his group were bypassing him because JFK *did not invite him* to a very crucial 7:30 PM meeting on October 27, 1962 in the Cabinet Room discussing *quid pro quo* i.e. Khrushchev's offer to pull the mid-range ballistic nuclear missiles from Cuba in lieu of pulling Jupiter missile system from Turkey and Italy that was aimed to the Soviet Union [182]. However, Khrushchev was a trustworthy international leader, when he came under political attack by his opponents in Kremlin for mishandling the Cuban Missile Crisis he did not disclose the deal that the US would dismantle Jupiter nuclear missile from Europe. The decision of JFK to skip Director of CIA from a very crucial meeting was an example of distorted communication system among the president's men; the other example was Bill Harvey's decision to invade Bay of Pig without clear order from President Kennedy [183].

Fidel Castro the Cuban Prime Minister and President for long time outlived President Kennedy while the US has ten Presidents since the Cuban Missile Crisis. On July 16, 2010 he unexpectedly showed up to publicly warn Cuba's Foreign Ministry about an impending devastating nuclear war if the United States, in alliance with Israel, tries to enforce international sanctions against Iranian nuclear power project [184][185]. His leadership is still strong; he also has predicted that the United States will attack North Korea to stop its nuclear program despite a fact that Korean needs more food than weapon.

[*] September 11 always became significant moment for violence?
[175] http://en.wikipedia.org/wiki/Cuba_Missile_Crisis
[176] http://en.wikipedia.org/wiki/Penkovsky
[177] http://en.wikipedia.org/wiki/Cuba_Missile_Crisis
[178] *ibid.*
[179] Spies, *ibid.* p. 109-115
[180] Spies, *ibid.*
[181] *quid pro quo* does mean "a favor for a favor", a mutual agreement over a very important thing, "I do this and you do that". In 1962, this phrase does mean "Soviet Union to withdraw the nuclear weapon from Cuba in lieu of US Jupiter nuclear weapon withdrawal from Germany."
[182] Weiner, *ibid.*, p. 238
[183] http://en.wikipedia.org/wiki/Cuba_Missile_Crisis
[184] http://www.reuters.com/article/2010/07/16/us-cuba-castro-fidel-idUSTRE66F5UV20100716
[185] *republika.co.id*, July 15, 2010 (this date is equal to July 16, 2010 Cuban local time)

7. Crisis Time Table

October 14, 1962

The American U-2 surveillance airplane took the photographs over Cuba and found the evidence that the Soviet MRBM launching pads were under construction.

October 22, 1962

The US prepared 511 aircrafts including fighter jet, supporting tanker and reconnaissance airplane from Tactical Air Command ready to deploy to Cuba on one-hour alert status. Within one hour all aircrafts and personnel are combat ready.

October 25, 1962

At 1:45 AM EDT (Eastern Daylight Time), upon receiving Khrushchev's telegram, President Kennedy responded that the US was forced into action after realizing that the repeated assurances from the Soviet Union about "no offensive missiles in Cuba" turned to be false. He demanded the Soviet government to take necessary action to restore of the "earlier situation". Earlier situation is a diplomatic term; its real meaning is Cuba without nuclear missiles!

At 7:15 AM EDT, the US ships intercepted the foreign tanker and freighter within quarantine area and let them go through after the cargo being checked and no military equipments found. To deal with the mounting tension, the US requested the emergency meeting of the UN Security Council. During the UN Security Council session, Adlai Stevenson, US Ambassador to the UN displayed the aerial photograph of Cuban missiles and challenged Valerian Zorin the Soviet Ambassador to admit the existence of the missiles, but he refused to answer since he had no authority from his government.

At 5:00 PM EDT, CIA reported that the missiles in Cuba were still being prepared, and not dismantled. President

Kennedy responded by *issuing Security Action Memorandum Number 199 for the loading of nuclear weapons to strategic bombers ready to carrying out nuclear air strikes on the Soviet Union soil. The doomsday was counting down.* President JF Kennedy really prepared the nuclear war! The Soviets responded to the naval quarantine by turning back 14 ships apparently carrying Soviet weapons to Cuba.

October 26, 1962

In the morning, President Kennedy convinced the ExComm that invasion was the only solution to remove the missiles from Cuba. The ExComm responded to be given a little more time for diplomatic and military pressure as well. He also ordered to increase the spy flight over Cuba from two flights per day to once every two hours, or 12 flights a day; everybody could feel the atmosphere of war.

At 1:00 pm EDT, John Alfred Scali (1918 - 1995) a reporter for ABC News who became the US mediator to have a meeting with a KGB operative Colonel Aleksandr Fomin alias Alexander Feliksov for lunch at Fomin's request to discuss the tension between the US and Soviet Union citing the "**War seems about to break out**" and asked Scali to talk to the State Department for the possibility of **a diplomatic solution**. [Scali later became US Ambassador to the UN who in March 1973 raised the yellow flag for veto during the UN session on Panama canals].

At 6:00 PM EDT, the State Department received a message from Khrushchev; it was Saturday **2:00 AM** Moscow local time, a late night for Soviet Union people to know what's going on; when they wake up next day maybe the war erupted already.

> **October 26, 1962. Letter from Chairman Khrushchev to President Kennedy:**
>
> ```
> Mr. President, we and you ought not now to pull on
> the ends of the rope in which you have tied the knot
> of war, because the more the two of us pull, the
> tighter that knot will be tied. And a moment may come
> when that knot will be tied so tight that even he who
> tied it will not have the strength to untie it, and
> then it will be necessary to cut that knot, and what
> that would mean is not for me to explain to you,
> because you yourself understand perfectly of what
> terrible forces our countries dispose. Consequently,
> if there is no intention to tighten that knot and
> thereby to doom the world to the catastrophe of
> thermonuclear war, then let us not only relax the
> forces pulling on the ends of the rope, let us take
> measures to untie that knot. We are ready for this.
> ```
>
> Source: http://en.wikipedia.org/wiki/Cuba_Missile_Crisis

At 10:00 pm EDT, the US raised the war readiness to level 2 where B-52 bombers were fully prepared to take off and fully equipped on 15 minutes' notice [186]. 1,436 Strategic Air Command bombers were on high alert, around 145 (one hundred forty five) intercontinental ballistic missiles were also on high alert, Air Defense Command dispersed 161 nuclear-armed interceptors to 16 different fields within nine hours period with some of them were ready to deploy within 15-minute alert status. Twenty-three B-52 nuclear bombers were sent to the strategic point that would ready to strike the Soviet Union [187]. The war is coming, now even closer. On the other hand, Fidel Castro; a central figure in the Cuban Missile Crisis was so worry that the US invasion was imminent then he sent a telegram on October 26 to Khrushchev demanding a ***pre-emptive nuclear*** strike on the US. At this point, both the US and Soviet Union were ready for the nuclear war! Never be in the history, the nuclear war was closer than this moment, ever. It's a time for interim government or Supreme Committee or whatever the name to do anything necessary to stop the nuclear war at any cost; even to kill one person is still feasible than to let one hundred million Americans get killed.

The worst incident on Oct 26, 1962 was B-59 Soviet submarine pursuit. The USS Beale was tracking and dropping the depth bomb on a Soviet Union submarine at the blockade line off Florida coast without knowing that the submarine was armed with 15 kiloton nuclear missile. Captain **Valentin Savitsky** the submarine commander opted to launch the nuclear torpedo out of thinking that the real war already begun; and only after a heated argument with the other Soviet officers **Ivan Semonovich Maslennikov** a Political Officer on board, and Captain **Vasili Arkhipov** Deputy Brigade Commander, then the launching of nuclear torpedo was aborted. The world was really on the brink of nuclear war.

October 27, 1962

At 00:12 AM EDT early morning of October 27, 1962 the US officially informed North Atlantic Treaty Organization (NATO) allies that the situation was getting worst and a military action may be necessary.

At 6:00 AM EDT the CIA reported that the missile sites at **San Cristobal** and **Sagua la Grande** were fully operational. The report also noted that the Cuban military were on high alert and combat ready.

At 9:00 AM EDT Radio Moskwa broadcasted Khrushchev's message that was different with the previous letter received by State Department. He offered a new deal that the missiles on Cuba would be removed if the US removed the Jupiter missiles from Italy and Turkey.

At 10:00 AM EDT, "the War Committee" discussed the latest situation especially about the difference between Khrushchev's first and second letters; they concluded that the difference was due to internal difference among the members of Soviet Politburo.

At 11:03 AM EDT a new harsh message arrived from Khrushchev. He was furious why did the US worry about the US missiles in Cuba while the US installed the missiles in Turkey and Italy just next to Moscow? After this message, the "War Committee" went on their meeting all the day. One thing the Soviet Union did not know, the Jupiter missiles were **obsolete** and due to replace with advanced missiles launched from the submarine!

At around 12:00 PM EDT, USAF Major Rudolf Anderson aboard a U-2 spy plane on a reconnaissance mission over Cuba was shot down. The stress in negotiations between the Soviet Union and the US was getting worst and almost going off. Later, the Soviets acknowledged that the shooting down was decided by a local commander on his own idea which was not authorized by the Soviet high commander in Moscow.

At 4:00 PM EDT, Kennedy summoned the EXCOMM members to the White House asking them to send an immediate message to the UN Secretary General **U Thant** to demand the Soviets suspending any missile activity while negotiation was on the way. Officially, during this meeting, General Maxwell Taylor reported that a U-2 was shot down; President Kennedy which vowed to invade Cuba if another U-2 were shot down, decided not to invade unless another shot happened. On the other hand, Khrushchev ordered the Soviet Commander in Cuba General Issa Pliyev not to shoot any U-2 while the negotiations were on the way.

Still on the same day Oct 27, 1962 at a far away a US U-2 spy plane made a crazy flight over Soviet Union's eastern coast for 90 minutes; it might be perceived as an act of provocation if the US did not abruptly apologize.

At evening of October 27, 1962, special envoys from the US and the SU agreed to meet at a restaurant in **Washington** DC. The US envoy conveyed JFK proposal that Khrushchev's offer to deal with the missiles was **accepted**, although the ExComm would oppose it since it would undermine NATO's authority. However, the new proposal discussed by the ExComm which would be sent in writing to Khrushchev did not contain the clear word of "withdrawal from Turkey", instead it should have been understood as **voluntary withdrawal**. At last, after long negotiation between the US and the SU, President JFK secretly agreed to remove all missiles from Turkey and Italy in a deal with the Soviet to remove all missiles from Cuba.

October 28, 1962

At 9:00 AM EDT, Radio Moskwa broadcasted a latest message from Khrushchev stating that "the Soviet government issued an order to dismantle the weapons from Cuba and to bring them back to the Soviet Union. President Kennedy responded with a statement that Khrushchev decision was an important and constructive contribution to the world peace. However, the naval quarantine was still in effect on the next day until all Soviet weapons were shipped out of Cuba; the blockade officially ended on November 20, 1962 at 6:45 EDT. Meanwhile the Jupiter missiles were totally dismantled from Turkey on April 24, 1963. The crisis ended on October 28, 1962; the UN Secretary General U Thant mediated the crucial deal between President JFK and Soviet Prime Minister Khrushchev. The deals covered two important things:

(1) Publicly the Soviet Union would dismantle their weapons including offensive missiles, defensive (anti-aircraft) missiles and fighter jets from Cuba; while the US would never invade Cuba.

(2) Secretly, US agreed to dismantle Jupiter missiles from Turkey and Italy.

By this agreement, the blockade was officially terminated. It's a win-win solution. When the conflict has ended on **Sunday October 28, 1962**; it does not mean that the similar situation **will not happen again** under the Kennedy administration; and therefore the special plan has to be meticulously planned within one year to avoid the nuclear war either intentionally or accidentally!

October 29, 1962

Although the crisis ended on October 28, "the War Committee" still convened in the White House Cabinet Room on October 29, 1962 for the final evaluation and marked the official end of the Cuban Missile Crisis. Unlike today's ultra modern communication system including satellite, internet and cell phone, in 1962 there were some obstacles in communication between the US and the SU which made the situation deteriorating.

No doubt, that the main objective of the nuclear missiles installation in Cuba is to force the US to withdraw the Jupiter nuclear missiles from Europe and Soviet border which were perceived as a direct threat to the Soviet Union. About JFK's respond to launch "full scale war", it was beyond Khrushchev's calculation who considered JFK as weak based on his reaction over the Bay of Pigs invasion and Berlin blockade; and therefore the end of Cuban Missile Crisis was a little different with Khrushchev's initial plan. However, Khrushchev was the winner since the basic purpose to eliminate Jupiter missile from Soviet border was successfully obtained.Thanks to Statesman Robert S. McNamara for his chilling account about how close we were in the brink of real nuclear war:

> "And the conventional wisdom is "don't make same mistake twice, learn from your mistakes", we all do, we make the same mistake three times, four, five; but will be no learning period with nuclear weapon; **you make one mistake you destroy the nation**... [188]

He paused, and as a Grand Old Statesman he seemed so guilty over what happened before his eyes while he has no power to stop. Then, he went on:

> "Soviet introduces nuclear weapon into Cuba targeting 90 million Americans. We mobilized 180,000 troops.... During Kennedy time we tested 100 megaton nuclear weapon in atmosphere. I remember that *) [189]"

Robert "Farook" Dickson Crane (1929-) a former adviser to President Nixon from 1963 to 1968, and the first US Muslim Ambassador to United Arab Emirate under President Ronald Reagan; has a awesome thought about the Cuban Missile Crisis, he thinks that the US would prevail for sure, but the main purpose of Khrushchev was not to intimidate the US since his main objective was to **consolidate** the communists in Cuba. By installing the MRBM as a bargaining power, Khrushchev successfully obtained the assurance from President Kennedy that the US would not bother Castro and would **never invade** Cuba again [190].

The JFK's order to launch a full scale war against Cuba during the Cuban Missile Crisis was obvious and very likely with a deadly consequence of dragging the Soviet Union into direct confrontation with the USA using the nuclear weapons. Moreover, John F. Kennedy reclusive meeting with Attorney General Robert Kennedy without the presence of National Security Adviser **McGeorge Bundy;** and Robert Kennedy reclusive meeting with White House Special Adviser **Ted Sorensen** to prepare draft to send to Khrushchev also without the presence of Bundy increased the ExComm's **suspicion** that JFK would surprisingly order the *full scale war against Cuba*. For this action, JFK actually **put his own life at risk**; and that what happened when "The Supreme Committee" which consists of individuals of various groups, decided to stop him for the sake of American safety. As we knew that HSCA concluded "could not rule out individual members of any of those groups acting together"; and this infers and refers to the "Supreme Committee" which consists of extraordinary individuals planning to assassin JFK to avoid the impending nuclear war.

Cuban Missile Crisis is another kind of Russian roulette; Khrushchev deliberately installed the nuclear weapons in Cuba to present JFK a *fait accompli* against the US decision to install Jupiter missiles in Turkey and Italy with the capability to reach Moscow within 18 minutes.

In this roulette, for sure, Khrushchev was the winner since JFK [secretly] dismantled Jupiter nuclear system from Turkey and Italy!

JFK's loss to Khrushchev was just like a real Russian roulette "if you win you get what you want, and if you lose you get a bullet." It's a matter of fact that the US Thor and Jupiter missiles were removed from Europe after the Cuban Missile Crisis, it's a clear proof that Khrushchev prevailed; that's the main purpose of nuclear deployment in Cuba; and that is the Russian roulette!

The History: Who wins and who loses?
Did the USA/British win Russian Roulettes, how the scores are?

1. Nuclear Weapon
USA: 0   Soviet Union: 1
The USA lost nuclear secret to the Soviet teams:
Fuchs, Rosenberg, Fisher, et.al.

2. Cuban Missile Crisis
USA: 1   Soviet Union: 3
US won 1: Soviet dismantled its nuclear weapon from Cuba
Soviet won 3: Jupiter dismantling, No Cuba Invasion, Berlin Wall Stood still

3. Spy Master (1)
USA: 2   Soviet Union: 4
USA won over Penkovsky and Kalugin but lost in Fisher, Johnson, Ames, and Hansen

4. Spy Master (2)
Britain: 1   Soviet Union: 4
Britain won over Gordievsky but lost in Philby, McLean, Burgess, and Blunt

5. Secret Barge
NATO: 0   Russia: 1
They now know what a secret barge looks like; they would manufacture a similar barge and may be better

6. Car Manufacturing
USA: 0   Japan: 1
USA car manufacturers would bankrupt without government help

> **7. Modern Gadgets**
> USA: 0   China: 1
> US markets are filled up with $1 merchandise. China now knows how to produce high technology products even without stealing USA secrets; instead USA disclosed them voluntarily by relocating the factories to China
> **8. Assad**
> USA: 0   Assad: 1
> Can do nothing, Russia and China Veto
> **9. Jonathan Pollard**
> USA: 0   Pollard: 1
> USA lost huge secret to Jonathan Pollard
>
> TOTAL SCORES for USA et. al. : 4; SOVIET UNION et. al. : 17
> The History taught us a lot of tips and tricks. Agile is good but rush is not.

*) never be announced, the public did not know until 2003 when *"The Fog of War"* movie released.

[186] http://en.wikipedia.org/wiki/Cuba_Missile_Crisis
[187] *ibid.*
[188] Errol Morris Film, *"The Fog of War"*, documentary 2003
[189] *ibid.*
[190] *"Republica"* Online newspaper, Monday, April 19, 2010

8. Assassination of JFK

> The assassination of President Kennedy was the assassination of the century; it had been meticulously planned, professionally carried out, and systematically covered up

John Fitzgerald Kennedy the 35th President of the United States of America was assassinated on Friday November 22, 1963 in Dealey Plaza, Dallas, Texas at 12:30 Central Standard Time while riding the open limousine on the way to attend the meeting with businessmen. His assassination became the world topic for years and is still considered the unsolved big mystery in 20th century.

The official investigation by Warren Commission in 1963 to 1964 concluded that President JFK was assassinated by Lee Harvey Oswald individually, and on November 24, 1963 Jack Ruby killed Oswald when he was arraigned in Dallas Police Station before standing for trial. By this conclusion, the Warren Commission wants us to know that Oswald was the assassin; and Jack Ruby killed Oswald to avenge over JFK assassination; and both acted alone without plan and help of anybody else. No conspiracy. This conclusion only generated the world wide conspiracy theory until today. However, the later polls from 1966 to 2004 concluded that majority of Americans thought that there was a **high-level plot** or –at least- the deliberate cover-up [191].

The curious Americans then authorized their representatives to establish the United States House Select Committee on Assassination [HSCA] in 1976 to investigate the assassinations of President JFK, Reverend Dr. Martin Luther King and Alabama Governor George Wallace (he survived but paralyzed). After two-year investigation, in 1979 the HSCA concluded that President John F. Kennedy was probably assassinated as a result of a conspiracy; it also found that the previous investigation was seriously flawed. While HSCA agrees with the Warren Commission over Oswald's [three] shots wounding JFK and Governor John Connally who was on the same limousine with JFK, it also provided the opinion that there were at least **four shots** and a high probability that **two gunmen** shot the President. The portion of the Zapruder film detailing the moments of JFK assassination could be found at youtube.com http://www.youtube.com/watch?v=K2oIAUz0drw.

The HSCA did not mention anyone or any group but Oswald. It specifically mentioned that the CIA, Soviet Union, organized crime and other groups were NOT involved, even though HSCA never ruled out the **individual involvement** of those groups.

CIA has nothing to do with JFK assassination; Mark Lane's explanation in *"Plausible Denial"* [192] about Edward Hunt's is inconclusive; Hunt's employment with CIA –if any-- did not necessarily mean his involvement in JFK assassination while no definitive proof that CIA was involved in JFK assassination. Lane is the lawyer of Liberty Lobby Inc. the publisher of *Spotlight* magazine which published the article written by a former CIA agent Victor Marchetti implicating Hunt for being involved in the assassination of JFK. Howard Hunt filed lawsuit against Liberty Lobby Inc and won, he was awarded $650,000. In the retrial of 1985, Mark Lane successfully defended *Spotlight* magazine "by producing evidence suggesting that Hunt had been in Dallas", and the jury rendered a verdict for Liberty Lobby [193]. However, most jurors in the court disregarded the conspiracy theory involving Hunt in the JFK assassination; they focused on whether the article in *Spotlight* magazine was published with "reckless disregard for the truth", **not regarding the conspiracy theory itself**. Lane in 1991 wrote his experience and opinion pertaining to this case in *"Plausible Denial"*; a note in this book cover reads:

"... **that the CIA had indeed killed President Kennedy**"

is actually **not** a court verdict; it is only **a comment** of a court employee outside the court and **not** a part of trial. However, the presence of Howard Hunt was disproved in 1992 by researcher Mary LaFontaine who discovered the document that Hunt was not among Dallas "three tramps" who were nabbed by the police on the day of JFK

203

assassination; instead they were Gus Abrams, Gedney and Doyle [194]. In 1975, the Rockefeller Commission already concluded that neither Hunt nor Sturgis were in Dallas at the time of the assassination.

The HSCA did not conclude the motive behind the attempt to kill Governor Wallace; yet based on some clues he might be considered as embarrassment to the American democracy and equality after refusing Vivian Malone admission to the University of Alabama.

Vivian Malone and James Hood were African-American students refused by Governor Wallace to enroll the Alabama University during the segregation era. Therefore, Wallace should have been stopped. Who did? Most probably the same actors who assassinated President Kennedy. The assassination of President Kennedy and the attempt to assassinate Wallace are **not** justified, but at least the public understand on why it happened (Part Three: Chapter 4. A Futuristic Daddy).

After some years, we still do not understand on why the President route from Love Field airport to Dallas Trade Mart was published in Dallas newspapers several days prior to the actual trip. The presidential route should had been kept in secret and never be disclosed to public and never ever be published in any newspaper. If the purpose of the publication was to draw more crowds then it drew more questions if it was intended to open the possibility for assassin(s) among the crowds to act, and to blur the assassination plot. This is the meaning of HSCA conclusion that it did not rule out the individual involvement of (any) group. However, the assassination of the 35th US President was meticulously planned and perfectly carried out which absolutely impossible to be done individually without any clear motive. The initial itinerary for President John F. Kennedy was from the Love Field airport in a motorcade through Dallas downtown Dealey Plaza to "Dallas Trade Mart". Riding on a 1961 Lincoln Continental open-top limousine were Kennedy along with First Lady Jacqueline, Texas Governor John

Connally, Sr. a former Secretary of US Navy and his wife Idanell Connally. The limousine driver is a Secret Service Agent William Greer; the presidential limousine was NOT a bulletproof vehicle while J. Edgar Hoover the Director of FBI already had 3 bulletproof cars [195]. The President main plan on Friday November 22, 1963 was to attend business luncheon at Dallas Trade Mart after a breakfast and meeting in Fort Worth Texas where the President spent overnight after visiting San Antonio, Houston and Washington DC. From Fort Worth Texas, the President departed to Love Field Dallas Texas aboard the Presidential Air Force One for 15 minutes, then riding open limousine while greeting the crowds all the way to Dallas Trade Mart.

There are three main reasons for John F. Kennedy to visit Dallas, Texas on November 22, 1963:

(1) To prepare his next campaign for 1964 presidential election;

(2) To rise more money for Democratic Party presidential campaign prior to the presidential election;

(3) In 1960 Kennedy-Johnson won Texas primary, Kennedy was so eager to maintain the readiness of Texas Democratic Party members for the 1964 election.

As the presidential motorcade entering Dealey Plaza area early afternoon on Friday, November 22, 1963 at 12:30 p.m. Central Standard Time (18:30 UTC), the assassination of John F. Kennedy took place.

He was wounded in several spots of his body: back, neck, throat, and head by bullets either coming from front or rear. Although his wounds were still disputed over the decades but the wound at the head was fatal; he never got his consciousness nor revived.

The controversy over the assassination is going on for 5 decades and maybe even longer.

Two official government investigations, the Warren Commission from 1963 to 1964 and HSCA from 1976-1979 concluded that Lee Harvey Oswald was involved in the assassination of US President John F. Kennedy; their conclusions are similar with only a slight different nuance, the Warren Commission reported in 1964 that Oswald acted alone while HSCA stated in 1979 "probably as a result of a conspiracy." Another bullet -or just the same bullet according a ridiculous theory- wounding Governor Connelly at his back, chest, right wrist, and left thigh. An unfortunate James Teague, a spectator and witness to the assassination, got a minor scratch on his right cheek while standing about 270 feet in front of the crime scene; his minor injury was superficial and coming from flying concrete curb hit by a fragment of bullet or a missing bullet or another "magic bullet".

The Zapruder movie recorded the assassination clearly, JFK was shot from the back side, and a couple minutes later he was shot from the front side; after first [round] of shots the President swayed left *forward* and held his neck which indicated that the shot(s) fired from the back side. As the limousine went on a couple seconds later a decisive shot was fired from his front side, on the impact his head was swayed *backward* to the opposite direction of limousine indicating that the powerful shot came from his front side. It's a simple truth; it's easy to recognize this account easily. Either Warren Commission or HSCA concluded that the first shots came from Oswald who was on the sixth floor of Texas Depository Building behind Kennedy motorcade; while the other shots were disputable especially about the presence of another decisive assassin standing on the grassy knoll in the Dealey Plaza in front of Kennedy motorcade. Who's this assassin has been a mystery for 31 years until March 22, 1994 when **James E. Files** confessed that he was the man who fired the fatal last shot onto the right temple of President Kennedy [196]. His confession conformed to the House Select Committee report that the final shot was a fourth shot and that there were two shooters. James E. Files' confession was videotaped by a TV producer Robert G. Vernon with cameraman Robert Baxter and Mike Krolikiewicz as witnesses. 14 Years later, Wim Dankbaar a Dutch writer published his book in 2008 disclosing the confession of James E. Files. The public information on how any legal action was ever taken after James Files confession is not available, and no confirmation or denial was issued whatsoever.

Even if his confession was true, it did not resolve on why President JFK was assassinated. James Files himself –if he was a true assassin- would never know the motive behind JFK assassination because he was only a triggerman who received the payment and then went to forget what he did.

The assassination of President John F. Kennedy had been meticulously planned, professionally carried out, and systematically covered up for a long time which had been unprecedented in the history. Every crime has a motive. The motive is a strong thrust to commit the crime, either hatred, jealousy, retaliation, "defending the dignity" and so forth.

In the case of John F. Kennedy assassination, there was absolutely no motive for Lee Harvey Oswald to kill the President or any motive either to kill police officer Jefferson Davis Tippit.

Oswald provided the different accounts about what happened at the time when President John F. Kennedy was shot. To the detective Jim Leavelle during the first interrogation on Friday November 22, 1963 Oswald said that he was having a lunch in the *first floor* of his workplace the Texas School Book Depository then he went up to the *second floor* for a bottle of soda in which he met face to face with the police officer. But, during the second -and last- interrogation on Sunday November 24, 1963 Oswald said he was working on the *upper floor* then went downstairs to the *second floor* and encountered the police officer (later was identified as Dallas police officer Marion Baker who was searching the shooter) [197].

Oswald was on the ***second floor*** drinking a bottle of soda ***two minutes*** after the shootings had ceased [198] when Officer Baker entered the Texas School Book Depository. The Texas Bok Depository Building then had no elevator; the question is how come Oswald reached second floor within two minutes from sixth floor where the shooting alleged came from; if so he might be run downstairs too fast as a young man of 24. Do we know how long to insert the coins into vending machine to buy a bottle of soda, to open it up and to drink its content? Mathew Smith, the author of "***Conspiracy, The Plot to Stop the Kennedys***" explained "to take coins, inserted in it or them, open a bottle and drink, was more than two minutes, not saying the trip from sixth to second floor.

Most reasonable human being should have declared this quite nonsense". Another witness said it was not Oswald who shot and killed Officer JD Tippit [199]. The other witness Warren Burroughs a Theatre Manager said Oswald was already in the theatre when the shooting on Office Tippit happened. The key word was "second floor". This contradictory account might be a sign of confusion because -if he were on the sixth floor- he had to protect someone, or the scenario he was playing was not working as planned before.

The scenario to protect someone was supported by the fact that the police detained three men who were on the adjacent area behind the Texas Book Depository and turned them to the Dallas Police Station, but their identities were disputed until now, are they Hunt et. al. from CIA or Gedney et. al. from the street [200].

The reasonable explanation is Oswald might had been instructed or intended to shoot Connally ONLY --from somewhere **not** from the sixth floor, might be the **second floor**-- because Oswald was very upset over Connally's refusal to reverse Oswald dismissal to "honorable discharged" from the Navy; as we knew that Connally was a Navy Secretary under President Eisenhower. This is the **key answer** why Oswald shot the motorcade when Connally was in the same car with President John F. Kennedy.

Oswald never had any intention to kill President Kennedy, but his intention was benefited by the plotter to do something else. The plotter might have known in advance about Oswald hatred toward Connally. Oswald **was confused** when he was accused of assassinating JFK. The indication of his confusion was his explanation to the reporters at the Dallas Police Station "I'm just a *patsy*!" If he was **not** a patsy, why did he have to be eliminated; to stop the further investigation over the involvement of someone else? This is the reasonable explanation of the House Select Committee on Assassination (HSCA) conclusion in 1979 "probably as a result of a conspiracy."

A ballistic expert, Howard Donahue gave a different account that a Special Agent George Hickey accidentally discharges his AR-15 rifle from behind John F. Kennedy limo when the escort car he rides on either accelerating or braking at once. There are two questions around this account:

(a) Did Special Agent bring a rifle with a finger on trigger any time?

(b) Could his bullet come out from the barrel flying upward hitting John F. Kennedy then going down and makes a right sharp turn to hit Governor Connally?

According the investigation, about ten minutes after the shooting or about 12:40 p.m. (CST), Oswald boarded a local bus where he met his former landlady; the heavy traffic and traffic jam forced him to request the bus driver to stop a couple of blocks later, the rode a taxi and intentionally stopped some yards beyond his boarding house then walked back at about 1:00 PM and went again, could be going to Texas Theatre. His housekeeper Earlene Roberts [201] later told the investigator that Oswald walking so fast and almost running; she was looking at him standing by the bus shelter across the street where he lived, that's last time she saw him. The traffic was not getting better or he thought it too long to wait a bus, he walked about a mile away from the bus shelter and reached Oak Cliff neighborhood when police officer Tippit encountered him and talked from inside the patrol car.

The conversation might be not clear and officer Tippit got out from his patrol car to talk to Oswald. According to a witness -not from a close range- Oswald shot officer Tippit with his .38 caliber hand gun. It's not clear how the witness knew the caliber of Oswald's hand gun. Some eyewitnesses said they heard the gun shot and some said they identified Oswald fleeing the scene. Officer Tippit got four shots and killed; the eyewitnesses found four cartridges at the scene (a ballistic expert at the Warren Commission testified that all four cartridges came from Oswald's hand gun and not from the other). After a few minutes, Oswald entered a shoe store to avoid the police then sneaked into a theater without realizing that several people had paid attention on him; his actions was suspiciously watched by the shoe store manager who had been listening to the radio and notified the ticket master who called the police. A group of police officers entered the theater and turned the light on. Officer Maurice N. McDonald was approaching Oswald who stated "It's all over now", he scuffled McDonald who with the help of other officer(s) to subdue Oswald in the theater. As he was led out from the theater passing through the onlookers, he said aloud that he was a victim of police abuse [202]. Oswald then was detained on the suspicion of shooting dead of Officer JD. Tippit and later was also suspected of assassinating President Kennedy. Oswald harshly denied killing either Officer Tippit or President Kennedy; at a press conference before reporters and photographers, he answered "I have not been accused of that" when a reporter asked him "Did you shoot the President?" When the reporters snapped him "You had been accused of (killing President John F. Kennedy)"; Oswald snapped back with a confidence **"In fact, I didn't even know about it until a reporter in the hall asked me that question"**. Later, he made more statement to the reporters "I didn't shoot anyone, they're taking me in because of the fact I lived in the Soviet Union. I'm just a patsy! [203]"

During his two-day detention at Dallas Police Station, Oswald was questioned by the Dallas police several times, and he consistently denied any wrongdoing either killing President Kennedy or Officer Tippit.

He denied owning a Carcano rifle and stated that the photograph showing him holding a shot gun was absolutely forged. He also denied knowing anything about "Alek J. Hidell" who ordered the rifle by mails; he also denied carrying a long object in a package to work in the morning prior to President Kennedy assassination.

The mystery of the assassination went deeply when Oswald was unexpectedly shot by **Jack Ruby** a Chicago native and the owner of a Dallas nightclub at 11:21 CST Sunday morning, November 24, 1963 while he was being transferred from the basement of Dallas Police Station to the Dallas County Jail. This tragic incident happened in front of some reporters and photographers and was aired live on the television. Oswald was rushed in the ambulance to Parkland Memorial Hospital where President John F. Kennedy had died a couple of days before.

Oswald was still unconscious when admitted and underwent the abdominal surgery, but the doctors were unsuccessfully operated him due to the severe damage of his blood vessel in the abdomen wounded by Ruby's single sharp shot. Oswald was pronounced dead 48 hours after the President John F. Kennedy's death in the same hospital.

Oswald's body was sent back to the grieving family; he was buried in the Rose Hill Memorial Park in Fort Worth, Texas [204] with a very simple headstone marking "Oswald".

Ruby's reasoning to kill Oswald was murky, he claimed to protect Jackie Kennedy from testifying at the trial; no doubt it seemed to be planned and not on impulse on the blink of eye as Ruby confessed later.

How Jack Ruby entered the basement of Dallas Police Station with a hand gun and what reason he came remained mystery; but when he was in the jail for the life sentence, a mysterious visitor [205] visited him and provided him the food that the conspiracy theorist believed to be either the poison or carcinogenic agent with a long term effect"; he died later from cancer.

The official investigations concluded that the alleged gunman was Oswald; most probably based on:

(1) Witnesses testimony that the fire came from Texas Book Depository

(2) Dallas Police found Italian Carcano M91 rifle on the sixth floor of Texas Book Depository -where Oswald worked- soon after the assassination of JFK

(3) The owner of this rifle turned to be Oswald who bought it and got mailed to his post office box address using the name of "A. Hidell"

(4) Soon after the assassination, Oswald was hiding in the nearby cinema after allegedly shot Office Tippit who confronted him

(5) Oswald ran away from Texas Book Depository soon after the shooting of JFK. During two-day interrogation, Oswald denied any involvement in the killings of patrolman JD Tippit and President Kennedy, and the Dallas Police Department paraffin test on Oswald to collect the remnant of bullet firing was **inconclusive**. The results were positive for Oswald hands but negative for his right cheek; therefore the Warren Commission did not use it as the credible evidence.

(6) A bullet found on hospital stretcher which used to transport Connally and two bullet fragments found in JFK limousine were matched to Oswald Carcano rifle. According to another account, the bullet found on Connally's stretcher was mysteriously found, a security officer just found it anyway without proper explanation on how come a lose bullet found on the hospital stretcher. It was actually found *next to Connally stretch, not on the stretch where Connally was*; this bullet was intact, no damage or deformation as the result of penetrating to human bone as the experts conclude.

Jim Garrison based on his investigation, did not believe Oswald was alone in the assassination of JFK. In his popular book, Garrison named Oswald "Scapegoat". Scapegoat is something or someone to sacrifice for the safety of the other person, or somebody who is made to take blame for others:

> "From our investigation so far, I knew that Oswald could not have shot President Kennedy alone, that some part of intelligence community had been guiding him, and that someone had been impersonating him. In other word, he had been just what he said he was when he was arrested—a patsy. [206]"

President JFK was declared dead when he arrived at Parkland Hospital emergency room. Vice President Lyndon B. Johnson was riding behind President JFK was safe and was sworn in at November 23, 1963 2:38 pm on board of Air Force One with JFK widow Jacqueline Kennedy among other witnesses. JFK was buried three days later on November 25, 1963.

As President Johnson started a new administration, a near miss incident occurred in his home which almost took his life. Brett Michael **Dykes** wrote in yahoo blog that **Gerald Blaine** a Secret Service agent in the ensuing power transfer after the assassination of John F. Kennedy recalled that he almost shot new President Lyndon B. Johnson when Blain misidentified President Johnson as an intruder inside Johnson's Washington DC home.

Blaine was watching the Johnson home the night after JFK assassination when he heard someone approaching him from behind. He instinctively grab his submachine gun while the silhouette keeps coming closer, then he yelled "Let me see your face, you %@&#@rd" while pointing the ready-to-shoot submachine gun directly to President Johnson's chest stepping in the darkness. Dykes wrote *"In the blackness of the night, Johnson's face went completely white.* [207]*"*

It's hard to imagine if Blaine were to gun down LBJ a day after JFK was shot, then the world would be in a total chaos to blame each other.

To investigate the assassination of JFK, President Johnson soon on November 29, 1963 established a special board lead by Chief Justice Earl Warren and later would be unofficially named after him "Warren Commission". This commission presented 888-page report to President Johnson on September 24, 1964 and later generated more controversy rather than explanation. Ironically, from this point; the conspiracy theory goes viral. The formation of HSCA in 1976 is a natural continuation of this theory since the American public was not satisfied with Warren Commission final report. After JFK assassination, several investigations were performed; in 1968, Attorney General Ramsey Clark appointed a medical panel to examine the medical documents related to the late JFK. The Clark Panel concluded that Kennedy was struck by two bullets fired from behind and above him, one of them went across JFK's base of the neck on the right side and the other one entered his skull from behind and destroyed its upper right side [208]. This conclusion was later undermined by the video evidence of Zapruder film.

In 1975, President Gerald Ford established a commission led by Vice President Nelson Rockefeller especially to clarify the presence of **E. Howard Hunt** and **Frank Sturgis** in Dallas at the time of JFK death –and the possibility of their involvement. The Rockefeller Commission concluded that both were NOT in Dallas at the time of the assassination. In 1975, the US Senate established the special committee led by Senator Frank Church a Democrat from Idaho to investigate the assassination of JFK. This committee was commonly known as Church Committee and refers to "the United States Senate Select Committee to Study Governmental Operations with Respect to Intelligence Activities". Church Committee concluded that JFK investigation by FBI and CIA were deficient and some facts were **not** reported to Warren Commission in 1963. The committee also concluded that "the higher government official" pressured FBI to conclude investigation early; and there was a high probability that both agencies decided to hold the important information [209].

The controversy of JFK assassination never ended, a controversial remark by lawyer Mark Lane former New York congressman alleged that James Angleton might have been involved in the Kennedy assassination since Angleton controlled a team of assassins under the counterintelligence command of Colonel Boris Pash; and this counterintelligence team "could not be tried in an open legal proceeding due to security risk and sensitivity" [198]. The other controversy was a questionable fact about the distribution of threatening flier prior to JFK visit to Dallas, why it was not investigated properly to prevent the worst. It's not just a freedom of speech; this flier conveyed the deep hatred against JFK and should have been investigated properly prior to the JFK arrival.

WANTED FOR T R E A S O N

THIS MAN is wanted for treasonous activities against the United States:

1. Betraying the Constitution (which he swore to uphold): He is turning the sovereignty of the U.S. over to the communist controlled United Nations.
   He is betraying our friends (Cuba, Katanga, Portugal) and befriending our enemies (Russia, Yugoslavia, Poland).
2. He has been WRONG on innumerable issues affecting the security of the U.S. (United Nations-Berlin wall-Missile removal-Cuba-Wheat deals-Test Ban Treaty, etc.)
3. He has been lax in enforcing Communist Registration laws.
4. He has given support and encouragement to the Communist inspired racial riots.
5. He has illegally invaded sovereign State with federal troops.
6. He has constantly appointed Anti-Christians to Federal office: Upholds the Supreme Court in its Anti-Christian rulings.
   Aliens and known Communist abound in Federal offices.
7. He has been caught in fantastic LIES to the American people (including personal ones like his previous **marraige** and divorce).

Replica of flier distributed in Dallas prior to JFK arrival in November 22, 1963. Why were we not aware? [The original text on flier has typo; "*marraige*" instead of **marriage**]

The public relentlessly demanded the explanation about the JFK assassination; they considered the previous official investigations are insufficient. In 1976 US House of Representative established the special committee the **United States House of Representatives Select Committee on Assassinations (HSCA)** to investigate the assassinations of Kennedy, Rev. Dr. Martin Luther King and the shooting to assassinate Alabama Governor George Wallace. The HSCA in 1979 concluded that the assassination of President John F. Kennedy "was very likely" a result of conspiracy of individuals and did not involved any group, official organization or government. Instead of being happy, the American public suffered a deeper upset with the result of The HSCA since it decided that all the evidence relating to the JFK assassination would be sealed from the public for 50 years. This decision was mandated by Congress the representative of American public. They were upset, but what they can do? While Congressional rule mandated 50-year seal on the evidence relating to JFK assassination, the unpublished records reviewed by Warren Commission which were sent to National Archives in 1964 would NOT be open for 75 years until 2039! Luckily, this rule does not apply longer, supplanted by the Freedom of Information Act of 1966 and JFK Record Act of 1992; eventually the most records were made public and only a small part still being kept until 2017.

In December 1991, Oliver Stone produced a popular movie "JFK" featuring Kevin Costner as New Orleans District Attorney **Earling Carothers "Jim" Garrison** (1921-1992) which generates a public outcry about JFK assassination. Jim Garrison steadily investigated the JFK assassination regardless of whether he was considered controversial or failed or blocked by the federal government. Jim Garrison wrote his investigation in *"On the Trail of the Assassins"*, this book later was transferred into "JFK" movie and successfully influenced the American public. As the impact of the public outcry, the US Congress in 1992 passed the bill of "President John F. Kennedy Assassination Records Collection Act of 1992" to be public law, and soon The

Assassination Record Review Board (**ARRB**) was created. As the result, from 1992 to 1998 about 60,000 documents of over 4 million pages were released, yet all remaining documents are still waiting to be released by 2017 when the most of those were involved had died, or to secure all those are involved died already.

The second opinion and more explanation about the mystery surrounding JFK assassination now available on youtube.com; although we do not have to believe but at least it will add up to our knowledge in the era of free information and modern technology. Here some of them:

http://www.youtube.com/watch?NR=1&v=yLiF4Jwvb0o&feature=endscreen
http://video.google.com/videoplay?docid=818267521031292324#
http://www.youtube.com/watch?v=TCVaYxOvcMs&feature=endscreen&NR=1
http://www.youtube.com/watch?v=Rp3P2wDKQK4&feature=related
http://www.youtube.com/watch?v=VI07govlUqI&feature=related
http://www.youtube.com/watch?v=bqL1ANq7VPM&feature=endscreen&NR=1

The persistence to keep the important records pertaining to JFK assassination from being released to the public only indicates that something very important happened out there which is not easy for every American to understand. What if it's the informal or formal resolution that made the assassination legitimate to prevent the nuclear war? Are the Americans ready to hear if the US Government to announce that JFK assassination was sadly decided by a group of concerned statesmen in order to prevent JFK from ordering a full scale war against Cuba that eventually would drag the Soviet Union into the mutual assured destruction of nuclear war? We think about it, especially why is there a perennial cover-up until today? The USA never stepped back against any adversary, but to let forty million innocent Americans die from Soviet's initial nuclear strike is not a good option. We never ruled any possibility out. Until today, nobody knows who the real assassin; yet the conspiracy theorists estimated about the planner to murder President John F. Kennedy; it's just their estimation, no legitimate evidence and no witness to support it:

(1) Marcello, Trafficante and Rosselli in Chicago, Illinois on November 2, 1963 planned to kill Kennedy [211]. According to an informant Ed Becker, Marcello in 1962 was heard to swear of killing Kennedy [212].

(2) The mob planned to murder Kennedy in Tampa, Florida on November 18, 1963. The would-be gunman was Gilberto Lopez a Cuban national lived in Tampa. He was a former defector who had been active at Fair Play for Cuba Committee (FPCC), he had also a Russian connection and was also linked to Oswald and Ruby [213]. There were some reports that Oswald and Ruby knew each other before the Kennedy assassination.

(3) Edward Lansdale and David Atlee Phillip were the planners of John F. Kennedy assassination [214].

There are still some another accounts about who planned the assassination; it's a matter of fact that the assassination of US President John F. Kennedy is important subject to discuss; however the motive behind the assassination is more important. Some people insist that Mafia was behind the assassination of JFK; if it's true then should Mafia be named the hero, and does it deserve the huge prize since it averted USA from the nuclear war? Had JFK not been murdered, he most probably would ordered to completely destroy Cuba and to launch the nuclear warhead to Soviet Union soil since the preparations to do so had been soundly ordered.

On October 25, 1962 at 5:00 p.m. President Kennedy issued **National Security Action Memorandum Number 199** to the Secretary of Defence Robert McNamara authorizing the loading of air launched ballistic missiles (ALBMs) onto strategic bombers ready to carry out the initial nuclear strikes to the Soviet Union. The initial nuclear strike might be followed by the next and also followed by the nuclear respond from the Soviet Union to the US soil. No doubt. This crucial moment was later described by McNamara a member of President Kennedy's Cabinet as "[the nuclear weapons] **to be launched by the decision of one human being**". If it happens then the world were totally in chaos and desperate as depicted in "*The Day After*" a Japan movie about the life one day after the nuclear war. This is President Kennedy Memo #199 [215]:

THE WHITE HOUSE
WASHINGTON

SANITIZED COPY

October 25, 1962

NATIONAL SECURITY ACTION MEMORANDUM NO. 199

TO: The Secretary of Defense

SUBJECT: Loading of SACEUR Land-Based Alert Strike Aircraft

Paragraph 4 in National Security Action Memorandum No. 143 is hereby rescinded.

Two-stage weapons may now be loaded on land-based alert strike aircraft on station in NATO. This decision shall be applicable to U. S. forces as well as non-U. S. forces when the specific QRA capability is achieved and dispersal authorization is granted. The yield of such weapons will be limited to that compatible with a .... probability of destruction of the target (assuming the carrier arrives) and will not exceed ------. It is understood that present targeting indicates that yields are in the order of ------ for most targets programmed for QRA aircraft and that the specific yield is subject to the type target, the delivery error of the system, the stockpile yield available and numbers on hand.

cc: Secretary of State
    Chairman, AEC

cc: Mrs. Lincoln
    Mr. Bundy
    Mr. C. Johnson
    NSC Files

SANITIZED
E.O. 12356, Sec. 3,4
NLK-94-5
By SKF NARA, Date 12/2/93

It reads:

> **THE WHITE HOUSE**
> **Washington**
>
> SANITIZED COPY
>
> October 25, 1962
>
> NATIONAL SECURITY ACTION MEMORANDUM NO. 199
>
> TO: The Secretary of Defense
> SUBJECT: Loading of SACEUR Land-Based Alert Strike Aircraft
>
> Paragraph 4 in National Security Action Memorandum No. 143 is hereby rescinded.
> Two-stage weapons may now be loaded on land-based alert strike aircraft in station in NATO. This decision shall be applicable to U.S. forces as well as non-U.S. forces when the specific QRA capability is achieved and dispersal authorization is granted. The yield of such weapons will be limited to that compatible with a ....probability of destruction of the target (assuming the carrier arrives) and will not exceed .... It is understood that present targeting indicates that yields are in the order of ....for most targets programmed for QRA aircraft and that the specific yield is subject to the type target, the delivery error of the system, the stockpiles yield available and numbers on hand.
>
> cc: signed,
> Secretary of State   Kennedy
> Chairman, AEC
>
>   cc: Mrs. Lincoln
>   Mr. Bundy
>   SANITIZED   Mr. C. Johnson
>   E.O. 12356 Sec. 3.4   NSC Files
>   NLK—94-55
>   By <u>SKF</u> NARA, Date 11/22/93

With this piece of paper, should the world be in total chaos with initial American casualties up to 40,000,000? They are innocent; they are our sons, daughters and relatives. Should they have been desperate refugees with no food, shelter and blanket during winter?

To prevent the nuclear tragedy in the future, an amendment to the US Constitution should have been created. This amendment should have restricted the authority of US President from authorizing to launch the nuclear weapon without prior approval of the US Senate and the US Congress except in the emergency situation where the adversary has launched the nuclear weapon first; especially in the wake of North Korean young leader Kim Jong-Un's threat in March 2013 to strike the US with the nuclear weapon. Basically, the North Korean threat is an imaginary missile attack on US government vital buildings in Washington DC including the White House and the Capitol as the symbols of democracy. This imagination was posted on http://www.youtube.com/user/uriminzokkiri on March 2013 with the White House on the digital cross hair for attack and then the Capitol dome was destroyed with a blast. This video was posted online after Kim Jong-Un threatened the US with nuclear missile a week before. To respond North Korean propaganda video threat with $1B shifted from European missile shield program as Secretary of Defense Chuck Hagel announced is unnecessary. Russia would be very happy if $1B missile shield program shifted from Europe to Alaska!

This video is propaganda only, and rhetoric to boost the leadership of young Kim; the South Korea would easily overcome Kim Jong-Un threat with Psy's Gangnam style which North Korea was worrisome about. It is better for South Korea and the US not to listen the young Kim illusion; he is learning to be an adult.

Any country attacks the US with the nuclear weapon; it should be wiped out from the world map for sure. By the way, who would so dare to start attacking the USA with a nuclear weapon, are they committing suicide? The US needs an amendment on the Constitution; it should cover the basic points:

> **Amendment XXVIII**
> **Section 1.**
> Congress shall make law respecting an executive order of US President to launch any nuclear weapon to the adversary, such an approval is necessary; there shall be no any nuclear launching prior to the US Congress approval.
>
> **Section 2.**
> Prior to issuing approval over President's executive order, Congress shall accordingly regard the considerations from the State Department, Department of Defense, and National Security Agency.

The crucial incidents happened over the times, and we may summarize the relevant and important incidents prior to and around the assassination of President John F. Kennedy:

#	Time	Incident
01	Aug. 6, 1945	USA dropped first atomic bomb over Hiroshima, and Aug. 9, 1945 on Nagasaki during WW II,
02	1945-1958	The espionage to steal the nuclear secret from America. Ethel Rosenberg and her husband was convicted of stealing the US nuclear secret; sentenced to death
03	June 21, 1957	The Soviet master spy Colonel KGB Vilyam Fisher aka Rudolf Abel was captured in New York. His main mission was to coordinate of stealing USA nuclear secret
04	1958-1960	The Soviet Union test the atomic bombs (it's amazing how fast it acquired the nuclear secret and tested it in the atmosphere)
05	May 1, 1960	U-2 the US spy plane was shot down over Sverdlovsk, Russia the pilot FG Powers was captured alive
06	May 16, 1960	The summit meeting between Khrushchev and Eisenhower was cancelled after U-2 incident
07	Apr 15, 1961	US bombed Cuban airfield
08	Apr 17, 1961	US invaded the Bay of Pigs, Cuba

09	Jun 3-4, 1961	Summit meeting between Kennedy and Khrushchev in Vienna, Austria
10	Aug 30, 1961	The Soviet Union announced the resume of nuclear test. JFK invented the name of "weapon of mass destruction" (WMD)
11	Feb. 10, 1962	Rudolf Abel was exchanged with FG Powers in Berlin
12	Oct. 16, 1962	U-2 spy plane took the photographs of Soviet missiles placed in Cuba
13	Oct. 20, 1962	US imposed the naval defensive quarantine over Cuba to prevent ships from delivering the supplies to Cuba. A huge amount of B-52 US bombers -some of them might be carrying the nuclear bombs- had been sent encircling near Cuban airspace; and 180 naval ships had been sent to Florida along with some hundreds of thousands of troops. Quarantine is a blockade, a blockade is a war
14	Oct. 26, 1962	Soviet Union Prime Minister Khrushchev sent a very important letter stating that it would be no more weapons shipping to Cuba
15	Oct. 27, 1962	Khrushchev under the pressure of the Soviet Union Politburo members sent another letter to demanded USA to remove the Jupiter nuclear missiles from Turkey
16	Oct. 27, 1962	U-2 US spy plane was shot down over Cuba
17	Oct. 27, 1962	President Kennedy asked the US Attorney General Robert Kennedy to call the Soviet Ambassador Anatoly Dobrynin to let him know that the USA declined the Soviet Union's request to remove the Jupiter nuclear missiles from Europe!
18	Nov. 1, 1963	*Coup d'etat* by General Duong Van Minh over Vietnamese President Ngo Din Diem, and the USA acknowledged the new Vietnamese military government under General Duong; the Soviet Union consider the *coup d'etat* in Asia as an American strategy to divide the concentration over its focus on American and European continents
19	Nov. '62 - Nov. '63	Between these months, it was decided that JFK had to be stopped to avoid the nuclear war between Soviet and America because no matter who's the winner, both sides would

			have been loosing millions of people
20	Nov. 22, 1963		President John F. Kennedy assassinated in Dallas, Texas; in the same day Vice President Johnson was swore in as US President inside the presidential airplane Air Force One
21	Nov. 24, 1963		Jack Ruby killed Lee Harvey Oswald; a suspect in Kennedy murder during a transfer from the police station to jail. The case of Kennedy assassination became complicated and shrouded with the secrets ever since
22	Nov. 29, 1963		President LB. Johnson formed a special commission lead by Supreme Court Chief Justice **Earl Warren** to investigate Kennedy assassination
23	Nov. 1963 – now		* The critics said there're some attempts to keep the assassination facts and files from the public reach to cover-up what really happened * The Warren Commission Report in 1966 concluded that Oswald was the lone assassin * The American had been saved from the nuclear disaster, JFK was a real hero, he was sacrificed and prevented from ordering the nuclear attack either to Cuba or Soviet Union
24	1945-1963		There were 336 nuclear explosion tests altogether in our planet conducted by Soviet Union, USA, Britain and France (two "small" atomic bombs for Hiroshima and Nagasaki Japan not included). After 1963, there are even more nuclear tests
25	1979		The House Select Committee on the Assassinations concluded at the assassination of President John F. Kennedy probably as a result of conspiracy

Some researchers expressed their displeasure and even the frustration over the consistent cover-up and destroying the records on the assassination of John Fitzgerald Kennedy, a sitting and democratically elected President of the United States of America the most democratic and free nation on this planet. Professor **James Fetzer** sarcastically narrated the nature of the "official" cover-up:

> "The presidency of the United States is decided by bullets rather than ballots cast by citizens….. The resurgent of interest of the death of John F. Kennedy have a repercussion when Congress passed the JFK Record Act in 1992 that created 5-civilian member board in trust with responsibility to review declassified documents were held by the government agents……. We know from the report, they have some significant failures; for example the Secret Service has deliberately destroyed the motorcade records that will reveal the motorcade in Dallas was a travesty of violation of at least fifteen different Secret Service policies for presidential protection. This behavior on their part raises the most serious disturbing question about their complicity in entire affair. [216]"

Meanwhile, **Vince Palamara**, an expert on Secret Service history, commented on the presidential motorcade movie:

> "There is last minutes change invoked by Secret Service involving President Kennedy security, specifically agents were told NOT to ride ON or NEAR the rear of limousine. These orders were funneled from the assistant specifically in charge of the White House … to one of his assistant by the name Amy Roberts who's in charge in the follow-up car.
>
> You can see an agent **Henry Rybka** doing his normal duty jogging beside the limousine when in the follow-up car, you can see, **Amy Roberts** stands up and waves him (Rybka) back in very perplexed agent **Rybka** waving his arms near several times and seeming disgusted… There is another last minutes change in the **Love Field** *) invoked by the Secret Service: the Dallas Police motorcycle outriders were told not be beside the car…[217]"

From this video display, with due respect to SS, DPD, and everybody else; we have a couple of questions: (1) Was this agent, either Rybka or Lawton, warned against the incoming danger, so better for him to stay away from the side of limousine? (2) Did someone know that bullets would be straying over the Presidential limousine? (3) Was this agent more valuable than US President John Fitzgerald Kennedy and Governor Connally?

The answer(s) of these questions could be the clue which a researcher should have never neglected, ever.

[191] http://en.wikipedia.org/wiki/JFK_assassination
[192] Lane, Mark, "*Plausible Denial*", Thunder's Mouth Press, New York 1991, pp. 1-5, 182-188
[193] http://en.wikipedia.org/wiki/Howard_hunt
[194] http://en.wikipedia.org/wiki/Three_tramps
[195] economicexpert.com/John:F:Kennedy:assassination.htm
[196] Wim Dankbaar, "*Files of JFK*", IPG Chicago Il, first edition 2008, p. 43
[197] Smith, Mathew, "*Conspiracy, the Plot to Stop the Kennedys*", Citadel Press Book, New York, 2005, p. 64
[198] Smith, *ibid.*
[199] Smith, *ibid.*
[200] http://en.wikipedia.org/wiki/JFK_conspiracy
[201] http://en.wikipedia.org/wiki/Lee_Harvey_Oswald
[202] *ibid.*
[203] *ibid.*
[204] Smith, *loc.cit.*
[205] Smith, *ibid.*
[206] Jim Garrison "*On the Trail of the Assassins*", Warner Book Edition, 1988; p. 70
[207] http://news.yahoo.com/s/yblog_upshot/20101020/od_yblog_upshot/ex-secret-service-officer-i-almost-shot-lbj
[208] President's Commission "*Warren Report*", The Associated Press, pp. 225 - 229
[209] http://en.wikipedia.org/wiki/JFK_assassination
[210] http://en.wikipedia.org/wiki/James_angleton
[211] Lamar Waldron/Thom Hartman, "*Ultimate Sacrifice*", Carol & Graf Publisher, New York, first edition 2005, p. 619 - 620.
[212] *ibid.*, p. 654
[213] *ibid.*, p. 653
[214] Dankbaar, *ibid.* p. 261.
[215] http://www.jfklibrary.org/Asset-Viewer/0BYhudts-E6hwG7-Hay9NQ.aspx
[216] http://www.youtube.com/watch?v=bqL1ANq7VPM&eature=endscreen&NR=1
[217] *ibid.*

9. Warren Commission

> How deep a truth was buried, some day it would come out
> to the public as the undisputable fact

The Warren Commission is a special commission appointed by President Johnson to investigate the assassination of President Kennedy; it was named after its chairman a former Chief Justice Earl Warren. Its official name is **The President's Commission on the Assassination of President Kennedy.** It was established on November 29, 1963 seven days after Kennedy's tragic death.

The core of Warren Commission's almost 900-page report is (a) the conclusion that Lee Harvey Oswald acted alone in the killing of Kennedy [he was a suspect, he never be tried and never be sentenced]; and (b) Jack Ruby who killed Oswald - before the crowd of journalists at a Dallas police station- also acted alone. This report was presented to President Johnson within one year since the assassination, and later became subject of perennial controversy for five decades and maybe more. The Warren Commission officially concluded that either Oswald or Ruby acted alone; and thus did not recognize the conspiracy theory. The history eventually would reveal the truth long time after the incident happened; some day it would come out to the public as the undisputable fact.

The very first known official attempt to obscure John F. Kennedy's assassination was the Katzenbach memo. Although the memo was initially a measurable effort to avoid the nuclear war just in case there were an undistinguished rumor that Russia was behind the assassination. As for Katzenbach memo turned to be a perennial cover up, it was not his initial intention. The House Select Committee on Assassination (HSCA) in 1979 discovered that on November 25, 1963 or three days after the assassination, Nicholas Katzenbach, then deputy Attorney general had written an official memo to the White House:

> "The public must be satisfied that Oswald was the assassin; that he had no confederates who are still at large; and that evidence was such that he would have been convicted at trial...Speculation about Oswald's motivation ought to be cut off...Unfortunately the facts on Oswald seem about too pat—too obvious (Marxist, Cuba, Russian wife, etc.)...We need something to head off public speculation or Congressional hearings of the wrong sort [218]"

Katzenbach was the main person behind the idea to create a special committee on the assassination that later was publicly knows as Warren Committee. Earl Warren, then-Chief Justice of Supreme Court on November 29, 1963 was appointed by President Lyndon B. Johnson as a chairman of the commission to investigate the assassination. The Warren Commission on September 24, 1964 presented the 888-page final report in 15 volumes to President Johnson, and it was made available to public on September 27, 1964; later on The Associated Press published it in a simplified 366-page format with double columns in every page. In November 1964 two months after the initial publication, the Commission published the additional 26 volumes of supporting documents including the testimony of more than 500 witnesses and more than 3,000 exhibits; one of the popular exhibitions is the exhibit #399 which was known as the magic bullet.

The commission has several extraordinary members including Gerald Rudolph Ford (1913 – 2006) who later became the 38th President of the United States after President Richard Milhous Nixon (1913 - 1994) resigned in the aftermath of burglary scandal of Democratic Party Headquarters at Watergate. This incident later was named after the city where the burglary took place, Watergate. Had the Warren Commission been formed after the Watergate, it could have been named Warrengate. HSCA criticized Warren Commission over the conspiracy "HSCA agreed to the Warren Commission which was reasonably thorough and acted in a good faith, but failed to adequately address the possibility of conspiracy".

Six days after being sworn in as 36th President of the United States, on November 29, 1963 Lyndon B. Johnson formed the Warren Commission which its members were the well-known citizens and proven public servants.

As of the publication of this book, all main 7 committee members had passed away including President Johnson (1908-1973) who appointed them.

The President's Commission on the Assassination of President Kennedy
1. Earl Warren (1891-1974), Chief Justice of Supreme Court; chairman
2. Senator Richard B. Russell (1897-1971), Democrat of Georgia, member
3. Senator John Sherman Cooper (1901-1991), Democrat of Kentucky, member; he was later popular with Cooper-Church Amendment
4. US Representative Hale Boggs (1913-1972), Democrat of Louisiana, member
5. US Representative Gerald Ford (1913-2006), Republican of Michigan, member who later became the US President succeeding Richard M. Nixon
6. Allen Welsh Dulles (1893-1969), former director of CIA, member
7. John McCloy (1895-1989), former director of the World Bank, member

The General Counsel, Assistant Counsel, and Staff Members
1. J. Lee Rankin, General Counsel
2. Francis WH Adams, Assistant Counsel
3. Joseph A. Ball, Assistant Counsel
4. David W. Belin, Assistant Counsel
5. William T. Coleman, Jr., Assistant Counsel
6. Melvin A. Eisenberg, Assistant Counsel
7. Burt W. Griffin, Assistant Counsel
8. Leon D. Hubert, Jr., Assistant Counsel
9. Albert E. Jenner, Jr., Assistant Counsel
10. Wesley J. Liebeler, Assistant Counsel
11. Norman Redlich, Assistant Counsel
12. W. David Slawson, Assistant Counsel
13. Arlen Specter, Assistant Counsel

14. Samuel A. Stern, Assistant Counsel
15. Howard P. Willens, Assistant Counsel and Liaison Officer between Commission and Department of Justice
16. Phillip Baron, Staff Member
17. Edward A. Conroy, Staff Member
18. John H. Ely, Staff Member
19. Alfred Goldberg, Staff Member
20. Muray J. Laulicht, Staff Member
21. Arthur Marmor, Staff Member
22. Richard M. Mosk, Staff Member
23. John J. O'Brien, Staff Member
24. Stuart Pollack, Staff Member
25. Alfredda Scobey, Staff Member
26. Charles N. Shaffer, Jr.
27. Lloyd L. Weinreb

In 1964 the Warren Commission concluded the bullets that killed JFK came from a 6.5 millimeter Italian carbine Carcano which Lee H. Oswald fired from a window on the sixth floor of the Texas Book Depository Building as Presidential motorcade went through Dealey Plaza in Dallas, Texas.

The bullet(s) struck and killed John F. Kennedy on Friday at 12:30 afternoon on November 22, 1963; while -according the Warren Report- the same bullet also struck Texas Governor John Connally who was on the same car with President Kennedy. The suspect, Oswald, in a news conference at Dallas Police Station on November 23, 1963 after midnight, consistently denied shooting and killing either Officer JD Tippit and/or President John F. Kennedy.

According to the Warren Commission report, as Oswald shot President John F. Kennedy, he hid his rifle behind the boxes and went downstairs through the rear stairwell. When he reached the lunch room on the second floor approximately 90 seconds after the shooting, he encountered Dallas police officer Marion Baker who was searching the shooter suspected of firing the gun from inside the Texas Book Depository Building. Baker parked his motorcycle outside the door of the building and ran upstairs.

With a pistol on his hand, Baker and Roy Truly the supervisor of Texas Book Depository let Oswald went because he was an employee. He went down stair and left the building through the front door on Elm Street a couple of minutes before Dallas Police sealed the building off. Because he was the only missing employee after the assassination; Roy Truly noticed the police who still in the Texas Book Depository Building.

The HSCA Report in 1979 said that based on the witness it believed that between late August and early September 1963 Oswald was in Clinton, Louisiana in the company of David Ferrie or/and Clay Shaw; but the witness did not know for sure what the kind of relationship between Oswald, Shaw and Ferrie was. It was about three months before the assassination of President John F. Kennedy [219], were they discussing a plan? The Warren Commission has made the extraordinary efforts; and one among its (disputable) conclusion was nobody participated in the assassination of John F. Kennedy but Lee Harvey Oswald himself.

The critics say the biggest flaw ever on the Warren Commission and HSCA accounts was the presence of an evidence which known as the exhibit #399 in a correlation with the single bullet theory. The Single-Bullet Theory or Magic-Bullet Theory or Ridiculous-Bullet Theory was credited to a then-young member of the Warren Commission Arlen Specter, later he becomes a US Senator from Pennsylvania. The theory was adopted by the Warren Commission to explain -or to blur- how one single non fatal shots fired by Lee Harvey Oswald from sixth floor of Texas Book Depository resulted in ALL non fatal wounds of the US President Kennedy and Texas Governor John Connally who was on the same car at the time of President Kennedy assassination. Specter was a Democrat when he started his political career; he worked work at the Warren Commission on the recommendation of then-US Representative of Michigan Gerald R. Ford.

Specter is the father of the "single bullet theory" a weird explanation over JFK's back wounds and John Connally's non-fatal wounds that caused by the same "magic" bullet [220] [221]. This theory is bizarre; had it been stated that President Kennedy and Governor Connally were wounded by the different bullet, then it implicated another shooter in a conspiracy. However the Warren Commission stayed away from mentioning that President Kennedy and Governor Connally were wounded by the ***different*** bullet although it is impossible for the "magic bullet" to make such trajectory to penetrate President Kennedy and Governor Connally consecutively. Nevertheless, the Kennedy's fatal head wound was caused by another bullet, but not a magic one.

The evidence which known as the "Warren Commission Exhibit 399" is absolutely flawed and within reasonable doubt, because it was not recovered from Connally wound during the medical procedure at Parkland Hospital. It was recovered by a Secret Service agent from a stretcher ever used to transport Connally from the ambulance to the hospital. What if this evidence was planted by someone and found by someone else to distract the investigation? What the ballistic and medical explanation of a single bullet traversed 15 layers of clothing belong to Kennedy and Connally plus 7 layers of skin belong to the both plus about 15 inches of human tissue of Kennedy's neck, then struck Kennedy's necktie, then upon exiting from Kennedy's body this extra naughty bullet abruptly turned right to slash 4 inches of Connally's rib, and shattered Connally's radius bone before hitting his thigh and finally resting on the stretch? C'mon, this is America; this story may sell in Neanderthal community but not in the modern civilization.

The exhibit #399 is a one-inch-long copper-jacketed lead-core rifle bullet with 6.5-millimeter diameter that allegedly fired from the sixth floor of the Texas School Book Depository and recovered from Parkland Hospital stretcher; since the bullet matches the Carcano rifle owned by Oswald, the conclusion was Oswald to fire the bullet.

What if Oswald or someone else fired Carcano rifle in another time another place then the rifle was brought to Texas Book Depository while the bullet was kept by someone to be put on stretch later to obstruct the justice?

If the bullet recovered from a Parkland Hospital stretcher is the bullet Oswald fired from sixth floor of the Texas School Book Depository then why it is still intact with a little deformation after traversing 15 layers of clothing, 7 layers of skin, 15 inches of human tissue, striking necktie, turning right to slash 4 inches of human rib, and shattering radius bone before hitting the thigh and finally resting on the stretch after exhausting? Did we ever hear a bullet hitting a target then afterward turning right after exit? The witness who recovered this agile bullet and the proponent of the single-bullet theory should have been grilled before the scientific commission prior to the public acceptance. Since the bullet was doubtful then the rifle which the bullet came from was also doubtful, then the owner of rifle was also doubtful; then the crime allegedly committed by the rifle owner was also doubtful. How deep a truth was buried, some day it would come out to the public as the undisputable fact!

Oliver Stone's "*JFK*" movie [222] [223] –inspired by Jim Garrison investigation-- drew the public fury and forced the US Congress to pass the 1992 JFK Assassination Records Collection Act (JFKRA). The implementation of JFKRA was to identify and declassify JFK assassination records, and as a continuation, the Assassination Records Review Board (ARRB) was created in 1994. Ever since, some millions pages of documents were declassified [224] [225].

According to ARRB, all Warren Report except the tax return information should be available to the public "with redaction", and the remaining document -about 2 percents- would available only in 2017, 25 years after the enactment of JFKRA. Although ARRB decision was questionable especially about the availability of Warren documents in 2017, it made a fair statement:

> "Doubts about the Warren Commission's findings were not restricted to ordinary Americans. Well before 1978, President Johnson, Robert Kennedy, and four of the seven members of the Warren Commission all articulated, if sometimes off the record, some level of skepticism about the Commission basic findings" [226].

The House Select Committee on Assassinations (HSCA) was formed in 1976 to reinvestigate the murders of John F. Kennedy and Martin Luther King, Jr., it worked until 1978; and in 1979 presented a Report plus twelve appendices which later were published by the US Congress.

One of the HSCA important findings was the assassination of John F. Kennedy resulted from a "probable conspiracy" [227] [228] without determining the kind of conspiracy or the participant(s); the Report did not excluded Oswald. Although the HSCA Report was better off than that of Warren, it still conveyed a disputable spot with regarding the fact that in the Zapruder movie -first publicly aired in 1975- the head of John F. Kennedy was moving *backward* against the direction of motorcade instead of forward. If the deadly bullet really came from the back side of John F. Kennedy, his head should had been leaning *forward* as an impact of bullet thrust from the back. The fact recorded on the movie is, his head was violently moving backward indicating that an object with a very strong thrust had been deployed from the front side maybe from the grassy knoll hitting JFK's head (see Zapruder Film, Part Five: Chapter 1).

It is not clear either why the Life magazine or the other party kept Zapruder movie for 12 years before release it. Moreover, according to Wim Dankbaar in **"Files on JFK"**, James E. Files an inmate in North American correctional facility has admitted that he fired the Remington Fireball gun from the grassy knoll killing John F. Kennedy [229]. A few years later, according to **"Files on JFK"**, Robert Tenenbaum the Chief Counsel for HSCA considered HSCA was "not designed to find the truth", he resigned over the HSCA decline to recall David Atlee Phillips on the suspicion of perjury on his testimony [230].

David Atlee Phillips was the government agency officer in Mexico City post when Lee Harvey Oswald allegedly visited the city [231]; another researcher claimed that it was not real Oswald but the impersonator.

The Warren Commission made the spectacular efforts and completed almost 900 pages of report on September 24, 1964 less than one year since it was ordered by President Johnson on November 29, 1963. The report was available to public 3 days later [232] and sparked the nationwide tumult about its accuracy. All documents collected by the Warren Commission went to National Archives and were deemed to be sealed for 75 years until 2039. It's something questionable, and after the enactment of Freedom of Information Act of 1966 and the JFK Record Act of 1992 the documents sealing for 75 years was legally changed. Up to 1992 almost all documents about 98% have been released to public, but another questionable 2% remained mystery. Let the public read and know the remaining 2 percents of the documents pertaining to the assassination of John F. Kennedy, let the documents released to the public without blackout and redacted, let all documents declassified; it has been 49 years more after the assassination and nobody would be prosecuted; and let John F. Kennedy be honorably acknowledged as a hero who bravely challenged the domination of Soviet Union in Latin America, and he forced Soviet to step back from Cuba for good, let John Fitzgerald Kennedy rest in honor, peace and dignity. The late US President John F. Kennedy deserved this **honor** without anybody losing anything.

In addition to 888-page report, the Warren Commission in November 1964 also published 26 volumes of important documents, including the testimony of 552 witnesses and more than 3,000 exhibits only to make the American more skeptical about the report. On November 23 all records were transferred to the National Archives with big question mark. The most questionable in the Commission conclusion is "the single bullet theory" devised by commission's Assistant Counsel Arlen Specter.

He later became Senator from Pennsylvania (1930 – 2013); who in a stunning move on April 28, 2009 after 44 years serving as Republican announced that he is switching side to the Democratic Party, and he sought for re-election in 2010 as a Democrat and lost. In 1992, the JFK Records Act created the Assassination Records Review Board to assemble the documents relating to JFK assassination. It issued a skeptical report:

> Doubts about the Warren Commission's findings were not restricted to ordinary Americans. Well before 1978, President Johnson, Robert Kennedy, and four of the seven members of the Warren Commission all articulated, if sometimes off the record, some level of skepticism about the Commission's basic findings [233].

Gerald Ford, a member of Warren Commission who later became the US President, sadly commented that the "CIA destroyed or kept from investigators critical secrets connected to the 1963 assassination of President John F. Kennedy." The critical secrets are still kept away from the public since the Warren Commission probe may put "certain classified and potentially damaging operations in danger of being exposed"; and the reaction "was to hide or destroy some information, which can easily be misinterpreted as collusion in JFK's assassination", Ford added [234].

After Warren Commission, three additional investigations have been completed; and all of them have agreed with the Warren Commission's conclusion that ONLY two shots struck JFK from the rear. The 3 investigations are:

(1) The Attorney General Ramsey Clark panel, in 1968

(2) The Rockefeller Commission, in 1975

(3) The House Select Committee on Assassination (HSCA), in 1978-79

HSCA reconsider the available evidence with the help of the forensics panel; it also involved Congressional hearings and at last concluded that Oswald's action to assassinate President Kennedy "probably as the result of a conspiracy".

It also concluded that Oswald fired *first*, *second* and *fourth* shots, and that an unidentified assassin fired *third* shot --but missed-- from near the corner of a picket fence above and to right front of JFK that was known as the grassy knoll at the Dealey Plaza. There is a big question "How did they know that the third shot missed JFK, while Zapruder movie as the strong evidence recorded that the head of JFK swayed backward as a bullet hit his right temple. The HSCA 1979 Final Report conformed to the Warren Report's 1964 conclusion about "magic bullet" which asserted that two bullets penetrated President Kennedy and Governor Connally were fired by Oswald from the 6th floor of the Texas School Book Depository. The HSCA also criticized the Warren Commission which failed to adequately consider the possibility of conspiracy.

[218] http://en.wikipedia.org/wiki/Nicholas_Katzenbach
[219] http://en.wikipedia.org/wiki/JFK_conspiracy
[220] http://en.wikipedia.org/wiki/Arlen_Specter
[221] http://en.wikipedia.org/wiki/Single_bullet_theory
[222] Spies, *ibid.*, p. 134
[223] history-matters.com
[224] *ibid.*
[225] Karen Bornemann Spies, "John F. Kennedy", Enslow Publishing Inc., Berkeley Height, NJ, 1999, p. 134
[226] http://en.wikipedia.org/wiki/Warren_Commission
[227] hystory-matters.com
[228] Spies, *op. cit.*, p. 132
[229] jfkmurdersolved.com
[230] *ibid.*
[231] http://en.wikipedia.org/wiki/David_Atlee_Phillips
[232] http://en.wikipedia.org/wiki/Lee_Harvey_Oswald
[233] http://en.wikipedia.org/wiki/Warren_Commission
[234] *ibid.*

Part Five: The Mystery Got Deeper

The more they investigate JFK assassination the deeper the mystery goes

Earl Warren as a Supreme Court justice was assumed to be aware that if his report was inaccurate he could have been labeled as "grossly inadequate"; but the fact is his report was far from accurate especially about the "single bullet theory" that penetrated President John F. Kennedy before wounding Governor John Connally.

The explanation of his decision to put his signature on the Warren Report could have been a simple truth and common sense "if something could happen to John F. Kennedy why not to himself if he should have declined the single bullet theory". The nature of bizarre Warren Report suggested that must be something or someone to protect, nobody knows until all files related to the assassination of President John F. Kennedy come to light and the case is reopened; the American public deserve to know what really happened to their legitimate President.

Earl Warren was a Supreme Court Justice when he was appointed as the chairman of Commission. He was a trial justice who knew the every aspect of law; and he knew he would not sacrifice his credibility by signing the bizarre report or signing without reading. The natural big question is on why did he accept the single bullet theory despite his awareness that it does not make any sense?

There must be a compelling situation for him to accept this bizarre theory; the question is who did force him to do so; it must be someone with higher rank than Warren himself. If he did not sign the report someday someone might have said: "Look, we could do it to JFK, we do not want it happen to you later", nobody blamed on him. However, when a Supreme Court justice had decided something, then who is more legitimate and trustworthy than him?

1. Zapruder Film

"One slip might have been accidental, but there were clearly intended to deceive" (Matthew Smith in "Conspiracy")

The story of Zapruder Film was legendary. Abraham Zapruder [1905-1970] was a businessman, he manufactured the woman clothing, and he was a democrat. When he knew that JFK would visit Dallas, Texas he prepared himself to record the historical moment with his brand new Bell-Howell movie camera. He was a common citizen, not a journalist or politician. He was just on the right time and right place but on the wrong moment. It's not clear, was Zapruder fortunate or unfortunate man. He was one and only person who through his camera witnessed the right side head of US President John F. Kennedy severely injured as a bullet hit him; he did want to share this horrible scene with anybody else. Therefore, as a part of deal on his famous film footage to **Life** Magazine, the frame number 313 should not be exposed, it was a frame which precisely recorded the assassination of President John F. Kennedy when his head *was leaning backward* hit by a fatal bullet.

Zapruder could not help himself, he wept in the court when he testified for the popular New Orleans District Attorney Jim Garrison on the trial of Clay Shaw who was prosecuted in the connection with assassination of US President John F. Kennedy. Later on, Shaw was found not guilty [235] of the charge. Zapruder donated $ 25,000.00 from his movie sale to the widow of police office JD Tippit. Four times Zapruder testified before the Warren Commission that the shot(s) came from the Grassy Knoll in front of President Kennedy, and NOT form the rear, the place from which Oswald was accused of having fired his Carcano rifle to kill President Kennedy. His famous photographic evidence later was altered to make an impression that the rearward movement of President John F. Kennedy's head has never happened at **all** [236]. This fact should have been an indication -not yet a proof- that there was a conspiracy, but the cover up was going on.

Another possibility of altering Zapruder film was questioned by Thomas Lipscomb who compared the Zapruder movie with another films taken at Dealy Plaza, Dallas Texas. He found on Zapruder movie that two women on the assassination site were wearing *white* shoes, while on the Polaroid photo they were wearing the *black* shoes [237]. "Shoesgate"? These shoes might be more popular than "shoes number 10" thrown by Al-Zaidi an Iraqi journalist to President George W. Bush at a press conference in Bagdad December 2008 (See the box: Cambridge Shoe).

Zapruder film is a piece of history; if there is someone to alter it must be for reason, either to conceal something or to blur the fact, and not just "printing error" [238] as J. Edgar Hoover easily answered.

Oliver Stone's "*JFK*" successfully reminds America on how much the nation and the world loved John F. Kenney and lost him when he died. "*JFK*" was based on the true story of independent investigator Jim Garrison, New Orleans District Attorney, who believed that the government agents were the key planners of the assassination. Stone believed, like other conspiracy theorists, that government agency or perhaps Lyndon B. Johnson himself might have been involved the assassination of President John F. Kennedy [239]. The reason for New Orleans, Louisiana District Attorney to investigate the assassination is, he believed that Oswald ever met a friend the **New Orleans** businessman Clay Laverne Show to discuss the assassination of President John F. Kennedy, and therefore he arrested Clay Show in 1967; but later he was acquitted by the jury in 1969. He became the only person ever prosecuted in connection with the murder of US President John F. Kennedy (see Box: Clay Laverne Show).

In 1992 The Congress passed the Assassination Materials Disclosure Act (AMDA) to preserve the historical evidence related to the President John F. Kennedy's assassination.

Under the AMDA, Zapruder film was preserved as the historic evidence, meanwhile Zapruder heirs were struggling to take back the film, and after the proper negotiation the government agreed to pay Zapruder heirs for $16 Million. In the Zapruder movie that could be reviewed on **jfkmurdersolved.com** and **YouTube.com**, the head of John F. Kennedy was hardly moving to left-backward indicating that the deadly bullet came from the right-front side to conform to James E. Files' confession in 2003 and Abraham Zapruder's testimony before the Warren Commission 1963-1964. The deadly bullet was really coming from the front-right side, it was not the first bullet; the first one -and was not decisive- came from the back side when the limousine passed the lamp post, and as soon the bullet hit John F. Kennedy his wife **Jacqueline** hold his shoulder with her right hand. Meanwhile, he was either pushed forward by the incoming bullet or was ducking slightly upon hearing a gun shot, he was the commandant of PT-109 naval ship and a veteran in the Pacific war, he knew how to intuitively duck to protect him self.

Cambridge Shoe

This incident inspired at least two another shoe throwing. According to Aljazeera website, one incident was in England on the first week of February 2009 where a protester shouting "Dictator" and threw a shoe at Wen Jiabao, the Chinese premier, during a speech at Cambridge University. Another incident was in Sweden February 4, 2009 when Benny Dagan the Israeli ambassador to Sweden was giving a lecture at University of Stockholm, a girl - maybe a student- has thrown a shoe at him hitting his chest. This daring girl then asked the policeman to give the shoe back to her; it was a pretty red shoe, an eyewitness said. It's no further information available whether Wen Jiabao or Benny Dagan recognized the shoe number as George W. Bush did "It number 10" and ducked to avoid the cold missile.

Two and one half seconds later when Jacqueline was embracing him he got a deadly shot; the splashing blood was visible from the hazy head; his head was uncontrollably moving slight left-backward and in a split second his body fell back altogether. Less than two seconds later Jacqueline Kennedy climbed up the limousine trunk to retrieve the fragment of her husband's head which was scattered on the trunk, and soon Secret Service agent Clint Hill put her back on the seat to prevent her from being ejected from the sudden accelerating limousine. It's clear that nobody used the seat belt. Her gown still laced with the blood when she attended the swearing in of Lyndon B. Johnson on Air Force One at 2:38 PM at the same day. Neither John F. Kennedy nor Emmet Till deserved the lynching, but the fact told us what happened.

Clay Laverne Show (1913-1974)

He retired in 1946 from the United States Army with a major rank, and upon retirement he became a successful businessman. His decorated records as a military man suggested that he was a very important person at the time; he might be a liaison officer who connected the USA with France and Belgium during the World War II. Three nations awarded him 3 different medals; the United States awarded him Legion of Merit and Bronze Star; the France awarded the Croix de Guere and appointed him Chevalier de l'Orde du Merite; while the Belgium awarded him Chevalier of the Order of the Crown of Belgium. Jim Garrison, New Orleans District Attorney prosecuted Shaw on the charge of being right-wing activist, he and his group including David Ferrie and Guy Banister were suspected of being involved in a conspiracy to kill President Kennedy [240]. On March 1, 1967 Shaw was arrested; Garrison has every confident that that Clay Shaw was Clay Bertrand the man named in the Warren Commission Report. Garrison believed that "Clay Bertrand" was Clay Shaw's pop name amongst the gay society in New Orleans, Louisiana. Garrison called Perry Russo an insurance salesperson as the main witness. Russo testified during January-February 1969 trial that he attended the party at David Ferrie's the apartment; Ferrie was an anti-Castro activist. Russo testified that at the party, Ferrie, Oswald, and "Clay Bertrand" aka Clay Shaw had discussed the assassination of John F. Kennedy. Garrison's preparation to prosecute Shaw seemed either in rush or in grief over the death of President John F. Kennedy; his main witness' story evolved from time to time.

Garrison's main record came form Shaw's first interrogation conducted by Andrew Sciambra the Assistant District Attorney who interrogated Shaw. It's not clear why Scimabra **did not include the party** attended by so-called "right-wing activists" Clay Shaw, Lee Oswald and David Ferrie in his interrogation memorandum. On another side Sciambra memorandum quoted that Russo met Shaw in two different times which "neither one was in the party". For the trial lawyer, this fact was like a piece of cake; it's pretty easy to shake the credibility of Russo before the jury. The jury deliberated less than sixty minutes to acquit Shaw. We can say now "*No party no guilty*". This case is almost like the OJ Simpson trial where his defense attorney said to the jury "If it (glove as the proof) does not fit (to OJS), you have to acquit". After the trial, Garrison wrote a book about the investigation and trial of Clay "***On the Trail of the Assassins***". Garrison insisted that Shaw had an "extensive international role as an employee of the CIA", it could be based on the international medals Shaw had received; while Shaw denied any connection with the CIA. There is a small note 5 years after Shaw died. Richard Helms the former director of the CIA testified under oath that Clay Laverne Shaw was "a part-time contact" of the CIA, in which he occasionally and voluntarily provided some information he obtained when he was traveling abroad in 1970's [241]. In that time so many American people who traveled abroad voluntarily provided such information, and it does mean that they're the CIA agents. The CIA -and other agencies- is not subject to blame. To blame on anybody does not resolve the problem, nor reveal the truth.

Here the frame-by-frame reviews on the famous Zapruder Film as available on YouTube.com, http://www.youtube.com/watch?v=1q91RZko5Gw

Frame #	Scene
1-132	Police motor cycles preceding the limo and other cars, most spectators were on the curb
133	Presidential limo coming from the curve, followed by the SS car
222	Someone standing on the green grass field across the limo, most spectators were on curb on the right side of limo
232	A man with white long sleeve waving to motorcade
253-258	JFK was still alive
262 - 268	JFK was leaning forward until passing the lamp post indicating he was hit by a bullet from the back, most probably the bullet hit his neck before exiting on the

		Adam apple. Frame #262 most probably was the very first shot
	272	Limo just passed the lamp post, JFK body already leaned against his wife indicating he was not able to control himself
	276	Jackie was embracing JFK with her left hand indicating that she held JFK from falling forward without knowing another bullet from another direction was ready for him
	285	Limo passing in front of the man with white long sleeve shirt and dark trouser
	291	JFK was leaning forward on Jackie's hand, might be he was unconscious
	297	Jackie was changing position, moving her body to see JFK from the front
	298 - 309	Limo passed the lady dressing red coat, on her left side was a man wearing white trouser and dark overall. Here Jackie embracing JFK with her right hand
	313 - 314	A blow on the head, JFK's head moved violently backward, blood splashing. Across the limo on the green field, a young girl (may be 6-year old) was running closer to find a better spot to see the President
	318-321	JFK body leaning backward against the car seat
	322-324	JFK body fell down backward against the car seat
	328	Jackie pushed JFK forward to put him for straight sitting
	342	Jackie climbed up the limo trunk to retrieve the fraction of JFK's head, limo passing in front of three men wearing dark jackets, one of them aiming the camera toward the motorcade. A SS agent put Jackie back to the car seat
	381-480	Limo speeding to hospital

Most of us think that the Zapruder film is pristine even its copies are still original as it was, but JFK researcher Matthew Smith in his book "*Conspiracy*" points out to some sequence have been changed in the Zapruder film. Smith came to this conclusion after comparing a copy presented to the Warren Commission with another copy.

Smith has found that the Zapruder frame 161 had been substituted for frame 168, frame 166 occupied frame 171, and frame 210 changed to be frame 208; he expressed his displeasure "One slip might have been accidental, but there were clearly intended to deceive" [242]. The latest development of the Zapruder movie saga is the discovery that some parts of it have been altered for the unknown purpose.

The original shoe color of two women on the crime scene was black, but they appeared as white in the Zapruder movie. The conviction of the color was obtained by **Thomas Libscomb** after comparing the movie with the Polaroid photograph for the very same shoes. The "deliberate alteration" of shoe color suggests that there was something to hide, may be the presence of other assassin as *US News and World Report* asserts [243]. Someone might have altered the Zapruder movie for reason, or to have it being considered as a hoax especially about the existence of spectators in certain frame and the different account about the spectators' color of shirt and shoes. Even if there are some deliberate alterations, Zapruder movie is still delivering the perfect evidence that President Kennedy was shot from the **back** and **front** within a split of second.

[235] http://en.wikipedia.org/wiki/Clay_Shaw
[236] Brian Sprinkle and James Butman, "*Armchair Detective*", Rainbow Books Inc., Highland City, Fla. 1992; p. 17.
[237] Paul Bedard, "*Tampering With the Zapruder Film?*", US News & World Report, May 22, 2006; p. 10
[238] Sprinkle and Butman, *ibid.*
[239] Karen Bornemann Spies, "*John F. Kennedy*", Enslow Publishing Inc., Berkeley Height, NJ, 1999, p. 134
[240] http://en.wikipedia.org/wiki/Clay_Laverne_Shaw
[241] *ibid.*
[242] Smith, *ibid.*, p. 116 - 117
[243] *US New and World Report,* May 22, 2009 p. 10

2. Dictabelt

The discussion about the obsolete dictabelt became hotter and more interesting

Dictabelt is recording machine commonly used in 1960's that recorded dictations or sounds in grooves on a celluloid, it is gramophone alike; it was produced by American Dictaphone in 1947. Dictabelt was used by police and court before replaced with more sophisticated digital recorder. Both gramophone and dictabelt use stylus, either to record the audio or to play the recorded audio. One dictabelt used by Dallas Police Department (DPD) at the time when President John F. Kennedy was assassinated in Dallas, Texas Friday November 22, 1963 was stuck in recording position and it recorded the "impulse of shootings". This dictabelt was later investigated by the House Select Committee on Assassinations (HSCA) to find evidence relating to the assassination of President Kennedy.

The DPD operated two channels of radio communication; Channel I was for daily normal police radio communication, and Channel II was specifically used for the presidential motorcade. Channel I and Channel II Radio Communications were recorded by a different recording system in the DPD radio operating room. **Dictabelt** was used to record Channel I communication, and an **Audiograph** machine was used to record Channel II communication.

The both machines used the stylus to engrave a track or groove into a plastic recording medium; the difference between two is: the Dictabelt using rotating cylinder and the Audiograph using a flat disk like gramophone record. The other difference is: Channel I was continuous recordings, and Channel II was voice-activated recordings (VAR); therefore the verbal communications on the two channels were **not** synchronized [in time] because Channel II recorded whenever in use only. This technical specification should have been assessed first before discussing further about Dictabelt which recorded the impulse of shootings.

A historic moment had been captured on Dictabelt when a defective microphone button of the communication system on one out of 18 DPD motorcycles was accidentally stuck in "transmit position" on 12:28 PM Friday November 22, 1963 2 minutes before the assassination of the millennium took place on Dealey Plaza, Dallas Texas. Why 12:30? Do we believe that 12:30 PM was a coincidence, and not a meticulously planned action? Was it a T-Time on a D-Day? In a big case, a small clue sometimes has a deep meaning. The dictabelt became a big issue when the HSCA used it to conclude that President John F. Kennedy was assassinated probably as a result of a **conspiracy**. The HSCA is an official agency established in 1976 by the United States House of Representatives to investigate the assassination of JFK and Martin Luther King Jr., although conspiracy theory have been looming, yet no one single government agency but the HSCA used the term of "conspiracy", ever. At the end of its investigations in December 1978, HSCA was preparing a final report which concluded that Oswald was a lone assassin when it learned that a dictabelt used on the day of assassination might have contained a clue. However, upon hearing a significant testimony regarding to the recently-found dictabelt that recorded a play back of the fourth shot, the HSCA changed its mind and concluded that there was the **second shooter** who had fired a fourth shot at President John F. Kennedy on a fateful day Friday November 22, 1963 in Dallas, Texas.

The important dictabelt was found by the researchers Mary Ferrell and Gary Mack [244] ten years after the Warren Commission concluded that Lee Harvey Oswald acted alone in the assassination of President John F. Kennedy. This disputable dictabelt DID NOT record an audible gunshots, instead the investigators compared the impulse patterns resulted from the gunshots and the following echo recorded on the dictabelt to those of recordings on firing test of Carcano rifle in 1978 from the 6th floor of Texas School Book Depository and from the grassy knoll on right front of where a presidential motorcade was traveling at Dealey Plaza in 1963; this is a comparative research.

A comprehensive and detailed analysis of the dictabelt was performed by a team at **Bolt, Beranek & Newman** (BB&N) acoustic firm under supervision of Dr. James E. Barger. Based on this comparative research, BB&N concluded that the **impulse pattern** [of 1st, 2nd, and 4th shots] were coming from Texas School Book Depository, while the **impulse pattern** [of 3rd shot was] coming from the grassy knoll with the probability of 50%.

On December 29, 1978 Dr. Weiss and Dr. Ashckenasy, acoustic experts, in a testimony before HSCA presented their finding that the third shot came from the grassy knoll "with a probability of 95 percent or better" [245]. Dr. Aschkenasy explained:

> "The numbers could not be refuted ... The numbers just came back again and again the same way, pointing in only one direction, as to what these findings were. [246]"

Dr. Ernest Aschkenasy and Dr. Mark Weiss confirmed this conclusion and determined that the probability was up to 95% [242] [248]; both Dr. Barger and Dr. Weiss testified before the HSCA. Dr. Barger testified before the HSCA that based on his analysis, the motorcycle with the "stuck open microphone" was about "120 to 138 feet" behind the President Kennedy's limousine [249]. There is no doubt that the dictabelt is important evidence and a turning point of HSCA conclusion. The question is who was using this very important dictabelt?

Based on the result of comparison between sound on Dictabelt and the sound from field test and an amateur film sequence, the HSCA concluded that the dictabelt recording must be from H.B. McLain's motorcycle. Officer McLain later testified before the HSCA that the microphone of dictabelt on his motorcycle was often stuck in "open" [recording] position. McLain himself never heard the actual dictabelt recording until after his testimony, and he denied that the recording originated from his motorcycle.

Without any clear motive, Officer McLain *revised* his story that **he was not in the plaza** when recording had been made, he said he followed the presidential car to the hospital [250]. If his revised story was accepted then it would discredit and undermine the dictabelt as acoustic evidence. However, upon combing all available photographs taken from Dealey Plaza *after* President Kennedy being taken to Parkland Hospital, it was revealed that **officer McLain was really where he first said he was;** and was **not accompanying** the Presidential motorcade to Parkland Hospital immediately after President Kennedy was shot; he was right here on the Elm Street [251]; who did ask him to revise his story and why?

Since the dictabelt became a turning point in the investigation -and evidence- of the Kennedy assassination, it is a matter of fact that the criticism, proponent and opponent sides are looming ever since. The discussion about the obsolete dictabelt became intense and more interesting since from this point the researchers and investigators are looking for the additional evidence in JFK assassination; here, what the experts say about the dictabelt; here their quoted notes:

[1] "In 2003, ABC News based on **Dale K. Myers** computer analysis, concluded that the recordings on the Dictabelt could **not** have come from Dealey Plaza, and Dallas Police Department (DPD) Police Officer **McLain** was **not** yet at Dealey Plaza at the time of the assassination." Jim Bowles -a Dallas police dispatcher in November 1963- believes that the sound recording originated from an officer on a three-wheeled motorcycle "at the Dallas Trade Mart", while McLain himself believes it was from another officer on a three-wheeler "near the Trade Mart". "A consultant to the HSCA **Richard E. Sprague** explained that McLain's motorcycle was actually 250 feet behind the presidential limousine, not 120 to 138 feet when the first shot was fired. On another part of dictabelt recording there was **Sheriff Bill Decker** voice "Hold everything secure" about a minute after the assassination at the point where the HSCA concluded the assassination shots were being recorded."

"The FBI disputed the validity of this acoustic evidence and therefore the Justice Department asked the National Academy of Sciences [NAS] to review it. Dr. Norman Ramsey and the panel of NAS scientists determined in 1982 that there was NO strong evidence for gunshots caught on the dictabelt recording, and that the HSCA assertion as the impulses [of gun shots] were actually recorded about a minute **after** the shooting, not at the time of shooting. **Dr. James E. Barger** of BB&N acoustic firm upon asked about the NAS analysis, responded that the **weak** phrase ["Hold everything secure"] which was also recorded on the Audiograph from Channel II DPD radio communication at the time of assassination was **caused by** the fourth shot. Therefore, it would seem that the sounds that we connected with gunfire were made about a minute **after** the assassination shots were fired. In March 2001 Dr. Donald B. Thomas analysis was published in **Science & Justice;** he used a different radio transmission synchronization to claim that the NAS analysis was error. In 2003, **Michael O'Dell** claimed that both NAS and Dr. Thomas had used incorrect timelines because they assumed that the Dictabelt ran continuously. The impulses actually recorded too late to be the real shots even with Thomas' alternative synchronization. A respond on O'Dell analysis by **CourtTV** channel in November 2003 asserted that "the gunshot sounds did not match test gunshot recordings fired on Dealey Plaza any better than random noise"; and right away in December 2003 Dr. Thomas pointed out to the error he claimed occurred in **CourtTV** analysis" [252].

[2] McLain a Dallas police officer, who rode the motorcycle, however without an explanation, revised his story; and on the other hand Matthew Smith in "*Conspiracy*" explained that McLain revised his story since he was NOT in the plaza at the time of the dictabelt recording [253] [254].

The mystery of dictabelt does not end, it is still continuing because it is one among preserved evidence that lead the HSCA to the conclusion there was a *conspiracy* in the assassination of President John F. Kennedy.

[3] In November 2003 the *CourtTV* program *Forensic Files* reported that a new study of the acoustical evidence by a signal analysis firm, *Sensimetrics Inc.* -used its computer program *Impulses*- had concluded that there is no valid evidence for gunshots on the DPD recordings, contrary to the findings of the HSCA in 1978. The actual test shot pattern from the grassy knoll **is not directly comparable** to the suspect pattern because it was recorded in August 1978 with **90** degree temperature while the assassination occurred in November with **65** degrees. The echoes of gunshot recorded at the microphone and the speed of sound are affected by air temperature.

The test was recorded on a *stationary* microphone, while sound was recorded by a system on a *traveling* police motorcycle, therefore HSCA consultants adjusted the analysis including to position of microphones; "the result is 10 coincidences among the 14 succeeding impulses and the 12 known echoes in the test shot pattern" before concluding that the DPD suspect pattern resembles a grassy knoll gunshot. On the other hand, *Sensimetrics* to apply "less subjective" criteria, only five coincidences are found; and therefore its analysis contained serious errors. *Sensimetrics* had applied the wrong criteria, as Indiana Jones said in *Raiders of the Lost Ark*: **"They're looking in the wrong place!"**

The *Sensimetrics* analysis had some problems: *first*, they used a different playback of dictabelt **not** used by HSCA. The pattern analyzed by the HSCA has the differences in the relative amplitudes of some impulses than of those analyzed by *Sensimetrics*.

251

Second, the HSCA used the re-recorded sound from the original, by analyzing the 60 Hertz power hum the HSCA concluded that the re-recorded sound is 5% faster, therefore the adjustment have to be made by correction factor of 1.05 because the time had been compressed to 95%. The example for the "time compression" is the time interval between the Sheriff Decker and Sgt. Bellah broadcast, it was 171 seconds while on the FBI version was 178 seconds.

Sensimetrics made mistake in the analysis, it used the wrong speed correction factor in the computer program *Impulses;* it used 0.95 instead of 1.05 factor which more compressing rather than decompressing. *Third*, *Sensimetrics* used "the wrong signal to noise ratio (S/NR) in establishing the threshold for inclusion of impulses for comparison". The threshold has to be applied to separate the suspect signals from the motorcycle noise, it was based on the noise level in the segment of recording *immediately prior to* the impulses assumed to be the shock wave and muzzle blast. "This S/N ratio left 14 impulses above the threshold and 12 impulses of similar amplitude on the test shot pattern.

Sensimetrics misunderstood the logic of this approach and used a threshold that left 26 impulses on the DPD pattern for comparison". Another error is they only entered 25 of the 26 echo delay times determined by the HSCA consultants. "The *Sensimetrics* and **CourtTV** folks also failed to understand that the matching data in and of itself does not establish evidence for gunfire on the recordings" [255] [256].

[4] Dr. Donald B. Thomas is a research entomologist at USDA Agricultural Research Service; he became interested in the John F. Kennedy assassination after reading an article about Oliver Stone's film ***JFK*** in *Newsweek* magazine. He wrote some scientific articles in British forensic journal ***Science & Justice*** [257].

(a) Dr. Thomas realized that his article published in **Science & Justice** had made a lot of people angry. The acoustic evidence does contradict the official version of events that there were exactly three shots. He explained that most conspiracy theorists are convinced that JFK received the frontal shot through the throat and the head, but the acoustical evidence indicates only one shot from the front. He is not going to try to convince those who do not believe to his explanation, but he wants us to know the facts; he wants to show how the "acoustical evidence meshes with the other crime scene evidence, particularly the Zapruder film". When the HSCA was first confronted with this acoustical evidence, they asked the Acoustical Society of America which refers to Bolt, Baranek & Newman (BB&N) of Cambridge, Massachusetts. BB&N found the "fingerprint" of a gunshot from the Grassy Knoll. The second expert opinion came from the Computer Science Department of Queens College, NY. Professor Mark Weiss and his assistant Arnold Aschkenasy "eliminated the cause of the uncertainty and concurred that there was scientific evidence of a shot from the Grassy Knoll on the police tapes. [258] [259]"

(b) The HSCA based on the acoustical evidence found that there was one shot fired from the Grassy Knoll, this important finding needs a second opinion and was *confirmed*. The finding led to "the official conclusion that there probably was a conspiracy behind the death of President Kennedy". After a formal request to the Department of Justice to reopen the case, it considered further study of the acoustical evidence. The third study conducted by National Research Council found that the HSCA conclusion **was not valid because the recordings occurred after the assassination was over**. Dr. Thomas wants to explain "how one might arrive at a different conclusion" [260] [261].

(c) Mary Ferrell, a Dallas legal secretary and JFK researcher, in 1977 told the HSCA that she'd heard the recording of DPD radio traffic around the time Kennedy died; and the HSCA retrieved the Dictabelt in May 1978. The HSCA's general counsel G. Robert Blakey a former federal prosecutor chose James Barger the audio scientist to assess the evidence. Barger compared the sound impulses on the recordings with the sound of real gunfire. In August 1978, he and his team performed the ballistics tests.

He set up 36 microphones along motorcade route at the Dealey Plaza to record the shots fired from the sixth-floor Texas Book Depository window and from the grassy knoll. The results then compared with the impulses on the Dictabelt; his findings "contrasted with those of the Warren Commission, which ruled that Oswald fired three shots at Kennedy's limousine". Barger identified *at least four sound-wave patterns*, three of them resembled shots fired from the sixth-floor window, and one resembled a shot from the grassy knoll. Two other acoustic experts, Prof. Weiss and Aschkenasy, supported Barger's conclusion. The acoustic evidence became the keystone of the House panel's finding in January 1979 that Kennedy had "probably" been killed by conspirators who, besides Oswald, couldn't be identified.

In May 1982, on the request of the Justice Department, a 12-scientist NRC panel ruled that Barger's supposed gunshots "came too late to be attributed to assassination shots." In 2001, Donald Thomas wrote in a British forensics journal an article, his conclusion: five shots had been fired at Kennedy's motorcade from two different directions [262] [263].

(d) "..... I should point out that the work that was originally done by BB&N, when they concluded that they had found the gunshots, the House Select Committee itself asked for a second opinion, so they had the Computer Science Department at Queens College - folks that are sonar experts - to review the evidence. They confirmed and actually extended the study to show that there was a gunshot from the Grassy Knoll among the shots that were identified by BB&N. Now, the explanation for what is happening here is - the approach to trying to debunk that evidence by - first by the FBI - well, pretty much simultaneously, the FBI and NRC panel kind of worked together on this, and yet came to different conclusions. The NRC panel, their primary argument was that these sounds are not synchronous with the time of the assassination.

That is, the sounds acoustically identified as gunfire, they claim were recorded about sixty seconds after the assassination..... I mean, the acoustics evidence itself doesn't stand alone, and it seems like it's corroborated by analysis of the Zapruder film. Can you elaborate on that?....

Now, since the acoustical experts didn't know where the motorcycle was, but they did know that the motorcade was first on Houston Street and then on Elm Street, what they did was they put out an array of 36 microphones in a row - in a line - on Houston Street and then on Elm Street..... And when they do, they find this, out of the 18 motorcycles that were in the motorcade, the filmed evidence eliminates all but one guy, a police officer named McLaine..... From his position, we can say that he is the one cop that was in the right place - that he could have been in the right place at the right time. [264] [265]"

(e) The Dictabelt #10 that recorded the gunshots had been a disputable topic among the scientists. Physicist Richard Garwin and his colleagues said the alleged gun shot sounds occurred approximately one minute after Kennedy was killed; they were not gunshots at all. He could not say what created such sound impulses. His article was a response to Dr. DB Thomas who in 2001 reviewed the findings of acoustic scientists by the HSCA in 1978.

So who's right? Garwin and colleagues focus on the timing of Dictabelt #10, while Thomas focuses on the nature of the sound impulses. We have the photographic evidence from the Zapruder film showing Kennedy's head backwards. The bullet fired from the knoll pushed Kennedy backward is plausible conjecture, regardless of the acoustic evidence. If FBI agents Sibert and O'Neill saw a more massive head wound, that's more evidence of a shot from the front [266] [267].

The HSCA in its investigation analyzed the dictabelt recording on November 22, 1962 to track the number, timing, and origin of the shots fired in Dealey Plaza on the day of JFK assassination.

The HSCA concluded that the recording came from microphone on McLain's motorcycle escorting the presidential motorcade. The Commission also concluded that it's a high probability that two gunmen fired at President Kennedy. There were *six impulse patterns* found on the dictabelt recording which indicated that up to 6 (*six*) shots have been fired from the Texas School Book Depository and the grassy knoll. "The acoustical analysis firm hired by the committee recommended that the committee conduct an acoustical reconstruction of the assassination in Dealey Plaza to determine if any of the six impulse patterns on the dispatch tape were fired from the Texas School Book Depository or the grassy knoll. [268]"

[244] Smith, *ibid.*, p. 69
[245] Scheim, David E., "Contract On America", Shapolsky Publishers, New York 1988, p. 27
[246] *ibid.*
[247] *ibid.*, p. 69-70
[248] http://en.wikipedia.org/wiki/Dictabelt_evidence_relating_to_the_assassination_of_John_F._Kennedy
[249] *ibid.*
[250] Smith, *ibid.*, p. 69 - 70
[251] *ibid.*, p. 69-70
[252] en.wikipedia.org/dictabelt
[253] http://pages.prodigy.net/whiskey99/courttv.htm
[254] http://pages.prodigy.net/whiskey99/courttv.htm under the title of Impulsive Behavior: The *CourtTV - Sensimetrics* Acoustical Evidence Study by D.B. Thomas (C) 2003 Donald B. Thomas
[255] http://pages.prodigy.net/whiskey99/courttv.htm
[256] http://pages.prodigy.net/whiskey99/ courttv.htm, the original article was written by Dr. Donald B. Thomas, published on Science & Justice December 2003 issue
[257] http://www.spartacus.schoolnet.co.uk/JFKthomasD.htm
[258] Jefferson Morley, *"The Man Who Did Not Talk"*, *Playboy* magazine, November 2007
[259] Thomas, Donald B., *"Hear no Evil: The Acoustical Evidence in the Kennedy Assassination"* (2001)
[260] Jefferson Morley, *ibid.*
[261] Thomas, Donald B., *"Crosstalk: Synchronization of Putative Gunshots with Events in Dealey Plaza"* (2002)
[262] Jefferson Morley, *ibid.*
[263] Jefferson Morley, *"The JFK Murder"*, *The Reader's Digest* magazine, March 2005
[264] efferson Morley, *ibid.*
[265] Interview with Donald B. Thomas by **Rex Bradford** on April 5, 2006
[266] efferson Morley, *ibid.*
[267] efferson Morley, *"The Man Who Did Not Talk"*, *Playboy* magazine, November 2007
[268] http://en.wikipedia.org/wiki/JFK_conspiracy

3. Autopsy

> John F. Kennedy rear head wound diameter was **two and three quarter inches,** the same wound "measuring five and one-eighth inches by seven inches".

Autopsy or post mortem examination is a comprehensive medical procedure on the corpse to determine the cause and kind of death and to evaluate any possibility of disease or injury; the autopsy should be performed by *certified* medical profession or pathologist. If a death is suspicious then the autopsy is mandatory to determine the cause of death. Autopsy is a medical-legal procedure and not a political-influential matter; after 50 years since the assassination of a sitting US President, the public should have had a certain assessment about the assassination and they have the rights to know. The autopsy of John F. Kennedy body was performed on November 22, 1963 8:00 PM at the Bethesda Naval Hospital, Bethesda, Maryland. The autopsy was performed by **Commander James J. Humes** and **Dr. J. Thornton Boswell**, both of them never conducted any autopsy before; the consultant of autopsy was **Colonel Pierre A. Fink**. None of them was a forensic pathologist [269].

A witness Lieutenant Richard A. Lipsey; said in 1979 that John F. Kennedy's body arrived in a body bag inside an unidentified **gray metal coffin** delivered to the back door. Around 20 minutes later, a *polished bronze coffin* was admitted at the front door accompanied by Jacqueline and Robert Kennedy [270]. Two Federal Agents James W. Siebert and Francis X. O'Neil witnessed the arrival of John F. Kennedy's body with more blood like a surgery on the head area, while the doctors at Parkland Hospital where the body arrived first, maintained that they **did not** perform surgery other than tracheotomy a small incision at "the front-entry wound to the throat by extension "to help John F. Kennedy breathe [271].

The both said Commander Humes removed the bullet from John F. Kennedy and handed it over to them, later on it had completely disappeared; nobody ever saw it again [272].

The doctors at Parkland Hospital provided a different account that (1) the bullet came from the front-right, (2) the second bullet came from behind, and (3) the third bullet came from the front-right again to blow President Kennedy's rear head out. A German computer expert, Joachim Markus who was known in Smith-Vidit study, confirmed the third fatal shot came from the grassy knoll in the front-right of the Presidential limousine; the acoustic evidence supported his conclusion.

Two shots at least came from behind limousine; one of them missed and hit the curb throwing a tiny fragment of concrete up then flying to make a scratch on James Tague [273]. He got a minor injury on his face; he was standing on a small concrete median near the underpass on the Elm Street Dallas, Texas where motorcade of President Kennedy was on their way. Tague's minor injury might be resulted from a fragment of flying concrete that struck by a bullet from the grassy knoll on the Elm Street. The spot at the curb where the concrete was hit by the bullet; now is marked with the new concrete mix that looks different with the rest of curb. The Kennedy's throat wound was allegedly resulted from the exit of first shot, and the wound on his back "was shifted" a couple inches upward to match the "single bullet theory" in the Warren Commission Report. According to Smith-Vidit study if a bullet had entered John F. Kennedy's back and exited at his throat, then the sniper should have been lying on the middle of Elm Street. John Connally wounds were resulted from *another two bullets*, one bullet came from behind and hit through his back and exited his chest, while the second bullet came from the grassy knoll hitting his wrist, went through, and hit his thigh; the second bullet rested here [274]. Contrary to the public opinion, the single bullet theory is a very smart scenario ever; otherwise it could not dupe so many gullible people for so long time.

How many of us did realize that the Warren Commission **never** saw the X-rays and medical photograph of John F. Kennedy's autopsy performed at Bethesda Naval Hospital, Maryland?

This special medical procedure was very important but never be a part of the Warren Commission. X-rays were missing or appeared to have been altered [275]. Even there was a suspicion that second brain -not belong to Kennedy- was used in the Kennedy's autopsy cover up [276]; it was unbelievable that John F. Kennedy's brain **disappeared** between April 1965 to October 1966 [277]. Agent O'Neil witnessed the brain of John F. Kennedy was removed [278], and it disappeared never be seen ever since.

The physicians at Parkland Hospital maintained their observation John F. Kennedy wound indicated that he must have been shot from the front NOT from the rear as Warren Commission told, but a Secret Service agent told them to say "it's form rear" [279]. HSCA appointed by the House of Representative in 1979 concluded that the shot(s) had come from two directions: book depository and grassy knoll although it could not identify the gunman or gunmen or the nature of plot to kill US President John F. Kennedy. Autopsy should have been an objective medical description of facts based on the comprehensive observation, but in the autopsy of John F. Kennedy there were at least two different descriptions over one single same fact.

According to the Parkland Hospital medical doctors, John F. Kennedy head wound diameter was **two and three quarter inches**, but the very same wound was "measuring five and one-eighth inches by seven inches" according to the doctors at Bethesda Naval Hospital [280]. This is an unacceptable discrepancy in the serious case related to the President of United States John F. Kennedy, his body should have been exhumed to determine the exact measure of his head wound and to confirm the allegedly penetrated neck by a magic bullet.

To trace back to the mystery of John F. Kennedy autopsy, there were some unusual incidents related to it:

(1) The body of John F. Kennedy was taken to Washington, DC; before autopsy performed in Texas, this action violated the Texas Law. The wounded body of President John F. Kennedy was rushed to Parkland Hospital and he was pronounced dead upon arrival. According to Texas Law, the autopsy should be performed in Texas, but the body of John F. Kennedy was immediately taken to the capital and transported on Air Force One altogether with new President Lyndon B. Johnson. President Kennedy's body underwent the autopsy at Bethesda Naval Hospital on Friday night of November 22, 1963.

(2) The pathologists at Bethesda Naval Hospital concluded that the deadly bullet had entered slightly above and 1 inch to the right of the external *occipital protuberance* (occiput = a part of back head; protuberance = the 'leading' curve), exiting through the right side of the skull above the ear. It does mean that the bullet entering from the back head, this is contrary to the evidence either autopsy photographs or frame #313 of Zapruder film or both. The physicians at Parkland Hospital maintained that the head wound of John F. Kennedy indicated that he was shot from the front, but the Secret Service told them to say "from the rear".

(3) The another bullet entered JFK's back about the level of **third thoracic vertebra** (chest section) as Dr. Burkley recorded on the death certificate, with the supporting evidence of the holes both on Kennedy's shirt and jacket; while three Bethesda Hospital doctors informed the HSCA that the wound was at the level of the *sixth cervical* **vertebra** (neck section), at the base of neck; the single same wound was viewed at two different places. However, there's still another effort to cover up this material evidence. In 2007 an "analysis" was made and determined that John F. Kennedy's (shirt and) "jacket was bunched below his neckline, and was not lying smoothly along his skin, so the clothing measurements have been subject to historical criticism as being untrustworthy on the matter of the exact location of the back wound" [281].

If Kennedy's shirt and suit jacket were bunched below his neckline, then the hole in his jacket and shirt should have been more than one each; the available material evidence was ONLY one bullet hole in his shirt and one bullet hole in his suit jacket; it definitively means that his shirt and suit jacket were NOT bunched below his neckline. These double holes were between 5 and 6 inches (12.5-15 cm) below Kennedy's collar.

(4) The Assassination Records Review Board in 1998 criticized the autopsy because the original draft of the autopsy made by Commander James Humes at the time of the autopsy at Bethesda Naval Hospital was burned out, as well the another autopsy materials.

(5) A mysterious bullet on the stretcher at Parkland Hospital was found by a Secret Service agent; it was neither obtained from Kennedy's nor Connally's body. Although it is a good job to find something; but the bullet could **not** be used as the legitimate evidence, because it could be a planted evidence to distract the investigation. Only the bullet removed by a pathologist from a victim would be the legal evidence.

(6) Commander James J. Humes the head of Bethesda Naval Hospital and Dr. J. Thornton Boswell NEVER conducted any autopsy before, nor did Colonel Pierre A. Fink [282] "a sudden consultant" for Kennedy's autopsy.

(7) Lieutenant Richard A. Lipsey in 1979 made a statement that he was present at the time of the Kennedy coffin delivered at Bethesda Naval Hospital, he said the Kennedy's body arrived at Bethesda Naval Hospital in an unmarked vehicle [283]; but twenty minutes later a polished bronze coffin was admitted at the front door of Bethesda Naval Hospital accompanied by Jacqueline Kennedy and Robert Kennedy. A staff member of the hospital recalled the arrival of second (ornate) coffin while he was ALREADY taking X-ray film of the President's body for development to another building of the hospital [284].

(8) John Stringer, a former US Navy photographer had denied that he made the photographs of President's brain; he used another film unlike the circulating photograph [285].

Gerald McKnight, the author of ***"Breach of Trust"*** wrote in anguish "This massive corruption of autopsy records was undertaken with one purpose to ensure that the medical evidence in the Kennedy assassination was consistent with the official government version of a lone assassin.... The overwhelming weight of evidence support the view the President Kennedy's official autopsy report was deliberately falsified to suppress the fact that he was the victim of conspiracy" [286].

It took fifteen years to acknowledge in a government report that the autopsy "had been incompetently conducted, full of gross errors and failure to carry out the standard forensic procedures, in the investigation of an 'unnatural' violent death [287]." The important medical evidence suggested that a five-inch-diameter hole was in the back right-hand side of the President's head as witness Roy Kellerman a Secret Service agent testified. He was in the front seat of presidential limousine next to the driver. Another Secret Service agent Clint Hill testified that "a portion of the President's head on the right rear side was missing".

Robert McClelland a doctor at Parkland Hospital who examined JFK body testified that JFK's back right head was blown out, with "posterior cerebral tissue and some cerebellar tissue missing." Douglas Horne a chief analyst of the Assassination Record Review Board said he was "90 to 95 percent certain" that the photographs of JFK's brain in the National Archives are not JFK's [288].

All testimonies indicated that the JFK's head wound was an exit wound, and it pointed to the existence of the second shooter from the front which shot the fatal head shot as depicted in the

Zapruder film. With this medical evidence, the single bullet theory should be rejected.

[269] Smith, Matthew, *"Conspiracy"*, Citadel Press Book, New York, July 2005, pp. **132 - 133**
[270] Smith, *ibid.*, p. 133
[271] Smith, *ibid.*, pp. 133 - 134
[272] Smith, *ibid.*, p. 134
[273] Smith, *ibid.*, pp. 134 - 135
[274] Smith, *ibid.*
[275] Spies, *ibid.* p.131
[276] Paul Bedard, *ibid.*
[277] Spies, *loc.cit.*
[278] Smith, *ibid.*, p. 136
[279] Spies, *ibid.*
[280] Smith, *ibid.*, pp. 132 - 133
[281] wikipedia.org
[282] Smith, *ibid.*, p. 132 - 133
[283] *ibid.*, p. 133
[284] *ibid.*, p. 133
[285] *ibid.*, p. 136
[286] McKnight, Gerald D., *"Breach of Trust"*, University Press of Kansas, 2005, p. 153
[287] McKnight, *ibid.*
[288] http://en.wikipedia.org/wiki/JFK_conspiracy

4. Mysterious Bullet

James Thomas Tague was a spectator on Elm Street when a bullet cut a small fragment of concrete and in turn hit his face. The bullet came from a mysterious weapon on a fateful day where a US President was killed nearby. Tague was standing on a small concrete median near the underpass on Elm Street in Dallas, Texas where motorcade of John F. Kennedy was on their way. A bullet struck the curb and cut a fragment of concrete median. The fragment of concrete -and not the bullet- then struck Tague's face and cut his right cheek. There was a report about the incident, but no further action had taken place. Had the incident been not important, nobody would have paid attention and nobody secretly repaired it; but an unknown person repaired the crack [289] without the consent of authority. Is it tampering with evidence?

The Warren Commission declared that the bullet killed President John F. Kennedy was a single bullet which made seven wounds altogether to John F. Kennedy and Texas Governor accompanying President on the same limousine. According to Warren Commission report, there were only 3 (three) bullets fired from *behind* President John F. Kennedy and *above* his car. **One** bullet hit all the way through John F. Kennedy's body then the same bullet hit Governor John Connally; the **second** bullet hit John F. Kennedy's head (from behind) and instantly killed him. The **third** bullet missed both John F. Kennedy and Governor Connally and hit the curb on the south of Main Street. The Warren Commission report also stated that Lee Harvey Oswald killed police officer JD Tippit and President John F. Kennedy, "no other than Oswald had planned and carried the assassination".

Navy pathologist James J. Humes accurately found the bullet hole on President Kennedy's back "below the shoulders and two inches to the right of the middle of spine". However, John Connally until his final day on June 15, 1993 maintained that President John F. Kennedy was killed by the first and third bullet, and Connally himself was hit by the second bullet [290].

What did the extraordinary single bullet hit both President John F. Kennedy and Governor John Connally, and what kind of wounds did John F. Kennedy and John Connally suffered from?

According to the medical report, Governor John Connally suffered from the wounds in his (1) back, (2) ribs, (3) wrist, and (4) thigh. This bullet later was removed from "his body" during a medical procedure on November 22, 1963. President John F. Kennedy suffered from wounds in his (1) back below the right shoulder, (2) throat just below Adam's apple, and (3) right front head. All these wounds were generated by one single bullet which was said it came from Carcano rifle fired by Lee H. Oswald on the window of Texas Book Depository Building; the bullet had first passed through JFK's back, going upward and came out from his throat, then make a sharp right turn to hit John Connally's back, and went through Connally's ribs to come out to hit his wrist and suddenly this special bullet changed its course back into Connally's thigh; as it exhausted then to take a rest on the final station, Connally's thigh.

It must be a naughty bullet; we should have found the manufacturer to buy a lot of such bullet in order to deter the enemy and to save money in the battle field. Josiah Thompson the researcher and author of "*Six Seconds in Dallas*" concluded that the shots fired on the presidential motorcade came from *three* different locations: (1) the **Texas School Book Depository**, (2) the area of the **grassy knoll**, and (3) the **Dal-Tex Building** [291] [292]. Acquilla Clemons, a witness who did not appear before the Commission, saw two men -- not Oswald-- near Tippit's car just before the shooting. As she ran outside of her house she saw a "heavy man" with a gun instructing to the second man to do something. Another witness Frank Wright observed a man with a long coat standing by Tippist's (dead) body then ran to waiting car and sped away [293]. Is the evidence presented before Warren Commission the same evidence recovered from the crime scene?

The answer is "not always". Witness Domingo Benavides found two bullet cases from the crime scene where Tippit died and turned them over to police officer J.M. Poe. Sergeant Gerald Hill from DPD later testified to the Warren Commission that he ordered police officer Poe to mark the shells with Poe's initial "JMP"; however when the two bullet cases were presented to the Warren Commission, Poe's initial "JMP" were not found [294]. How long the time to fire the shots to President Kennedy? The Warren Commission concluded that three shots were fired in a period of 4.8 to 7 seconds. Oswald's Carcano is not an automatic rifle, it is impossible to him to fire-reload-fire three (consecutive) bullets accurately within 7 seconds while the target was moving on the running car.

The critics said it must be a multiple shooters since the bullet also hit the presidential car and Governor Connally beside JFK in a very short time while the car was moving. Governor Connally who seated in the same limousine directly in front of Kennedy testified before the Warren Commission, he thought that "there were **either two or three people** involved, or more, in this—or someone was shooting with an **automatic** rifle. [295]"

The very startling evidence is the movie uploaded on youtube.com depicting the presidential motorcade on Dealy Plaza; a running agent behind JFK limousine turned his back and seemed to be upset; he opened his arms in displease indicating he received an instruction he does not happy with; it's most probably an instruction for him to move somewhere and not to block JFK while a sniper was peering from a telescope mounted on a rifle aiming to JFK. Before being removed, just watch this movie at:

http://www.youtube.com/watch?v=bqL1ANq7VPM&feature=endscreen&NR=1

In this movie with the title *"The Men Who Killed Kennedy; The Smoking Guns (full)"*, Professor James Fetzer of Duluth, MN narrating as transcribed below:

> "The resurgent of interest of the JFK death have a repercussion when the Congress passed the JFK Record Act in 1992 that created a five-civilian member Board in trust with responsibility to review declassified documents………. We know from the report that there are some significant failures, for example the *agency* deliberately destroy the motorcade records that will reveal the motorcade in Dallas was a travesty of violation of at least fifteen different Secret Service policies for presidential protection".

In another part of this movie we also learn from Vince Palamara a Secret Service expert, explaining:

> "There is last minutes change invoked by the *agency* involving President Kennedy security, specifically agents were told NOT to ride on or NEAR the rear of limousine. These orders were funneled from the assistant specifically in charge (of the) White House………..to one of his assistant……..Amy Robert who in charge in the follow-up car. You can see an agent, Henry Rybka; doing his normal duty jogging beside the limousine; when in the follow-up car, you can see Amy Robert stands up waves him (Rybka) back. In very perplexed, agent Rybka waving his arms several times and seeming disgusted. There is another last minutes change in the Love Field (airport where JFK landed in Dallas) invoked by the *agency*. The Dallas Police Department outriders were told not to be beside the car……"

A little content of this video was later corrected in Palamara's comment over another video http://www.youtube.com/watch?v=mCHGNvTvqU0; the name of Secret Service is Don Lawton, not Rybka but the action is still the same.

The origin and number of bullet are subject to the perennial controversy, the Warren Commission concluded that there're three bullets fired from the Texas Book Depository building while the HSCA concluded four, three came from the Texas

Book Depository building with one came from the grassy knoll. However, the critics said there are some "suspected firing points" in Dealey Plaza, including multiple locations in the Texas School Book Depository, not just on the 6th floor, and on its roof, the Dal-Tex Building, and the Dallas County Records Building, the railroad overpass, a storm drain of Elm street, and another spots next to the grassy knoll. Some witnesses reported that they heard the gunfire from Dal-Tex Building located across the Texas School Book Depository [296]. A researcher in 1997 inserted himself into the storm drain at Elm Street; and proved that the assassin might have fired from the storm drain near the grassy knoll and then could have escaped by crawling through twelve inch drain pipe. This pipe goes through under Elm Street and is connected to larger one under Main Street, and this pipe goes along the way one half mile to Trinity River [297].

Either way the assassin(s) fired the deadly weapon(s), it must be meticulously planned for a long time within a special team with the high skill capability, and then implemented under an extraordinary synchronization like a famous orchestra under the legendary conductor, exactly at 12:30 PM; within six minutes everything was done, completely and perfectly.

The Warren Commission, the first official committee established by the US government, has some controversial conclusions; it was either misinformed by the information sources or deliberately misinformed the public. It is hard to say that the Single Bullet Theory was a truthful one; this theory was attributed to the Warren Commission staffer Arlen Specter who explained that one single same bullet made all wounds to Governor Connally and President Kennedy. According to Specter as concluded in the Warren Commission report, this magic bullet was fired by Oswald from 6th floor of the Texas School Book Depository building successfully hit President Kennedy's neck, exited and went through Connally chest and still went through to hit his wrist and after making a sharp turn then took a final rest in Connally thigh. Is that sounds marvelous or ridiculous?

This crazy bullet was not recovered from Connally's body; instead it was found at Dallas Parkland Hospital gurney by someone after the assassination; this magic bullet is still intact and only has a small deformity. However, the Warren Commission acknowledged that it is not a unanimous decision by all members, yet all of them have no doubt that all shots were fired from 6th floor of the Texas School Depository building [298]. This statement was only intended to point out that Oswald was the only assassin. What if the other shots were fired from Dal-Tex Building?

Whosoever the sniper on the sixth floor of Texas Book Depository Building was, it would be easy to shoot President Kennedy *when he was on Houston Street*, since the view from sniper nest is wide open to the target without any blocker such as trees and spectators.

When JFK motorcade made a left on Elm Street the view from the sniper nest was blocked by the tree, at this point the only good spot to shoot JFK was *from Dal-Tex Building* since the view from here was wide open to the target without any blocker such as trees and spectators.

The plans should have been, (a) Plan A, Job for Assassin at Texas Book Depository Building: if JFK arrived at Houston Street at 12:30 PM then shoot him here, (b) Plan B, Job for Assassin at Dal-Tex Building: if JFK arrived at intersection of Houston Street – Elm Street at 12:30 PM then shoot him here, (c) Plan C, Job for Assassin at Grassy Knoll and Storm Drain on Elm Street: if JFK arrived at Dealey Plaza on Elm Street at 12:30 PM then shoot him here, no matter which one came first, the final job should have been done here. As we know, Plan A did not work since JFK arrived at Houston Street *before* 12:30 PM; Plan B worked since at 12:30 JFK was on Elm Street right after Houston Street intersection, and Plan C worked anyway since here was the final job for the Assassin(s).

Did Oswald fire Carcano rifle from 6th floor of TBDB? Absolutely no (the paraffin test was inconclusive, by the law it does mean NO), someone at Dal-Tex did instead. He was put as patsy, he was ordered to go out from TBDB to enter the theatre to shift the police focus from either Dal-Tex Building or/and Grassy Knoll sites. By the law, Oswald had had a perfect alibi as Texas Theatre manager Warren Burroughs witnessed [299].

At the time of Officer Tippit was shot to death at 1:10 PM, Oswald *was already inside* the Texas Theatre building since 1:00 PM; at 1:15 PM he went downstairs to buy popcorn from Burroughs. A victim died and a suspect also died before put on trial, no witness no proof. A perfect murder of the century!

[289] Brian Sprinkle and James Butman, "*Armchair Detective*", Rainbow Books Inc., Highland City, Fla. 1992; p. 17.
[290] Karen Bornemann Spies, "*John F. Kennedy*", Enslow Publishing Inc., Berkeley Height, NJ, 1999, p. 130
[291] http://en.wikipedia.org/wiki/John_F._Kennedy_assassination_conspiracy_theories
[292] http://www.jfk-info.com/thomp2.htm
[293] http://en.wikipedia.org/wiki/John_F._Kennedy_assassination_conspiracy_theories
[294] *ibid.*
[295] *ibid.*
[296] *ibid.*
[297] Dealy Plaza Special Edition, p. 21
[298] http://en.wikipedia.org/wiki/Single_bullet_theory
[299] Groden, *ibid.*

5. The HSCA

"President John F. Kennedy was assassinated probably as a result of a conspiracy", HSCA notes

At the very same day John F. Kennedy assassination, Vice President Lyndon B. Johnson was sworn in on board of Air Force One at Love Field as the 36th President of United States. At 7:30 PM the new President returned to the White House and called the Director of FBI J. Edgar Hoover and ordered the investigation of John F. Kennedy's assassination. Although the assassination of the sitting President was not ruled as a federal crime yet, but from that point; the full responsibility of investigation of Kennedy's assassination would be on the Federal Agency. A couple days later [300] after considering the suggestion of Nicholas Katzenbach and J. Edgar Hoover, President Johnson established the Warren Commission. In 1976, due to public demand and critics about the accuracy of the Warren Commission, then the US House of Representative established the **US House of Representatives Select Committee on Assassinations** (HSCA) to investigate the assassinations of JFK, ML King and Alabama Governor George Wallace [301]. As the public know, only Wallace survived but paralyzed; the other two were mysteriously killed. They were the public figure and popular, why they were shot?

The HSCA worked for two years and in its 1979 final report, concluded that President Kennedy was assassinated by Lee Harvey Oswald "probably as a result of a conspiracy", but it was unable to identify the member(s) of the probable conspiracy. The HSCA believed that the conspiracy did **not** include the governments of Soviet Union or Cuba, or the government agencies such as the FBI, the CIA, or the Secret Service. The involvement of the organized crime and anti-Castro exiles was also ruled out, but the HSCA **did not rule out** the individual participation of either of those groups acting together.

When the HSCA was investigating the assassinations, at the same time some private researchers were working hard to disclose the mystery of assassination; the most important note is at that time James E. Files has not claimed yet as the assassin. The HSCA itself worked in secret atmosphere and kept the evidence in secret. Under the public pressure which demanded more disclosure, in 1992 the Congress passed legislation to collect and open up the evidence and documents relating to John F. Kennedy's death; and the **Assassination Records Review Board** (ARRB) was created thereafter. The HSCA was a continuation of Church Committee a 1975 **United States Senate Select Committee to Study Governmental Operations with Respect to Intelligence Activities**; it was named after its chairman Frank Church a Democratic Senator from Idaho.

The committee was also a precursor to the **U.S. Senate Select Committee on Intelligence** to investigate the legality of intelligence gathering by the government agencies in the wake of Watergate scandal, a breach into the Headquarter of Democratic Party at Watergate by Richard M. Nixon's special team. The HSCA was also an outcome of public pressure after the publication of books, magazine articles, and video documentary pertaining to the assassination of US President Kennedy especially after the Zapruder Film aired in March 1975.

The members of HSCA were Thomas N. Downing of Virginia, the First Chairman, Louis Stokes of Ohio, Second Chairman; L. Richardson Preyer of North Carolina, Walter E. Fauntory of D.C., Yvonne Brathwaite Burke of California, Christopher Dodd of Connecticut, Harold Ford Sr. of Tennessee, Floyd Fithian of Indiana, Robert W. Edgar of Pennsylvania, Samuel L. DeVine of Ohio, Stewart McKinney of Connecticut, Charles Thone of Nebraska, and Harold S. Sawyer of Michigan.

After working for about two years, in 1979 the HSCA made a report to the US House of Representative, the excerpts of its report [302]:

(1) **Three** shots were fired at President John F. Kennedy by Lee Harvey Oswald, the **second** shot hit the President and **third** shot killed him. There were **four** shots were fired altogether.
(2) A **high probability** was established based on the [scientific acoustical] evidence that **two gunmen** fired at President John F. Kennedy, and he was probably assassinated as a result of an unidentified conspiracy. The other shot came from a second assassin on the grassy knoll but **missed.**
(3) The Soviet and Cuban Governments were **not** involved in the assassination of President Kennedy.
(4) The groups of anti-Castro Cuban and the national syndicate were **not** involved in the assassination of President Kennedy, but the possibility of individual involvement of the group member(s) was not precluded.
(5) The Secret Service, FBI, and CIA were **not** involved in the assassination of President Kennedy.
(6) The Committee agreed with the single bullet theory, although it slightly differed with those of the Warren Commission.

The recent survey conducted by Wim Dankbaar revealed that Lee Harvey Oswald *did not fire* any shot at President John F. Kennedy, instead the shot from the grassy knoll was perfectly fired by James E. Files hitting the front right temple of John F. Kennedy and killing him; and the single bullet theory is a nonsense at all [303].

The HSCA also appointed 9 forensic pathologists to review the previous autopsy conducted by the doctors at Bethesda Naval Hospital; these forensic pathologists revealed some stunning facts never reported before [304]:

(1) The fatal head wound of John F. Kennedy was incorrectly reported, the official autopsy recorded that the wound was one hundred millimeters or four inches *lower* that the real point of entry.
(2) The lacerated brain of John F. Kennedy was *not* adequately examined to determine that only one bullet hit him.

(3) The extremities John F. Kennedy was *not* X-rayed to determine that no other bullet(s) hit them.
(4) The doctors at Bethesda Naval Hospital *knew* exactly that there are other additional fragments of bullet(s) on John F. Kennedy's **lower arm, wrist, hand, lower leg, and ankle.** They kept silence because revealing these facts would raise the suspicion of conspiracy.
(5) John F. Kennedy's neck wound was *not* properly examined to determine the direction of bullet.
(6) Lieutenant-Colonel Pierre A. Fink, a "prosector" of US Army *was prevented* from examining John F. Kennedy's clothes. He also complained about the crowded autopsy room by the military officers.
(7) The Navy pathologist Lieutenant Commander Dr. J. Thornton Boswell who was one of the doctors conducted autopsy complained that Bethesda Naval Hospital was only the training school for medical technologists and has no sufficient facility. He, as Lt. Col. Fink did, complained about the *noisy* autopsy room.
(8) John T. Stringer, a Navy photographer complained "the scene in morgue resembled the circus"; when the "prosectors" initially failed to find the bullet of Kennedy's *back wound*, the onlooker suggested the use of a metal detector.
(9) Admiral David Osborne recalled a pressure on the pathologists to do their job quickly.
(10) The Navy pathologist James J. Humes found a bullet wound on John F. Kennedy's back "below the shoulder and two inches to the right of middle spine".
(11) A copper-jacketed 6.5 mm bullet found on a stretcher at Parkland Hospital, not during autopsy.
(12) Admiral CD. Galloway, the commanding officer of Bethesda Naval Hospital had ordered the full autopsy, but he prohibited it from dissecting the bullet track on the back of John F. Kennedy upon learning about the stretcher bullet.

(13) The doctors who performed the autopsy of John F. Kennedy's body had no previous experience; even Navy Commander John H. Ebersole had not yet board certified. He admitted that the extremities of John F. Kennedy were not X-rayed because lack of equipment.
(14) None of medical "prosector" was qualified as forensic pathologist; Lt. Cmd. James J. Humes only had one-week course in forensic pathology at the Armed Forces Institute of Pathology (AFIP).
(15) March 16, 1964 Lt. Cmd. Dr. James J. Humes told Arlen Specter the Warren Commission assistant that he had burned the first draft of autopsy report at his fireplace, while he had no any warrant to destroy. Lt. Cmd. Dr. Humes and Lt. Cmd. Dr. J. Thornton Boswell later before the Assassination Records Review Board (ARRB) informed that they had had lot of sessions with Specter before they testified to the Warren Commission.
(16) Colonel Pierre A. Fink complained to his colleagues that his autopsy records had disappeared before he left morgue at the night of autopsy. Someone stole it.
(17) Lt. Cmd. Dr. Humes in March 1979 testified before the HSCA that he burned all autopsy notes because they were stained with the John F. Kennedy's blood and body fluid, but he assured that word by word was copied on the fresh papers.
(18) Lt. Cmd. Dr. Humes in 1996 prior to his death testified before the ARRB that he was not sure about the notes of autopsy, when T. Jeremy Gunn of ARRB reminded Dr. Humes about his 1979 testimony before the HSCA, he thought he handed them over to Cmd. Dr. Burkley who later burned them out.
(19) Dr. George Burkley, the President's personal physician determined that the head wound on John F. Kennedy was the cause of death; he had signed the death certificate of John F. Kennedy *one day* prior to the announcement of official version of the assassination.

He never be asked to testify before the Warren Commission, neither by the HSCA; he had considered that the Warren Commission report is "a conscious falsification of the history".
(20) Lt. Cmd. Dr. Humes used the term of puncture instead of *puncture wound,* and "puncture" was replaced twice with "lacerated".
(21) On Saturday morning, one day after assassination of John F. Kennedy, Dr. George Burkley notified Walter Jenkins a Presidential Aide that he wants to resign. President Johnson called him, before the meeting he was the Rear Admiral and soon after the audience with the President, Burkley becomes Vice Admiral; he became the first and only White House physician to carry this rank; no one before him no one after him.
(22) Before his death in 1991, Admiral Dr. George Burkley confided to the writer Henry Hurt that *President John F. Kennedy was a victim of conspiracy*; later in another interview he abruptly refused [the conspiracy theory]. The death certificate of John F. Kennedy which was signed by Dr. Burkley never appeared on the Warren Commission report.

The death certificate of John F. Kennedy contained the word of "third thoracic vertebra"; the wound at his back was one among the crucial wounds on his body, this back wound on the Warren Commission report became the neck wound, it shifted from the level of **third thoracic vertebra** (on the chest section) as Dr. Burkley recorded on the death certificate to the level of the **sixth cervical vertebra** (on the neck section), at the base of the neck. Only the exhumation of John F. Kennedy's remain would have ended the controversial version of his wounds; and we know it's impossible. At the time of John F. Kennedy's autopsy, no one doctor at Bethesda Naval Hospital had an experience in autopsy, nor one of the medical "prosector" was qualified as the forensic pathologist. It is clear that the body of late US President Kennedy was not on the right hand and not on the right place either.

He should have been alive at the White House to lead the nation for his second term; instead his body landed at the morgue with so many mysteries shrouded his unnatural death. Nobody will blame anybody else who wept on his tragic death. The mystery of the disappearance of John F. Kennedy brain might have been connected to the finding of the second bullet, his brain was the medical-legal evidence but someone intentionally made it disappeared, for what reason other than covering-up the existence or trace of the second bullet on his brain?

Everybody who watched the Zapruder film will be convinced that the initial movement of John F. Kennedy body was leaning forward, it may have been from the first shot at his head and then for the next, his body was leaning backward when he got the second head shot from the grassy knoll.

In 1979 report the HSCA concluded that:

1. Oswald fired three shots from his rifle at President JFK. The second and third shots hit the President JFK; and the third shot killed him.
2. Based on scientific evidence; it's a high probability that at least two gunmen fired at President JFK.
3. Probably, President JFK was assassinated as a result of a conspiracy. The Soviet Government, the Cuban Government, anti-Castro Cuban groups, the syndicate of organized crime, the Secret Service, Federal Bureau of Investigation, and Central Intelligence Agency as the organizations were NOT involved.
4. The protection of President JFK and the investigation to reveal the possibility of conspiracy are inadequate.
5. There are four shots; the missed third shot, came from a second assassin on the grassy knoll.

Source: http://en.wikipedia.org/wiki/HSCA

---

[300] According to wikipedia.org it was November 29, 1963; and according to McKnight in "*Breach the Trust*" it was November 24, 1963
[301] http://en.wikipedia.org/wiki/HSCA
[302] Summarized and simplified from many sources
[303] Dankbaar, *ibid.*, pp. 250
[304] Summarized from McKnight's "*Breach of Trust*", pp. 153 - 180

6. The Possible Motives of Assassination

President Kennedy's Executive Order No. 11110 is still valid

On June 4, 1963 President Kennedy signed the Executive Order Number 11110 that mandated the U.S. Treasury a power *"to issue silver certificates against any silver bullion, silver, or standard silver dollars in the Treasury."* The significant meaning of this Executive Order is *for every single ounce of silver the US Government keeps in the Treasury's vault, the government might issue new money into circulation.* The public enactment –not a restricted one- would bring back the US government to its authority to issue US currency and strip the Federal Reserve's authority to loan money with interest to the US government. Now, the US dollar bill is not belong to the US government, it belongs to the Federal Reserve Bank; on every single dollar bill there is **"FEDERAL RESERVE NOTE"**. Whenever there is enough of silver certificate [paper money that certifies a value of silver bullion] on circulation then the demand of US government for Federal Reserve notes would be eliminated; this is the meaning of Executive Order Number 11110. President Kennedy's Executive Order No. 11110 is still valid [305].

The original single dollar bill was a "silver certificates against any silver bullion", it does mean that by the law the Federal Reserve Bank has to give you a silver bullion upon receiving one (old) single dollar bill that certified (to have a value as a silver bullion). Who did say that? The old dollar bill itself did. On the old dollar bill there was the print:

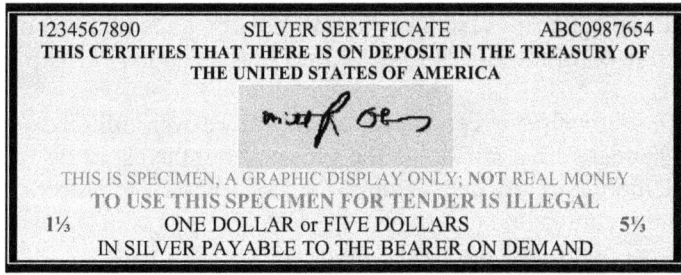

Illustration of US dollar silver certificate

However, as of 1962 there were no more old dollar bill that certified as a "silver certificate", then President Kennedy issued the executive order to the Treasury to issue silver certificate i.e. the dollar bill that stated it has a value as a silver bullion; his order still in effect hitherto.

This is the most startling possibility or impossibility to think that President Kennedy might have been assassinated because of his Executive Order Number 11110. All possibilities would be considered accordingly and would not be ruled out until the definitive motive of his assassination to be unearthed. President Kennedy was the last president that authorized the issuance of the silver dollar bill; no other presidents after him did ever. **This order was not enacted until the time of President Reagan.** Unfortunately, this old single dollar bill does not exist anymore, or is very rare now.

This is the Executive Order Number 11110:

AMENDMENT of EXECUTIVE ORDER No. 10289 AS AMENDED, RELATING TO THE PERFORMANCE OF CERTAIN FUNCTIONS AFFECTING THE DEPARTMENT of THE TREASURY

By virtue of the authority vested in me by section 301 of title 3 of the United States Code, It is ordered as follows:
SECTION 1. Executive Order No. 10289 of September 19, 1951, as amended, is hereby further amended –

a) By adding at the end of paragraph 1 thereof the following subparagraph (j):
"(j) The authority vested in the President by paragraph (b) of section 43 of the Act of May 12, 1933, as amended (31 U.S.C. 821
(b)), to issue silver certificates against any silver bullion, silver, or standard silver dollars in the Treasury not then held for redemption of any outstanding silver certificates, to prescribe the denominations of such silver certificates, and to coin standard silver dollars and subsidiary silver currency for their redemption," and

> (b) By revoking subparagraphs (b) and (c) of paragraph 2 thereof.
> SECTION 2. The amendment made by this Order shall not affect any act done, or any right accruing or accrued or any suit or proceeding had or commenced in any civil or criminal cause prior to the date of this Order but all such liabilities shall continue and may be enforced as if said amendments had not been made.
>
> JOHN F. KENNEDY
> THE WHITE HOUSE,
> June 4, 1963

John F. Kennedy assassination was an example of perfect murder with perennial cover up; yet some people were hesitant to call it conspiracy or the perfect conspiracy. John Kennedy was a flamboyant hawk, a real deal American who did not want his name would be tarnished with a failure to repulse against adversary no matter the cost. He was not a bellicose, but letting America being intimidated was not an option and never be blinking in his mind. His iconic inaugural speech –with a quote from *Kahlil Gibran,* a Lebanese poet-- "Ask not what your country can do for you, ask what you can do for your country" was not an empty slogan. It was proven true before, during and after his tenure as a President of the United States of America. Had he known he was sacrificed for his country he would be happy to do it once more time, ask him any time you would meet him over there.

There were some precedents in Kennedy's life that became strong factor for a young and flamboyant President to challenge the Soviet Union that no other US President ever did. All moments in his life sated with the bravery to serve the country since his PT-109 boat slashed by Japanese Amagiri destroyer in Pacific, campaigning while he's still limping, donating his presidential salary for the needy until his ultimate sacrifice to save America from nuclear catastrophe, that's his total loyalty to United States of America.

Meanwhile, Nikita S. Khrushchev was worry about the US pre-emptive attack; from the previous incidents Khrushchev knew the US is always combat ready against the Soviet Union. The incident of Garry Powers where he was shot down over Sverdlovsk Soviet, Bay of Pigs incident and Jupiter missiles installation in Europe which ready to attack Moscow are the clear evidence over what Khrushchev to worry about. Khrushchev was a bellicose like Yuri Andropov; they were obsessed to an imagination that the US would attack Soviet Union, any time.

From so many books, articles, films, re-enactments and other publications there are some theories pertaining to the assassination of US President John F. Kennedy beyond the possibility of his Executive Order No. 11110:

(1) The governments of Soviet Union and Cuba were suspected of being involved in the Kennedy's assassination; both governments have boasted to destroy the USA and considered it as a main enemy under John F. Kennedy administration. Kennedy's successful handling of Cuban Missile Crisis had made them very upset and should have retaliated. The main basis of the suspicion is the fact that Lee Harvey Oswald was a supporter of Fair Play for Cuba Committee (FPCC), a pro-Castro organization.

This theory could be flawed, the accusation that Oswald as the lone assassin was never be beyond reasonable doubt. Moreover, his membership of FPCC was inconsistent. In a same time he was a supporter of pro-Castro and anti-Castro organizations. His ambiguous participation in two contradictory organizations is either to infiltrate or to disintegrate the both. Oswald on August 5, 1963 visited **Carlos Jose Bringuier** a Cuban lawyer and member of anti-Castro organization ***Directorio Revolucionario Estudiantil*** (the Student Revolutionary Directorate, DRE) in New Orleans. Oswald offered his support and wanted to join DRE.

But, 4 days later on August 9, 1963 he was spotted of handing out FPCC leaflets; FPCC is a pro-Castro organization. Upon his action, Bringuier, Celso Macario Hernandez and Miguel Mariano Cruz confronted Oswald and fought him. They all were arrested, a couple days later Oswald was found guilty and paid the $10.00 fine. After this incident, Bringuier released a public warning about mysterious Oswald. Bringuier also testified before Warren Commission, and in 1967 was helping New Orleans District Attorney Garrison's investigation of the Kennedy's assassination.

(2) The Cuban exiles -most of them settled in Miami, Florida- were suspected to get involved in the Kennedy's assassination, the main basis of the suspicion is the fact that they were involved in the ***Bahia de Cochinos*** invasion to topple Castro but John F. Kennedy did not adequately support them. The reluctance of John F. Kennedy to support the invasion was a main cause of the failure and more than 100 casualties plus more than 1,000 captured. The Cuban exiles were poor, they were dependent to the US government aid; they did not have the capability to influence Warren Commission nor the expertise to cover up. None of them was in Dallas at the time of assassination.

(3) The organized crime was suspected involved in the Kennedy's assassination, the main basis of the suspicion is the fact that President John F. Kennedy and US Attorney General Robert Kennedy were so eager to destroy the organized crime in USA. Robert Kennedy (1925-1968) had Carlos Marcello (1910-1993) deported to Guatemala on April 4, 1961. Marcello in 1938 was arrested and charged with the possession and sale of more than 23 pounds of marijuana. He was a "Father of New Orleans Family" for 30 years [306], although he was born in Tunisia he claimed to "be born later in Guatemala", and therefore he was deported to Guatemala instead of Tunisia.

The main basis of the suspicion is the fact that the "animosity" between the Kennedys and Marcello dated back to March 24, 1959 when he appeared before a US Senate Committee investigating the organized crime. Robert F. Kennedy was a Chief Counsel to the committee and Senator John F. Kennedy was a member. To curtail the Kennedys' effort to battle the organized crime and to comply with the *omerta*, Marcello simply invoked the Fifth Amendment of the Constitution; he refused to answer any question about his associates and his activities as "a tomato salesman". Contrary to the reality, in the Mario Puzo screenplay of Coppola movie, Sony (Al Pacino) was portrayed to testify although in a brief word before the government committee. Another basis was **Robert Blakey**'s assertion that Marcello, Trafficante, and Chicago boss Sam Giancana were complicit in planning the assassination. Blakey, chief counsel to HSCA, in 1981 published a book "The Plot to Kill the President" explaining he believes that Oswald was involved in JFK assassination but there was still one another assassin firing JFK from the grassy knoll [307]. The organized crime did not have the long and strong relationship with the officials in the government to make Kennedy's brain disappeared which was the very sensitive evidence in the investigation. The organized crime did not have the capability to influence Warren Commission with "the single bullet theory". The fact that Kennedy's assassination was meticulously coordinated, perfectly implemented and perennially covered-up was beyond the organized crime tradition. The FBI investigated Marcello after Kennedy's assassination; and it concluded that Marcello was not involved.

(4) The individuals within the Central Intelligence Agency (CIA) who were embarrassed by the failure of Bahia de Cochinos invasion. Chauncey Marvin Holt testified that he went to Dallas, Texas with Charles Nicoletti and Leo Moceri.

Along with Charles Harrelson and Charles Rogers he was nabbed and detained by the Dallas Police; they were known as "the three tramps". The individuals within the CIA have no ability to orchestrate the plan, coordinate it, implement it, and cover it up for five decades in row; nor the capability to influence the Warren Commission. The covering up for more than 49 years needs a lot of money to pay a various individuals off in order to keep them quiet; the individuals within the CIA have no enough money for this.

(5) The racist group, especially in the South when segregation was still in effect; they were embarrassed by John F. Kennedy who advocated the civil rights, equality in all sectors and equal opportunity in all jobs (See Box: Rosa Parks).

The main basis of the suspicion is the fact that John F. Kennedy on June 11, 1963 appointed himself as temporary registrar for University of Alabama in the incident of African-American student registration at the all-white university to enable Vivian Malone and James Hood enrolling at University of Alabama. The racist group -and even former Governor Wallace were included- absolutely have no a billion dollar on hand and keep the money for 50 years ready to cover up the assassination. The racist group, if any, in turn has no capability to influence the powerful Warren Commission and President Johnson altogether.

Some conspiracy theorists considered the government agency got involved in the JFK assassination. The HSCA concluded that **no** one single US Government Agency such as FBI, CIA, Secret Service, Department of State and the others was involved in the assassination of US President John Fitzgerald Kennedy, nor any of foreign governments such as Cuba and Soviet Union involved in this assassination, and no any organization and/or any business company was involved whatsoever.

However, the HSCA in 1979 officially issued a final report concluding that President John F. Kennedy was assassinated probably as a result of an [unidentified] conspiracy. According to *Washington Post* in 1973; the initial intention of New Orleans District Attorney Jim Garrison in March 1971 is to accuse General Charles Cabell of involvement in the conspiracy to kill John F. Kennedy. The prosecution was cancelled because it was without any evidence and not substantiated; and the CIA is not a scapegoat, either. **Charles Cabell** was the brother of Earle Cabell the Mayor of Dallas Texas at the time of John F. Kennedy assassination; Charles Cabell was also the second man after the CIA Director Allen Dulles. Both Dulles and Cabell were forced to resign by President Kennedy in the wake of failed invasion on Bay of Pigs to topple Fidel Castro. Jim Garrison in 1967 unsuccessfully prosecuted Clay Shaw on the allegation of complicity with Lee H. Oswald in the assassination of John F. Kennedy (see Box: Clay Laverne Shaw).

[305] http://en.wikipedia.org/wiki/JFK
[306] http://en.wikipedia.org/wiki/Carlos_Marcello
[307] *ibid.*

7. The Conspiracy Theory

The conspiracy theory surrounding the death of President Kennedy was so vary and sometimes looks weird, complicated, sometime does not make sense at all, and sometime hard to belief; here the summary:

7.1. New Orleans Conspiracy

New Orleans District Attorney Jim Garrison, in 1966, investigated the assassination of President Kennedy; he concluded that right-wing extremists such as David Ferrie and Guy Banister were involved in a conspiracy to kill President Kennedy. Garrison also concluded that New Orleans businessman Clay Shaw was involved in the conspiracy based on Clay Shaw's pseudonym "Clay Bertrand" who on November 1963 called New Orleans attorney Dean Andrews asking him to be a lawyer for Oswald. The call was on the same day with the JFK assassination. Garrison on March 1, 1967 arrested Shaw, charged him and brought to trial. The jury found him **not** guilty.

7.2. CIA Conspiracy

When the HSCA was established, Gaeton Fonzi an investigator, wrote that investigators were pressured not to look into the relationship between Oswald the prime suspect and the CIA while he stated that David Atlee Phillips a CIA agent using alias "Maurice Bishop" was involved with Oswald in connection with anti-Castro Cuban groups prior to the JFK assassination. Somehow, John M. Newman, a former US Army Intelligence officer and National Security Agency assistance, in 1995 published "evidence" that both the CIA and FBI had deliberately tampered with their files on Lee Harvey Oswald either before or after the assassination. The weird part of Newman assertion that James Angleton "was probably the key figure of assassination… However the control ….. was not under James Angleton, but under Allan Dulles (the former

CIA director who had been dismissed by Kennedy after the failed Bay of Pig [308]." However, The HSCA concluded that Oswald never had any contact with the Agency, and it concluded that the CIA and the FBI were not involved in the assassination of Kennedy.

7.3. Shadow Government Conspiracy

The secret government including wealthy industrialists and right-wing politicians ordered and financed the assassination of Kennedy. Peter Dale Scott a former professor at University of California, Berkeley, asserts that after JFK, the secret government successfully escalated US involvement in Vietnam. The war is profitable, yet no proof of this theory.

7.4. Military-industrial Complex

The war is a success for the politics planner, profit for the military industry, and misery for the people. The end of Vietnam War (and any war) as planned by President Kennedy would not be god for the military industry; and therefore JFK should be stopped, since the war is profitable. Even though he war is profitable, yet no proof of this theory.

7.5. Secret Agency Conspiracy

Vince Palamara a researcher who interviewed Secret Service agents assigned to protect President Kennedy, narrated in a youtube.com movie that **Sam Kinney** Secret Service agent and limousine driver told him that the requests (1) to remove the bubble top from the presidential limousine in Dallas, (2) not placing the agents beside limousine's rear bumper, and (3) reducing the number of DPD police motorcycle outriders near or beside the presidential limousine's rear bumper were **not** ordered by Kennedy (see Part Five Chapter **4. Mysterious Bullets**).

When the Assassination Records Review Board (ARRB) was created by Congress in 1992 to collect and release [from 1992 to 1998] all US Government records related to the assassination of President Kennedy on November 22, 1963, the ARRB was informed that in January 1995 the Secret Service destroyed protective survey reports that covered President's trips from September 24 to November 8, 1963 [309] [310].

The HSCA declared in 1979 report that "the Secret Service was deficient in the performance of its duties" since the agents in the motorcade were not ready to protect the President from a sniper; but was **not** involved in the assassination.

7.6. Cuban Exiles Conspiracy

The Fidel Castro' revolution let thousands of Cubans abandon their homeland and properties to run to Florida, US, they hoped someday to go home; they participated in the Bay of Pigs Invasion in 1961 but failed. Many Cuban exiles blamed on President Kennedy for this failure; and therefore they planned to assassinate him. The HSCA concluded "anti-Castro Cuban groups, as groups, were not involved in the assassination of President Kennedy, but that the available evidence does not preclude the possibility that individual members may have been involved [311]."

7.7. Organized Crime Conspiracy

The Castro revolution in 1959 brought down the casino business; the businessmen want to get the casino reopened; and they need to topple Castro but failed because JFK stopped the Bay of Pigs invasion; therefore they disliked him. They also disliked JFK brother, the Attorney General Robert Kennedy, who busted the organized crime and deported the mob figure Carlos Marcello to Guatemala (see Part 3 Chapter 7. Marilyn Monroe).

The HSCA concluded that the national organized crime, as a group, was not involved in the JFK assassination, but it does not preclude the possibility that individual members may have been involved".

7.8. Lyndon Baines Johnson Conspiracy

Lyndon B. Johnson was the 36th President of the USA the successor of Kennedy. According to Gallup poll in 2003, nearly 20% of Americans suspected Lyndon Johnson involvement in the assassination of President Kennedy. Critics of the Warren Commission have also accused Johnson of planning the assassination because he hated the powerful Kennedy clan and feared being dropped from the Democratic vice presidential nomination for the 1964 Election [312]. E. Howard Hunt, a former CIA agent and Watergate "plumber" accused Lyndon Johnson of complicity in the assassination of President Kennedy. Before his death in 2007, Hunt confessed that Johnson had plotted the JFK assassination with the help of CIA agents who were disturbed by Kennedy. Hunt implicated several CIA agents David Atlee Phillips, **Cord Meyer**, Bill Harvey, Frank Sturgis, David Sanchez Morales and also a French assassin who fired a deadly shot to Kennedy from the grassy knoll [313]. If his confession were true, it contradicts to James E. File's confession who said he was the sharp shooter at the grassy knoll [314]. However, historian Michael L. Kurtz wrote that there is no evidence that Johnson orchestrated the JFK assassination of Kennedy; instead Johnson believed that Fidel Castro was responsible for the assassination.

7.9. Cuban Conspiracy

Jack Anderson, an investigative reporter concluded that Castro hired the organized crime figures to assassinate Kennedy. He interviewed Johnny Roselli who detailed him the plot; Anderson acknowledged that he could not confirm Roselli's confessions; and Anderson also wrote in his published report that Oswald played a role in the assassination, and there was more than one gunman. The Warren Commission which investigated the allegations of contact between Oswald and the Cuban agents, found no evidence that Cuba was involved in the JFK assassination. Another investigation by the HSCA also concluded that the Cuban Government was not involved in the JFK assassination. Castro himself in 1977 in an interview with newsman Bill Moyers denied any involvement in Kennedy's death.

7.10. Soviet Conspiracy

Nikita Khrushchev had KGB arranged the JFK assassination as a revenge for the humiliation of the Cuban Missile Crisis. This information came from a high level Romanian defector General Ion Mihai Pacepa. The other information came from CIA agent Cord Meyer before his death that CIA knew KGB organized the JFK assassination as revenge for the embarrassment of the Cuban Missile Crisis, meanwhile Cord Meyer himself was implicated in the JFK assassination by the confession of other CIA officer E. Howard Hunt (see Lyndon B. Johnson Conspiracy). The Warren Commission concluded that no evidence of the Soviet Union involvement in the assassination of President Kennedy. The HSCA also concluded the same.

7.11. Israeli Conspiracy

This weird theory asserts that the Israeli government was upset with Kennedy for his pressure over Israeli pursuit of a top-secret Dimona nuclear program.

7.12. Federal Reserve Conspiracy

President Kennedy's Executive Order 11110 mandated the Secretary of the Treasury to print additional silver certificates. This order might be a first step for the US Government to be independent from the Federal Reserve; therefore Kennedy should have been stopped, actually the order was not officially repealed some years later until the Reagan Administration. Jim Marrs, Richard Belzer and Craig Roberts theorized that the assassination of Kennedy might have been related to his Executive Order 11110.

7.13. Decoy Casket

While the body of JFK was on Air Force One on the way from Dallas to Washington, the conspirator removed Kennedy's body from the original bronze casket into a shipping casket for the wound alteration to make the wound looks like from a rear shot while it was from the front from the grassy knoll. This is a story presented by David Lifton in his book *"Best Evidence: Disguise and Deception in the Assassination of John F. Kennedy"*. However, researcher David Wrone rejected the theory that Kennedy's body was secretly removed from the Air Force One since the coffin and lid were tightly held by steel cables to prevent unnecessary moving during takeoff and landing or air disturbances. The plane was always on the watch of television camera and thousands of spectators that would impossible any effort to snatch JFK body [315].

7.14. Moon Flight

The "moon landing" may be a wrong term since "landing" refers to the earth; let us use the term of "Moon embankment". As the world knew John F. Kennedy won Pulitzer Prize for publishing his thesis "Profiles in Courage" he was a dependable Harvard Scholar and international writer before taking office at the White House. This is the fact not everybody remembers.

When the Soviet Union launched *Sputnik* the first artificial earth satellite on October 4, 1957 which marks the beginning of space age; the US feels defeated and therefore it was pursuing the space technology.

It was John F. Kennedy who declared that the USA would defeat the Soviet Union in the space race. National Aeronautics and Space Act was established on July 29, 1958 and since October 1, 1958 National Aeronautics and Space Administration [NASA] becomes operational. The USA ambitious program is to put the first human being stepping on the moon. **Neil Armstrong**, 82, who passed away on August 25, 2012; was the first American and first human being to step on the moon at 02:56 UTC on July 21, 1969. This moon embankment was credited to JFK; even though he passed away 6 years before, he was confident that someday the USA will prevail over the Soviet Union in the space race.

The critics said that the "moon landing" is an international hoax; the evidence is the waving US flag, how come a flag is waving if no wind in the moon. This hoax, as the conspiracy theory goes, was planned during Kennedy administration; and since Kennedy was a good international writer and the Pulitzer Prize winner, the hoax planners were so worry that someday he would write another international best seller "The Moon Landhoaxing" and therefore before it happens, he should have been stopped. The "Moon Landing" later inspired Michael Jackson to dance the famous "Moon Walking"; every time the world enjoy Jackson's dance, the hoax planners feel being nudged and scolded; therefore Jackson should have been stopped, too. That's what the conspiracy theory says; and it's going viral.

7.15. Korean Air Lines Flight 007

Only **James Bond** is licensed to bear the insignia of **"007"**, anybody else would die like 269 passengers of Korean Air Lines Flight 007 on September 1, 1983. All 269 passengers were killed including Lawrence "Larry" McDonald a member of US Congress from Georgia. The conspiracy theory says, Larry McDonald was deliberately put on peril because he had had the evidence including audio tapes linked to the JFK assassination, and he was going to reveal them right away; therefore he had to be stopped. Korean Air Lines' Boeing 727-230B was shot down by Major Gennadi Osipovich one among 3 Sukhoi Su-15 fighter pilots who together with a Mig-23 were intercepting a civilian KAL 007 strayed over the prohibited Soviet airspace. The shooting down of a civilian aircraft occurred when the tension between the Soviet Union and the US was high; and Soviet was just done with Operation RYAN while the US was preparing Operation Able Archer 83. The civilian commercial KAL 007 was suspected to be used as a spy plane to monitor the military exercise on the Sakhalin Island.

The theories may go wild over the time and make the JFK assassination getting murky. Forget Mafia, Castro, Soviet, and Israel etc. in conspiracy theory; the death of JFK is our fault, since we failed to protect him. It's a time now for national reconciliation, the US used to be a brilliant negotiator and mediator for another nation, now they should have been the negotiator and mediator between themselves. The US created the HSCA and ARRB, now is the time to create the US Senate for **Arbitration and Reconciliation Board** (ARB). We do not need prosecution, we need reconciliation and resolution.

[308] http://en.wikipedia.org/wiki/John_F._Kennedy_assassination_conspiracy_theories
[309] ibid.
[310] http://www.youtube.com/watch?v=bqL1ANq7VPM&feature=endscreen&NR=1
[311] http://en.wikipedia.org/wiki/John_F._Kennedy_assassination_conspiracy_theories
[312] *ibid.*
[313] *ibid.*
[314] Dankbaar, *ibid.*, p. 250
[315] http://en.wikipedia.org/wiki/John_F._Kennedy_assassination_conspiracy_theories

8. Perennial Cover up

Since day one until today for fifty years, some facts of the Kennedy assassination has been covered up, it must be for reason

The plan to stop JFK was starting from the day of Cuban Crisis, and the cover-up of the conspiracy starting from the morgue when Colonel Pierre A. Fink lost his autopsy records before he left morgue at the time of JFK autopsy on Friday night November 22, 1963. Although the killing of Oswald was successful yet it was too late; he should have been shot inside the theater for resist the arrest.

If since beginning the authority wants to reveal who is behind JFK assassination; it should have been done a long time ago on the Day One just a couple hours after incident when the Dallas Police Department nabbed three "tramps" hiding inside the box car on the railway next to Dealy Plaza. DPD should have not released these guys regardless of whether who ordered to release them; but it turned to be released and it was another clue that there was something more powerful than DPD. On the other side, the deliberate destroy of motorcade records is also indicating that there is something powerful than SS. Another clue is a 50-year restriction to open the JFK records even though it was limited later until 2017 after the enactment of 1992 AARB.

The finding of the dictabelt is an "accident" for those who want to keep the cover-up to proceed. Mary Ferrell and Gary Mack found Dictabelt on their research. They tried to find out who accidentally recorded the shot impulse at Dealey Plaza on the day of Kennedy assassination; and it was found that Dallas Police Officer **HB McLain** is most probable officer whose communication system stuck on "On" position to record the impulses. He denied of using the communication system that was recorded on the dictabelt in the Police communication room, however after a comprehensive check through photographs taken at Dealey Plaza after the President had been rushed to Parkland Hospital revealed that McLain was at Dealey Plaza instead at Elm Street as he claimed before [316].

The acoustic is not the mere evidence as discussed in previous Part Five "Chapter 2. **Dictabelt**"; there are another evidence such as the Zapruder movie, amateur film, and the witnesses. Any clue the witness provided, will help to a better understanding to the assassination of President Kennedy:

(1) Caroline Walter was at Houston Street next to the Elm Street when President John F. Kennedy was murdered. She clearly looked at *two men* visible over the Texas Book Depository Building window just before the presidential motorcade arrived and the shooting occurred. One of them in the brown suit coat, and the other in white shirt to hold a rifle, he has the colored hair; they were at 4th or 5th floor, not 6th, at right side of the building. However, this witness was omitted by the Warren Commission [317] without any explanation.

(2) Sam Holland, a railroad worker and his co-workers watched the motorcade from railway overpass; he saw a puff of smoke from behind the fence of the grassy knoll when the shooting occurred. To see what happened, he and his co-workers ran down within two minutes to the spot next to the grassy knoll, they found (a) the foot print, (b) a cigarette butt, and (c) a parked car facing the fence with a muddy bumper, someone had stood up on the car to see over the fence [318]. This car might belong to anybody not related to the murder, but without the consent of its owner it could have been used by someone else. Holland said to hear FOUR shots, his account was recorded in the Warren Commission as "Holland immediately after the shots, ran off the underpass to see if there was anyone behind the picket fence on the north side of Elm Street but he did not see anyone behind the parked cars". Although his testimony was included in the Warren Commission Report; but the shots became THREE only [319]. Where is one other shot?

(3) Ed Johnson, a Fort Worth reporter said "Some of us saw little puffs of white smoke that seemed to hit the grassy area". His testimony was also ignored [320].

(4) Jean Hill was at another side of the grassy knoll when President Kennedy was murdered, she was the closest witness ever, only some feet across the scene of crime. When looking across the Presidential motorcade **she spotted a sniper** on the grassy knoll fired at the President. Although she said to see the smoke, but she was omitted from the witness list [321].

(5) Jean Hill was standing next to the other witness, Mary Moorman who snapped a Polaroid picture, her picture depicting a sniper dressed like a policeman and therefore so-called "a badgeman" toward the corner of picket fence. Her Polaroid photograph was asked by someone but never be included in the Warren Commission Report, it was missing and omitted [322].

(6) Julia Ann Mercer was driving down Elm Street around thirty minutes before the Presidential motorcade was due; she had to wait to pass a weird pickup car parked "half-on and half-off" the pavement at the foot of grassy knoll. She saw a man with gray jacket and brown trouser taking a case from the pickup that looked like a rifle. The driver of the pickup car was a heavy set white man in 40's, faired hair wearing a green jacket; Mercer to call police after witnessing the both. When Mercer saw the picture of the Oswald murderer at the Dallas Police Department, she recognized "ever saw this man before"; and she recalled he was turned to be Jack Ruby [323].

(7) Mercer said she saw the "Air Conditioning" sign on the truck; she was called to identify a series of photographs, and she thought the data of identification have been altered and she could make a proper identification. A signed affidavit had been altered, she complained [324].

(8) Helen Markham was waiting a bus and standing next to the junction of Tenth Street and Patton Avenue in the Oak Cliff neighborhood when Officer Tippit was gunned down by unidentified suspect, not Oswald. She witnessed Tippit walked around the car and was shot four times by a five feet eight inches man aged around 25 to have the brown hair and white jacket at 1:06 PM [325].

(9) Markham's testimony did not match to the color of Oswald's jacket that was black according to Oswald's landlady Earlene Roberts. Markham also said that the killer was heavy with the bushy hair, while Oswald was not [326]. The Warren Commission just declared that she was "unreliable" [327] to set her testimony aside; because "in her various statement and testimony, Mrs. Markham was uncertain and inconsistent in her recollection of the exact time of the slaying", and because the "reliable witness" was the Warren Commission only.

It is clear to us, based on the witness account and evidence that the cover up had been starting from the Day One until today, it is for reason and not a coincidence.

Despite the misery and pain of loosing a sitting President, the US found the valuable lesson for some developments on how to manage a better government; among other things:

(1) The creation of the situation room to handle the crisis, it was not established yet during the Cuban Missile Crisis.

(2) The crime against the US President becomes a federal crime; it was a state crime where it happened.

(3) The establishment of hot line between Kremlin and the White House, the hot line communication with the red phones.

(4) To prevent the Soviet submarines from sneaking into US territory, the array of electronic ears were planted on the sea bed some miles from US coasts. The confrontation between USS Beale and a Soviet submarine under the command of Savitsky which loaded with the nuclear torpedo several miles south of Florida coast on October 26, 1962 had taught an expensive lesson to the USA.

(5) More spy satellites were launched into orbit to monitor the suspicious activity of the adversaries around the globe. Among its early achievement is to catch the specific ray from a nuclear weapon test of South Africa during the Apartheid government. Under the pressure of US and Europe, the nuclear program was voluntarily cancelled.

(6) The invention of the global wireless phone for an urgent communication between the government agents around the globe. Unfortunately, this very sophisticated technology was leaked in its early time to the Soviet Union by William B. Kampiles; as well other sensitive information e.g. the existence of the underground tunnel under the Soviet Embassy in Washington that its presence was compromised by Robert Hansen. The other sensitive information was passed to the Soviet Union by **Aldrich Hazen Ames**. It is a time now to invent the radical disciplinary rules similar to *omerta* pledge applied to any government agent to keep their mouths well closed at any situation. The government agents should be notified the difference between the freedom of speech, money and the government secrets.

The available evidence is sufficient to conclude that the assassination of US President John F. Kennedy is a very unusual action which is carefully planned and meticulously executed. If there is any collaboration between insider and outsider in his assassination, it must be carried on in a very limited time; and as the main purpose was successfully achieved then the collaboration might have been dismissed.

Since beginning, it seems that investigation of JFK assassination was deliberately distracted from the right path to shield some "semi-official" secrets from the American public.

The true story of weird autopsy, the missing autopsy records just inside Bethesda Naval Hospital, the saga of two different coffins for one JFK body, the destruction of motorcade records, the finding of a bullet on the stretcher, the "resignation" of Dr. George Burkley a White House Physician who checked the JFK body after assassination, and the resignation of frustrating Robert Tenenbaum the HSCA Chief Counsel over his consideration that HSCA was "not designed to find the truth" and over the HSCA rejection to recall David Atlee Phillips on the suspicion of perjury, have been the long list of perennial cover-up and never ending frustration.

The time of secrecy surrounding the death of late President Kennedy is over, the truth has been revealed, the motive behind his assassination has been disclosed; what we do need now is to release all remaining records and to make national reconciliation. The Republicans and Democrats should have signed the national agreement pertaining to *the successive term of US presidency among them. Let GOP to hold US presidency for 8 years and next time let Democrat to hold the US presidency for eight years, no single US President would be replaced before his term ends unless he breaks the law. This term will continue over and over to save money for the American education and senior medication rather than spending billions of dollar for political campaign. Americans spent too much money for presidential campaign; and when a legitimate **president was elected** then he was assassinated.*

The statute of limitation to prosecute those who were involved in the assassination of US President has expired; the American public wants to know and to forgive. That's it. The time of witness intimidation, and foul play is over.

The American public and the world already knew that that main reason of Kennedy assassination is to prevent the nuclear war which he was about to authorize at the peak tension during the Cuban Missile Crisis; they can understand even though they do not agree. The Congress should have passed the law to prevent those who got involved in Kennedy assassination from the prosecution since they need the peace of mind, let them all to confess and not just partial confession like **Chauncey Holt, James Files** etc. did. The assassination is wrong, but this one was very different in a very special case i.e. to safe the innocence American citizens from the devastation of nuclear war. If the world is now safe, it is a part of Kennedy's sacrifice. The past of America is important, but its future is more important; forgive and forget the past, a new leading generation of Americans should be up front in every development as they used to be before they are defeated by the other nation.

[316] Smith, ibid. pp. 69 - 70
[317] Smith, ibid., pp. 117 - 118
[318] *ibid.*, p. 118
[319] *ibid.*, pp. 118 - 119
[320] *ibid.*, p. 119
[321] *ibid.*, p. 119
[322] *ibid.*, p. 119
[323] *ibid.*, p. 120
[324] *ibid.*, p. 121
[325] *ibid.*, pp. 120 - 121
[326] *ibid.*, pp. 121 - 123
[327] *ibid.*, pp. 123 - 125

Epilogue
Part Six: The Nuclear Jeopardy

We have humanitarian institutions to help the near death people from starving only to kill them later as they are healthy and wealthy

From the Part Four we know that the World War III was overdue; only by the mercy of God we are safe now and our tiny planet is still intact. Over the time the civilized people are pursuing the tools to make easy killing fellow people to satisfy their passion and to feel to be victorious and happy; such a fragile and volatile happiness on the cost of suffering people.

From the day one of the nuclear age where the paradigm of **mass killing** starts, the effort to obtain the weapons for more sophisticated mass killing is going on and on. Since the first nuclear bomb detonated several feet over Hiroshima to ensure its deadly effect of some kilotons explosive over the live Japanese bone and flesh, until now, the power of mass killing weapon is increasing steadily. During Kennedy administration the US tested 100 megaton nuclear bomb dropped from the strategic plane to know how deadly this super powerful bomb was. It's an old fashioned way of mass killing when the nuclear bomb deployment was still very simple; to load it on the aircraft, to fly aircraft over the target and drop the bomb. Now, with the thermonuclear warhead with the power of ten thousand times more deadly than Hiroshima's nuclear, the deployment is very sophisticated. The nuclear weapons might be loaded on the state-of-the-art missile either from the land or the sea, on the fixed silo or from mobile launcher or from the submarine.

How much is the cost to produce a nuclear bomb? A cost to produce every single deadly nuclear weapon is more than the living cost of whole people of Burundi or Eritrea Africa for a year. And all costs to produce the 7,500 nuclear weapons and their additional tools which are now operational are more than the living cost of all human being in this planet for 20 years.

This tiny blue planet has the humanitarian institutions to help the near death people from starving only to kill them as they are healthy and wealthy. It has also the religious and peace preachers, but it has also the civilized people whose jobs are only to kill another people, no matter you like or not.

The paradigm of pure self defense when the civilized people created the first nuclear bomb does not exist anymore; the new paradigm is to use the nuclear weapon as the deterrence and at the same time to threat the weak nations to surrender their scarce natural resources. Among the powerful nations themselves, they are fighting each other to grab the bigger chunk of these scarce natural resources belong to the weak nations. On the other side, the weak nation is pursuing the nuclear technology despite of fact that its people need more food instead of the weapon, yet its leader argues that he is protecting the people from marauding belligerents.

The time of jungle law is back where "the stronger rules"; the democracy, socialism, communism, and the other doctrine are labels only, the perpetual goal of any doctrine now is to create the latest method to deceive another deceit and to cheat another cheating in order to gain a pinch of daily food only. From this point, it is easy to understand what's behind any deadly conflict in the world. However, it is not easy for the world leaders to understand this shifting paradigm; if there is an exception, he's Ronald Reagan. He was the leading statesman in 20th century; he made GPS (global positioning system) free for everybody to avoid the accident similar to KAL 007; we are proud of him. He understood well the nature of arm racing and nuclear deterrence. When the Soviet leaders were worry about the ruse of war, he issued a peaceful statement later ".... we had no designs on the Soviet Union and Russians had nothing to fear from us".

1. The Little Naughty Boy

The war is cruelty over another cruelty; it is a natural continuation of the arrogance among the so-called civilized human being. No matter who did start the war, the end result would be the same: the misery for civilian, women and children. In March 1945 the US fire-bombed the city of Tokyo, killing at least 100,000 people. At another place, after Nazi's bombing on London, the British and the US bombers dropped the incendiary bombs on German cities Hamburg, Dresden, Kassel, Darmstadt, and Stuttgart. The website of nuclear alert www.nucleardarkness.org under the title of "Nuclear Darkness, Global Climate Change & Nuclear Famine: the Deadly Consequences of Nuclear War" displayed the horrible victims of the fire bombs, they were piled up after being burnt out alive [328].

Tokyo and its vicinity had been bombed for months in early 1945 prior to atomic bombing which the world never knew until McNamara revealed it in *"Fog of War"*. When the major cities of Japan were already devastated by the fire bomb where in a single night 100,000 civilians killed, then for what reason the atomic bombs were dropped over Hiroshima and Nagasaki? This startling question came in 1999 from a Grand Old Statesman the former US Secretary of Defense Robert S. McNamara. There are still several questions surrounding the use of atomic bombs on the Japanese cities of Hiroshima and Nagasaki on August 6 and August 9, 1945 respectively, and why not on the German cities; it sounds discriminative:

(1) When one half of Japanese most populated cities were destroyed already, then for what purpose two atomic bombs were dropped over Hiroshima and Nagasaki?
(2) Why did Hiroshima receive a package of **uranium** deadly weapon and why did Nagasaki receive the **plutonium** lethal weapon?
(3) Why not 2 uranium bombs or 2 plutonium bombs?
(4) Is the Potsdam declaration to ask Japan to surrender was just the pretext of the atomic bomb attack?

(5) Why the atomic bomb was not dropped on any German city?
(6) Is it because the Nazi surrendered on May 7, 1945 or because the atomic bomb on Germany would contaminate the civilized Europe for decades?
(7) It is a matter of fact that atomic bomb was not dropped over Europe; is it to prevent the radiation from Europe, and not from Japan?
(8) Why was the atomic bomb not used against the Germany to immediately stop the World War II?
(9) Why was the atomic bomb not used against China during Korean War despite of the urgent request from General McArthur?
(10) Vietnam War was the longest war in the modern history. Why was the atomic bomb not used against Vietnam to avert the 19-year war and the death of around 3,000,000 Vietnamese soldiers and civilians, 300,000 Cambodians, 200,000 Laotians, plus 58,220 US service members, at least 3,600,000 altogether?
(11) Who is the next after Hiroshima and Nagasaki?
(12) What **pretext** will be used?

The end winner of World War II between the Allied Forces versus Japan–Germany is Japan-Germany. Japan-Germany did not have the atomic bomb yet at that time; and after the war it was banned under the international treaty, but Japan-Germany to strike the Allied back by dropping the peaceful and luxury cars with very good price, and suddenly in 2008 the CEOs of US car maker became beggars in Washington to ask help from Obama administration. Yes, the Allied Forces won the battle and Japan-Germany won the war. The Japan-Germany car makers never asked the help from their governments; however the US car makers got $700 billion *Troubled Asset Relief Program*. The difference between **cap***italism* and so*cialism* is now vague. Is "capicialism" the end result of the World War II and Cold War?

The end result of every war --regardless of whether the belligerents are, either between the socialist and capitalist, or between fascist and allied forces, or other parties-- is the death of the nice girls and boys their parents loved dearly. The nature of their deaths was terrible; sometimes dismembered and sometimes burn out while they did not know why they were burned out alive with the technology products the ultra modern civilization ever invented.

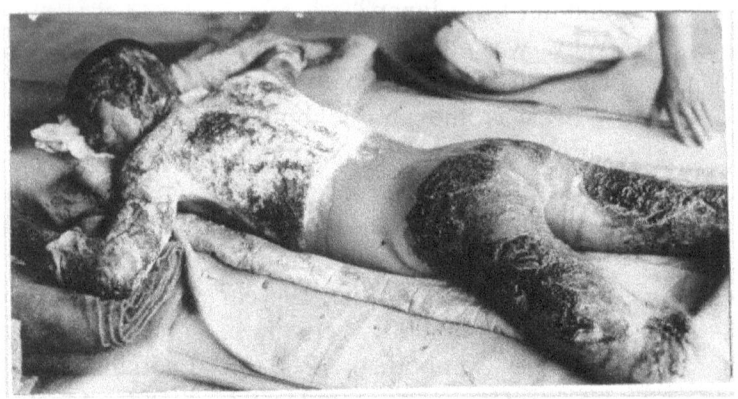

The victim of Atomic bomb in Hiroshima, August 6, 1945.
Photo by Masami Onuka, courtesy of **Hiroshima Peace Memorial Museum**, Japan

When a US airman was shot down while bombing a Japanese city, then General Curtis LeMay ordered to burn Tokyo with the incendiary bombs as "retaliation". Who can survive and endure a six-month bombing? Let's read this quotation "*For six months before the atomic bombings, the United States intensely fire-bombed 67 Japanese cities*" [329].

Is that necessary? That's the question from a former US Secretary of Defense McNamara; let's listen to his narration in "*Fog of War*":

> "The issue is in argue of killing one hundred thousands people in one night by fire or other; LeMay clearly said 'Yes'....And then have our soldiers crossed beach of Tokyo and slaughtered ten thousands Japanese?"

"Is that what you proposing? Is that moral? Is that wise? ***Why is it necessary to drop nuclear bomb*** if [US Air Force General] LeMay was bring up Japan and he went on from Tokyo to fire bomb other cities."

[Documentary displaying the devastation of 67 Japanese cities] "... 58% Yokohama, Yokohama is roughly the size of Cleveland, and [imagine] 58% of Cleveland was destroyed! Tokyo is the size of New York, 51% of New York was destroyed! 99% Chattanooga which is the size of Toyama and 99% destroyed!" [McNamara, in exclamation, his voice was raising and it sounds so angry to LeMay], "This is all done **before** the dropping of nuclear bombs which by the way were dropped by LeMay's command. Proportionality should be a guide in war. Killing 50-90% of people of 67 Japanese cities and then bombing them with 2 nuclear bombs is **not** proportional. [330]"

McNamara clearly implied General Curtis LeMay who was behind this mass devastation, to see how bad the six-month fire bombing over 67 Japanese cities, let's check the following statistics:

#	Japanese City	Size of US City	Devastation
1	Akashi	Lexington	50.2%
2	Amagasaki	Jacksonville	18.9%
3	Aomori	Montgomery	30%
4	Chiba	Savannah	41%
5	Chosi	Wheeling	44.2%
6	Fukui	Evansville	86%
7	Fukuoka	Rochester	24.1%
8	Fukuyana	Macon	80.9%
9	Gifu	Des Moines	69.6%
10	Hachioji	Galveston	65%
11	Hamamatsu	Hartford	60.3%
12	Haratsuka	Battle Creek	48.4%
13	Himeji	Peoria	49.4%
14	Hiroshima	Cambridge	11.9%
15	Hitachi	Little Rock	72%
16	Ichinomiya	Springfield	56.3%
17	Imabari	Stockton	63.9%
18	Iumazu	Waco	42.3%

19	Isezaki	Sioux Falls	56.7%
20	Kagoshima	Richmond	63.4%
21	Kawasaki	Portland	35.2%
22	Kobe	Baltimore	55.7%
23	Kochi	Sacramento	55.2%
24	Kofu	South Bend	78.6%
25	Kumagaya	Kenosha	55.1%
26	Kumamoto	Grand Rapids	31.2%
27	Kure	Toledo	41.9%
28	Kuwana	Tucson	75%
29	Maebashi	n/a	64.2%
30	Matsuyama	Duluth	64%
31	Mito	Pontiac	68.9%
32	Miyakonojo	Greensboro	26.5%
33	Miyazake	Davenport	26.1%
34	Moji	Spokane	23.3%
35	Nagaoka	Madison	64.9%
36	Nagoya	Los Angeles	41%
37	Nara	Boston	69.3%
38	Nobeoka	Augusta	25.2%
39	Ogaki	Corpus Christi	39.5%
40	Oita	St. Joseph	28.2%
41	Okayama	Long Beach	68.9%
42	Okazaki	Lincoln	32.2%
43	Omura	Santa Fe	33.1%
44	Omuta	Miami	35.9%
45	Osaka	Chicago	35.1%
46	Saga	Waterloo	44.2%
47	Sakai	Fort Worth	48.2%
48	Sasebo	Nashville	41.4%
49	Sendai	Omaha	21.9%
50	Shimizu	San Jose	42.1%
51	Shimonoseki	San Diego	37.6%
52	Sizuoka	Oklahoma City	66.1%
53	Takamatsu	Knoxville	67.5%
54	Tokushima	Fort Wayne	85.2%
55	Tokuyama	Butte	48.3%
56	Tokyo	New York	51%
57	Toyama	Chattanooga	99%
58	Toyohashi	Tulsa	67.9%
59	Tsu	Topeka	69.3%
60	Tsuruga	Middleton	65.1%
61	Ube	Utica	20.7%

62	Ujiyamada	Columbus	41.3%
63	Utsunomiya	Sioux City	43.7%
64	Yawata	San Antonio	21.2%
65	Yokkaichi	Charlotte	33.6%
66	Yokohama	Cleveland	58%
67	Wakayama	Salt Lake City	50%

This is the statistics. This is the fact. Do you believe the victims in Hiroshima and Nagasaki were "only" 200,000 Japanese? McNamara estimated in a single night there were sometime up to 100,000 victims, how much for 67 cities? When the average damage of every city was 50%; is it possible that the number of victims in every city were only 50,000? Is there any Japanese city with only 100,000 residents? Do you believe the devastation of Hiroshima with an **atomic** bomb was only 11.9% [eleven point nine percent] while Toyama suffered 99% [ninety nine percents] with the **conventional** bomb? Which is more powerful, conventional or atomic bomb? The amount of victims died from the fire bombs in 67 Japanese cities during a six-month bombing is huge, huge, is there still enough alive resident to kill in Hiroshima and Nagasaki? McNamara had had the biggest question ever "Is it necessary to drop the atomic bombs in Hiroshima and Nagasaki?" General Curtis LeMay never be able to answer, nor we do. Do we need another war?

> "By the time the atomic bombs were dropped on Japan, **50 million people** had already died in World War II. The bombing/murder of civilian populations had occurred so many times that it **was no longer even regarded as unusual**. I believe this is perhaps **the greatest tragedy of the war**, and it set the stage for the Cold War and the nuclear arms race that followed. [331]"

The victims of two atomic bombs in Hiroshima and Nagasaki were "only" 200,000 civilians; and it was **NOT** because the bombs were unsuccessful or harmless or failed, it was because there were no more living people available within these two cities to kill; most of their residents already died after heavy bombardment since six months earlier.

Only the residents of Hiroshima and Nagasaki ever suffered from the radiation of atomic bomb detonated some feet above their cities to make the effect more deadly, while General LeMay and the other war planners were looking at the mushroom cloud like a huge toy rising 60,000 feet into the Japanese air. Why does the war always come over and over and over?

Is it true that the war is our self destruction mechanism, an intrinsic factor within our body and soul, and we shall not stop until extinct? Why do we happy with the death of women and our beloved children?

[328] http://www.nucleardarkness.org/hiroshima/
[329] http://en.wikipedia.org/wiki/Nuclear_winter
[330] Error Morris Film, *"The Fog of War"*, documentary, 2003
[331] http://www.nucleardarkness.org/hiroshima/

2. "Abel Archer" War Game

Do we remember Sherlock Holmes' trick, a character created by Sir Arthur Conan Doyle, in "*A Scandal in Bohemia*" to find out a proof of King's scandal with Irene Adler a prima Donna Imperial Opera of Warsaw?

The US never forgave the Soviet Union over the theft of nuclear secret, ever. In fact, the "**Able Archer**" war game is the "**Irene Adler**" modern war game, the basic plot are the same, nothing new. If there is something new, it is the Soviet Union fiasco to translate the war game from "Irene Adler" into "Able Archer" or vice versa. Please take a look, "Able Archer" is another name and spelling of "Irene Adler" each entry consists of exact 10 letters, no more and no less. "**Able Archer**" is the Sherlock Holmes' pretty fire cracker on the stage of Kremlin to find out where the Soviets keep their secret arsenal! During Able Archer 83, the NATO knows that the Soviet arsenal was secretly spread in the Baltic Military District, Czechoslovakia, Poland and East Germany. The NATO won over the Soviets as Holmes did over Irene Adler. If "**Able Archer**" is the fire cracker, so what the Soviet scandal is? It was Ethel Rosenberg, prima donna of nuclear theft!

"**Able Archer 83**" was comprehensive NATO rehearsal to test the combat readiness of NATO military power in the case of critical situation where the possibility of conflict between NATO and Soviet Union block escalated and culminated in a coordinated nuclear launching. This rehearsal started on November 2, 1983, lasted for ten days and involved the participation of government leader of NATO members [332]. The coordinated military exercises covered Western Europe and under the command of Supreme Headquarters Allied Powers Europe [SHAPE] in Belgium. It was a breath-taking rehearsal since it was made as actual as possible including military operating procedure at any stage of real war such as radio silence, encrypted communication, authorization of every government leader and the critical stages of nuclear launching.

Several factors in "**Able Archer 83**" exercise such as its natural procedure and the deteriorating US - SU relation, altogether with the arrival of new Pershing II nuclear missiles in the Europe had led the Soviet Union Block to think that it was real war preparation disguised in the military exercise to avoid suspicion, as Soviet did in Cuban. It's another moment where the world was on the brink of nuclear disaster after the Cuban Missiles Crisis. When the Soviet Union sent MRBM to Cuba in 1962, it was done in maximum secrecy; the soldiers had to dress the winter uniform to make them (and their family) thinking that they were going to Vladivostok, and the military missile technicians were sent under the disguise of Soviet-Cuban farming cooperation.

Finally, the Soviet Union Block was taking back its breath after "Able Archer 83" exercise ended without incident on November 11, 1983.

Sir Arthur Conan Doyle's [1859-1930]
"A Scandal in Bohemia"

A sad love story of a Prince **Irene Adler** was a young and beautiful Prima Donna Imperial Opera of Warsaw when she met a young and handsome **Prince of Bohemia**, Wilhelm Gottsreich Sigismond von Ormstein, Grand Duke of CasselFelstein, and hereditary King of Bohemia [333]; then happened what happened and they were both in a photograph, the hard evidence of old style scandal. Now, the Prince is going to get married and he was so worry that his photograph with Irene would be used against him to ruin his future and his plan to marry **Clotilde Lothman** von Saxe-Meningen, second daughter of the King of Scandinavia whose family principles were very strict. Any previous scandal of the groom candidate may ruin the matrimony.

A photograph tells more than one thousand words, and Irene Adler would not sell it at any price, some attempts have been made to steal it but always failed. In a desperate, the Prince asked Sherlock Homes' advice, even though he was wearing the mask when visiting Holmes, the latter was still recognized!

> Sherlock Holmes was the best spy in the Great Britain ever, he was even better than any **MI5** or **MI6** agent, nobody was able to bribe or threaten him, nor did he betray his country to sell the British secret to **KGB**. To him, the Prince asked the strategic advice about his past mistake with a young and talented Irene Adler. This delicate case for the Prince; is only a piece of cake for Sherlock Holmes. The only way to know where the photograph is being kept is to incite the fire during Adler performance. A natural reaction for someone during the arson or danger is to run and grab the most valuable thing for him/her; it could be money, jewelry or just photograph. From this point, our spy Sherlock Holmes knew for sure where the Adler-Prince photograph is. Had the KGB agents been not too busy reading **"Gulagtanamo ArchipeLagoon"** and had had a little time to read "A Scandal in Bohemia" then they might solve the mystery of "Able Archer 83". [333]
>
> http://www.mysterynet.com/holmes/01scandalbohemia/

While all activities were monitored and recorded from the orbiting satellites for later review and improvement, what did NATO find from Able Archer 83 exercise?

(1) They knew that the Soviet prepared the nuclear missiles and Air Force in East Germany and Poland as well; therefore the two points which are closest to NATO defense i.e. East Germany and Poland should have been taken over first to eliminate the Soviet's front defense line.

(2) The NATO knew where the KGB agents are stationed across Europe and even around the globe since they were very active to monitor the Able Archer 83 exercise.

(3) When the satellite recorded the images of thermal tracks, most probably resulted from the helicopter encircling over the Barents Sea near Greenland, the NATO knew for sure that beneath the sea under the chopper, a nuclear submarine was exercising at a certain coordinate on GPS.

(4) By sending the mock sortie over Soviet airspace and abruptly turning back home after detecting where and when the anti air aircraft missiles are, NATO knew the vulnerability of Soviet's radar. From this point, do we believe that **Mathias Rust**, then-19 year-old German amateur pilot who flew his Cessna and illegally landed next to the Kremlin wall on May 28, 1987 was creating "imaginary peace bridge"[334] to the East as he claimed? He was a young smart pawn to test the Soviet radar vulnerability and he made it, therefore the Soviet Defense Minister General Sergei Sokolov and the Head of Soviet Air Defense General Aleksandr Koldunov were fired. The Kremlin considered the both are numb and dumb.

Oleg A. Gordievsky

Oleg Antonovich Gordievsky (1938-) is a former high rank of KGB stationed in London and became a secret agent of MI6 the British Secret Intelligence Service from 1974 to 1985. His most important contribution to the West is his potential aversion of nuclear confrontation between the NATO and the Soviet Union when Able Archer 83 war game was considered by the Soviet Union as a ruse of nuclear war. He also provided the crucial information that the Soviet leaders were worrisome about the NATO nuclear strike; and therefore President Reagan arranged a special meeting with Gordievsky. Reagan, in his memoir, wrote "....I was even more anxious to get a top Soviet leader in a room alone and try to convince him we had no designs on the Soviet Union and Russians had nothing to fear from us. [335]" On 22 May 1985 Gordievsky was ordered back to Moscow; he was interrogated by Soviet counterintelligence about the possibility of his treason; the intelligence sources speculated that it was apparently as a result the very sensitive information leaked by Ames a CIA officer who sold the US secret to KGB. With a spectacular move he evaded the KGB surveillance and defected to England. Later he was united with his wife and 2 children after British Prime Minister Margaret Thatcher extensively lobbied the new Kremlin leader Mikhail Gorbachev [336].

The obsolete Kremlin leaders were so numb to excessively respond to Able Archer exercise, no wonder a few years later the Soviet Union collapsed; now the Soviet-built modern airfield in Semey Kazakhstan becomes a temporary US air force base, something unimaginable during the Cold War.

Before the Able Archer 83 exercise, the same situation actually happened 2 years earlier on the NATO side when in 1981 the Kremlin leaders Brezhnev and Andropov ordered the Soviet military operation code-named Operation RYAN, the largest coordinated war preparation during the Cold War. The origin of this operation is the erroneous intelligent gathering either due to the misinformed KGB field agents or the direct result of NATO disinformation program that makes the Kremlin thinking of NATO attack on Soviet Union. Once more time the world was on the brink of nuclear disaster.

Since both side of NATO and Soviet Block knew that there would be no winner in the nuclear war, then the war planners invented a new doctrine of "Pre-emptive Strike" where the one who strikes first would win a half. That is the main purpose of Operation RYAN since the Kremlin war committee was thinking that the NATO was going to attack the Soviet Union. The Soviet's suspicion was based on the NATO approval in 1979 to install the Pershing II missiles in the Europe replacing the Jupiter missiles that were dismantled after the Cuban Missile Crisis. The US under Ronald Reagan leadership was developing a new strategy of Strategic Defense Initiative [SDI] which was dubbed "Star Wars" in 1983 by using the ground and space-based defense system to prevent the US from the sudden attack of ballistic missile. The SDI was designed to protect the US from Soviet's SS-20 ballistic missiles; however the Soviets considered SDI as a step forward to win the nuclear war; and therefore the world once more time was on the brink of the nuclear war.

The US was taking a closer attention on the Soviet's SS-20 since it was the sophisticated missile with peculiar capability to deliver three different warheads to three different targets

[Multi Independently Reentry Vehicle, MIRV]. Meanwhile the Soviets were taking a closer attention on Pershing II which installed on the west side of their border with the capability within four to six minutes to destroy SS-20 while it's still in its hard covered silo. With the deployment of Pershing II missile, there is no more save bunker to protect the Kremlin leaders; and from this point they think that the only way to tame Pershing is to pre-empt it, by this doctrine the Kremlin has the good reason to start the nuclear war even before the NATO does. The Soviets were actually fearful of the US sudden aggression. Is there still any save place in this planet for us to live?

The imminent danger of nuclear weapon seems does not last; one after another. On September 26, 1983 the Soviet satellite early warning system detected a single ICBM launched from the US soil; should the Soviets retaliate? Luckily they did not; and it was not because they gave up their lives; it's just because they did not know, since the commander of radar station Colonel Stanislav Petrov intentionally did not report the missile launch he saw on his radar to Kremlin leaders! The missile launch from the US soil headed to the Soviet Union turned to be false due to the satellite malfunction, that's what Petrov believed; and he's right.

He was still sane to think otherwise; his decision not to report to Kremlin was based on:

(1) the negative detection from the ground radar, and

(2) the US attack on the Soviet Union should have **not** been carried out by a single missile; and

(3) the satellite was known before to have a malfunction. This is what McNamara most worried about, the nuclear weapon "**to be launched by the decision of one human being.**"

> **Stanislav Yevgrafovich Petrov**
>
> Stanislav Yevgrafovich Petrov (1939-) is a lieutenant colonel of the Soviet Defense Forces who on September 26, 1983 when worked at the command center for nuclear early warning system spotted "the small launch from the United States" on the Soviet defense computer system. He correctly considered that the warning was wrong; and it was a false alarm [337]. His decision had prevented the mistaken retaliatory nuclear launching against the USA. His supervisors later confirmed his decision that the satellite early warning system was in malfunction. The decision to launch the retaliatory attack was not his authority, but had he reported that there was a nuclear launching from the US then the chain of command would have decided an erroneous nuclear revenge since the Soviet generals only had had a couple minutes to make a fateful decision. From this point we might respect his decision not to report the "US nuclear launching against Soviet Union" to his supervisors. However, he had had a crucial role in averting the MAD nuclear war. He deserved an International Peace Award, even a Nobel; but who would file a petition to the Noble Prize Committee?

The threat of war is one among one thousand methods of product marketing; without arm business the unemployment will be higher, the hedonists become the regular worker to sustain their lives with the minimum wage; the sovereignty of a country will be abused, etc. Any merchandise has its own standard price except for the military arms. The arm production does not have the price standard; the more tension the higher the price, the more conflicts the more value; and therefore the arm producers, arm dealers and politicians might join hand in hand to create the crisis; from this business they became rich. We have too many bank surpluses; we may print the paper money anytime without causing inflation and without real gold backup, we have too much oil, gold and silver deposit, farm produce, trade surplus against another country. It's too easy to print electronic circuit board and packing it to be the modern gadgets such as calculator, scales, game box, smart phone, GPS, blood pressure monitor, PC, tablet etc. and people keep buying it every single season. It's too easy to make millions even billions of dollar by fixing the bank rate, or hiding billions of dollars to avert the owner from paying taxes, or duping the gullible customers in their mortgage, or robbing the whole money from other bank by inviting its young inexperienced manager into speculative profitable trading and investing etc. etc. to generate the multiple loss. It's too easy to make money within an hour by selling our stock to rake some million dollars, our lives are too easy and we need our kids to taste our experience as we did when we're the baby boomers when everything was difficult and expensive. Yes, we definitely need war to drain our money and to taste a pinch of poverty and pass it on to our kids to feel the same because we are jealous since they are born in the peace time when everything is available. As they grow and become mature, in turn they will do the same to create the vicious cycle. Are we convinced that after the nuclear war there will be no more Superpower, there will be Superpoor only instead?

[332] http://en.wikipedia.org/wiki/Able_Archer_83
[333] http://www.mysterynet.com/holmes/01scandalbohemia/
[334] http://en.wikipedia.org/wiki/Mathias_Rust
[335] http://en.wikipedia.org/wiki/Able_Archer_83
[336] http://en.wikipedia.org/wiki/Oleg_Gordievsky
[337] http://en.wikipedia.org/wiki/Stanislav_Petrov

3. Worst scenario: nuclear warfare

August 6, 1945. The new paradigm of war was born. The war planners decided the nuclear weapon should be detonated behind the battle line to kill a lot of civilian to destroy the soldier moral on the front line. Their choice was Hiroshima. This is an imbalance war, since under the strong request of General LeMay, the nuclear weapon was used behind the battle line; had the nuclear weapon been used on the battlefield such Okinawa, Saipan, Midway etc., it would be understandable. The vast majority of victim is not the soldier but civilian. The use of nuclear weapon would yield a very different effect if the both adversaries have the nuclear weapon. No matter the cause, if an adversary already launched a nuclear weapon against the other, then the latter would respond immediately with the another nuclear weapon. The aftermath could be very devastating; this kind of nuclear exchange at least has the potential to kill 200,000,000 [two hundred million] people. This would be real nuclear warfare with unlimited damage and possibility for very very long time since the main purpose of the nuclear weapon is to inflict maximum destruction against the adversary with the minimum retaliatory effect; therefore the prominent doctrine in a nuclear warfare is *pre-emptive strike*, it does mean kill them first before they kill you. The Soviet's SS-20 ICBM with MIRV capability and the US Pershing II also with the MIRV capability were created based on this doctrine to hit the adversary's WMDs while they are still sitting in their silos.

The latest information revealed what would happen if a nuclear war erupted. The Soviet Union in 1962 beyond the US knowledge, also deployed 100 additional tactical nuclear weapons to Cuba, and the Soviet Commander General Issa Pliyev was authorized to launch them **without** additional command from Moscow. This chain of command is quite different with the US method where the last command is on the President's hand.

The key person of 1962 "nuclear confrontation" was Vasili Arkhipov who stopped Valentin Savitsky, a submarine captain, from launching the nuclear weapon from B-59 submarine when he was cornered off Florida coast and he thought that the real war erupted already, and the key date was October 26, 1962. Had the nuclear confrontation erupted, at least 100 million American would be killed and 100 million Soviets would also be killed. We know later that the tally is too low, based on the latest information we need to recalculate the number of victims who lost their lives during and after the nuclear war.

The 2010 report indicates that around 8,000 nuclear weapons still remain today; 1,459 out of them should have been deployed against 654 targets in Soviet Union and China during the Cold War to eliminate at least 175 millions lives [338] in the so-called communist countries. Would the communist countries respond with their nuclear weapons, and how much another lives lost? Our next generation would ask us "Is this the end result of capitalism and communism?"

40 Years after the Cuban Missile Crisis, former Secretary of State Robert McNamara on the documentary movie "***The Fog of War***" said "[If] you make a wrong decision, you destroy the nation".

He's right. The person, who supposed to make wrong decision to launch the nuclear missile while the adversary had also the same weapon, should have been stopped first to save hundred millions of lives. The war planners know for sure that the nuclear warfare is the ultimate misery for the mankind, but they execute the plan anyway like what happened to Hiroshima and Nagasaki in August 1945. If being compared to the latest version, the uranium weapon dropped on Hiroshima on August 6, 1945 and plutonium weapon dropped on Nagasaki on August 9, 1945 were like a small spark. Both weapons killed 200,000 Japanese people with the destroying power of only 15 kiloton each; while the Titan II ICBM carried 9 megaton warhead or around 10,000 times more powerful than those of Hiroshima's.

Titan II is the most powerful nuclear weapon ever developed by the US during the Cold War with the capacity of wiping Moscow out of the world map within six minutes. Meanwhile the Soviet SS-20 ICBM was designed to wipe Washington DC out from the continent map within 15 minutes or less. The method to kill the other people was significantly increasing, from duel one by one, to one group by one group, to one country by one country, and to one single man by one hundred million people yet they proud of it.

The human being is always maintaining and developing the self-destruction mechanism which they disguised under the luxury label of "national pride", "pre-emptive strike", "war on the aggressor", "annihilating the imperialist", "maintaining the freedom and peace", etc.

During the Korean War in 1951, General Douglas McArthur consistently requested President Harry Truman's permission to use his own authority to launch the atomic weapon on the China Mainland to win the war. This request was one among other reasons for President Truman to fire McArthur, and it's also the reason on why he was not elected a US President. McArthur was the Army general who knew the battle only, not the war, not the politics. However, the China who was behind the North Korean 260,000 soldiers and mobilizing 1.3 million soldiers, signaling to welcome the US decision to use the atomic weapon since the China Chairman Mao Zedong was seriously considering to use the same atomic bomb against the US to "annihilate imperialist system." Once more time the world was on the brink of the nuclear war. Mao Zedong was also quoted to be optimistic to have the chance to build the socialist world after razing the imperialist down:

> "Let us imagine how many people would die if [nuclear] war breaks out. There are 2.7 billion people in the world, and a third could be lost. If it is a little higher it could be half ... I say that if the worst came to the worst and one-half dies, there will still be one-half left, but imperialism would be razed to the ground and the whole world would become socialist. After a few years there would be 2.7 billion people again. [339]"

Mao Zedong was the one and only world leader to welcome the nuclear war; China has more than four hundred fifty million people in 1951; and it's not easy to feed these people before the Chinese economic boom in 2000s, therefore on one side he welcomed the nuclear war which would help him to resolve the population problem. On the opposite side, the hedonists who are worshipping the luxury life; should have been discouraged to know Mao Zedong casual attitude toward loosing one half of the world population. He did not just talk but did implement his bright idea, he encouraged the growth of Chinese population just in case the nuclear war erupts, China still has enough population; under his leadership the Chinese people increasing from 550 million to 900 million. Mao maybe right, in 2012 according to the World Bank China has 1.3 billion people and becomes the most populous country in the world. What if President Truman granted General McArthur's request, how much the US population would be now?

The world after World War II is not better off than before it, since several nations are competing to produce the nuclear weapons. Nuclear age has delivered a new paradigm, a new age of disguised colonialism. For them, the nuclear weapon is a ticket to force their political expansion over the non-nuclear nations and at the end to capture the rich natural resources. When the nuclear countries retained their nuclear arsenal, South Africa becomes the only country to voluntarily disassemble its nuclear weapon; it is the one and only the nation to do such action. Since 1945, around 2,000 (two thousands) nuclear weapons have been detonated either for "scientific testing" or to really killed people.

According to the military theory there are two kinds of nuclear war, limited nuclear war [LNW] and full-scale nuclear war [FNW]. A LNW could be intended to destroy the military and limited civilian facilities, or as a starting point for the regular forces to invade. The LNW and FNW could arise during an *accidental nuclear war* where the use of nuclear weapons is activated either by accident or coincidence. In September 26, 1983, the Soviet radar commander **Stanislav Petrov** observed on his radar system that an US ICBM was heading the Soviet Union but he smartly think it must be a false warning due to malfunction. Another accidental nuclear war may result from the undetermined mishaps; or from deliberate twist by the bellicose Generals who persistently requested permit(s) to launch the nuclear weapon, and the leaders like Mao Zedong who casually welcomed the US nuclear weapon during 1951 Korean War. Luckily although some accidental scenarios already occurred during the past Cold War, yet no real nuclear launching ever happens. The FNW involves the large numbers of nuclear weapons to deliberately destroy military and civilian targets including (1) space centers such as NASA, Xichang Space Center, Guizhou Aerospace Industrial Center, and Baikonur Cosmodrome even it is now not a part of Russia; (2) economics centers such as Wall Street, Silicon Valley, Shanghai, Tianjin, and Moscow; (3) infrastructures, even entertainment or civic centers such as Disney Land and Hollywood or Beijing's Forbidden city; or the historic sites such as Kremlin Palace, Bolshoi Opera House, Buckingham Palace, 10 Downing Street, Madame Tussauds Museum, Champs-Elysees, Louvre Museum or another targets within a whole country. Jerusalem? It would be safe since it is a holy city for 3 major religions.

Every nuclear-owning country has its own favorite target; the Soviet Union may strike the Washington DC first while the US in favor of the silos surrounding Moscow. The US and Soviet leaders may build the underground bunker some miles below the mountain rock, but for how long they may survive; soon they will be boring since they need the open space to live, they need the live TV show, bar and grill, they need internet and entertainment that no longer available, they are not Flintstone family, they need to come out but the fallout prevents them, and soon they die in the narrow modern cave named bunker.

The LNW is only a theory, when the US dropped the first atomic bomb in Hiroshima August 6, 1945 actually Japan was in an intensive research to acquire its atomic bomb. The

Soviet Union, the prominent US adversary during Cold War also has the nuclear bomb; any time the US attack Moscow with a nuclear bomb, or any time the Soviet attacks Washington then the FNW will ensue for sure. Therefore, the LNW is on the paper only; however limited nuclear attack would eventually lead to the unlimited nuclear exchange until all nuclear weapons in the arsenal become zero. At this point this tiny blue planet becomes uninhabited; the civilization would be totally destroyed, the next generation –if any- would be the crippled generation with so many genetic defects, the natural resources become the source of perennial poison for centuries; and no more car, cell phone, computer, airplane, movie, bar, fast food restaurant, and school. No doctor, no engineer and no any modern gadgets since all infrastructures have been completely destroyed. The human being then would be very idling and they can see the real effect of their self-destruction mechanism, not on the paper only.

In the nuclear war there is no optimistic prediction and calculation, everything should be put in the maximum estimate of loss, even to extinction. If there is any survivor, it would the Eskimos in the remote area and they do not want to live in our present place since it will be totally messed up, in rubble, hot and no fresh animal available to hunt. Fire arm? They did not need, with their spears they sustained the live since centuries ago and will be for the other centuries; and wait; where are we? Extinct!

The end of World War II is not the **end** of enmity between nations; it turns be a **beginning** of new and long proxy war between the former friends which costs each belligerent unprecedented military spending along the history. The money they spent is more than enough to feed the human being in this planet and educate them for free for 10 years. The end of WW II is a beginning of competition to inherit Nazi's technology to produce the more powerful tools to kill the other people on the behalf of "ideology", an abstract word that does mean nothing but "kill them before they kill you." The Nazi created the popular 9mm Parabellum *) cartridge, they won over the other European countries including the Soviet Union before being defeated by the Allied Forces where the Soviets and the US are included. The Nazi developed Vergeletung-1 a first ballistic missile that unexpectedly hit London, they invented the "heavy water" from a very sophisticated reactor a precursor of nuclear weaponry, they organized the best spy ring ever, they manufactured the sophisticated car without the water cooler which endured the desert where the water is more important for soldier rather than for the car, the one and only car of this kind; they invented the crypto communications, and much more.

Upon finding this treasure, the Soviets and the US start the competition to grab it first, and after an intensive dispute it became the Cold War and the number of victims never be announced. As they found the bounty and the huge spoil of war including the high technology, they start the prolonged altercation for 40 years. To ensure their superiority over the adversary, they created a very expensive weapon on the expense and sacrifice of their people. One of their most expensive killing machines is a nuclear-powered submarine with the capability to launch the nuclear warhead to kill as much as 40 million people for a single warhead.

How much the cost for each killing machine? It costs more than the annual budget of Somalia government. Who does get the benefit and profit? The arm producers and dealers do. To be the arm producer and arm dealer is more profitable than to be drug producer and drug dealer. The local police, international police, state and country are always fighting drug producer and drug dealer, while the arm producer and arm dealer are always welcomed by any country although the end result of drug and arm is same, the death.

Thanks to the civilized nations in the UN General Assembly who voted overwhelmingly on early April 2013 to approve a dare treaty aimed at regulating the lavish global trade in conventional killing weapons. What about the unconventional weapons, like chemical, biology, nuclear?

The most worrisome scenario for the US is the Soviet's tank battalion which expected to roam the Europe after an initial nuclear launchings to takeover the Western Europe. Meanwhile the most worrisome for both the Soviet Union and the US is the pre-emptive strike which would destroy the nuclear weapons while they are still sitting in the silos; and therefore the both side considered the nuclear war would be conforming the MAD [mutually assured destruction] doctrine, where no one will be the winner. With the MAD doctrine, each belligerent would destroy not the military targets only but the civilian targets including business, entertainment centers and the enemy population to make sure the enemy's spirit of war would be eliminated. From this point we may understand the nuclear shelters were built across the country in both the Soviet Union and the USA. The both side fully understood that they had had enough nuclear warheads to wipe the other population out completely. Among the nuclear countries; only China and India to openly declare that they would not adopt the pre-emptive nuclear strike.

To prevent the nuclear arsenals from the possibility of pre-emptive strike, both the Soviet Union and the US moved their nuclear forces to the sea; they invented and produced a large amount of nuclear powered submarines armed with the SLBM [Submarine Launched Ballistic Missile] to make sure the nuclear retaliation would be accomplished as one adversary starts the nuclear war. These submarines were able to sneak into the adversary's coast to aim more accurately to the targets. In order to protect the civilian targets, each side invents the defense system including early warning satellite system [EWSS] to detect the pre-emptive strike. Unfortunately, more than one hundred error detections happened even with very sophisticated satellite; only God knows why the real nuclear war did not happen after so many detections including the notorious detection of "US pre-emptive nuclear launching" on September 26, 1983 "discovered" by Stanislav Petrov the Soviet radar commander. The similar error also happened on the US side as if "the Soviet's ICMB is heading to US soil."

This tiny planet in the same time was officially ever recorded by the United Nation in 1980 to have 40,000 nuclear warheads with the capability of producing 13,000 megatons total explosion [340] more than 800,000 times than the atomic bomb dropped over Hiroshima in 1945. This explosive is more than enough to make the human being species to extinct.

Three nuclear-related incidents took place during Ronald Reagan presidency in 1983; it was a nuclear crazy year which generated the nuclear fever:

(1) September 1, 1983; KAL 007 fate. Korean Air Line 007, Boeing commercial jumbo jet was shot down by the Soviet's jet fighter while straying over the Sakhalin restricted airspace. All 246 passenger and 23 crews on board were dead. The Soviet Union despite its acknowledgment that KAL 007 was a passenger airplane but it did not take a risk that the plane was equipped with a military surveillance gadgets to monitor the nuclear readiness and ongoing military exercise on the Sakhalin Island.

(2) September 26, 1983; Stanislav Petrov wisdom. He spotted a launching of "a US nuclear ballistic missile" on the radar screen; he decided not to report to his supervisors and considered one missile launching from the US is not feasible, since the pre-emptive strike would be always with several nuclear weapons or at least the simultaneous strike. He was right and therefore averted the real nuclear war. What if he reported to Kremlin?

(3) November 2 - 11, 1983; Able Archer nuclear war exercise. Amid Reagan's military buildup and war rhetoric, the Soviet Union was considering that Able Archer nuclear war exercise was a disguised preparation for a real war. The Soviet military forces were fully prepared to face the worst possibility.

During Reagan presidency the US military underwent the most significant buildup ever to be ready for nuclear war; the production of new strategic bomber was revived after suspended by preceding President Jimmy Carter. Reagan's rhetoric was also threatening; at least in three different occasions his remarks were sharp against the Soviet Union:

(1) On March 3, 1983 he said that the communism would collapse;

(2) and on March 8, 1983 he called the Soviet Union "evil empire".

(3) In his wide covered address before the British Parliament on June 8, 1983 he declared "freedom and democracy will leave Marxism-Leninism on the ash-heap of history." To anticipate all possibilities, the Soviet Union was on its highest alert at the time of Reagan, never be in any preceding US President, ever.

[338] TIMES magazine, September 27, 2010 page 38
[339] http://en.wikipedia.org/wiki/Nuclear_warfare
[340] *ibid.*
 *) The word of parabellum is not the German language, it comes from the Latin proverb *"Si vis pacem para bellum"*, if you want the peace prepare for the war.

4. Global Cooling

Today, the heated debate about global warming suggesting that the global temperature is rising up compared to the previous decades, while some critics say the global warming is just a hoax. It's a systematic method to shift the global focus on injustice, poverty, conflicts, crimes and drugs as happened in Y2K hoax prior to year 2000. The Y2K does mean Y = Year, 2 is two and K is Kilo or thousand; it stands for "Year2000". The Y2K hoax is a made-up issue that all computers were set to start the year of twentieth century from 1900 with double zero digits, and in year 2000 the computer would reset themselves into year 1900 instead of 2000; this condition would affect or destroy the data stored in all computer as the hoax suggested. The truth is nothing happened with Y2K, it is a pure hoax but it affected the behavior of the computer owners around the globe. The global incest actually is more serious than global warming. The global incest which caused the baby boomers around the globe already happened post World War II. Since the relationship between man and woman is more permissible than ever, so the baby birth of unmarried couple is soaring ever since.

When this kind of baby in his adulthood –say he is Bobby- meets a woman –say she is Annie- who was also born out of wedlock from a very same father then they produce an incest baby either out of wedlock or within a legitimate marriage. Unbeknown by each side Annie and Bobby have the same father.

This case happened already over and over and nobody paid the attention; what if this incest baby later in his or her adulthood does the same thing, and who would perform the medical research to determine if *the incest babies are more susceptible against cancer*, and if they were, should the medical coverage be excluded or more premium be collected and so on and so forth? This is serious case either from medical or legal perspective since the main purpose of insurance is protection for the insured people and for the health insurance company as well.

The health insurance company would save billions of dollars or make more billion dollars if they have the *medical proof* that the incest people are more susceptible against cancer or any possibility of *congenital defect* and genetic mutation. The "congenital defect" is a keyword in the next insurance policy. The legal reasoning is simple "the insured people have to complete all information on insurance applications and they leave the incest information blank or N/A" then the insurance benefit would be reduced accordingly; and if they check the incest field with "Yes" then the premium would be increasing; this is a simple way for the health insurance company to add up some billion dollars.

On the other side, the insurance company could not be accused of discrimination against the incest if medical facts become the legal and medical proof that the persons who are product of incest are more susceptible against cancer and congenital defects.

The global warming, if any, is not an excuse for creating "global cooling". However, all scientists did agree that the nuclear war would lead to the global cooling due to the blocked sun ray by the debris and soot. The scientists have conducted numerous scientific calculations concerning the impacts on ecology and economics after the nuclear war; and nothing of their research recommended the nuclear war; all scientists were skeptical and worrisome toward the nuclear war.

On March 23, 1983, US President Ronald Reagan announced the Strategic Defense Initiative [SDI], a coordinated program to use land and space to protect the US from the attack by Inter Continental Ballistic Missiles [341]. Although this program was not implemented yet during Reagan presidency, yet it made the Kremlin leaders worrisome since it brought the US a step ahead of launching and counter attacking the ballistic missiles. Ronald Regan, in his memoirs, wrote:

> "Three years had taught me something surprising about the Russians: Many people at the top of the Soviet hierarchy were genuinely afraid of America

and Americans. Perhaps this shouldn't have surprised me, but it did ... During my first years in Washington, I think many of us in the administration took it for granted that the Russians, like ourselves, considered it unthinkable that the United States would launch a first strike against them. But the more experience I had with Soviet leaders and other heads of state who knew them, the more I began to realize that many Soviet officials feared us not only as adversaries but as potential aggressors who might hurl nuclear weapons at them in a first strike ... Well, if that was the case, I was even more anxious to get a top Soviet leader in a room alone and try to convince him we had no designs on the Soviet Union, and Russians had nothing to fear from us." [342]

Michael Gorbachev, a peaceful Soviet leader, in 2000 said "Models made by Russian and American scientists showed that a nuclear war would result in a nuclear winter that would be extremely destructive to all life on Earth; the knowledge of that was a great stimulus to us, to people of honour and morality, to act in that situation. [343]" The world leaders were talking about the horrible account after the nuclear war, yet they produced the nuclear warheads instead of dismantling them to avoid the nuclear war. It is simple, without nuclear warhead there is no nuclear war. No nuclear war no global cooling. The worst possibility for mankind today and tomorrow is nuclear war, nothing else. The following list is only some of the bad possibilities of nuclear war:

1) soot was ejected into stratosphere 6-30 miles above the earth surface, there will be the perennial or even eternal night and chilling temperature
2) with global eternal nights, there will be more gas and electric bills if there is still any power company to operate
3) soaring price, any price except the price of dignity
4) scarcity of healthy resources

5) low civilization, everything should start from scratch again
6) no more economics, entertainment, and education centers
7) no scientific research, the people do not want to do any scientific research since at last it was used to kill each other
8) no car, no plane, no train; people back to the ancient method of transportation using the cattle and wind as machine
9) no phone, no internet, no satellite
10) no farm and mass produce
11) no more international representatives in the UN
12) no more international monetary regulation, no IMF, no World Bank
13) if there is still the human being alive, their quality of life would be like in the ancient or prehistoric age
14) no TV show, no Oscar, no American Idol, no Hollywood, no Disney, no Madame Tussauds, no Forbidden City, no Kabuki, no Bolshoi, no Arc de Triomphe, no Middle Eastern belly dance
15) hunger and famine, people would do anything including prostitution to survive
16) defective generation
17) no fast food restaurant, no livestock, almost all of them are contaminated, no tools to detect the contamination since all Geiger counters were destroyed
18) no doctors, no hospitals, no medical schools; everything will be destroyed
19) ozone destruction, the earth inhabitants including the livestock and human will be in a great danger from sun's ultra violet radiation if there is any sun ray on the earth after being blocked by the soot and debris
20) suicide rate will be soaring
21) crime, any crime rate will be soaring; the crime is everywhere and even will not be considered as crime anymore, it becomes "common sense" in a such situation
22) people have no more feeling of shame, everything will be considered as necessity

23) marijuana, drug and hallucinogenic agents will be used as the daily consumption to escape from painful life; most countries, if still any, will legalize the tranquilizers and hallucinogenic agents; they will be the legitimate and profitable export commodity
24) the trading of drugs and hallucinogens would be the major trigger to local and regional conflicts
25) shorter life expectancy
26) human trafficking
27) total chaos everywhere

In 1992 Havana Meeting commemorating the Cuban Missile Crisis, attended by Fidel Castro and former US Secretary of Defense Robert McNamara, Castro disclosed that there were not only 9 nuclear warheads in Cuba but 162 nuclear warheads including 90 tactical warheads which McNamara initially considered he was mistranslated since he could not believe what he already heard.

McNamara at this point asked 3 questions to Castro as a former adversary; (1) "Mr. President, do you know that nuclear warheads out there?" (2) "If you did, what do you have recommended to Khrushchev in the face of US attack?" (3) "If you have to use them [nuclear warheads], what would happen to Cuba?" Castro said #1 I knew they were there, #2 'I have not recommended [to Khrushchev, and it does mean Castro would let Khrushchev to launch nuclear warheads to US] and #3 we are totally destroyed [Castro used '*We*' and not '*I*'];" and it does mean all belligerents including Cuba, the Soviet Union and the US [Part 4: Chapter 1].

The Cuban Missile Crisis of 1962, almost bring the world to the global cooling, and since the Cuban leader Fidel Castro was still upset with the US, he suggested the Soviet Union leaders to take a hard stance against the US and to launch the nuclear warhead if necessary. He insisted that the US should have been taught the meaning of receiving nuclear weapon and not just sending it to Hiroshima and Nagasaki. His pressure stopped after Kremlin officials provide him a short course on the ecological impact over Cuba after a nuclear detonation on the US soil [344]. He is completely silent afterward. The other world leaders especially Kim Jong-Un should have been taught as well. Castro, 51 years later, criticized North Korea over its taking "the gravest risk of nuclear war since Cuban Crisis of 1962"; he has now "the wisdom of age". The world leaders who knew the real and close danger of nuclear war provided the chilling account about it, while the common people who do not know anything about it were calm until the real war erupts.

Jonathan Pollard

The USA had lost a lot of security secrets since the theft of nuclear secret by Klaus Fuchs and the Rosenbergs in 1950's; even though, it is not dull and tired to get duped by the top spies. **Jonathan Jay Pollard** (1954-) is one of the top spies who steal and sell the US government secrets for money to the foreign governments. In 1987 he received a life sentence for his treason to USA; he was a former intelligent analyst who convicted of spying for Israel. His treason was dubbed as "one of the most devastating cases of espionage in US history" for the fact that he stole over "one million classified documents" [345] which *enabled Israel to monitor the surveillance system around the globe and to jam it if necessary.* In 1985 Jonathan Pollard was captured, in June 1986 he pleaded guilty; and on March 4, 1987 was sentenced to life in prison for espionage. TIME Magazine made several reports on Pollard case since 1985 until 2009; it was considered an important issue [346].

The importance of Pollard role in the espionage should be considered accordingly in accordance with several serious attempts by the high profile politicians to lobby the US government to release him. He must be a top rated spy, otherwise why did at least two prime ministers insist and were so eager to get him released. In 1995, Prime Minister Yitzhak Rabin asked President Bill Clinton to release Pollard. The request was declined.

Even in the Palestine peace conference at Wye River, Maryland on October 23, 1998 Prime Minister Benjamin Netanyahu tried to insert the release of Pollard as a prerequisite of the peace agreement which was declined by US President Bill Clinton. After Netanyahu's unsuccessful attempt to release Pollard, there is another relentless effort to release him. On September 2005 President George W. Bush rejected the request to release Pollard. Still, there was another Prime Minister to request the release of Pollard. During a Presidential visit to Israel on January 10, 2008, George W. Bush was asked by Prime Minister Ehud Olmert to release Pollard. Again, this request was rejected. Some attempts to release Pollard had made CIA Director George Tenet upset, it was reported he would resign if Pollard was released. The relentless efforts by at least three Prime Ministers only presented the clear evidence that Pollard is a Master Spy [347]. The story of top spies stealing the secrets of US government would never be ending from time to time. But, the US government never took the lesson on how to protect its secrets from the top spies.

[341] http://en.wikipedia.org/wiki/Able_Archer_83
[342] *ibid.*
[343] http://en.wikipedia.org/wiki/Nuclear_winter
[344] *ibid.*
[345] http://en.wikipedia.org/wiki/Jonathan_Pollard
[346] TIME Magazine 12/16/1985; March 16, 1987; July 22, 1991; December 13, 1993; January 10, 1994; April 4, 1994; April 13, 1995; October 23, 1998.
[347] http://en.wikipedia.org/wiki/Wye_River_conference

5. Cyber War vs. Nuclear War

> Which is more dangerous, the nuclear war or cyber war?

In September 2010 the cyber attack on the Iranian computer system became the world top news [348]. It was reported that Stuxnet computer virus attacked 30,000 Iranian computers; the Iranian government was on high alert and the necessary steps if the computer artificial virus infected the Iranian nuclear power system. Iran Daily newspaper on Sunday September 26, 2010 edition quoted the Secretary of Industry Mahmoud Liayi as to say that the computer virus was created by the adversary to disturb Iran as a part of electronic warfare. The experts are considering the computer virus named Stuxnet was created by a certain country targeting the Iranian nuclear power program [349]. Liayi was also quoted that Stuxnet was a sophisticated computer virus and it brings the footprint of the certain government with special agenda, if the computer IP was activated, Stuxnet starts to transfer the various important data from the infected computer to the Stuxnet operator; and after data retrieval then they are sent back to the computer source to attack it.

The Iranian Secretary of Information Technology Reza Taqipour explained that Stuxnet has not infected the Iranian industrial system, but the necessary precaution was taken; the ongoing virus cleaning is on the way.

Thomas Rid, a computer virus observer, wrote on 28 September 2010 "So what does all this mean? The CCC's Frank Rieger thinks that the Stuxnet attack will write history as the first offensive use of a cyber weapon by a state. That is a daring assessment. In the past, "cyber weapons" have been used prior to military operation, for instance during Operation Orchard when Israel disabled the air defense radar at Syria's suspected nuclear site before bombing it on September 6, 2007. And then, of course, there are probably numerous attacks we just don't know anything about. [350]"

Eugene Kaspersky, Co-founder and Chief Executive Officer of Kaspersky Laboratory, who is recently active to fight the computer virus said that today is the decisive moment for us to enter a new world, in the past we knew the cyber criminal, and now we know the cyber terrorist, cyber weapon and cyber war [351].

The list of country and number of computer infected by Stuxnet according to Kaspersky Lab [352]:

Country	# of Users
India	86,258
Indonesia	34,138
Iran, Islamic Republic of	14,171
Russian Federation	7,904
Kazakhstan	6,316
Afghanistan	3,081
Syrian Arab Republic	2,926
Uzbekistan	2,798
Pakistan	2,758
Azerbaijan	2,566
Bangladesh	2,489
Malaysia	1,691
Iraq	1,593
Nepal	1,453
Belarus	1,238
United Arab Emirates	1,206
Kyrgyzstan	1,097
United States of America	805
Turkmenistan	796
Tajikistan	780

The latest report indicates that the number of computer infected by Stuxnet is increasing. Symantec, a US security software maker estimated that as of August 6, 2010 the infected computer in Iran is 62,867; Indonesia 13,336; India 6,552; the US 2,913; Australia 2,436, Britain 1,038; Malaysia 1,013 and Pakistan 993; the number is still changing.

Symantec also estimates that Stuxnet needs a group of 5-10 well organized computer programmers and experts working hard at least for 6 months with unlimited fund which indicates that it is not a fledgling hacker operating from the basement of his mom's house [353].

Stuxnet is a new form of cyber terrorism, according to Kaspersky; however it is debatable. The Stuxnet attack augmented the speculation over the main purpose, origin, identity of the provider of malicious software [malware]. The target is clear, Iran and Middle Eastern countries; the purpose is clear, it is the sabotage; but the origin and the provider are still in a question mark. The sophisticated worm is a highly specialized malware that is designed to target only Siemens' Supervisory Control and Data Acquisition [SCADA] systems that are configured to control and monitor specific industrial processes in Iran plants [354].

The designer of Stuxnet must be the expert(s) who understood well the Siemens SCADA and must be supported by the huge amount of manpower with unlimited time and finance which no any private organization can do. In a recent computer security symposium in Munich Germany, Kaspersky said that **Stuxnet** was not designed to steal the money from the bank; instead it was designed to sabotage the target country. The sabotage is included but not limited to industry, infrastructure, processing facility, power line, communication, airport, shipping and even military installation. The airport as a Stuxnet target would bring the total chaos to the civil aviation and may generate the fatal accident which takes the civilians as the victim.

Kaspersky was worrisome that in 2012, the cyber war and cyber terrorism have begun while in 1990's there was only the cyber vandals, and 2000's is the cyber crime. He believes that Stuxnet is a prototype of cyber weapon which lead to a new competition to acquire the new power in the cyber world [355]. Kaspersky Computer Laboratory's experts believe that Stuxnet reveals the beginning of the new age of dangerous cyber-warfare.

Kaspersky Laboratory has not identified the Stuxnet origin, but he confirms that it is a sophisticated malicious software (malware) attack backed by a well-funded, highly skilled attacker team with sound knowledge of SCADA technology. Kaspersky, in a Munich symposium also said "I think that this is the turning point, this is the time when we got to a really new world, because in the past there were just cyber-criminals, now I am afraid it is the time of cyber-terrorism, cyber-weapons and cyber-wars." "I am afraid this is the beginning of a new world. 90s were a decade of cyber-vandals, 2000's were a decade of cyber criminals, I am afraid now it is a new era of cyber-wars and cyber-terrorism. [356]"

Kaspersky Lab in June 2010 discovered **Stuxnet** computer virus, the later version of it which is known as **Duqu** discovered in September 2011 by Budapest University of Hungary [357]; and latest version aka **Flame** discovered by Kaspersky Lab in June 2012. Stuxnet and Flame are designed by the same computer attacker; Kaspersky Lab confirms that Stuxnet is a weapon to damage uranium enrichment centrifuges in Iran. *Flame* malware as a cyber-espionage to infiltrate the computer systems through hundreds of possible vulnerabilities, it records almost all users' information including printed documents and voices recorded on the computer microphone [358].

The computer security experts consider *Flame* is one of the most sophisticated computer virus ever discovered until today. They are still intensively investigating the virus which they believe was created and released to particularly attack the computers in Iran and the Middle East. Therefore, Eugene Kaspersky, whose computer laboratory discovered Flame, urged the nations to halt "cyber terrorism"; he sends the message that they must talk on how to halt it. He told reporters at a cyber security conference in Tel Aviv June 6, 2012 "It's not cyber war, it's cyber terrorism, and I'm afraid the game is just beginning. Very soon, many countries around the world will know it beyond a shadow of a doubt. I'm afraid it will be the end of the world as we know it, I'm scared, believe me. [359] [360]"

Stuxnet and *Flame* success story to infect target computers without being detected for a long time because the both used the very smart way, even it was unthinkable by the computer experts. According to a computer expert, *Flame* uses Secure Socket Layer (SSL) port 443 to conceal its traffic which is normally used for e-banking service. A smart way, since most anti-virus software never scanned the traffic on port 443. On the other side, *Flame* uses the programming language *LUA Scripting*, an expensive and rare tool which is used by the big corporate only [361].

The computer experts said that technical evidence suggests *Flame* was built for the same nations that commissioned the *Stuxnet* worm that attacked Iran's nuclear power program in 2010. Tova Cohen and Maayan Lubell wrote for Reuter news agency June 6, 2012:

> "In recent months U.S. officials have become more open about the work of the United States and Israel on Stuxnet, which targeted Iran's Natanz nuclear enrichment facility. [362][363]"

That is because the US and Israel suspecting Iran of having developed atomic weapons which Iran harshly refutes and says the project is enriching the uranium for civilian purpose only. Basically, the US officials have NOT really "become more open about the work" on Stuxnet targeting Iran, it was a fatal leak and soon became the commodity of political campaign. CNN reported on June 6, 2012 that according a US official, the government investigation agency has launched the investigation into the leaking possibility of classified information involving a cyber warfare program against Iran. Furthermore CNN reported:

> "[The] spokesman Paul Bresson had no comment on the reported investigation. Senator Saxby Chambliss, ranking Republican on the Senate Intelligence Committee, said he was informed that an inquiry was under way. The senator from Georgia and other leaders of the House and Senate Intelligence Committees issued a joint statement Tuesday

340

deploring the apparent leaks. In recent weeks, we have become increasingly concerned at the continued leaks regarding sensitive intelligence programs and activities, including specific details of sources and methods," said Chambliss; Chairwoman Dianne Feinstein, Democrat of California; Chairman Mike Rogers, Republican of Michigan; and Ranking Member C.A. "Dutch" Ruppersberger, Democrat of Maryland, in the statement. "These disclosures have seriously interfered with ongoing intelligence programs and have put at jeopardy our intelligence capability to act in the future. Each disclosure puts American lives at risk, makes it more difficult to recruit assets, strains the trust of our partners and threatens imminent and irreparable damage to our national security in the face of urgent and rapidly adapting threats worldwide. The House and Senate Intelligence Committee leaders said they intended "to review potential legislation to strengthen authorities and procedures with respect to access to classified information and disclosure of it, as well as to ensure that criminal and administrative measures are taken each time sensitive information is improperly disclosed."

"We also intend to press for the executive branch to take tangible and demonstrable steps to detect and deter intelligence leaks, and to fully, fairly, and impartially investigate the disclosures that have already taken place."

"The committee is expected to add leak provisions later this month, when it takes up the FY13 intelligence authorization bill. The plan is for the Senate to vote on the measure before the summer recess. Although the House has already passed a version of the bill without the leak provisions, they would likely be added during a conference with the Senate. Spy ware [is] infiltrating Iranian computers. The White House pushed back against suggestions it could be leaking classified information for political purposes. [364]"

Meanwhile, Mitt Romney, the Republican presidential candidate embraced the leaking issue as a monumental point in his campaign to reach the White House. He is soon to join the Republicans demanding the independent investigation into the serious intelligence leaks since it indirectly becomes the [un]official and [in]direct acknowledgement of the US involvement in Stuxnet. On July 25, 2012 **MSNBC** TV reported:

> "The leaking info about the cyber war against Iran soon became the campaign issue for 2012 Republican Presidential candidate Mitt Romney who's on his trip to London pointing "Exactly who is in the White House who betrayed this secret?", and immediately Obama senior campaign advisor David Axelrod denied from the White House, he said "I can tell you the President of United States did not leak classified info as Mitt Romney suggested. [365]"

Today is the information age, as Alvin Toffler suggested, and today is also the cyber age; it is very hard to conceal any secret and it is extremely hard to correct a slip-lip. The heyday of leaking information about *Stuxnet* could be traced back to White House Coordinator for Arms Control and Weapons of Mass Destruction; in May 2011 the PBS TV program *"Need To Know"* cited his statement "We're glad they [the Iranians] are having trouble with their centrifuge machine and that we – the US and its allies – are doing everything we can to make sure that we complicate matters for them" [366]. This is not a smart and tactful comment, because:

> "[is] offering 'winking acknowledgement' of US involvement in Stuxnet. According to *The Daily Telegraph*, a show reel that was played at a retirement party for the head of the *Israel Defense Forces* (IDF), **Gabi Ashkenazi**, included references to Stuxnet as one of his operational successes as the IDF chief of staff."

"On 1 June 2012, an article in The New York Times said that Stuxnet is part of a U.S. and Israeli intelligence operation called "Operation Olympic Games", started under President George W. Bush and expanded under President Barack Obama. [367]"

The recent move of US politicians who do not understand the high level politics, especially presidential candidate Mitt Romney, did not help to correct and to fix the deteriorating situation; instead it's implicating and incriminating the certain people. The US and Israeli government should have issued the statement to refute, and should not let it becomes a political commodity.

Mr. Obama senior campaign advisor, who denied the accusation, was quoted to say "I can tell you the President of United States did not leak classified info as Mitt Romney suggested"; he did a mistake anyway. The leak already happened; he should have not issued this statement because it implicates and incriminates the other person; his statement "the President of United States did not leak classified info" might be politically translated into "Yes, there is the leaking information, but the President of United States did not do that, maybe someone else". As an advisor, he should have said **"We do not have any information that there is or there is not any leaking; we do not know what Mitt Romney was talking about. You may ask him to elaborate."** Period. It is so unfortunate on the politicians today; they do not understand what the politics is; be silent, it is golden.

[348] "Kompas" online newspaper, Monday September 27, 2010
[349] *ibid.*
[350] http://kingsofwar.org.uk/2010/09/stuxnet/
[351] "Kompas" online newspaper, October 4, 2010
[352] *ibid.*
[353] *ibid.*
[354] http://en.wikipedia.org/wiki/Stuxnet
[355] "Kompas" online newspaper, October 4, 2010
[356] http://www.kaspersky.com/news?id=207576183
[357] http://en.wikipedia.org/wiki/Duqu
[358] http://rt.com/news/flame-stuxnet-kaspersky-iran-607/

[359] http://in.reuters.com/article/2012/06/06/net-us-cyberwar-flame-kaspersky-idINBRE8550HM20120606
[360] http://rt.com/news/kaspersky-fears-cyber-pandemic-170/
[361] "Kompas" online newspaper, June 4, 2012
[362] http://in.reuters.com/article/2012/06/06/net-us-cyberwar-flame-kaspersky-idINBRE8550HM20120606
[363] http://www.alarabiya.net/articles/2012/06/06/219054.html
[364] http://articles.cnn.com/2012-06-06/politics/politics_white-house-leaks_1_leaks-sensitive-information-intelligence-authorization-bill?_s=PM:POLITICS
[365] http://video.msnbc.msn.com/mitchell-reports/48321651#48321651
[366] http://en.wikipedia.org/wiki/Stuxnet
[367] *ibid.*

Closing Note

"I keep thinking about the children whose lives would be wiped out", JFK.

If the JFK assassination is not justified, at least it decided together by the insider planners, how come to protect the secret so long, and how come to decide keeping secret for 50 years even after 1978, not after 1963; it does mean 65 years from 1963 to make sure that those who were involved had gone long time before.

The promise John F. Kennedy pledged on the inauguration day January 20, 1961 "Ask not what your country can do for you, ask what you can do for your country" was proven to be true when he was sacrificed for the safety of all Americans. He was a real hero, all American generations should be thankful to him. America has taken from him more than it could give to him. To considering the American safety is the most important thing and looking back at the available evidence, with all due respects to the late legendary US President John F. Kennedy who fell in the line of duty, it's so sorry for being compelled to draw an inconvenience conclusion that his assassination most probably was designed to save at least 40,000,000 fellow American lives. This conclusion does **not** imply that the assassination is legitimate, it's a better off condition; the assassination of a legitimate US President is bad but the nuclear war is worst, the conclusion is merely in the context of saving America from nuclear war, nothing else. This is the ultimate sacrifice John F. Kennedy could do. The USA is never be the same ever since.

The "better off" -not the legitimacy- of John F. Kennedy assassination does not necessarily imply that any agency, any organization nor any administration was involved. The John F. Kennedy case was solely aimed to save 40,000,000 American lives; as of the main purpose was successfully carried on, then the group of individuals or "the emergency committee", or the individuals who had the mutual goal which planned and implemented the assassination of John F. Kennedy dismissed themselves.

Although the existence or the legitimacy of these individuals is always disputable and open to refute, at least it worked as we see now that no one single American died from a Russian nuclear attack on American soil. It is the fact. Nobody can deny that it was a sacrifice of John F. Kennedy.

After a bizarre Warren Report with a magic bullet theory that duped hundreds of million Americans for five decades and maybe more, the history should have been rewritten -even after HSCA report- to put the sacrifice of John F. Kennedy on the stage of world history. Are we so gullible? America is a super powerful country, and John F. Kennedy was one of those who worked hard to make American safe, powerful and prosperous, he had a special share in the USA. He fulfilled his promise to American next generation "I keep thinking about the children whose lives would be wiped out"; "Ask not what your country can do for you, ask what you can do for your country". America is a great country everybody dreaming to be a part of, America should open all documents pertaining to the sacrifice of John F. Kennedy; he was a legitimate President of the United States of America when he was being sacrificed. He was democratically elected; America should have been daring to admit that John F. Kennedy had been honorably sacrificed to save more than one hundred millions people of USA, Soviet Union and Cuba in the case of the nuclear war crupts.

To place the medium-range nuclear weapon on the American backyard was an intimidation and nuclear terrorism, America would not be quiet under any pressure, intimidation and terrorism; America never gave up. Under the strategic calculation and under the pressure of USAF General Curtis LeMay -who could not accept the lost of USAF Major Anderson during Cuban Missile Crisis- although strongly contended by Secretary Robert McNamara, John F. Kennedy might have been inclining to order deploying the nuclear missiles to Cuba in **a pre-emptive strike** to prevent the initial deployment of Soviet nuclear missiles from Cuba to American soil where America under no any circumstances does have the time to evade the sudden deadly attack.

General LeMay was known to adopt the pre-emptive strike, and President Kennedy did first step of nuclear war by issuing the National Security Action Memorandum Number 199 to prepare the nuclear war on October 25, 1962.

Although with the great risk, a **pre-emptive war** against a nation which installed the MRBM ready to launch to the US cities maybe justifiable; but **pre-emptive war** based on the falsified documents was put on the big question mark, especially [if] it costs thousands or even millions of American lives who did not aware the reality behind the staged war.

Here some critical points which should have been the *clear signs* that President John F. Kennedy had been **inclining** to order attacking Cuba over the missile crisis:

(1) On October 25, 1962 at around 5:00 p.m. President John F. Kennedy issued National Security Action Memo Number 199 authorizing the loading of air launched ballistic missiles (ALBM) onto strategic bombers under the command of Supreme Allied Commander Europe (SACEUR) which had the duty to carry out the initial air strikes on the Soviet Union. It's a preparation if the Soviet Union would have been attacking Europe in the escalation of the US invasion against Cuba. Memo #199 is first step to the nuclear war!

(2) In the morning of October 26, 1962; President Kennedy informed the ExComm that he was sure that only an invasion would remove the missiles from Cuba. Nevertheless, he was advised to spend a little more time to let the military and diplomatic process to proceed;

(3) President Kennedy ordered the surveillance over Cuba to be increased from two flights a day to twelve flights a day, a 600% increase;

(4) President Kennedy also ordered a special arrangement to form a new civil government in Cuba to replace Castro after invasion was done;

(5) The members of ExComm **unanimously recommended** the invasion to Cuba;

(6) The CIA memo of October 27, 1962 clearly reported that missile sites at ***San Cristobal*** and ***Sagua la Grande*** were in combat ready.

Had Cuba with any reason been hit by a nuclear weapon, the Soviet Union should subsequently have a legitimate reason under the international law and bilateral treaty to deploy the intercontinental ballistic missiles; and within minutes the Jupiter missiles should have been deployed from Turkey to the Soviet Union as well. Therefore, John F. Kennedy should have been stopped from imposing such order which in turn could trigger a chain reaction of war, since every body knows that in the nuclear war there would be no winner whatsoever, both sides would be the losers with the economic and environmental devastation for very long time.

The planner and executioner to stop John F. Kennedy was an intangible group which had had the concern about the American safety where in the meantime the world was on the brink of nuclear war. This group was so powerful and had such influence everywhere including Warren Commission; otherwise it did not have the perennial influence hitherto. Such an influence will be unnecessary in 2017 where the most of participants would have been totally gone and the statute of limitation expired. It is the time when we need to open this book once more time.

This group was voluntarily and unobtrusively preventing the nuclear war at any cost without any intention that its presence will be recognized or even rewarded later in the history, its volunteer consists of the influential people in any position who did not want their establishments and luxurious lives got disturbed with the economic dismay and global disaster as ever happened before in the World War II. For them, however, to be hedonist to enjoy the life in peace is better off than to be the derelict and bellicose. We may respectfully name this group "The Supreme Committee", or something like that, or what is in a name?

The UN should have issued the resolution to reprimand the nuclear-owning nations and declared them as "special note nations" since they owned the weapon with capability to wipe another nation out and for genocide purposes. Let Hiroshima and Nagasaki the first and the last victim of the nuclear weapon. It is a time for us to make a moment of silence for three seconds to honor John Fitzgerald Kennedy since he was sacrificed to avert the nuclear war. It's his ultimate sacrifice "Ask not what your country can do for you; ask what you can do for your country"; he sacrificed his presidential salary, his life and everything he had to his country instead of asking from it.

This planet has several organizations to preserve the nature, wildlife and primate but it does not have a single organization to preserve the human being from extinction. The perennial war seems to be designed to speed up the extinction of human being, or at least to temporarily solve the population problem by utilizing the self destruction mechanism i.e. to kill each other.

As we know by generating a local conflict the demand on arms will soar and their price will be so good, and no single local conflict on this earth without the involvement of arm merchandiser. Every single human being loves peace, only this creature has concern with the peaceful earth; the other creatures do not even have the ability to make the weapon of mass destruction; what should do to prevent the human being from extinction?

(1) The mutual understanding among the nations that the earth is only one. If there is another inhabitable planet somewhere, but now is impossible to find and to reach it. Even if we are able to reach it then it takes some generations since it is too far, while the nuclear war may destroy this planet right here right now. Every nation has the obligation to preserve the world for the next generation. Once this earth is destroyed by the massive nuclear weapon, there will be no any human power to replace it.

(2) All nations with the capability to deploy the nuclear weapon should hold itself from any conflict which leads to the nuclear war.

(3) All nuclear nations, no exception, should have voluntarily dismantled their nuclear arsenals as the South Africa did.

(4) The nations pursuing nuclear weapon should stop their efforts to produce the nuclear weapon or any another tools of mass destruction.

(5) The independent world forum on the nuclear weapons should be formed under the United Nations. The members may be selected from the Noble Laureates, world dignitaries and celebrities to ensure the neutrality. This forum should make annual report to the world over their supervision and investigation.

(6) The defiant owning-nuclear nations under the Charter of United Nation should have been labeled as the dangerous country and been persuaded to dismantle their nuclear arsenal.

(7) The UN should establish a special organization to fight the cyber terrorism.

(8) To stop the space exploration; it just wasting money and inciting the arm race. The space exploration to find the planet to live beyond the earth is naïve. There is absolutely no infrastructure and no earth-like resources available; if we found one or some earth-resembling planets and we decide to live over there, it does mean we go back to the prehistoric age where nothing available to support our modern and luxury lives today.

The discovery of —or illusion to discover— the inhabitable planet in the other galaxy does not justify destroying this earth, our earth. With our limited span of life, how long the journey would be, and how short we would live there? If the bellicose successfully destroyed the planet earth and escaped to the other planet, then they would make another war anyway, either because of oxygen or water competition. These two important basic necessities are free in our planet, but they are the most expensive commodity in the other planet.

The astronomer in December 2012 announced the "discovery" of **Tau Ceti** star with 5 planets which one of them is most inhabitable with conditions "conducive to life"; it's not so far, only 12 light years away. The estimate cost in 2013 to stay in the space for 60 days only will be $25 million for living expense including food and oxygen, plus $27.5 million for round trip transportation, plus $17.8 million for the price of an inflatable portable house as big as 7 feet. Anytime you are ready, enrol to SpaceLife of Washington, or to KremLeinsure of Moscow, or TriompheTour of Paris. Now, the detail of your living cost in space is $25M + $27.5M + $17.8M = $50.3 millions just for 60 days. Everyday you have to spend $50.3M : 60 = $838,333; and every hour you have to pay $838,333 : 24 = $34,930.55. Your living cost per hour in space would be equal to average living cost in Cleveland Ohio for one year where the Federal minimum wages is $7.25 per hour. Do you want to live in one of Tau Ceti's planets? To reach it, the cost after the discount will be $800,000 per day, you need $800,000 x 365 x 12 = $3,504,000,000. The travel cost per day is very expensive since your space ship has the speed of light 186,000 miles per second, not per hour. It will be no pilot no technician and no room service; if your spaceship needs any technical maintenance, there will be no parts supplier; the imported parts from the earth need a 12-year delivery. Everything is automatic and self service including the coffin and bay to deport the corpse to the outer space. Just click.

Three and half billion dollars just to go to Tau Ceti; the living expense, medication for heart attack, and insurance over explosion during travel are not included. After 12 years travelling in the speed of light and still wealthy and healthy without suffering from "speed compression", you reach Tau Ceti only to find rock and dust, no green golf course, no blue pool, no red mall. No white hospital; no colourful entertainment centre, no factory, no production facility either, no nothing. Please be advised that your canned foods, bottle waters and medication pills you bring along from the earth would be expired after 2 years while you have 10 years more to go or 22 years more to go and back to the earth; no superstore no drugstore and no rest area. The rest of your travel will depend upon your portable farm if you have time and expertise to sustain your lives. Without any drug factory, you would be required to invent your own medication, and if you need any organ transplantation you have to be cannibal since no organ supply from the earth; and at this situation there will be no the safety and no peace of mind, everybody suspects each other even between the spouses. Just in case you are boring and tired or depressed, then the suicide always welcomed since the spaceship passengers are waiting for harvesting your body organ for transplantation. The suicide during a space travel will be considered a heroic action to save a life of fellow passenger. The plaques, certificates, praises, diplomas and eulogy are always available for recognitions. Just click.

As you reach Tau Ceti, any time you miss your close relatives, you may call them but your voice will reach them after 12 years and their respond will reach you 24 years after your initial call; nobody knows if they still alive when you get their respond from back home, the faraway blue earth you miss every single minute. The space exploration to find the new and more peaceful planet to live and escape from the nuclear war whenever it erupts maybe not a hoax, and you are selected to stay out there because you're the most charismatic and distinctive person in the community; but this is the situation, and this is the objective condition. Think about. The war is a clear sign of uncivilized action. Why not living here peacefully after dismantling all nuclear weapons under supervision of UNO?

We are the civilized human being; our civilization has been built some million years ago since our forefathers inhabited this tiny blue planet for the first time. We, the civilized human being, came from the very same ancestor Adam and Eve; we do not need the deadly gadgets and weapon of mass destruction to hurt our cousins and siblings. We need a lot of weapon of mass construction. What's wrong with us, what's wrong if we live together side by side peacefully with our intrinsic differences?

AR. Bahry
abahry@hotmail.com

Appendix

The Transcript of Colin Powell address at the UN Assembly

Under the Freedom Information Act, the US State Department sent to the author the copy of Powell's transcript. Powell addressed the Security Council on Wednesday February 5, 2003.

Transcript of Powell's U.N. presentation

Following is a transcript of U.S. Secretary of State Colin Powell's presentation to the U.N. Security Council on the U.S. case against Iraq.

Part 1: Introduction

Thank you, Mr. President.

Mr. President, Mr. Secretary General, distinguished colleagues, I would like to begin by expressing my thanks for the special effort that each of you made to be here today. This is important day for us all as we review the situation with respect to Iraq and its disarmament obligations under U.N. Security Council Resolution 1441. Last November 8, this council passed Resolution 1441 by a unanimous vote. The purpose of that resolution was to disarm Iraq of its weapons of mass destruction. Iraq had already been found guilty of material breach of its obligations, stretching back over 16 previous resolutions and 12 years.

Resolution 1441 was not dealing with an innocent party, but a regime this council has repeatedly convicted over the years. Resolution 1441 gave Iraq one last chance, one last chance to come into compliance or to face serious consequences. No council member present in voting on that day had any illusions about the nature and intent of the resolution or what serious consequences meant if Iraq did not comply. And to assist in its disarmament, we called on Iraq to cooperate with returning inspectors from UNMOVIC and IAEA. We laid down tough standards for Iraq to meet to allow the inspectors to do their job.

This council placed the burden on Iraq to comply and disarm and not on the inspectors to find that which Iraq has gone out of its way to conceal for so long. Inspectors are inspectors; they are not detectives.

I asked for this session today for two purposes: First, to support the core assessments made by Dr. Blix and Dr. ElBaradei. As Dr. Blix reported to this council on January 27th, "Iraq appears not to have come to a genuine acceptance, not even today, of the disarmament which was demanded of it." And as Dr. ElBaradei reported, Iraq's declaration of December 7 "did not provide any new information relevant to certain questions that have been outstanding since 1998."

My second purpose today is to provide you with additional information, to share with you what the United States knows about Iraq's weapons of mass destruction as well as Iraq's involvement in terrorism, which is also the subject of Resolution 1441 and other earlier resolutions.

I might add at this point that we are providing all relevant information we can to the inspection teams for them to do their work. The material I will present to you comes from a variety of sources. Some are U.S. sources. And some are those of other countries. Some of the sources are technical, such as intercepted telephone conversations and photos taken by satellites. Other sources are people who have risked their lives to let the world know what Saddam Hussein is really up to. I cannot tell you everything that we know. But what I can share with you, when combined with what all of us have learned over the years, is deeply troubling. What you will see is an accumulation of facts and disturbing patterns of behavior. The facts on Iraq's behavior demonstrate that Saddam Hussein and his regime have made no effort -- no effort -- to disarm as required by the international community.

Indeed, the facts and Iraq's behavior show that Saddam Hussein and his regime are concealing their efforts to produce more weapons of mass destruction.

Part 2: Hiding prohibited equipment

Let me begin by playing a tape for you. What you're about to hear is a conversation that my government monitored. It takes place on November 26 of last year, on the day before United Nations teams resumed inspections in Iraq. The conversation involves two senior officers, a colonel and a brigadier general, from Iraq's elite military unit, the Republican Guard.

[Following is a U.S. translation of that taped conversation.]

GEN: Yeah.

COL: About this committee that is coming...

GEN: Yeah, yeah.

COL: ...with Mohamed ElBaradei [Director, International Atomic Energy Agency]

GEN: Yeah, yeah.

COL: Yeah.

GEN: Yeah?

COL: We have this modified vehicle.

GEN: Yeah.

COL: What do we say if one of them sees it?

GEN: You didn't get a modified... You don't have a modified...

COL: By God, I have one.

GEN: Which? From the workshop...?

COL: From the al-Kindi Company

GEN: What?

COL: From al-Kindi.

GEN: Yeah, yeah. I'll come to you in the morning. I have some comments. I'm worried you all have something left.

COL: We evacuated everything. We don't have anything left.

GEN: I will come to you tomorrow.

COL: Okay.

GEN: I have a conference at Headquarters, before I attend the conference I will come to you.

Let me pause and review some of the key elements of this conversation that you just heard between these two officers.

First, they acknowledge that our colleague, Mohamed ElBaradei, is coming, and they know what he's coming for, and they know he's coming the next day. He's coming to look for things that are prohibited. He is expecting these gentlemen to cooperate with him and not hide things. But they're worried. "We have this modified vehicle. What do we say if one of them sees it?"

What is their concern? Their concern is that it's something they should not have, something that should not be seen. The general is incredulous: "You didn't get a modified. You don't have one of those, do you?"

"I have one."

"Which, from where?"

"From the workshop, from the al-Kindi Company?"

"What?"

"From al-Kindi."

"I'll come to see you in the morning. I'm worried. You all have something left."

"We evacuated everything. We don't have anything left."

Note what he says: "We evacuated everything."

We didn't destroy it. We didn't line it up for inspection. We didn't turn it into the inspectors. We evacuated it to make sure it was not around when the inspectors showed up. "I will come to you tomorrow."

The al-Kindi Company: This is a company that is well known to have been involved in prohibited weapons systems activity. Let me play another tape for you. As you will recall, the inspectors found 12 empty chemical warheads on January 16. On January 20, four days later, Iraq promised the inspectors it would search for more. You will now hear an officer from Republican Guard headquarters issuing an instruction to an officer in the field. Their conversation took place just last week on January 30.

Let me pause again and review the elements of this message.

"They're inspecting the ammunition you have, yes."

"Yes."

"For the possibility there are forbidden ammo."

"For the possibility there is by chance forbidden ammo?"

"Yes."

"And we sent you a message yesterday to clean out all of the areas, the scrap areas, the abandoned areas. Make sure there is nothing there."

Remember the first message, evacuated.

This is all part of a system of hiding things and moving things out of the way and making sure they have left nothing behind.

If you go a little further into this message, and you see the specific instructions from headquarters: "After you have carried out what is contained in this message, destroy the message because I don't want anyone to see this message."

"OK, OK."

Why? Why?

This message would have verified to the inspectors that they have been trying to turn over things. They were looking for things. But they don't want that message seen, because they were trying to clean up the area to leave no evidence behind of the presence of weapons of mass destruction. And they can claim that nothing was there. And the inspectors can look all they want, and they will find nothing.

This effort to hide things from the inspectors is not one or two isolated events, quite the contrary. This is part and parcel of a policy of evasion and deception that goes back 12 years, a policy set at the highest levels of the Iraqi regime.

Part 3: Attempt to thwart inspection

We know that Saddam Hussein has what is called "a higher committee for monitoring the inspections teams." Think about that. Iraq has a high-level committee to monitor the inspectors who were sent in to monitor Iraq's disarmament. Not to cooperate with them, not to assist them, but to spy on them and keep them from doing their jobs.

The committee reports directly to Saddam Hussein. It is headed by Iraq's vice president, Taha Yassin Ramadan. Its members include Saddam Hussein's son Qusay.

This committee also includes Lt. Gen. Amir al-Saadi, an adviser to Saddam. In case that name isn't immediately familiar to you, Gen. Saadi has been the Iraqi regime's primary point of contact for Dr. Blix and Dr. ElBaradei. It was Gen. Saadi who last fall publicly pledged that Iraq was prepared to cooperate unconditionally with inspectors. Quite the contrary, Saadi's job is not to cooperate, it is to deceive; not to disarm, but to undermine the inspectors; not to support them, but to frustrate them and to make sure they learn nothing.

We have learned a lot about the work of this special committee. We learned that just prior to the return of inspectors last November the regime had decided to resume what we heard called, "the old game of cat and mouse."

For example, let me focus on the now famous declaration that Iraq submitted to this council on December 7. Iraq never had any intention of complying with this council's mandate.

Instead, Iraq planned to use the declaration, overwhelm us and to overwhelm the inspectors with useless information about Iraq's permitted weapons so that we would not have time to pursue Iraq's prohibited weapons. Iraq's goal was to give us, in this room, to give those of us on this council the false impression that the inspection process was working.

You saw the result. Dr. Blix pronounced the 12,200-page declaration, rich in volume, but poor in information and practically devoid of new evidence. Could any member of this council honestly rise in defense of this false declaration?

Everything we have seen and heard indicates that, instead of cooperating actively with the inspectors to ensure the success of their mission, Saddam Hussein and his regime are busy doing all they possibly can to ensure that inspectors succeed in finding absolutely nothing.

My colleagues, every statement I make today is backed up by sources, solid sources. These are not assertions. What we're giving you are facts and conclusions based on solid intelligence. I will cite some examples, and these are from human sources. Orders were issued to Iraq's security organizations, as well as to Saddam Hussein's own office, to hide all correspondence with the Organization of Military Industrialization. This is the organization that oversees Iraq's weapons of mass destruction activities. Make sure there are no documents left which could connect you to the OMI.

We know that Saddam's son, Qusay, ordered the removal of all prohibited weapons from Saddam's numerous palace complexes. We know that Iraqi government officials, members of the ruling Baath Party and scientists have hidden prohibited items in their homes. Other key files from military and scientific establishments have been placed in cars that are being driven around the countryside by Iraqi intelligence agents to avoid detection.

Thanks to intelligence they were provided, the inspectors recently found dramatic confirmation of these reports. When they searched the home of an Iraqi nuclear scientist, they uncovered roughly 2,000 pages of documents. You see them here being brought out of the home and placed in U.N. hands. Some of the material is classified and related to Iraq's nuclear program.

Tell me, answer me, are the inspectors to search the house of every government official, every Baath Party member and every scientist in the country to find the truth, to get the information they need, to satisfy the demands of our council? Our sources tell us that, in some cases, the hard drives of computers at Iraqi weapons facilities were replaced. Who took the hard drives? Where did they go? What's being hidden? Why? There's only one answer to the why: to deceive, to hide, and to keep from the inspectors. Numerous human sources tell us that the Iraqis are moving, not just documents and hard drives, but weapons of mass destruction to keep them from being found by inspectors.

While we were here in this council chamber debating Resolution 1441 last fall, we know, we know from sources that a missile brigade outside Baghdad was disbursing rocket launchers and warheads containing biological warfare agents to various locations, distributing them to various locations in western Iraq. Most of the launchers and warheads have been hidden in large groves of palm trees and were to be moved every one to four weeks to escape detection.

We also have satellite photos that indicate that banned materials have recently been moved from a number of Iraqi weapons of mass destruction facilities.

Let me say a word about satellite images before I show a couple. The photos that I am about to show you are sometimes hard for the average person to interpret, hard for me. The painstaking work of photo analysis takes experts with years and years of experience, pouring for hours and hours over light tables. But as I show you these images, I will try to capture and explain what they mean, what they indicate to our imagery specialists.

Let's look at one. This one is about a weapons munitions facility, a facility that holds ammunition at a place called Taji (ph). This is one of about 65 such facilities in Iraq. We know that this one has housed chemical munitions. In fact, this is where the Iraqis recently came up with the additional four chemical weapon shells. Here, you see 15 munitions bunkers in yellow and red outlines. The four that are in red squares represent active chemical munitions bunkers. How do I know that? How can I say that? Let me give you a closer look. Look at the image on the left. On the left is a close-up of one of the four chemical bunkers. The two arrows indicate the presence of sure signs that the bunkers are storing chemical munitions. The arrow at the top that says security points to a facility that is the signature item for this kind of bunker. Inside that facility are special guards and special equipment to monitor any leakage that might come out of the bunker.

The truck you also see is a signature item. It's a decontamination vehicle in case something goes wrong. This is characteristic of those four bunkers. The special security facility and the decontamination vehicle will be in the area, if not at any one of them or one of the other, it is moving around those four, and it moves as it needed to move, as people are working in the different bunkers. Now look at the picture on the right. You are now looking at two of those sanitized bunkers.

The signature vehicles are gone, the tents are gone, it's been cleaned up, and it was done on the 22nd of December, as the U.N. inspection team is arriving, and you can see the inspection vehicles arriving in the lower portion of the picture on the right. The bunkers are clean when the inspectors get there. They found nothing.

This sequence of events raises the worrisome suspicion that Iraq had been tipped off to the forthcoming inspections at Taji. As it did throughout the 1990s, we know that Iraq today is actively using its considerable intelligence capabilities to hide its illicit activities.

From our sources, we know that inspectors are under constant surveillance by an army of Iraqi intelligence operatives. Iraq is relentlessly attempting to tap all of their communications, both voice and electronics.

I would call my colleagues attention to the fine paper that United Kingdom distributed yesterday, which describes in exquisite detail Iraqi deception activities. In this next example, you will see the type of concealment activity Iraq has undertaken in response to the resumption of inspections. Indeed, in November 2002, just when the inspections were about to resume this type of activity spiked. Here are three examples.

At this ballistic missile site, on November 10, we saw a cargo truck preparing to move ballistic missile components. At this biological weapons related facility, on November 25, just two days before inspections resumed, this truck caravan appeared, something we almost never see at this facility, and we monitor it carefully and regularly. At this ballistic missile facility, again, two days before inspections began; five large cargo trucks appeared along with the truck-mounted crane to move missiles. We saw this kind of house cleaning at close to 30 sites.

Days after this activity, the vehicles and the equipment that I've just highlighted disappear and the site returns to patterns of normalcy. We don't know precisely what Iraq was moving, but the inspectors already knew about these sites, so Iraq knew that they would be coming. We must ask ourselves: Why would Iraq suddenly move equipment of this nature before inspections if they were anxious to demonstrate what they had or did not have?

Remember the first intercept in which two Iraqis talked about the need to hide a modified vehicle from the inspectors. Where did Iraq take all of this equipment? Why wasn't it presented to the inspectors? Iraq also has refused to permit any U-2 reconnaissance flights that would give the inspectors a better sense of what's being moved before, during and after inspectors. This refusal to allow this kind of reconnaissance is in direct, specific violation of operative paragraph seven of our Resolution 1441.

Saddam Hussein and his regime are not just trying to conceal weapons; they're also trying to hide people. You know the basic facts.

Iraq has not complied with its obligation to allow immediate, unimpeded, unrestricted and private access to all officials and other persons as required by Resolution 1441.

Part 4: Access to scientists

The regime only allows interviews with inspectors in the presence of an Iraqi official, a minder. The official Iraqi organization charged with facilitating inspections announced, announced publicly and announced ominously that, quote, "Nobody is ready to leave Iraq to be interviewed."

Iraqi Vice President Ramadan accused the inspectors of conducting espionage, a veiled threat that anyone cooperating with U.N. inspectors was committing treason. Iraq did not meet its obligations under 1441 to provide a comprehensive list of scientists associated with its weapons of mass destruction programs. Iraq's list was out of date and contained only about 500 names, despite the fact that UNSCOM had earlier put together a list of about 3,500 names. Let me just tell you what a number of human sources have told us.

Saddam Hussein has directly participated in the effort to prevent interviews. In early December, Saddam Hussein had all Iraqi scientists warned of the serious consequences that they and their families would face if they revealed any sensitive information to the inspectors. They were forced to sign documents acknowledging that divulging information is punishable by death. Saddam Hussein also said that scientists should be told not to agree to leave Iraq; anyone who agreed to be interviewed outside Iraq would be treated as a spy. This violates 1441. In mid-November, just before the inspectors returned, Iraqi experts were ordered to report to the headquarters of the special security organization to receive counterintelligence training. The training focused on evasion methods, interrogation resistance techniques, and how to mislead inspectors.

Ladies and gentlemen, these are not assertions. These are facts, corroborated by many sources, some of them sources of the intelligence services of other countries. For example, in mid-December weapons experts at one facility were replaced by Iraqi intelligence agents who were to deceive inspectors about the work that was being done there. On orders from Saddam Hussein, Iraqi officials issued a false death certificate for one scientist, and he was sent into hiding.

In the middle of January, experts at one facility that was related to weapons of mass destruction, those experts had been ordered to stay home from work to avoid the inspectors. Workers from other Iraqi military facilities not engaged in illicit weapons projects were to replace the workers who'd been sent home. A dozen experts have been placed under house arrest, not in their own houses, but as a group at one of Saddam Hussein's guest houses. It goes on and on and on. As the examples I have just presented show, the information and intelligence we have gathered point to an active and systematic effort on the part of the Iraqi regime to keep key materials and people from the inspectors in direct violation of Resolution 1441.

The pattern is not just one of reluctant cooperation, nor is it merely a lack of cooperation. What we see is a deliberate campaign to prevent any meaningful inspection work.

My colleagues, operative paragraph four of U.N. Resolution 1441, which we lingered over so long last fall, clearly states that false statements and omissions in the declaration and a failure by Iraq at any time to comply with and cooperate fully in the implementation of this resolution shall constitute -- the facts speak for themselves --shall constitute a further material breach of its obligation. We wrote it this way to give Iraq an early test -- to give Iraq an early test. Would they give an honest declaration and would they early on indicate a willingness to cooperate with the inspectors? It was designed to be an early test.

They failed that test. By this standard, the standard of this operative paragraph, I believe that Iraq is now in further material breach of its obligations. I believe this conclusion is irrefutable and undeniable.

Iraq has now placed itself in danger of the serious consequences called for in U.N. Resolution 1441. And this body places itself in danger of irrelevance if it allows Iraq to continue to defy its will without responding effectively and immediately. The issue before us is not how much time we are willing to give the inspectors to be frustrated by Iraqi obstruction. But how much longer are we willing to put up with Iraq's noncompliance before we, as a council, we, as the United Nations, say: "Enough. Enough."

The gravity of this moment is matched by the gravity of the threat that Iraq's weapons of mass destruction pose to the world. Let me now turn to those deadly weapons programs and describe why they are real and present dangers to the region and to the world.

Part 5: Biological weapons program

First, biological weapons. We have talked frequently here about biological weapons. By way of introduction and history, I think there are just three quick points I need to make.

First, you will recall that it took UNSCOM four long and frustrating years to pry -- to pry -- an admission out of Iraq that it had biological weapons.

Second, when Iraq finally admitted having these weapons in 1995, the quantities were vast. Less than a teaspoon of dry anthrax, a little bit about this amount -- this is just about the amount of a teaspoon -- less than a teaspoon full of dry anthrax in an envelope shutdown the United States Senate in the fall of 2001. This forced several hundred people to undergo emergency medical treatment and killed two postal workers just from an amount just about this quantity that was inside of an envelope. Iraq declared 8,500 liters of anthrax, but UNSCOM estimates that Saddam Hussein could have produced 25,000 liters.

If concentrated into this dry form, this amount would be enough to fill tens upon tens upon tens of thousands of teaspoons. And Saddam Hussein has not verifiably accounted for even one teaspoon-full of this deadly material.

And that is my third point. And it is key. The Iraqis have never accounted for all of the biological weapons they admitted they had and we know they had. They have never accounted for all the organic material used to make them. And they have not accounted for many of the weapons filled with these agents such as there are 400 bombs. This is evidence, not conjecture. This is true. This is all well-documented.

Dr. Blix told this council that Iraq has provided little evidence to verify anthrax production and no convincing evidence of its destruction. It should come as no shock then, that since Saddam Hussein forced out the last inspectors in 1998, we have amassed much intelligence indicating that Iraq is continuing to make these weapons. One of the most worrisome things that emerge from the thick intelligence file we have on Iraq's biological weapons is the existence of mobile production facilities used to make biological agents.

Let me take you inside that intelligence file and share with you what we know from eye witness accounts. We have firsthand descriptions of biological weapons factories on wheels and on rails. The trucks and train cars are easily moved and are designed to evade detection by inspectors. In a matter of months, they can produce a quantity of biological poison equal to the entire amount that Iraq claimed to have produced in the years prior to the Gulf War.

Although Iraq's mobile production program began in the mid-1990s, U.N. inspectors at the time only had vague hints of such programs. Confirmation came later, in the year 2000.

The source was an eye witness, an Iraqi chemical engineer who supervised one of these facilities. He actually was present during biological agent production runs. He was also at the site when an accident occurred in 1998. Twelve technicians died from exposure to biological agents. He reported that when UNSCOM was in country and inspecting, the biological weapons agent production always began on Thursdays at midnight because Iraq thought UNSCOM would not inspect on the Muslim Holy Day, Thursday night through Friday.

He added that this was important because the units could not be broken down in the middle of a production run, which had to be completed by Friday evening before the inspectors might arrive again. This defector is currently hiding in another country with the certain knowledge that Saddam Hussein will kill him if he finds him. His eye-witness account of these mobile production facilities has been corroborated by other sources.

A second source, an Iraqi civil engineer in a position to know the details of the program, confirmed the existence of transportable facilities moving on trailers. A third source, also in a position to know, reported in summer 2002 that Iraq had manufactured mobile production systems mounted on road trailer units and on rail cars.

Finally, a fourth source, an Iraqi major, who defected, confirmed that Iraq has mobile biological research laboratories, in addition to the production facilities I mentioned earlier.

We have diagrammed what our sources reported about these mobile facilities. Here you see both truck and rail car-mounted mobile factories. The description our sources gave us of the technical features required by such facilities are highly detailed and extremely accurate. As these drawings based on their description show, we know what the fermenters look like, we know what the tanks, pumps, compressors and other parts look like. We know how they fit together. We know how they work. And we know a great deal about the platforms on which they are mounted.

As shown in this diagram, these factories can be concealed easily, either by moving ordinary-looking trucks and rail cars along Iraq's thousands of miles of highway or track, or by parking them in a garage or warehouse or somewhere in Iraq's extensive system of underground tunnels and bunkers. We know that Iraq has at lest seven of these mobile biological agent factories. The truck-mounted ones have at least two or three trucks each. That means that the mobile production facilities are very few, perhaps 18 trucks that we know of -- there may be more -- but perhaps 18 that we know of.

Just imagine trying to find 18 trucks among the thousands and thousands of trucks that travel the roads of Iraq every single day. It took the inspectors four years to find out that Iraq was making biological agents. How long do you think it will take the inspectors to find even one of these 18 trucks without Iraq coming forward, as they are supposed to, with the information about these kinds of capabilities?

Ladies and gentlemen, these are sophisticated facilities. For example, they can produce anthrax and botulism toxin. In fact, they can produce enough dry biological agents in a single month to kill thousands upon thousands of people. And dry agent of this type is the most lethal form for human beings. By 1998, U.N. experts agreed that the Iraqis had perfected drying techniques for their biological weapons programs. Now, Iraq has incorporated this drying expertise into these mobile production facilities.

We know from Iraq's past admissions that it has successfully weaponized not only anthrax, but also other biological agents, including botulism toxin, aflatoxin and ricin. But Iraq's research efforts did not stop there. Saddam Hussein has investigated dozens of biological agents causing diseases such as gas gangrene, plague, typhus, tetanus, cholera, camel pox and hemorrhagic fever, and he also has the wherewithal to develop smallpox.

The Iraqi regime has also developed ways to disburse lethal biological agents, widely and discriminately into the water supply, into the air. For example, Iraq had a program to modify aerial fuel tanks for Mirage jets. This video of an Iraqi test flight obtained by UNSCOM some years ago shows an Iraqi F-1 Mirage jet aircraft. Note the spray coming from beneath the Mirage; that is 2,000 liters of simulated anthrax that a jet is spraying. In 1995, an Iraqi military officer, Mujahid Sali Abdul Latif, told inspectors that Iraq intended the spray tanks to be mounted onto a MiG-21 that had been converted into an unmanned aerial vehicle, or a UAV. UAVs outfitted with spray tanks constitute an ideal method for launching a terrorist attack using biological weapons.

Iraq admitted to producing four spray tanks. But to this day, it has provided no credible evidence that they were destroyed, evidence that was required by the international community.

There can be no doubt that Saddam Hussein has biological weapons and the capability to rapidly produce more, many more. And he has the ability to dispense these lethal poisons and diseases in ways that can cause massive death and destruction. If biological weapons seem too terrible to contemplate, chemical weapons are equally chilling. UNMOVIC already laid out much of this, and it is documented for all of us to read in UNSCOM's 1999 report on the subject. Let me set the stage with three key points that all of us need to keep in mind: First, Saddam Hussein has used these horrific weapons on another country and on his own people. In fact, in the history of chemical warfare, no country has had more battlefield experience with chemical weapons since World War I than Saddam Hussein's Iraq.

Part 6: Chemical weapons

Second, as with biological weapons, Saddam Hussein has never accounted for vast amounts of chemical weaponry: 550 artillery shells with mustard, 30,000 empty munitions and enough precursors to increase his stockpile to as much as 500 tons of chemical agents. If we consider just one category of missing weaponry -- 6,500 bombs from the Iran-Iraq war -- UNMOVIC says the amount of chemical agent in them would be in the order of 1,000 tons. These quantities of chemical weapons are now unaccounted for.

Dr. Blix has quipped that, quote, "Mustard gas is not (inaudible) You are supposed to know what you did with it." We believe Saddam Hussein knows what he did with it, and he has not come clean with the international community. We have evidence these weapons existed. What we don't have is evidence from Iraq that they have been destroyed or where they are. That is what we are still waiting for. Third point, Iraq's record on chemical weapons is replete with lies. It took years for Iraq to finally admit that it had produced four tons of the deadly nerve agent, VX. A single drop of VX on the skin will kill in minutes. Four tons.

The admission only came out after inspectors collected documentation as a result of the defection of Hussein Kamal, Saddam Hussein's late son-in-law. UNSCOM also gained forensic evidence that Iraq had produced VX and put it into weapons for delivery. Yet, to this day, Iraq denies it had ever weaponized VX. And on January 27, UNMOVIC told this council that it has information that conflicts with the Iraqi account of its VX program. We know that Iraq has embedded key portions of its illicit chemical weapons infrastructure within its legitimate civilian industry. To all outward appearances, even to experts, the infrastructure looks like an ordinary civilian operation. Illicit and legitimate production can go on simultaneously; or, on a dime, this dual-use infrastructure can turn from clandestine to commercial and then back again. These inspections would be unlikely, any inspections of such facilities would be unlikely to turn up anything prohibited, especially if there is any warning that the inspections are coming.

Call it ingenuous or evil genius, but the Iraqis deliberately designed their chemical weapons programs to be inspected. It is infrastructure with a built-in ally.

Under the guise of dual-use infrastructure, Iraq has undertaken an effort to reconstitute facilities that were closely associated with its past program to develop and produce chemical weapons. For example, Iraq has rebuilt key portions of the Tariq state establishment. Tariq includes facilities designed specifically for Iraq's chemical weapons program and employs key figures from past programs. That's the production end of Saddam's chemical weapons business. What about the delivery end?

I'm going to show you a small part of a chemical complex called al-Moussaid (ph), a site that Iraq has used for at least three years to transship chemical weapons from production facilities out to the field. In May 2002, our satellites photographed the unusual activity in this picture. Here we see cargo vehicles are again at this transshipment point, and we can see that they are accompanied by a decontamination vehicle associated with biological or chemical weapons activity.

What makes this picture significant is that we have a human source who has corroborated that movement of chemical weapons occurred at this site at that time. So it's not just the photo, and it's not an individual seeing the photo. It's the photo and then the knowledge of an individual being brought together to make the case.

This photograph of the site taken two months later in July shows not only the previous site, which is the figure in the middle at the top with the bulldozer sign near it, it shows that this previous site, as well as all of the other sites around the site, have been fully bulldozed and graded. The topsoil has been removed. The Iraqis literally removed the crust of the earth from large portions of this site in order to conceal chemical weapons evidence that would be there from years of chemical weapons activity.

To support its deadly biological and chemical weapons programs, Iraq procures needed items from around the world using an extensive clandestine network.

What we know comes largely from intercepted communications and human sources who are in a position to know the facts.

Iraq's procurement efforts include equipment that can filter and separate micro-organisms and toxins involved in biological weapons, equipment that can be used to concentrate the agent, growth media that can be used to continue producing anthrax and botulism toxin, sterilization equipment for laboratories, glass-lined reactors and specialty pumps that can handle corrosive chemical weapons agents and precursors, large amounts of vinyl chloride, a precursor for nerve and blister agents, and other chemicals such as sodium sulfide, an important mustard agent precursor. Now, of course, Iraq will argue that these items can also be used for legitimate purposes. But if that is true, why do we have to learn about them by intercepting communications and risking the lives of human agents? With Iraq's well documented history on biological and chemical weapons, why should any of us give Iraq the benefit of the doubt? I don't, and I don't think you will either after you hear this next intercept.

Just a few weeks ago, we intercepted communications between two commanders in Iraq's Second Republican Guard Corps. One commander is going to be giving an instruction to the other. You will hear as this unfolds that what he wants to communicate to the other guy, he wants to make sure the other guy hears clearly, to the point of repeating it so that it gets written down and completely understood. Listen.

(BEGIN AUDIO TAPE)

(Speaking in Foreign Language.)

(END AUDIO TAPE)

Let's review a few selected items of this conversation.

Two officers talking to each other on the radio want to make sure that nothing is misunderstood:

"Remove. Remove."

The expression, the expression, "I got it."

"Nerve agents. Nerve agents. Wherever it comes up."

"Got it."

"Wherever it comes up."

"In the wireless instructions, in the instructions."

"Correction. No. In the wireless instructions."

"Wireless. I got it."

Why does he repeat it that way? Why is he so forceful in making sure this is understood? And why did he focus on wireless instructions? Because the senior officer is concerned that somebody might be listening. Well, somebody was.

"Nerve agents. Stop talking about it. They are listening to us. Don't give any evidence that we have these horrible agents."

Well, we know that they do. And this kind of conversation confirms it. Our conservative estimate is that Iraq today has a stockpile of between 100 and 500 tons of chemical weapons agents. That is enough agents to fill 16,000 battlefield rockets.

Even the low end of 100 tons of agent would enable Saddam Hussein to cause mass casualties across more than 100 square miles of territory, an area nearly five times the size of Manhattan. Let me remind you that, of the 122 millimeter chemical warheads, that the U.N. inspectors found recently, this discovery could very well be, as has been noted, the tip of the submerged iceberg. The question before us, all my friends, is when will we see the rest of the submerged iceberg?

Saddam Hussein has chemical weapons. Saddam Hussein has used such weapons. And Saddam Hussein has no compunction about using them again, against his neighbors and against his own people. And we have sources who tell us that he recently has authorized his field commanders to use them. He wouldn't be passing out the orders if he didn't have the weapons or the intent to use them.

We also have sources who tell us that, since the 1980s, Saddam's regime has been experimenting on human beings to perfect its biological or chemical weapons.

A source said that 1,600 death row prisoners were transferred in 1995 to a special unit for such experiments. An eye witness saw prisoners tied down to beds, experiments conducted on them, blood oozing around the victim's mouths and autopsies performed to confirm the effects on the prisoners. Saddam Hussein's humanity -- inhumanity has no limits.

Part 7: Nuclear weapons

Let me turn now to nuclear weapons. We have no indication that Saddam Hussein has ever abandoned his nuclear weapons program.

On the contrary, we have more than a decade of proof that he remains determined to acquire nuclear weapons.

To fully appreciate the challenge that we face today, remember that, in 1991, the inspectors searched Iraq's primary nuclear weapons facilities for the first time. And they found nothing to conclude that Iraq had a nuclear weapons program.

But based on defector information in May of 1991, Saddam Hussein's lie was exposed. In truth, Saddam Hussein had a massive clandestine nuclear weapons program that covered several different techniques to enrich uranium, including electromagnetic isotope separation, gas centrifuge, and gas diffusion. We estimate that this illicit program cost the Iraqis several billion dollars.

Nonetheless, Iraq continued to tell the IAEA that it had no nuclear weapons program. If Saddam had not been stopped, Iraq could have produced a nuclear bomb by 1993, years earlier than most worse-case assessments that had been made before the war. In 1995, as a result of another defector, we find out that, after his invasion of Kuwait, Saddam Hussein had initiated a crash program to build a crude nuclear weapon in violation of Iraq's U.N. obligations.

Saddam Hussein already possesses two out of the three key components needed to build a nuclear bomb. He has a cadre of nuclear scientists with the expertise, and he has a bomb design. Since 1998, his efforts to reconstitute his nuclear program have been focused on acquiring the third and last component, sufficient fissile material to produce a nuclear explosion. To make the fissile material, he needs to develop an ability to enrich uranium. Saddam Hussein is determined to get his hands on a nuclear bomb.

He is so determined that he has made repeated covert attempts to acquire high-specification aluminum tubes from 11 different countries, even after inspections resumed. These tubes are controlled by the Nuclear Suppliers Group precisely because they can be used as centrifuges for enriching uranium. By now, just about everyone has heard of these tubes, and we all know that there are differences of opinion.

There is controversy about what these tubes are for. Most U.S. experts think they are intended to serve as rotors in centrifuges used to enrich uranium. Other experts, and the Iraqis themselves, argue that they are really to produce the rocket bodies for a conventional weapon, a multiple rocket launcher.

Let me tell you what is not controversial about these tubes. First, all the experts who have analyzed the tubes in our possession agree that they can be adapted for centrifuge use. Second, Iraq had no business buying them for any purpose. They are banned for Iraq. I am no expert on centrifuge tubes, but just as an old Army trooper, I can tell you a couple of things: First, it strikes me as quite odd that these tubes are manufactured to a tolerance that far exceeds U.S. requirements for comparable rockets. Maybe Iraqis just manufacture their conventional weapons to a higher standard than we do, but I don't think so.

Second, we actually have examined tubes from several different batches that were seized clandestinely before they reached Baghdad. What we notice in these different batches is a progression to higher and higher levels of specification, including, in the latest batch, an anodized coating on extremely smooth inner and outer surfaces.

Why would they continue refining the specifications, go to all that trouble for something that, if it was a rocket, would soon be blown into shrapnel when it went off? The high tolerance aluminum tubes are only part of the story. We also have intelligence from multiple sources that Iraq is attempting to acquire magnets and high-speed balancing machines; both items can be used in a gas centrifuge program to enrich uranium.

In 1999 and 2000, Iraqi officials negotiated with firms in Romania, India, Russia and Slovenia for the purchase of a magnet production plant. Iraq wanted the plant to produce magnets weighing 20 to 30 grams.

That's the same weight as the magnets used in Iraq's gas centrifuge program before the Gulf War. This incident linked with the tubes is another indicator of Iraq's attempt to reconstitute its nuclear weapons program.

Intercepted communications from mid-2000 through last summer show that Iraq front companies sought to buy machines that can be used to balance gas centrifuge rotors. One of these companies also had been involved in a failed effort in 2001 to smuggle aluminum tubes into Iraq. People will continue to debate this issue, but there is no doubt in my mind, these illicit procurement efforts show that Saddam Hussein is very much focused on putting in place the key missing piece from his nuclear weapons program, the ability to produce fissile material. He also has been busy trying to maintain the other key parts of his nuclear program, particularly his cadre of key nuclear scientists.

It is noteworthy that, over the last 18 months, Saddam Hussein has paid increasing personal attention to Iraqi's top nuclear scientists, a group that the governmental-controlled press calls openly, his nuclear mujahedeen. He regularly exhorts them and praises their progress. Progress toward what end?

Long ago, the Security Council, this council, required Iraq to halt all nuclear activities of any kind.

Part 8: Prohibited arms systems

Let me talk now about the systems Iraq is developing to deliver weapons of mass destruction, in particular Iraq's ballistic missiles and unmanned aerial vehicles, UAVs.

First, missiles. We all remember that before the Gulf War Saddam Hussein's goal was missiles that flew not just hundreds, but thousands of kilometers. He wanted to strike not only his neighbors, but also nations far beyond his borders.

While inspectors destroyed most of the prohibited ballistic missiles, numerous intelligence reports over the past decade, from sources inside Iraq, indicate that Saddam Hussein retains a covert force of up to a few dozen Scud variant ballistic missiles. These are missiles with a range of 650 to 900 kilometers. We know from intelligence and Iraq's own admissions that Iraq's alleged permitted ballistic missiles, the al-Samud II and the al-Fatah , violate the 150-kilometer limit established by this council in Resolution 687. These are prohibited systems.

UNMOVIC has also reported that Iraq has illegally important 380 SA-2 rocket engines. These are likely for use in the al-Samud II. Their import was illegal on three counts. Resolution 687 prohibited all military shipments into Iraq. UNSCOM specifically prohibited use of these engines in surface-to-surface missiles. And finally, as we have just noted, they are for a system that exceeds the 150-kilometer range limit.

Worst of all, some of these engines were acquired as late as December -- after this council passed Resolution 1441.

What I want you to know today is that Iraq has programs that are intended to produce ballistic missiles that fly over 1,000 kilometers.

One program is pursuing a liquid fuel missile that would be able to fly more than 1,200 kilometers. And you can see from this map, as well as I can, who will be in danger of these missiles.

As part of this effort, another little piece of evidence, Iraq has built an engine test stand that is larger than anything it has ever had. Notice the dramatic difference in size between the test stand on the left, the old one, and the new one on the right. Note the large exhaust vent. This is where the flame from the engine comes out. The exhaust on the right test stand is five times longer than the one on the left. The one on the left was used for short-range missile. The one on the right is clearly intended for long-range missiles that can fly 1,200 kilometers.

This photograph was taken in April of 2002. Since then, the test stand has been finished and a roof has been put over it so it will be harder for satellites to see what's going on underneath the test stand.

Saddam Hussein's intentions have never changed. He is not developing the missiles for self-defense. These are missiles that Iraq wants in order to project power, to threaten, and to deliver chemical, biological and, if we let him, nuclear warheads. Now, unmanned aerial vehicles, UAVs. Iraq has been working on a variety of UAVs for more than a decade. This is just illustrative of what a UAV would look like.

This effort has included attempts to modify for unmanned flight the MiG-21 and with greater success an aircraft called the L-29. However, Iraq is now concentrating not on these airplanes, but on developing and testing smaller UAVs, such as this. UAVs are well suited for dispensing chemical and biological weapons.

There is ample evidence that Iraq has dedicated much effort to developing and testing spray devices that could be adapted for UAVs. And of the little that Saddam Hussein told us about UAVs, he has not told the truth. One of these lies is graphically and indisputably demonstrated by intelligence we collected on June 27, last year.

According to Iraq's December 7 declaration, its UAVs have a range of only 80 kilometers. But we detected one of Iraq's newest UAVs in a test flight that went 500 kilometers nonstop on autopilot in the race track pattern depicted here. Not only is this test well in excess of the 150 kilometers that the United Nations permits, the test was left out of Iraq's December 7th declaration. The UAV was flown around and around and around in a circle. And so, that its 80 kilometer limit really was 500 kilometers unrefueled and on autopilot, violative of all of its obligations under 1441.

The linkages over the past 10 years between Iraq's UAV program and biological and chemical warfare agents are of deep concern to us. Iraq could use these small UAVs which have a wingspan of only a few meters to deliver biological agents to its neighbors or if transported, to other countries, including the United States. My friends, the information I have presented to you about these terrible weapons and about Iraq's continued flaunting of its obligations under Security Council Resolution 1441 links to a subject I now want to spend a little bit of time on. And that has to do with terrorism.

Part 9: Ties to al Qaeda

Our concern is not just about these illicit weapons. It's the way that these illicit weapons can be connected to terrorists and terrorist organizations that have no compunction about using such devices against innocent people around the world.

Iraq and terrorism go back decades. Baghdad trains Palestine Liberation Front members in small arms and explosives. Saddam uses the Arab Liberation Front to funnel money to the families of Palestinian suicide bombers in order to prolong the intifada. And it's no secret that Saddam's own intelligence service was involved in dozens of attacks or attempted assassinations in the 1990s. But what I want to bring to your attention today is the potentially much more sinister nexus between Iraq and the al Qaeda terrorist network, a nexus that combines classic terrorist organizations and modern methods of murder.

Iraq today harbors a deadly terrorist network headed by Abu Musab Zarqawi, an associate and collaborator of Osama bin Laden and his al Qaeda lieutenants. Zarqawi, a Palestinian born in Jordan, fought in the Afghan war more than a decade ago. Returning to Afghanistan in 2000, he oversaw a terrorist training camp. One of his specialties and one of the specialties of this camp is poisons. When our coalition ousted the Taliban, the Zarqawi network helped establish another poison and explosive training center camp. And this camp is located in northeastern Iraq. You see a picture of this camp.

The network is teaching its operatives how to produce ricin and other poisons. Let me remind you how ricin works. Less than a pinch -- image a pinch of salt -- less than a pinch of ricin, eating just this amount in your food, would cause shock followed by circulatory failure. Death comes within 72 hours and there is no antidote, there is no cure. It is fatal. Those helping to run this camp are Zarqawi lieutenants operating in northern Kurdish areas outside Saddam Hussein's controlled Iraq. But Baghdad has an agent in the most senior levels of the radical organization, Ansar al-Islam; hat controls this corner of Iraq. In 2000 this agent offered al Qaeda safe haven in the region. After we swept al Qaeda from Afghanistan, some of its members accepted this safe haven. They remain their today.

Zarqawi's activities are not confined to this small corner of northeast Iraq. He traveled to Baghdad in May 2002 for medical treatment, staying in the capital of Iraq for two months while he recuperated to fight another day.

During this stay, nearly two dozen extremists converged on Baghdad and established a base of operations there. These al Qaeda affiliates, based in Baghdad, now coordinate the movement of people, money and supplies into and throughout Iraq for his network, and they've now been operating freely in the capital for more than eight months. Iraqi officials deny accusations of ties with al Qaeda. These denials are simply not credible. Last year an al Qaeda associate bragged that the situation in Iraq was, quote, "good," that Baghdad could be transited quickly.

We know these affiliates are connected to Zarqawi because they remain even today in regular contact with his direct subordinates, including the poison cell plotters, and they are involved in moving more than money and materiel. Last year, two suspected al Qaeda operatives were arrested crossing from Iraq into Saudi Arabia. They were linked to associates of the Baghdad cell, and one of them received training in Afghanistan on how to use cyanide. From his terrorist network in Iraq, Zarqawi can direct his network in the Middle East and beyond. We, in the United States, all of us at the State Department, and the Agency for International Development -- we all lost a dear friend with the cold-blooded murder of Mr. Lawrence Foley in Amman, Jordan, last October -- a despicable act was committed that day. The assassination of an individual whose sole mission was to assist the people of Jordan. The captured assassin says his cell received money and weapons from Zarqawi for that murder.

After the attack, an associate of the assassin left Jordan to go to Iraq to obtain weapons and explosives for further operations. Iraqi officials protest that they are not aware of the whereabouts of Zarqawi or of any of his associates. Again, these protests are not credible. We know of Zarqawi's activities in Baghdad. I described them earlier. And now let me add one other fact. We asked a friendly security service to approach Baghdad about extraditing Zarqawi and providing information about him and his close associates. This service contacted Iraqi officials twice, and we passed details that should have made it easy to find Zarqawi. The network remains in Baghdad. Zarqawi still remains at large to come and go.

As my colleagues around this table and as the citizens they represent in Europe know, Zarqawi's terrorism is not confined to the Middle East. Zarqawi and his network have plotted terrorist actions against countries, including France, Britain, Spain, Italy, Germany and Russia. According to detainees, Abu Atia, who graduated from Zarqawi's terrorist camp in Afghanistan, tasked at least nine North African extremists in 2001 to travel to Europe to conduct poison and explosive attacks.

Since last year, members of this network have been apprehended in France, Britain, Spain and Italy. By our last count, 116 operatives connected to this global web have been arrested.

The chart you are seeing shows the network in Europe. We know about this European network, and we know about its links to Zarqawi, because the detainee who provided the information about the targets also provided the names of members of the network. Three of those he identified by name were arrested in France last December. In the apartments of the terrorists, authorities found circuits for explosive devices and a list of ingredients to make toxins.

The detainee who helped piece this together says the plot also targeted Britain. Later evidence, again, proved him right. When the British unearthed a cell there just last month, one British police officer was murdered during the disruption of the cell. We also know that Zarqawi's colleagues have been active in the Pankisi Gorge, Georgia and in Chechnya, Russia. The plotting to which they are linked is not mere chatter. Members of Zarqawi's network say their goal was to kill Russians with toxins. We are not surprised that Iraq is harboring Zarqawi and his subordinates. This understanding builds on decades long experience with respect to ties between Iraq and al Qaeda.

Going back to the early and mid-1990s, when bin Laden was based in Sudan, an al Qaeda source tells us that Saddam and bin Laden reached an understanding that al Qaeda would no longer support activities against Baghdad. Early al Qaeda ties were forged by secret, high-level intelligence service contacts with al Qaeda, secret Iraqi intelligence high-level contacts with al Qaeda.

We know members of both organizations met repeatedly and have met at least eight times at very senior levels since the early 1990s. In1996, a foreign security service tells us, that bin Laden met with a senior Iraqi intelligence official in Khartoum, and later met the director of the Iraqi intelligence service.

Saddam became more interested as he saw al Qaeda's appalling attacks. A detained al Qaeda member tells us that Saddam was more willing to assist al Qaeda after the 1998 bombings of our embassies in Kenya and Tanzania. Saddam was also impressed by al Qaeda's attacks on the USS Cole in Yemen in October 2000.

Iraqis continued to visit bin Laden in his new home in Afghanistan. A senior defector, one of Saddam's former intelligence chiefs in Europe, says Saddam sent his agents to Afghanistan sometime in the mid-1990s to provide training to al Qaeda members on document forgery.

From the late 1990s until 2001, the Iraqi embassy in Pakistan played the role of liaison to the al Qaeda organization. Some believe, some claim these contacts do not amount to much.

They say Saddam Hussein's secular tyranny and al Qaeda's religious tyranny do not mix. I am not comforted by this thought. Ambition and hatred are enough to bring Iraq and al Qaeda together, enough so al Qaeda could learn how to build more sophisticated bombs and learn how to forge documents, and enough so that al Qaeda could turn to Iraq for help in acquiring expertise on weapons of mass destruction.

And the record of Saddam Hussein's cooperation with other Islamist terrorist organizations is clear. Hamas, for example, opened an office in Baghdad in 1999, and Iraq has hosted conferences attended by Palestine Islamic Jihad. These groups are at the forefront of sponsoring suicide attacks against Israel. Al Qaeda continues to have a deep interest in acquiring weapons of mass destruction. As with the story of Zarqawi and his network, I can trace the story of a senior terrorist operative telling how Iraq provided training in these weapons to al Qaeda.

Fortunately, this operative is now detained, and he has told his story. I will relate it to you now as he, himself, described it. This senior al Qaeda terrorist was responsible for one of al Qaeda's training camps in Afghanistan.

His information comes firsthand from his personal involvement at senior levels of al Qaeda. He says bin Laden and his top deputy in Afghanistan, deceased al Qaeda leader Mohammed Atef, did not believe that al Qaeda labs in Afghanistan were capable enough to manufacture these chemical or biological agents. They needed to go somewhere else. They had to look outside of Afghanistan for help. Where did they go? Where did they look? They went to Iraq.

The support that (inaudible) describes included Iraq offering chemical or biological weapons training for two al Qaeda associates beginning in December 2000. He says that a militant known as Abu Abdullah Al-Iraqi (ph) had been sent to Iraq several times between 1997and 2000 for help in acquiring poisons and gases. Abdullah Al-Iraqi (ph) characterized the relationship he forged with Iraqi officials as successful.

Part 10: Conclusion

As I said at the outset, none of this should come as a surprise to any of us. Terrorism has been a tool used by Saddam for decades. Saddam was a supporter of terrorism long before these terrorist networks had a name. And this support continues. The nexus of poisons and terror is new. The nexus of Iraq and terror is old. The combination is lethal.

With this track record, Iraqi denials of supporting terrorism take the place alongside the other Iraqi denials of weapons of mass destruction. It is all a web of lies. When we confront a regime that harbors ambitions for regional domination, hides weapons of mass destruction and provides haven and active support for terrorists, we are not confronting the past, we are confronting the present. And unless we act, we are confronting an even more frightening future. My friends, this has been a long and a detailed presentation.

And I thank you for your patience. But there is one more subject that I would like to touch on briefly. And it should be a subject of deep and continuing concern to this council, Saddam Hussein's violations of human rights.

Underlying all that I have said, underlying all the facts and the patterns of behavior that I have identified as Saddam Hussein's contempt for the will of this council, his contempt for the truth and most damning of all, his utter contempt for human life. Saddam Hussein's use of mustard and nerve gas against the Kurds in 1988 was one of the 20th century's most horrible atrocities; 5,000 men, women and children died.

His campaign against the Kurds from 1987 to '89 included mass summary executions, disappearances, arbitrary jailing, ethnic cleansing and the destruction of some 2,000 villages. He has also conducted ethnic cleansing against the Shiite Iraqis and the Marsh Arabs whose culture has flourished for more than a millennium. Saddam Hussein's police state ruthlessly eliminates anyone who dares to dissent. Iraq has more forced disappearance cases than any other country, tens of thousands of people reported missing in the past decade. Nothing points more clearly to Saddam Hussein's dangerous intentions and the threat he poses to all of us than his calculated cruelty to his own citizens and to his neighbors. Clearly, Saddam Hussein and his regime will stop at nothing until something stops him. For more than 20 years, by word and by deed Saddam Hussein has pursued his ambition to dominate Iraq and the broader Middle East using the only means he knows, intimidation, coercion and annihilation of all those who might stand in his way.

For Saddam Hussein, possession of the world's most deadly weapons is the ultimate trump card, the one he most hold to fulfill his ambition.

We know that Saddam Hussein is determined to keep his weapons of mass destruction; he's determined to make more.

Given Saddam Hussein's history of aggression, given what we know of his grandiose plans, given what we know of his terrorist associations and given his determination to exact revenge on those who oppose him, should we take the risk that he will not some day use these weapons at a time and the place and in the manner of his choosing at a time when the world is in a much weaker position to respond?

The United States will not and cannot run that risk to the American people. Leaving Saddam Hussein in possession of weapons of mass destruction for a few more months or years is not an option, not in a post-September 11th world. My colleagues, over three months ago this council recognized that Iraq continued to pose a threat to international peace and security, and that Iraq had been and remained in material breach of its disarmament obligations. Today Iraq still poses a threat and Iraq still remains in material breach. Indeed, by its failure to seize on its one last opportunity to come clean and disarm, Iraq has put itself in deeper material breach and closer to the day when it will face serious consequences for its continued defiance of this council.

My colleagues, we have an obligation to our citizens, we have an obligation to this body to see that our resolutions are complied with. We wrote 1441 not in order to go to war; we wrote 1441 to try to preserve the peace. We wrote 1441 to give Iraq one last chance. Iraq is not so far taking that one last chance.

We must not shrink from whatever is ahead of us. We must not fail in our duty and our responsibility to the citizens of the countries that are represented by this body.

Thank you, Mr. President.

Note: *After May 1, 2003 the world became the witness over what really happened especially about the Iraqi weapon of mass destruction, and the case of Al-Janabi family would not happen without Powell's share.*

Abeer Qassim Hamza al-Janabi

Do you memorize all words in the Webster Dictionary? If so, you are still not be able to describe how horrible is the gang-rape over a 14-year old innocent Iraqi girl Abeer Qassim Hamza al-Janabi. Five US soldiers of 502 Infantry Regiment were charged with gang-rape in Yousoufiyyah village of Mahmudiyah town about 20 kilometers south of Bagdad, Iraq on March 12, 2006. They are **Pfc. Steven D. Green, Pfc. Bryan L. Howard, Pfc. Jesse V. Spielman, Sgt. Paul E. Cortez, and Spc. James Baker.**

They were sentenced to life, 27 months, 110 years, 100 years, and 90 years respectively for their crimes; the total of more than 300 years only in worldly prison but nobody knows for how long they will be in the hellfire.

Abeer was raped and later killed along with her mother Fakhriyah Taha Muhsin, 34, her father Qasim Hamza Raheem, 45; and 5 year-old sister Hadeel Qasim Hamza.

The crime has never been disclosed until 22 June 2006 when Pfc. Justin Watt of the 502nd Regiment told the horrible story during a psychological health counseling session. He got "medical discharge".

The five soldiers were so eager to become insurgents in the house of al-Janabis instead of finding out the allegedly insurgents. Abeer's mother was wary of her daughter safety and asked her to sleep at a neighbor house at night, but the gang-rape happened on a bright daylight! Only Mohammed, 13, Abeer's brother survived the brutal and inhumane killings, he and another brother were at school.

The nature of cruelty and brutality committed against an innocent young girl never could be explained in the polite language. The horror Abeer underwent is beyond the ability and endurance of any civilized people, even the victims of atomic bombs at Hiroshima and Nagasaki still could share the horror they survived from.

Someone forced a girl supine on the floor, another man hold her hands, another man forcefully open her clothing up and gang-raped her, and another man killed her later; they might be simultaneously raping her before killing and burning her altogether with the three victim bodies and left the scene with the satisfactory sensation because they tasted a virginity they never found before during their lifetime; and this is the missing link we were not aware of before prosecuting the culprits. No other word was available but "uncivilized", it's rape and lynching. 1,000 year-sentence will not suffice nor death penalty. Even if all five villains were put in death, it would not revive single one out of four lives they took from Mahmudiyah.

On May 21, 2009 **Steven D. Green,** 24, was sentenced in US Court to life in prison without (possibility of) parole, a verdict that sparked a Iraqi nation-wide rage as it was aired in a Iraqi national television. The rape, killing, and burning of the al-Janabi family members were so wild, inhumane and uncivilized that the US commanders initially thought it was an action by the insurgents (consider why the "insurgent" and did the "insurgent" ever rape anybody?). A Janabi tribal leader at the Anbar province, Sheikh Fadhil al-Janabi bitterly said "There is no comparison between the crimes and sentence. That soldier entered an Iraqi house, raped their daughter and burned her with her family, so this sentence is not enough, and it is insulting for Iraqi's honor". However, everybody should have respected the US court, can you imagine what happened if Abeer were your lovely daughter or Jena or Mary?

Although they acted individually, never be ordered nor supported by the US Army; but they were in Iraq after Powell's address to the UN Security Council on Wednesday February 5, 2003.

(Compiled from many sources)

Bibliography

1. Bahry, Abdul R., "*Jihad: Struggle or Terrorism*" 1stBook Library, Bloomington IN, 2002
2. Brian Sprinkle and James Butman, "*Armchair Detective*", Rainbow Books Inc., Highland City, Fla. 1992
3. Dankbaar, Wim (ed.), "*Files on JFK*", (c) 2007-2008 Wim Dankbaar, IPG distribution, Chicago, Ill., 2008
4. Edward Klein, "*The Kennedy Curse*", Thorndike Press, Waterville Maine, 2003
5. Epstein, Edward Jay, "*Legend: The Secret World of Lee Harvey Oswald*" McGraw-Hill, 1978
6. Errol Morris Film, "*The Fog of War, eleven lessons from the life of Robert S. McNamara*", documentary 2003
7. Fetzer, James H. (ed.), "*Murder In Dealy Plaza*", Catfeet Press, Chicago, 2000
8. Fred Kaplan, "*The Tragedy of Colin Powell. How the Bush presidency destroyed him*", Slate Magazine website, Thursday, Feb. 19, 2004
9. Groden, Robert J. "*The Search for Lee Harvey Oswald*", Penguin Studio Books, New York 1995
10. Interview with Donald B. Thomas by **Rex Bradford** on April 5, 2006
11. James McConnachie and Robin Tudge, "*The Rough Guide to Conspiracy Theory*", Rough Guided Ltd., London, 2005
12. Jim Nelson, *Globe* Magazine, April 13, 2009 edition
13. Jim Garrison "*On the Trail of the Assassins*", Warner Book Edition, New York 1988
14. Jefferson Morley, "*The Man Who Did Not Talk*", Playboy magazine, November 2007
15. Jefferson Morley, "*The JFK Murder*", The Reader's Digest magazine, March 2005
16. Karen Bornemann Spies, "*John F. Kennedy*", Enslow Publishing Inc., Berkeley Height, NJ, 1999
17. "*Kompas*" online newspaper, June 4, 2012
18. "*Kompas*" online newspaper, Monday September 27, 2010
19. "*Kompas*" online newspaper, October 4, 2010
20. Lamar Waldron and Thom Hartman, "*Ultimate Sacrifice*", Carol & Graf Publisher, New York, first edition 2005, p. 619 - 620.
21. Mark Lane "*Plausible Denial*", Thunder's Mouth Press, New York 1991, pp. 1-5, 182-188
22. McKnight, Gerald D., "*Breach of Trust*", University Press of Kansas, 2005
23. "*Newsweek*" Magazine, February 16, 2009
24. O'Brien, Michael, "*John F. Kennedy*", Thomas Dunne Books, St. Martin's Press, NY 2005

25. Paul Harris, "*How Condoleezza Rice became the most powerful woman in the world*", The Observer, Sunday January 1, 2005.
26. Paul Bedard, "*Tampering With the Zapruder Film?*", US News & World Report, May 22, 2006
27. PBS TV documentary, aired on January 26, 2009
28. Posner, Gerald "Case Closed", Random House, New York 1993
29. President's Commission "*Warren Report*", The Associated Press
30. "*Republica*" Online newspaper, Monday, April 19, 2010
31. "*Republika*" online newspaper; Republika.com, June 06, 2012
32. Scheim, David E., "Contract On America", Shapolsky Publishers, New York 1988
33. Smith, Mathew, "*Conspiracy, the Plot to Stop the Kennedys*", Citadel Press Book, New York, 2005
34. Thomas, Donald B., "*Hear no Evil: The Acoustical Evidence in the Kennedy Assassination*" (2001)
35. Thomas, Donald B., "*Crosstalk: Synchronization of Putative Gunshots with Events in Dealey Plaza*" (2002)
36. Tim Weiner, "*Legacy of Ashes, the History of CIA*", Anchor Books, New York 2008, ISBN 978-0-307-38900-8
37. "*TIMES*" magazine, September 27, 2010
38. "*US New and World Report*" Newspaper, May 22, 2009
39. "*USA Today*" newspaper, Friday June 4, 2010
40. http://assassinationresearch.com/v3n2/v3n2holt.pdf
41. http://abcnews.go.com/US/wireStory/colombia-general-pleads-guilty-drug-case-16725433, July 6, 2012
42. http://articles.cnn.com/2012-06-06/politics/politics_white-house-leaks_1_leaks-sensitive-information-intelligence-authorization-bill?_s=PM:POLITICS
43. http://history-matters.com
44. http://in.reuters.com/article/2012/06/06/net-us-cyberwar-flame-kaspersky-idINBRE8550HM20120606
45. http://jfkmurdersolved.com
46. http://kingsofwar.org.uk/2010/09/stuxnet/
47. http://nndb.com
48. http://pages.prodigy.net/whiskey99/courttv.htm
49. http://pages.prodigy.net/whiskey99/courttv.htm under the title of Impulsive Behavior: The *CourtTV - Sensimetrics* Acoustical Evidence Study by D.B. Thomas (C) 2003 Donald B. Thomas
50. http://pages.prodigy.net/whiskey99/ courttv.htm, the original article was written by Dr. Donald B. Thomas, published on Science & Justice December 2003 issue
51. http://TODAY.com, 2/9/2012
52. http://en.wikipedia.org/wiki/1964_Brazilian_coup _d%27%C3%A9tat
53. http://en.wikipedia.org/wiki/2002_Venezuelan_ coup_d%27%C3%A9tat_attempt
54. http://en.wikipedia.org/wiki/Able_Archer_83
55. http://en.wikipedia.org/wiki/Anatoliy_Golitsyn

56. http://en.wikipedia.org/wiki/Arlen_Specter
57. http://en.wikipedia.org/wiki/Autonomism_(political_doctrine)
58. http://en.wikipedia.org/wiki/Cambridge_Five
59. http://en.wikipedia.org/wiki/Carlos_Marcello
60. http://en.wikipedia.org/wiki/CIA_activities_in_Argentina
61. http://en.wikipedia.org/wiki/CIA_activities_in_Bolivia
62. http://en.wikipedia.org/wiki/CIA_activities_in_Brazil
63. http://en.wikipedia.org/wiki/CIA_activities_in_Chile
64. http://en.wikipedia.org/wiki/CIA_activities_in_Colombia
65. http://en.wikipedia.org/wiki/CIA_activities_in_the_Dominican_Republic
66. http://en.wikipedia.org/wiki/CIA_activities_in_Guatemala
67. http://en.wikipedia.org/wiki/CIA_activities_in_Guyana
68. http://en.wikipedia.org/wiki/CIA_activities_in_Haiti
69. http://en.wikipedia.org/wiki/CIA_activities_in_Honduras
70. http://en.wikipedia.org/wiki/CIA_activities_in_Nicaragua
71. http://en.wikipedia.org/wiki/CIA_activities_in_Peru
72. http://en.wikipedia.org/wiki/CIA_activities_in_Venezuela
73. http://en.wikipedia.org/wiki/Clay_Shaw
74. http://en.wikipedia.org/wiki/Chauncey_Marvin_Holt
75. http://en.wikipedia.org/wiki/Communism
76. http://en.wikipedia.org/wiki/Cuban_Missile_Crisis
77. http://en.wikipedia.org/wiki/David_Atlee_Phillips
78. http://en.wikipedia.org/wiki/Democracy
79. http://en.wikipedia.org/wiki/Dialectical_materialism
80. http://en.wikipedia.org/dictabelt
81. http://en.wikipedia.org/wiki/Dictabelt_evidence_relating_to_the_assassination_of_John_F._Kennedy
82. http://en.wikipedia.org/wiki/Duqu
83. http://en.wikipedia.org/wiki/Ethel_Rosenberg
84. http://en.wikipedia.org/wiki/ExComm
85. http://en.wikipedia.org/wiki/Gary_Powers
86. http://en.wikipedia.org/wiki/George_Koval
87. http://en.wikipedia.org/wiki/Guyana
88. http://en.wikipedia.org/wiki/Hedonism
89. http://en.wikipedia.org/wiki/History_of_Argentina
90. http://en.wikipedia.org/HSCA
91. http://en.wikipedia.org/wiki/Hugo_Spadafora
92. http://en.wikipedia.org/wiki/Hugo_Ch%C3%A1vez
93. http://en.wikipedia.org/wiki/Humberto_de_Alencar_Castelo_Branco
94. http://en.wikipedia.org/wiki/James_angleton
95. http://en.wikipedia.org/wiki/James_Byrd,_Jr.
96. http://en.wikipedia.org/wiki/James_Fetzer
97. http://en.wikipedia.org/wiki/JFK
98. http://en.wikipedia.org/wiki/JFK_assassination
99. http://en.wikipedia.org/wiki/JFK_conspiracy
100. http://en.wikipedia.org/wiki/John_F._Kennedy_assassination_conspiracy_theories

101. http://economicexpert.com/John:F:Kennedy:assassination.htm
102. http://en.wikipedia.org/wiki/John_F._Kennedy
103. http://en.wikipedia.org/wiki/John_Roselli
104. http://americanrhetoric.com/jfkamericanuniversityaddress.html
105. http://en.wikipedia.org/wiki/Joe_1
106. http://en.wikipedia.org/wiki/Jo%C3%A3o_Goulart
107. http://en.wikipedia.org/wiki/Kennedy_Curse
108. http://en.wikipedia.org/wiki/Kitty_Harris
109. http://en.wikipedia.org/wiki/Klaus_Fuchs
110. http://latino.foxnews.com/latino/news/2012/07/06/colombian-genl-pleads-not-guilty-to-us-drug-charges/ July 6, 2012
111. http://en.wikipedia.org/wiki/Lee_Harvey_Oswald
112. http://en.wikipedia.org/wiki/Lend-Lease_Act
123. http://en.wikipedia.org/wiki/Lev_Vasilevsky
114. http://en.wikipedia.org/wiki/Liberalism
115. http://en.wikipedia.org/wiki/Lobotomy, http://en.wikipedia.org/wiki/Kennedy_Curse
116. http://en.wikipedia.org/wiki/Lobotomy
117. http://en.wikipedia.org/wiki/Manuel_Noriega
118. http://en.wikipedia.org/wiki/Mathias_Rust
119. http://en.wikipedia.org/wiki/Monroe_doctrine
120. http://en.wikipedia.org/wiki/Morton_Sobell
121. http://en.wikipedia.org/wiki/Neo_liberalism
122. http://en.wikipedia.org/wiki/Nicholas_Katzenbach
123. http://en.wikipedia.org/wiki/Nuclear_warfare
124. http://en.wikipedia.org/wiki/Nuclear_winter
125. http://en.wikipedia.org/wiki/Oleg_Penkovsky
126. http://en.wikipedia.org/wiki/Panama
127. http://en.wikipedia.org/wiki/Panama_Invasion
128. http://en.wikipedia.org/wiki/Penkovsky
129. http://en.wikipedia.org/wiki/Peter_Dale_Scott
130. http://en.wikipedia.org/wiki/Pinochet
131. http://en.wikipedia.org/wiki/PRRI
132. http://en.wikipedia.org/wiki/Rafael_Trujillo#The_Downfall_and_Assassination
133. http://en.wikipedia.org/wiki/Ren%C3%A9_Barrientos
134. http://en.wikipedia.org/wiki/Rudolf_Abel
135. http://en.wikipedia.org/wiki/Rudolf_Anderson
136. http://en.wikipedia.org/wiki/Saville_Sax
137. http://en.wikipedia.org/wiki/Single_bullet_theory
138. http://en.wikipedia.org/wiki/Socialism
139. http://en.wikipedia.org/wiki/S-75_Dvina
140. http://en.wikipedia.org/wiki/Starfish_Prime
141. http://en.wikipedia.org/wiki/Statism_in_Sh%C5%8Dwa_Japan
142. http://en.wikipedia.org/wiki/Stuxnet
143. http://en.wikipedia.org/wiki/Theodore_Hall
144. http://en.wikipedia.org/wiki/Thor_IRBM

145. http://today.msnbc.msn.com/id/46325984/ns/today-today_news/t/former-intern-jfk-affair-was-imbalanced-not-abusive/
146. http://en.wikipedia.org/wiki/U-2_Dragon_Lady
147. http://en.wikipedia.org/wiki/Vasily_Arkhipov
148. http://en.wikipedia.org/wiki/Warren_Commission
149. http://hubpages.com
150. http://www.jfklibrary.org/Asset-Viewer/0BYhudts-E6hwG7-Hay9NQ.aspx
151. http://jfkonline.com
152. http://jfkmurder.com
153. http://jflmurdersolved.com
154. http://mcadams.posc.mu.edu
155. http://mayferrell.org
156. http://news.yahoo.com/s/yblog_upshot/20101020/od_yblog_upsht/ex-secret-service-officer-i-almost-shot-lbj
157. http://nymag.com
158. http://republika.co.id, July 15, 2010
159. http://rt.com/news/flame-stuxnet-kaspersky-iran-607/
160. http://rt.com/news/kaspersky-fears-cyber-pandemic-170/
161. http://spartacus.schoolnet.co.uk
162. http://sport.acorn.net/JFKplace/09/Kelin34/fear.html
163. http://sport.acorn.net
164. http://video.google.com/videoplay?docid=818267521031292324#
165. http://video.msnbc.msn.com/mitchell-reports/48321651#48321651
166. http://www.alarabiya.net/articles/2012/06/06/219054.html
167. http://www.bbc.co.uk/news/world-europe-11804398
168. http://www.cnn.com/2012/01/09/world/americas/venezuela-ahmadinejad/index.html
169. http://www.gwu.edu/~nsarchiv/NSAEBB/NSAEBB223/ index.htm
170. http://www.huffingtonpost.com/2012/03/09/pope-denounces-gay-marriage_n_1334504.html
171. http://www.huffingtonpost.com/2012/02/06/mimi-alford-jfk-affair_n_1257759.html
172. http://www.jfk-info.com/thomp2.htm
173. http://www.kaspersky.com/news?id=207576183
174. http://www.lifenews.com/2011/02/28/pope-benedict-delivers-abortion-message-to-pro-life- leaders/
175. http://www.mysterynet.com/holmes/01scandalbohemia/
176. http://www.nucleardarkness.org/hiroshima/
177. http://www.nytimes.com/2008/07/03/world/americas/03colombia.html?_r=1&hp
178. http://www.reuters.com/article/2010/07/16/us-cuba-castro-fidel-idUSTRE66F5UV20100716
179. http://www.spartacus.schoolnet.co.uk/JFKthomasD.htm
180. http://www.state.gov/j/ct/rls/other/des/123085.htm
181. http://www.youtube.com/watch?v=bqL1ANq7VPM&feature=endscreen&NR=1

182. http://www.youtube.com/watch?v=K2oIAUz0drw
183. http://www.youtube.com/watch?NR=1&v=yLiF4Jwvb0o&feature=endscreen
184. http://www.youtube.com/watch?v=Rp3P2wDKQK4&feature=related
185. http://www.youtube.com/watch?v=TCVaYxOvcMs&feature=endscreen&NR=1
186. http://www.youtube.com/watch?v=VI07govlUqI& feature=related

Index

Able Archer ... 294, 311, 312, 313, 314, 315, 327

Abraham 3, 105, 115, 239, 241

Adam Malik 34, 36

AK-47 41

ALBM .... xix, xxiv, 143, 347

Aleksandr Fomin 193

Al-Janabi 385

Anderson ..... xx, xxvi, xxxi, xxxii, xxxiii, xxxiv, 50, 63, 181, 186, 196, 290, 346, 391

Anthony Blunt 57, 59

Arkhipov xx, 46, 47, 63, 195, 320, 392

Assassination .. 25, 202, 209, 216, 227, 229, 233, 236, 240, 257, 262, 263, 273, 276, 279, 289, 292, 389, 391

Autopsy 158, 258, 260

Bahia de Cochinos . xxv, 169, 171, 172, 283, 284

Bear .... xxv, 143

Boeing .... xxv, 166, 294, 327

Bullet 161, 231, 269

Bush 19, 32, 78, 132, 133, 134, 135, 137, 138, 139, 140, 141, 142, 182, 240, 241, 335, 343, 388

Castro .. xxv, 8, 12, 27, 33, 44, 45, 53, 99, 101, 111, 120, 122, 124, 125, 150, 151, 164, 169, 170, 174, 177, 182, 189, 191, 194, 199, 242,

272, 274, 278, 282, 283, 286, 287, 289, 290, 291, 294, 333, 347

charismatic 352

China . xix, xxi, xxiv, xxviii, xxix, xxx, xxxi, 23, 27, 33, 34, 56, 68, 84, 201, 305, 320, 321, 322, 326

coffin 27, 258, 262, 292, 351

Cold War ..... **xxv, xxix, 4, 7, 8, 12, 15, 17, 32, 33, 34, 46, 50, 117, 119, 124, 125, 129, 130, 169, 170, 173, 174, 305, 309, 315, 320, 321, 323, 324, 325**

Colin Powell .. 133, 134, 135, 137, 142, 353, 388

Communist ..... xxi, 20, 24, 32, 34, 40, 43, 44, 45, 48, 54, 144, 146, 215

Condoleezza Rice .. 132, 136, 138, 139, 140, 142, 389

congenital 330

Congress .iii, 9, 18, 43, 68, 80, 83, 105, 119, 145, 216, 221, 222, 225, 233, 234, 240, 268, 273, 289, 293, 301

Connally 154, 155, 156, 159, 161, 202, 205, 208, 209, 212, 226, 230, 231, 232, 237, 238, 259, 262, 265, 266, 267, 269, 270

Conspiracy 98, 100, 110, 168, 208, 226, 239, 244, 250, 264, 291, 388, 389

Crisis .. xxvi, xxix, xxxii, xxxiv, 6, 7, 23, 31, 44, 46, 50, 52, 63, 80, 81, 119, 120, 124, 135, 171, 174,

394

177, 184, 186, 190, 191, 194, 198, 199, 200, 201, 282, 291, 295, 298, 301, 312, 315, 320, 333, 346, 390

Cuba ... ii, xix, xx, xxii, xxv, xxvi, xxix, xxx, xxxi, xxxii, xxxiii, 6, 8, 12, 14, 16, 27, 33, 44, 45, 46, 47, 50, 51, 52, 53, 101, 120, 121, 122, 123, 124, 125, 162, 169, 170, 171, 172, 174, 175, 176, 177, 178, 179, 180, 182, 183, 184, 185, 186, 187, 188, 190, 191, 192, 193, 194, 195, 196, 197, 198, 199, 200, 201, 215, 217, 218, 222, 223, 224, 228, 235, 272, 282, 285, 291, 312, 319, 333, 346, 347, 348

Cyber War 336

Dallas xviii, xxiii, xxvi, xxxiii, 44, 90, 93, 97, 111, 112, 113, 114, 115, 151, 152, 153, 154, 159, 164, 165, 167, 186, 189, 202, 203, 204, 205, 207, 208, 209, 210, 211, 212, 214, 215, 224, 225, 227, 230, 239, 240, 246, 247, 249, 250, 254, 259, 265, 266, 268, 269, 270, 283, 284, 286, 288, 292, 295, 297

Dealey Plaza.xxiii, 111, 113, 114, 115, 118, 152, 153, 156, 202, 204, 205, 206, 230, 237, 247, 249, 250, 254, 256, 257, 269, 270, 295, 389

Democracy ... 3, 24, 108, 146, 390

Democrat... 76, 93, 136, 214, 229, 231, 236, 300, 341

Dickson Crane 199

Dictabeltxxvi, 246, 247, 248, 249, 250, 254, 256, 257, 295, 296, 390

Doctrine i, 2, 3, 4, 5, 6, 7, 8, 9, 12, 17, 18, 21, 22, 23, 26, 30, 65, 70, 73, 76, 85, 89, 99, 104, 110, 119, 132, 143, 169, 174, 185, 192, 202, 227, 239, 246, 258, 265, 272, 279, 287, 295, 304, 311, 319, 329, 336

drug . 5, 14, 15, 18, 19, 25, 61, 96, 100, 325, 333, 352, 389, 391

Dvina.. xxix, xxxiv, 177, 187, 391

Eisenhower 31, 33, 34, 43, 50, 78, 86, 144, 146, 170, 171, 174, 176, 180, 208, 222

Estudiantil 282

EXCOMM 178, 193, 196

Federal Reserve 279, 291

Fejos 70

Fisher 50, 52, 55, 56, 200, 222

Garrison xix, 160, 213, 216, 226, 233, 239, 240, 242, 243, 283, 286, 287, 388

Gary Powers.. 49, 50, 51, 56, 131, 144, 163, 181

gay 7, 24, 108, 242, 392

George McBundy 171

global warming 329, 330

Golitsyn 59, 60, 64, 389

Guy Burgess 57, 58, 59, 60

Hero 62, 73

Hiroshima ... iii, iv, x, xxviii, xxix, 22, 30, 47, 56, 128, 178, 222, 224, 302, 304, 305, 306, 307, 309, 310, 319, 320, 323, 327, 333, 349, 386

hoax 245, 293, 329, 352

horror *4, 386*

HSCA 102, 119, 131, 165, 173, 199, 202, 203, 204, 206, 209, 214, 216, 227, 228, 231, 234, 236, 246, 247, 248, 249, 251, 253, 254, 256, 260, 261, 268, 272, 273, 274, 276, 277, 278, 284, 285, 287, 289, 290, 291, 294, 300, 346, 390

Ibn Khaldoun 5

ICBM .. xix, xxviii, 188, 316, 319, 320, 323

incest 4, 329

IRBM 51, 63, 391

395

Ireland..................................65, 66
Jack Ruby.....151, 159, 165, 167, 202, 211, 224, 227, 297
Jacqueline 32, 78, 92, 93, 96, 204, 213, 241, 258, 262
James E. Files 111, 152, 153, 206, 234, 241, 273, 274
JFK..........xviii, xxiii, xxvi, xxxii, xxxiii, xxxiv, 6, 32, 44, 50, 51, 52, 65, 78, 79, 81, 83, 84, 104, 110, 112, 117, 119, 120, 123, 131, 132, 147, 153, 154, 155, 156, 159, 160, 161, 170, 171, 173, 177, 180, 183, 184, 185, 186, 189, 190, 196, 197, 198, 199, 202, 203, 206, 212, 213, 214, 215, 216, 217, 218, 223, 224, 225, 226, 230, 233, 234, 235, 236, 237, 238, 239, 240, 243, 244, 247, 249, 252, 253, 254, 256, 257, 261, 263, 264, 267, 268, 270, 272, 278, 284, 285, 286, 287, 288, 289, 290, 291, 292, 293, 294, 295, 300, 345, 388, 390
Joe Kennedy...67, 70, 75, 76, 80, 86, 89, 91, 92
John Alfred Scali...................193
Johnson...xxvii, xxxiii, 12, 41, 48, 79, 81, 86, 97, 99, 120, 124, 166, 176, 182, 200, 205, 213, 214, 220, 224, 227, 228, 229, 234, 235, 236, 240, 242, 261, 272, 277, 285, 290, 291, 293, 297
KAL 007 ....294, 303, 327
Kennedy.i, ii, xi, xviii, xxii, xxiii, xxvii, 6, 28, 29, 32, 33, 40, 41, 43, 44, 65, 66, 67, 68, 69, 70, 71, 72, 73, 74, 75, 76, 77, 78, 79, 80, 81, 82, 83, 84, 85, 86, 87, 88, 89, 90, 91, 92, 93, 94, 95, 96, 97, 98, 99, 100, 101, 102, 104, 110, 111, 115, 117, 119, 120, 121, 122, 123, 124, 125, 126, 147, 151, 152, 153, 154, 155, 164, 165, 166, 167, 168, 169, 170, 171, 172, 173, 174, 175, 177,

180, 181, 182, 183, 184, 185, 186, 187, 188, 190, 191, 192, 193, 194, 196, 197, 198, 199, 202, 203, 204, 205, 206, 207, 208, 209, 210, 211, 212, 213, 214, 215, 216, 217, 218, 219, 220, 222, 223, 224, 225, 226, 227, 229, 230, 231, 232, 234, 235, 236, 237, 238, 239, 240, 241, 242, 245, 246, 247, 248, 249, 251, 252, 253, 254, 256, 257, 258, 259, 260, 261, 262, 263, 265, 266, 267, 268, 269, 270, 271, 272, 273, 274, 275, 276, 277, 278, 279, 280, 281, 282, 283, 284, 285, 286, 287, 288, 289, 290, 291, 292, 293, 294, 295, 296, 297, 299, 300, 301, 302, 345, 346, 347, 348, 349, 388, 389, 390, 391
Khrushchev xx, xxii, xxxii, 6, 32, 33, 34, 42, 43, 44, 50, 51, 54, 121, 122, 124, 125, 126, 174, 175, 177, 180, 183, 184, 186, 187, 190, 192, 193, 194, 195, 196, 197, 198, 199, 222, 223, 282, 291, 333
Kim Jong-Un 221, 334
Kim Philby.............57, 58, 59, 60
Kitty Harris 55, 56, 61
Klaus Fuchs 52, 53, 55, 60, 62, 63, 334
Koval 48, 61, 62, 64, 390
Last Tango...............................104
Lawrence McDonald......166, *See* McDonald
Lenin..31
life expectancy......................333
MacLean 57, 58, 59, 60, 163
MAD ....xxiv, 128, 317, 326
malware...............*xv, xvi, 338, 339*
Marilyn Monroe 93, 99, 100, 102, 289
Martin Luther King 29, 202, 216, 234, 247

McCone............xxvii, 13, 189, 190
McDonald...............167, 210, 293
McGeorge Bundy..........xxvii, 199
McNamara.......i, xxvii, 120, 121, 122, 123, 124, 125, 131, 177, 182, 198, 218, 304, 306, 307, 309, 316, 320, 333, 346, 388
Medicare...................................80
Mikoyan...................................41
Missile.xxvi, xxix, xxxii, xxxiv, 6, 7, 23, 44, 46, 50, 52, 63, 80, 81, 119, 120, 124, 171, 174, 176, 177, 184, 186, 190, 191, 192, 194, 198, 199, 200, 201, 215, 282, 291, 298, 301, 315, 320, 326, 333, 346, 390
Mohamad Hatta.....................40
Morton Sobell...................55, 61
Moscow .40, 51, 58, 83, 122, 123, 124, 149, 154, 176, 187, 193, 196, 199, 282, 314, 319, 321, 323, 324, 351
MRBMxxix, xxxii, 179, 192, 199, 312, 347
Nagasaki....30, 47, 128, 222, 224, 304, 305, 309, 310, 320, 333, 349, 386
NATOxxix, xxx, 31, 59, 181, 186, 195, 196, 200, 220, 311, 313, 314, 315, 316
North Koreaxxviii, xxix, xxx, 33, 84, 134, 191
Nuclear........iii, 61, 128, 200, 302, 304, 310, 322, 328, 335, 336, 373, 374, 391
Obama. 3, 7, 8, 28, 29, 77, 82, 96, 105, 107, 108, 136, 182, 305, 342, 343
Onassis 95, 96
Oppenheimer... 47, 48, 49, 63, 128

Oswald.... xxiii, xxvi, 34, 97, 144, 145, 146, 147, 148, 149, 150, 151, 152, 154, 155, 156, 159, 160, 161, 162, 163, 164, 165, 167, 168, 202, 203, 206, 207, 208, 209, 210, 211, 212, 213, 218, 224, 226, 227, 228, 230, 231, 232, 234, 235, 236, 237, 239, 240, 242, 243, 247, 254, 265, 266, 267, 269, 270, 271, 272, 274, 278, 282, 284, 286, 287, 290, 291, 295, 297, 298, 388, 391
Penkovsky . xxvi, xxxii, xxxiv, 45, 46, 47, 63, 179, 191, 200, 391
Petraeus................................ 105
Philby................. 57, 58, 60, 200
phobia 49
Pope 7, 83, 146, 147, 148, 150, 151
pre-emptive .... xxi, xxiv, 22, 73, 194, 282, 319, 321, 326, 327, 346
Pulitzer 78, 80, 83, 85, 87, 292, 293
Radar................................... **146**
Reagan.....19, 132, 142, 280, 292, 314, 327, 328, 330
Republic.15, 25, 27, 39, 145, 148, 185, 337, 390
Robert F. Kennedy .. xxvii, 93, 95, 190, 284
Rockefeller 204, 214, 236
Romney.8, 77, 105, 106, 342, 343
Ronald Reagan..18, 44, 132, 167, 182, 199, 303, 315, 327, 330
Rose Cherami153, 159, 160, 161, 165, 173
Rosenberg..52, 54, 55, 61, 62, 64, 200, 222, 311, 390
S-75 ...... xxx, xxxi, xxxiv, 49, 187, 391

Sakhalin 166, 182, 294, 327
Sally Hemings 105
San Cristobal ...... xxxii, 176, 183, 195, 348
Saville Sax 55, 61
Savitsky xx, 46, 47, 180, 195, 299, 320
Senate 76, 77, 78, 99, 119, 140, 145, 214, 221, 273, 284, 294, 340, 341, 365
Senator .... xxii, 13, 54, 66, 76, 77, 78, 79, 85, 86, 87, 91, 93, 94, 95, 96, 99, 136, 140, 214, 229, 231, 236, 273, 284, 340
silo .... xxix, 302, 316
silver 279, 280, 291, 317
SLBM .... xix, xxv, xxix, 326
Soeharto 9, 11, 34, 35, 36, 37, 38, 39, 40, 41, 127, 146
Soekarno ... 34, 35, 36, 40, 41, 72, 126, 144, 145, 146, 147, 148, 151
Sorensen xxviii, 68, 77, 78, 85, 86, 88, 171, 199
Soviet.. i, ii, xiii, xix, xx, xxi, xxii, xxv, xxvi, xxvii, xxviii, xxix, xxx, xxxi, xxxii, xxxiii, 2, 4, 6, 7, 8, 9, 12, 15, 16, 20, 27, 31, 32, 33, 40, 41, 43, 44, 45, 46, 47, 48, 49, 50, 51, 52, 53, 54, 55, 56, 57, 58, 59, 60, 61, 62, 63, 68, 77, 81, 110, 120, 121, 124, 125, 128, 129, 130, 143, 144, 148, 149, 150, 154, 155, 162, 163, 166, 167, 169, 171, 172, 174, 175, 176, 177, 178, 179, 180, 181, 182, 183, 184, 185, 186, 187, 188, 190, 191, 192, 193, 194, 195, 196, 197, 198, 199, 200, 203, 210, 217, 218, 222, 223, 224, 235, 272, 274, 278, 281, 282, 285, 291, 292, 294, 299, 303, 311, 312, 313, 314, 315, 316, 317, 319, 320, 321, 322,
323, 324, 325, 326, 327, 328, 330, 331, 333, 346, 347, 348
Stanislav Petrov 316, 323, 326, 327
STD 4
Stevenson .... xxvii, 78, 192
Stuxnet ...... xv, 336, 337, 338, 339, 340, 342, 343, 344, 391
Superstition 89
Supreme Committee .... xxi, 114, 119, 120, 123, 126, 132, 133, 134, 136, 169, 174, 182, 186, 189, 192, 194, 199, 227, 239, 246, 258, 265, 272, 279, 348
tank 326
Tau Ceti 351, 352
Theodore Hall 55, 61
Thomson .... xxvii, 122
Thurmond 106
trajectory 158, 232
tramps ... 111, 112, 113, 114, 115, 118, 154, 203, 226, 285, 295
triskaidekaphobia 97
Truman .... xxi, 15, 49, 321, 322
U.S. Treasury 279
U-2 ... xx, xxvi, xxxi, xxxii, xxxiii, xxxiv, 43, 46, 49, 50, 51, 52, 67, 124, 143, 144, 150, 151, 163, 174, 177, 178, 179, 180, 181, 182, 183, 187, 192, 196, 222, 223, 362, 392
UAV .... xxxiii, 368, 377, 378
Vasilevsky 57, 60, 64, 391
Vivian Malone ... 82, 84, 204, 285
Wallace .. 82, 84, 85, 87, 202, 204, 216, 272, 285
Warren .. 102, 118, 119, 124, 144, 154, 155, 157, 164, 165, 168, 202, 206, 208, 210, 212, 214, 216, 224,

226, 227, 228, 229, 230, 231, 232, 233, 234, 235, 236, 237, 238, 239, 241, 242, 244, 247, 254, 259, 260, 265, 266, 267, 268, 269, 270, 271, 272, 274, 276, 277, 283, 284, 285, 290, 291, 296, 297, 298, 346, 348, 389, 392

Washington .... xx, xxi, 13, 14, 28, 41, 58, 70, 81, 93, 100, 101, 102, 107, 129, 130, 138, 147, 151, 155, 171, 176, 188, 196, 205, 213, 220, 221, 261, 286, 292, 299, 305, 321, 323, 324, 331, 351

woman . 28, 41, 71, 102, 103, 104, 105, 106, 107, 142, 159, 239, 329, 389

World War .. 2, 13, 23, 26, 29, 30, 31, 45, 47, 52, 57, 58, 62, 68, 74, 75, 81, 91, 92, 118, 121, 178, 188, 189, 242, 302, 305, 309, 322, 324, 329, 348, 369

wound .. i, 30, 113, 144, 149, 159, 205, 232, 256, 258, 259, 260, 261, 263, 274, 275, 276, 277, 292

youtube ... 139, 140, 142, 203, 217, 221, 226, 243, 267, 268, 288, 294, 392, 393

Zapruder 156, 203, 206, 214, 234, 237, 239, 240, 241, 243, 244, 245, 253, 255, 256, 261, 264, 273, 278, 296, 389

About the Author

Abdul Rahman Bahry graduated in the Arabic Literature (1979); he also holds Master degree in the Public Administration (1996). He works as religious provider for 2 US Government Correctional Centers in Ohio; and blends his expertise in Political Science and his long experience to write ***"John F. Kennedy's Nuclear War"***. He is also the author of ***"Jihad: A Struggle or Terrorism?"***

www.ingramcontent.com/pod-product-compliance
Lightning Source LLC
Chambersburg PA
CBHW050119170426
43197CB00011B/1635

9780989298803